The Guide to
The House of Commons

New Parliament

Edited by Martin Linton

FOURTH ESTATE *London*

First published in Great Britain in 1992 by
Fourth Estate Limited
289 Westbourne Grove
London W11 2QA

Copyright © 1992 Guardian Newspapers Ltd
A catalogue record for this book is available from the British Lbrary

ISBN 1-85702-068-5

All rights reserved. No part of this publication may be reproduced, transmitted, or stored in a retrieval system, in any form or by any means, without permission in writing from Fourth Estate Limited.

Designed and produced by PDU, The Guardian London.
Editor: Clive Graham-Ranger. **Picture research:** Georgina Fagelson.
Computer analysis: Computer Newspaper Services Ltd. **Graphics:** Jenny Ridley.
Additional research: David McKie. **Photographs by:** Martin Argles, Jon James, Frank Martin, Don McPhee, Popperfoto, Press Association, Rex Features, Jeremy Sutton-Hibbert, Syndication International, Denis Thorpe, Roger Tooth, Graham Turner, Universal Pictures

Cover picture: 'Mr Gladstone in the House of Commons during the debate on the Home Rule Bill 1893' The Hulton-Deutsch Collection

Printed in Great Britain by Cromwell Press Ltd

CONTENTS

Introduction Ian Aitken	5
Fear at the eleventh hour Michael White	9
Long day's journey into night Hugo Young	13
Dream team or just jobs for the boys? Sarah Benton	17
On the stump Andrew Rawnsley	21
Press-ganged at the polls Martin Linton	25
Late swings, early results John Curtice	35
Reform – the key to No 10 Patrick Dunleavy, Helen Margetts and Stuart Weir	41
A time for change David McKie	49
Debate: John Biffen and Tony Benn	52
House of Commons: Seat-by-seat guide	57

Analysis:

New Cabinet **276** Government ministers and departments **277** Cabinet Committees **279** Opposition front bench **283** Votes cast region by region **286** Wasted votes **290** Highest swings 1987-1992 where seats have changed parties **292** Highest swings since 1983 which resulted in a change of sitting party **292** 1992 winners from 3rd or lower position **292** Largest electorates **293** Smallest electorates **294** Highest and lowest turnouts **295** Largest majorities **296** The marginals **297** Lowest winning share of the vote **300** Miscellany **301**

Alphabetical index of all MPs   **306**

INTRODUCTION

FOR a newspaper to offer a book about the 1992 general election may look a bit like chutzpah. It was, after all, the newspapers that published all those opinion polls which got the result so spectacularly wrong and caused leader writers and self-appointed pundits like myself to forecast at least a minority Labour government. You could therefore argue it was largely our fault so many members of the voting public, not to mention most of the politicians, were astonished by what happened on April 9.

But at least we newspaper pundits have been relatively honest about the extent of our error. Indeed, we had very little choice in the matter, since our mistaken predictions were there, in black and white, pinning us to our ill-chosen words. My own pathetic forecast, offered in the final week of the campaign, was that Labour would at worst emerge as the largest single party in a hung parliament and might even manage a small overall majority. So much for my *amour-propre*.

But not everyone has been as honest as the hacks. The last constituency result had scarcely been announced on Friday afternoon before the retreat from reality began. By the following week it was difficult to find a politician willing to admit surprise at the outcome. Now, still further beyond the event, it is astonishing how prescient most politicians appear to have been. We now know that all of them – or almost all of them – felt in their innermost souls that something must be gravely wrong with the polls, because their findings didn't match up to experience on the door knocker. We have their word for it – and in some cases even their betting slips.

For myself, I plead a severe attack of poll-o-mania for my failure to share this admirable, if belated, scepticism. I did not even place much weight on the proposition that the Labour lead was mostly within the pollsters' declared margin of error, since it seemed unlikely that this error could all be in the same direction. Indeed, if the polls had been "all over the place" (as John Major frequently claimed) then one would certainly have been less inclined to treat their message as conclusive. But they weren't all over the place. Apart from a single hiccup in mid-campaign, when three polls on the same day suggested that Labour had achieved a breakthrough, they produced almost unanimous figures making Labour the largest single party. To have ignored such persistent evidence would have demanded a direct line to some infallible spirit guru.

Well, that's my excuse. But even I began to feel just a trace of professional colliwobbles on the Wednesday evening when the final poll results were announced. Though they still recorded a small Labour lead, and it remained consistent with a hung parliament, the gap had visibly narrowed. And since there had been a time lag – albeit a brief one – between interviewing and publication of the results, it remained a strong possibility that the fall in the Labour lead might continue through Wednesday and into polling day. In other words, it could easily have vanished by the time the last voters were walking to the polling stations.

So I can truthfully claim that the fateful early result at Basildon, which told most observers not hypnotised by the exit polls that Labour's game was up, didn't take me totally by surprise. I now believe the opinion polls were broadly right when they were done and that there really was a late Conservative swing, perhaps brought on by the sheer enormity of voting for the unknown after 13 years of Conservative rule. If that message was hard to read in advance, then it was because it was written in invisible ink.

Even the oft-quoted proposition that no party had ever climbed an electoral mountain as high as the one facing Labour (a swing of 8 per cent) was balanced against the equal and opposite proposition that no party this century had ever won four elections in a row. Add to that the fact that my local constituency was among those recording a 7 point swing to Labour and I begin to feel quite prescient after all.

Besides, it would be wrong to believe that 1992 was a uniquely dreadful year for general election forecasters. There was, for instance, the extraordinary business of 1964, when the entire nation confidently looked forward to the obliteration of Harold Macmillan's candy-floss society by Harold Wilson and his white-hot technological revolution. There was no doubt in anyone's mind that Macmillan's successor in Downing Street, Alec Douglas-Home, was even more closely linked to the grouse moor and the aristocratic image than Supermac. With a touch that P.G. Wodehouse would have envied, Home even confessed to needing a box of matches to add up the balance of payments, the budget deficit and other unfamiliar economic concepts.

Yet, in the event, the apparently hapless Home came within a whisker of beating off Wilson's challenge. Far from achieving the landslide victory everyone had forecast, the former 14th earl managed to restrict Labour to a majority of three. All Harold Wilson's skills as a master fixer were needed to keep his government together until he could go back to the country in 1966 with a reasonable expectation of winning the majority that had eluded him at the first attempt. It would have needed only a handful of voters to behave differently for 1964 to have been an upset of 1992 proportions.

Four years later we got just such an upset, when Wilson's decision to cash-in early on his (or rather Roy Jenkins's) apparent success with the economy, blew up in his face. As with John Major this spring, the then Tory leader (Ted Heath) was almost alone in believing throughout the campaign of June 1970 that he was going to win. Nor was it just a matter of the pundits predicting a narrow Labour victory: the opinion polls put Wilson almost out of sight. I vividly remember sitting in the Prime Minister's first class rail compartment (it was before the days of battle buses, and anyway, Wilson liked trains) on the day that one poll had given him a 13 point lead. With barely a week to go, it looked like a formality.

But the sun continued to beat down, the walkabouts were untroubled by security arrangements and Wilson urged everyone he encountered to call on him at his home if they ever came to London. "Ten Downing Street's the address," he would say, "that's where we live."

Almost the only thing banned from Wilson's personal campaign was politics. There was almost an atmosphere of a Bateman cartoon when a member of the public asked anything so vulgar as a political question. Assured of victory, the PM busily fostered the image of Labour as "the natural party of government". This complacency survived right up to the final day, when the campaign reached its climax with the traditional eve-of-poll rally in Liverpool's magnificent St George's Hall.

But something was already going wrong, even in the Victorian splendour of that packed and euphoric building. Wilson was late – ominously late – and it turned out that he had just been handed news of the final opinion polls putting Heath ahead for the first time. When the rally was over we walked out into the first rain we had seen for weeks. By the time we reached the Adelphi Hotel, drenched, the mood in the Wilson entourage was unmistakable: Labour was about to lose an election everyone said they would win at a canter.

INTRODUCTION

Perhaps such an experience should have made the survivors of that debacle stop and think before we committed ourselves to a similar misjudgment 22 years later. But on the other hand, it would have denied our friends and neighbours a great deal of innocent pleasure. Folk get a lot of fun out of seeing the experts get it just as wrong as everyone else and it is the sovereign right of the people to make fools of us when they feel like it.

I'm just sorry I can't say "better luck next time", for that was my last election as a fully-fledged pundit. In 1996 or 1997 I will be just another punter, doing my best to make fools of the pundits.

But before I hand in my notebook and pencil I am tempted to have one final stab at election forecasting.

Although I have no means of knowing who will win the 1996 or 1997 general election and do not even feel confident that John Major will hold out that long, I predict that the "discredited" opinion polls will again play a significant part in the election campaign. This may seem incredible to anyone who remembers their performance in the 1992 campaign. But the reality is that those nice ladies with the clipboards provide the only empirical alternative to a crystal ball or the pricking in our thumbs. Like the Treasury and those notoriously inaccurate statistics, the polls remain the best evidence we possess.

But there is an even better reason why the polls will continue to make headlines during an election campaign. Painful experience tells me that even a journalist who is wary about polls will crack when he is presented with their latest findings half an hour before the next edition of his newspaper. The figures may be wrong, but they remain news – which is why the likes of Bob Worcester seem likely to stay in business for quite a long time to come. ●

Ian Aitken
The Guardian, London

'If you vote for Kinnock you are voting against Christ'
Dame Barbara Cartland

FEAR AT THE ELEVENTH HOUR

Michael White

NO SOONER had the outcome of the general election become clear beyond doubt, early on April 10, than politicians, pundits and voters began wondering whether the longest campaign in living memory had all been a dream in which a Conservative defeat had never really been likely.

Labour's target was a swing of 8 per cent – no modern Opposition has ever achieved such a figure – and it was being attempted after three humiliating defeats in a world utterly changed by widening prosperity and a resurgence of *laissez faire* individualism shrewdly harnessed by Margaret Thatcher.

Left-wing idealists might bemoan the lost solidarity of the industrial working class, of council houses and factory life, especially when they saw it replaced by the "shell suit and two rottweilers" culture of the Sun. But they could not turn the clock back on the new materialism of the C2s. Thatcher's children were, after all, Attlee's grandchildren.

In the event, four weeks of expensive huffing and puffing produced a swing of just 2 per cent, albeit enough to gain Labour 42 seats.

From the Government's point of view the campaign started badly. Chancellor Lamont's budget was judged economically worrying and politically disappointing by the City despite its new 20p tax band. A week later, the shadow chancellor, John Smith, delivered his own well-received "budget". Smith appeared to neutralise the Tory tax campaign by promising that nobody earning less than £21,000 a year would be worse off under his plans to abolish the ceiling on national insurance contributions – long an ambition among tax buffs – and impose a 50 per cent income tax rate at gross incomes around £40,000.

In reality, the crude Tory poster depicting "Labour's Tax Bombshell", which had first appeared in January, was more of a time bomb than an old-fashioned thousand-pounder. Although Labour moved ahead (by up to 7 per cent in some opinion polls) after February's economic data confirmed the persistence of the longest depression since 1945, Tory ministers and strategists, led by Chris Patten, insisted that the tax-and-spending issue would work by polling day. They were right. They had, Patten confessed, timed the campaign to get through the unavoidable bad news (and Mrs Thatcher's statutory appearance) early on. They were right on that, too.

After yet another lacklustre and negative press conference at Central Office I asked a senior Tory what he was banking on to turn the tide. "Fear," he replied. Fear that, whatever restraint Smith promised, a Kinnock government and its union sponsors would unleash public spending so lavish as to put up income tax by 10p – £1,250 a year on the average tax bill in Basildon and Bury rather than upmarket Didsbury and Dulwich.

It was preposterous, but so was much else that came out of a government determined to run not on its record but on what the Sun and John Major called "Nightmare on Kinnock St".

Throughout the campaign, the media and voters were regaled with denunciations of Labour's past and future. Even the fastidious Douglas Hurd dirtied his hands. All this from a Cabinet that had precipitated a recession, caused chaos in the housing market, presided over a 16 per cent increase in crime in 1991 alone and driven through rapid, radical and destabilising changes in health and education.

The Tory manifesto claimed to be bursting with ideas, centred around the Citizen's Charter – itself widely publicised at the taxpayer's expense – and Major's post-Thatcherite ambition to make public services more efficient so that the lower tax circle really could be squared with decent schools and hospitals for everyone in his classless meritocracy. But the Tory manifesto proved to be a damp squib and the more positive themes seemed to be coming from Labour and – under Paddy Ashdown's relentlessly wholesome leadership – the LibDems.

Day after day at press conferences there was Smith's pensions and child benefit pledges, which came to look expensive to taxpayers without looking attractive enough to recipients. Enough of them voted Labour, but there were never enough of them.

On top of it came extra funding for education and health, greater commitment to European integration and more money for training as part of Labour's modest £1 billion "Recovery Package" for industry. And, of course, constitutional reform.

On all sides it was a fast-moving, tightly controlled agenda, fought by well-scrubbed and disciplined armies in their red roses and power suits aided by the technologies of the mobile phone, fax machines and computer mailshots.

While winning only half its target seats, Labour achieved a higher swing in the marginals and the LibDems hung on to most of their seats. Results varied widely, but the basic failure was not one of money or organisation. As usual, the Tory campaign was judged the clumsiest, not least by ousted Thatcherites. But they won.

Two issues, plus a rally and a soapbox, disrupted the party managers' scripts. One was the furore over Labour's "Jennifer's Ear" election broadcast, in which three days were wasted on the "leaks row" after identification of the child whose glue ear operation was postponed by the NHS.

The second emerged after Labour had deliberately made overtures to the centre ground by choosing Charter 88's "Democracy Day" – April 2 – to highlight constitutional change and consensual government, albeit short of an outright pledge to endorse proportional representation for Westminster. As an issue it ran for several days, damaging Labour's hopes of projecting education in the crucial run-up to polling day.

It enabled Patten, a man who (as Roy Jenkins disapprovingly put it) came late to the politics of abuse, to run hard on the "Trojan Horse" theme: that a LibDem vote was a vote for a Kinnock minority government. More important, it encouraged Major, a man of Wilsonian instinct in politics, to defy his minders and highlight the Tory case for "stable government" against the coalition-mongers.

With low cunning he did so by linking PR with the twin constitutional themes of devolution for Scotland and Euro-federalism, declaring himself the champion of the Union. "It seems to have worked, too," a Tory MP said later as he picked up the echo on the doorstep. "He must be a bloody genius, because I never spotted it."

Major increasingly made his pitch from the top of a bespoke soapbox. He had been intended to campaign in a highly-protected environment, on a bar stool in a mobile theatre-in-the-round, surrounded by respectful questioners. It was much mocked and after Trotskyite hecklers jostled him in Bolton he reappeared in Luton on a soapbox to defend his street cred.

Like ex-marine Ashdown hopping over every five-bar gate, it was laughable, but few seemed to laugh. Major the Underdog looked and sounded more convincing. By contrast Kinnock's high-gloss Sheffield rally, intended as a mid-campaign gesture to the theatricality of Euro-left politics, made some people uneasy.

It had another attraction; it was an easily scapegoated target. Coinciding as it did with Labour's apparent peak in the polls it was seen, even by insiders, as "cynical manipulation and triumphalism" rather than an excitement-generating "time for change". As bad luck and timing would have it, the late TV news bulletins were left short of editing time and transmitted boisterous images that may have reinforced well-documented doubts about Kinnock's suitability as Prime Minister.

None of which would have mattered if Labour had been on a winning streak. Smith would later say that recessions make it harder for reformist parties of the left to win, because people become more cautious and fearful. True enough, but it was hard to avoid concluding that the voters judgment in 1992 more accurately reflected what they wanted than critics of the first-past-the-post system would allow.

Labour's successes in 1989-90 had already achieved "time for change" by driving out Margaret Thatcher and her poll tax and installing a more emollient Tory regime. Now they voted to trim its majority: no more poll taxes!

Kinnock had fought more heroically than any predecessor to modernise his party after its lurch to the left in the wake of the 1979 defeat, to bring its concerns and priorities more into line with what interested ordinary voters of every class. But many voters did not warm to him. Some blamed his prolixity, others his Welshness. More important, time and time again events showed that Labour had not changed far enough or, in the case of its new Euro-enthusiasm and concern for constitutional reform, changed too far, too fast. Thus voters preferred Major's caution and responded to jibes that Kinnock was untrustworthy because he would do any U-turn necessary to win power.

In fact, the Labour leader's deep desire to prove his party's renewed respectability, symbolised by his own improbable switch to double-breasted suits, frequently proved an inhibiting handicap. Determined to master his own past passions, Kinnock eschewed the wit or radical populism that still lurked beneath the regimental ties.

Still fighting to reconcile its history and its union ties to the Thatcherite agenda, Labour often seemed the more backward-looking and conservative, its hard-won new agenda too inflexible to respond to events, its vision of hope drowned out by the Tories' more resonant evocations of fear – and the threat to fragile prosperity.

That is what accounted for the late swing the polls failed to quantify, because much of it took place at the moment of truth: inside the polling booth. But if Labour remained a paroled prisoner of its past, the lurking irony in Major's promises was that, for all its reforming rhetoric in the eighties, the Tory escape plan for the nineties would also fail to liberate the electorate from the gilded cage of Britain's past. ●

LONG DAY'S JOURNEY INTO NIGHT

Hugo Young

ONE survivor from the election campaign was the reputation of Neil Kinnock. After Labour's defeat, he had no alternative but to quit the leadership. He did so, indeed, in unseemly circumstances, hastening away faster than the party would have liked. But before the election, and intermittently over a period that lasted many years, he was often identified as the sole impediment to a Labour victory. The result made clear that this was not the case. Something far deeper than the frailties of one man accounts for the tenacious inability of the Labour Party to secure more than 35 per cent of the popular vote.

Kinnock may have been over-promoted, but he was also underestimated. He was patronised by some of his friends, despised by most of his enemies. He needed the thickest skin of any man alive and over eight years developed this impregnable carapace. But it did not secure him against insidious attack, year after year, for not being a winner. Where his talents were conceded, as in the business of party management and reform, they were decreed not to be a qualification for government. He was not fit to be Prime Minister, many a hostile pundit decided. It was a verdict that attracted credence, rather than provoking revision, when the fateful possibility of his accession to the post finally made itself apparent.

Yet Kinnock had done some extraordinary things. His period as the longest-serving Opposition leader in the history of British politics was not wasted. It effectively began in 1985 when he opened in the most public manner a successful campaign to extirpate the Militant Tendency from power in the party. It continued with a series of reforms, laboriously forced through the party machine, to remove the perversions of "democracy" by which modernisation had long been obstructed.

The party was modernised. It became an efficient fighting machine and throttled the ambitions of third-party politics in the process. Kinnock was instrumental in all this. He was equally crucial to the evolutions of policy that concluded with a party that presented itself, in 1992, as pro-Europe, pro-nuclear deterrence, pro-market economics and against public ownership.

All this, moreover, was mobilised into a campaign that, by any conventional test, was highly credible. Under Kinnock, Labour abandoned its aversion to modern techniques, its contempt for the methodology of populism. It knew every trick and its leader was the master conjuror. Much more than in 1987, he was visibly in charge of his team. He was not cursed by division behind him and did not himself have to be hidden. He grew in the estimation of his colleagues and his personal ratings with the people improved as the campaign went on. By most of the outward signs he therefore gave the lie to those who had said for so long that, but for its leader, Labour would now be taking its rightful place as the alternative party of government.

All the same, that did not happen. And even though one may reject the temptations of simplistic analysis, the result exposed the limitations of the leader as well as his party. The leader was unable to transcend the party's shortcomings. Somehow he failed to transform what needed to be transformed. However complex a political problem may be, the leader faces a judgment if he fails to solve it. For victory is what his life is about.

Where can one say that Neil Kinnock ultimately failed? In two respects, the negative and the positive.

First, he did not succeed in erasing the feature in the public mind that most probably produced the fourth Conservative term. This was fear of the Labour Party. Despite the reforms Kinnock masterminded, popular feeling evidently remained in the grip of history: the history of the Labour governments that most people could remember, those of Wilson and Callaghan between 1974 and 1979, which terminated in industrial and social breakdown; and the history of Labour in the early 1980s, when it was torn apart by rival political gangs, one of which, still represented in some cities, desired to overturn the capitalist system.

Kinnock was too much the child of that era to personify its passing with real conviction. He had taken all the right steps inside the party. For the most part he had obliterated his enemies and the fears from history were now mostly phantom fears. But he had his own past to account for. His role at those moments had been, each time, on what he would now call the wrong side. Against Wilson and Callaghan he had been a left-wing rebel. During the 1979 Government, he was not the first to attack the importunate demands of his militant cronies. His speeches from those years were littered with proof that he had been a reflex-action leftie on every issue where he now took the opposite position.

He would not have been elected leader without this pedigree. Any leader elected in 1983 had to be acceptable to the left, while being least unacceptable to the right. Which emphasised another Kinnock limitation. He was not only a creature of his time, but entirely a product of his party. His whole identity was gained from his standing as a Labour politician. He had had no other meaningful employment. His intense commitment as a Welshman further narrowed his horizons, to those of the Valleys where neither the justice nor the electability of socialism was ever questioned.

Although Kinnock attempted to rise above this formation, he could not escape its shackles. Labourism was what he understood in his bones. And the particular instrument of Labourism, in the shape of the trade unions, was the weapon that became as integral to the mechanics of his political programme as it continued to be to the emotional purpose he was dedicated to fulfil: the reaffirmation, alongside a prudent new respect for individual rights, of the politics of collectivism and community. Kinnock was a union man. His party reforms depended on undemocratic manipulation by trade union bosses. He was at heart a collectivist more than he was an individualist. In each respect this militated against the widening of Labour support, which was the purpose of the exercise. As a creature of the Labour culture, Kinnock was simply unable to present himself as what he was not. He could not attract the extra 5 per cent who were not natural Labour sympathisers, who especially disliked trade union power, yet who would and will determine whether Labour ever governs again.

This was Kinnock's negative failure. He could not escape his past and for this he was not entirely to blame. But his positive failure was a matter of more reproach. It went to the heart of the most constructive criticism usually heard of his leadership.

If there is one function of party leaders that nobody else can perform, it is to articulate the message by which the party seeks to inspire support. Only the leader, in the end, can lead. In his person and from his voice the electorate is supposed to find the essence of what it is being asked to vote for. This is the benign side of the much-despised politics of personality.

Any Labour leader in the 1980s was confronted with deep problems in fulfilling this role satisfactorily. The zeitgeist was against them, having been captured by a politician with a talent for simplifying down to bare moral essentials the message she wished to convey. The state of Labour was also against them, because reform could not be accomplished overnight and there was always the necessity to keep opposing factions sweet until they were weak enough to be ignored.

By the late eighties, however, this had been achieved. Kinnock held sway. But Kinnockism remained a concept hard to define and harder still to warm to. The message could never be reduced to its essentials because, one suspected, the leader was uncertain what they were. His gift for explanation was limited, which was especially unfortunate since he had a lot of explaining to do. Having changed his mind, however sensibly, on matters at the centre of the political programme, he then declined to address the puzzlement this inevitably provoked even among well-disposed observers, let alone among the sworn enemies who abounded in the media. But inspiration also eluded him. He could make very good speeches to Labour audiences: funny, passionate, courageous. Yet addressing the nation, he somehow failed to touch the hearts and minds of the undecided. He delivered serious lectures, but without persuading the world that they came from his own brain or spoke for his own passion. He could express his outrage at the deplorable state to which Thatcherism had brought the country, without finding the words or ideas that might persuade people, who were keen enough to be persuaded, that under Labour it would all be different. To shift the public mood required the talents of a Lloyd George or a John Kennedy. Kinnock, in common with every one of his colleagues, did not have them.

He was, even so, remarkable in more ways than one. The obvious way was failure. He is the only leader in Labour's history never to have served in government: a telling expression, perhaps, of the regression from power, rather than its gradually increasing normality, that Labour's history consists of. On the other hand, he leaves a deeper mark on the party's character than any leader since Attlee. Little that he did, moreover, will have to be undone. It will need to be extended further, in directions that nobody can yet describe. Leaving the leadership will have been hard for him. He had become part of the furniture of British politics and did, when all is said and done, wipe 80 seats off the Conservative majority. It is not obvious what he might do next. Going so swiftly was perhaps a reflection of how shattered he felt by defeat: a peremptory decision to have done with it, knowing the task could never now fall to him to finish. It was a faintly undignified way to go.

The base point will be Kinnock's work. What remains to be seen is whether anyone else, with any other combination of talent and fallibility, can do more for the Labour Party than he did. ●

Back row (from left): Lord Dean (Labour peers' representative), Tony Blair, Donald Dewar, Chris Smith, Marjorie Mowlam, Jack Straw, Michael Meacher, Tom Clarke, Bryan Gould, Harriet Harman, David Clark, Lord Graham (Lords' whip), Doug Hoyle (Chairman of the Parliamentary Labour Party).
Front row (from left): Gordon Brown, Ann Clwyd, Frank Dobson, Jack Cunningham, John Prescott, John Smith, Margaret Beckett, Robin Cook, Ann Taylor, David Blunkett, Derek Foster (Labour chief whip).

DREAM TEAM OR JUST JOBS FOR THE BOYS?

Sarah Benton

There is only one principle new political leaders hold in common, and that is to avoid the mistakes of those they have replaced. For at least three years before his election as new leader, John Smith had been schooled in how he should differ from Neil Kinnock.

Among the Kinnockian errors he wished to avoid are the exclusion of the politically incorrect (mainly the one-time left) and the rendering of the Parliamentary Labour Party into a series of fiefdoms round the front bench stars. This alienated the host of backbenchers as well as the horde of wannabe political advisers and helpers on the outside. "Kinnock used to study the division lists late at night to see the right/left divide," said one northern MP, "and his first instinct was to look for the 30 per cent who hadn't supported him and hunt them down. John Smith's not like that at all."

But before looking at how these faults influenced Smith's choices, what are the more positive reasons a leader might follow in creating his team? First, and a highly rated value on the left, is a *strategic plan.* Here the leader defines the terrain that must be captured (eg the intellectual high ground, the economic hinterland, the Big Idea), has a rough idea of how to move towards that terrain and chooses those people most likely to produce policies and a style of politics that will advance that movement.

Nobody believes Smith had strategic objectives in mind when choosing his team. This is most evident in the top-level appointments; making Jack Cunningham Shadow Foreign Secretary is as good as declaring that Labour is not going to engage in new thinking on foreign relations and Britain's role in the world. And given how much the intellectual malcontents believe new foreign policy should be at the heart of Labour's strategy, it also tells us something about John Smith's attitude to that extra-parliamentary circle. Similarly, the team around David Clarke at the suggestively retitled Defence, Disarmament and Arms Control brief are solid supporters of leader and party, not bright sparks from the movement for disarmament.

Gordon Brown, no great chum of Smith, but rewarded for loyalty with the Shadow Chancellorship, is famous for liking clever people and new ideas around him, but equally famous for not letting any clever ideas trip him up. However, in Harriet Harman and Alistair Darling, his team is drawn more from the social and political modernisers than the solid economic managers. They will keep their boss in touch with fresh thoughts rather than derail him with subversive ones. Tony Blair has a team of one-time troublemakers (though in Graham Allen's case, more on the issue of how the party functions than on policy), but any difficulties are more likely to revolve around Blair's leadership than Smith's. Still, as their appointments are promotions for all three, that should keep them quiet for some time. Joan Ruddock's reputation is now as a competent, not a challenging, person.

Robin Cook, who was once the standard bearer for the idea that strategic policy thinking was important, appears to have despaired of incorporating new thinking into Labour's parliamentary work and tucked himself in with Smith to make a solid parliamentary marriage. He has accommodated one of the left's hate figures – Stuart Bell – in his team, as well as a critic of Smith in Jim Cousins. Cook may use his team to support Smith and prevent Brown or Blair getting too uppity (one of the reasons why he was Smith's campaign manager in the first place); otherwise he may have difficulty making anything original out of them.

The one obvious demotion for a "strategic thinker" is Bryan Gould, shuffled off to never-never land with the Heritage box. In theory, this will give him the space to think strategically, though as one of his supporters said: "Bryan won't be silent, but he won't lead a rebellion." The exclusion of Mark Fisher is also a loss for the "let's think" camp.

The second possible objective in choosing a team is *impressing the public*, which essentially these days means impressing the media. This, agree many in the PLP, will have been a factor behind Smith's choices, though not the overwhelming one. His task was made easier by Gerald Kaufman's decision not to stand (Kaufman's high standing in the PLP mystifying journalists who never experienced the charm he exercised on fellow MPs). He was also helped by the fact that the 1980s reduced the more flamboyant members of the left to impotence.

Increasingly, the bright ones are discovering how to use their time as backbenchers, on select committees or with House facilities, to do political work. Thus Chris Mullin – one-time rebel, but undoubtedly talented – turned down the post Smith offered him as housing spokesman in preference for his new position on the Home Affairs Select Committee. Peter Hain, new boy to parliament, though not to politics, was not offered a post, but he has plenty to do reviving the Tribune group. Ken Livingstone has nestled down with the Treasury Model in a mammoth computer; Diane Abbott and Jeremy Corbyn are both now on select committees. Michael Meacher has been demoted to Development and Co-operation, but that was easy because he is weak and isolated. Tony Benn has become an honourable English eccentric, a candidate for the Heritage box rather than leadership.

The last factor, *keeping the party peace*, seems to have been the dominant one. This is not, at first sight, obvious, given that, as one backroom boy acerbically pointed out, the PLP is "apolitical now".

However, having fought an apolitical campaign, Smith is well aware that parties can divide on non-political issues. One MP who was passed over thought Smith's choices were "exclusively to do with internal party dynamics. That's the criterion". As the Japanese know, where there are no politics around which to organise, large political parties will organise around people or places. Maintaining homogeneity in anything other than a constantly self-purifying sect is almost impossible; even the smallest, women's consciousness-raising group will find an issue on which to divide and divide again into new cells.

Kinnock may have handed Smith a party in which the far left was effectively defeated; but in its place he handed over a party with all the makings of an apolitical faction-based organisation. Long before this election, Shadow Cabinet members sniped at each other for empire building, the warfare spreading to whispering campaigns against their supporters in the PLP and, especially, their paid staff.

This sort of rendering down into factions can be avoided by a powerful political drive, lifting people out of the sniping and backbiting that marred Kinnock's last years as party leader, making the PLP a most inhospitable place. But in lieu of a political overdrive, the alternative is to reward as many factions as possible, with preferment for one's own supporters, however dull they may be. This appears to have been Smith's overwhelming concern in making his appointments.

In a party of personal rather than political factions, using posts to reward and sustain loyalty becomes dominant. Smith's need to secure his own base can be seen not only in the star postings, but also filtering through the lower appointments.

Thus Kevin Barron is off the front bench, not because he had to be punished for his left-wing politics, but because he wanted to be energy spokesman and didn't want the portfolio offered by Smith. Energy was offered to Martin O'Neill, who had a stronger claim for reward. Stuart Bell was rewarded less for his undoubted talents than for the substantial chunk of votes he got in Shadow

Cabinet elections from right-wing and northern MPs – potential backers for a Blair leadership bid.

The result of these deliberations – a mix of the new leader's gravamen, caution and affability – is a three-part parliamentary team. There are solid mainliners, who will be expected to sustain an effective attack on the government's economic policies. This is a war of position rather than manoeuvre. They will use the skills of a well-briefed forensic defence. The leaders in this will be Brown, Blair and Cook. Then there is the new chic Labour Party, the Citizen's Rights post given to Marjorie Mowlam and Environment to Chris Smith, for instance. In the new leader's book, these are not true front-line appointments; they will have a freedom to take risks, because they cannot undermine the central economic message. They maintain the edge of Labour's modernity. Indeed, the large number of women rewarded essentially reflects their role as the bearers of modernity rather than factions to be placated.

And then there are the holding pens, in which Smith supporters will quietly and, it is hoped effectively, do nothing of great interest. They include Cunningham at Foreign Affairs, Ann Taylor at education, Donald Dewar at Social Security (no opening for the new thinking on welfare there.)

The wild card is the health brief given to David Blunkett. He chose Dawn Primarolo, the Campaign group co-chair, as his number two and has already told his team that they can think everything afresh on health.

Perhaps it is too late. Cook effected a truce on health, extracting manifold promises from the government to maintain a National Health Service, while putting himself so much in hock to the medical profession that he left himself no room for manoeuvre. It is hard to see how Blunkett's team can manoeuvre out of this. But perhaps it no longer matters. ●

'Worth at least an Oscar nomination for best use of a child actress in a party political broadcast'

ON THE STUMP

with Andrew Rawnsley

FIFTY years from now they will probably still be setting the 1992 election as an exam question for students of politics, trainee opinion pollsters, TV commentators and newspaper pundits. The question could be couched in such terms as: "Paddy Ashdown won in the campaign, Neil Kinnock won in the polls, but John Major won in the end. Explain."

Late swings, gender gaps, tax policies, voter-preference for unassuming accountants over balding Welshmen, historical, economic and demographic forces . . . wide, deep, myriad and possibly even true are the reasons and excuses already advanced. But two images from the campaign are likely to abide longer in the national memory than the post-mortem arguments that have raged since, or during, the election about wealth or health. These images may be just as important in trying to answer the question. Because, in an election dominated by the photo-snack and the sound-opportunity, they were pictures that said more than a thousand academic theses about the parties' campaigns and the men who led them.

One image is of Neil Kinnock strutting before an all-ticket audience of strobe-lit supporters in the Sheffield Arena. The President Kinnock rally was the red rose party taken to its apotheosis and, as it turned out, hubris: the leader landing by helicopter, indoor fireworks exploding out of the ceiling, the audience singing to a jazz improvised version of Jerusalem. Kinnock was emboldened to use the word socialism – which had been deleted from his manifesto – 30 times. High on the atmosphere and the applause, he burst out of his double-breasted suit crying "Wellll Allll-Right!" like one of the rock celebrities who had just promised him their votes from giant video screens. The second image is of a beleaguered John Major standing in the middle of a Luton shopping precinct, spattered with eggs and heckles hurled from a crowd of the distinctly unconverted. Laughed off the Val Doonican stool from which he had begun his campaign crooning to selected Tory supporters, this was the first outing of the celebrated soap-box. The occasion seemed to be the. Tory campaign taken to its logical extension. Chaotic, defensive, its leader put on a platform as wooden as his oratory, forced to resort to crying "Wake up people of Britain!" halfway through his speeches. The professional political observers almost unanimously knew what to make of this contrast. The Labour leader was swishing from one adulatory Kinnockfest to another masterfully manipulated media event. Jack Cunningham, his director of campaigns and ferocious press conference bouncer, was throwing out any question which might pick a fight with the leader. John Smith was winning all the points for style and content in his duels with Norman Lamont, producing the marvellous spectacle of an election campaign in which a Labour Chancellor came across as someone who would invest your savings in a high interest building society account and a Tory Chancellor who came across as someone who would pop down the bookies and gamble it all on a doped nag.

As Kinnock swaggered across the country acting as Prime Minister, the pollsters said he shortly would be and the pundits treated him as if he already was. Contrast that with Major, embarked on a leader's tour apparently deliberately designed to put some more grey into his image, taking him from a railway marshalling yard to a DIY store via a brief visit back to Brixton to buy some kippers and check that his old house was still there. On the fifth take, he confirmed that it was. Chris Patten, the Tory cerebralist turned party chairman, was acting like a teetotaller coming late to drink, dropping crude "tax bombshells", which had a habit of exploding in his face, serving up indigestible Double Whammies and unleashing the Dogs of War only to find that they went round biting each other instead of the opposition. Margaret Thatcher – who had been consigned in the Tory manifesto to a footnote on page four – was desperately resurrected to rampage around half the country as if she were still Prime Minister. The party's other wild blond, Michael Heseltine, was encouraged to rampage around the other half pretending that he was Prime Minister. And as Major stumbled about the country playing the Leader of the Opposition, the pollsters said he shortly would be and the pundits treated him as if he already was. It is rare, if not unique, in a general election for the voters to be afforded an advance glimpse of the role reversal they could execute at the ballot box before they have actually done it. For a sufficiently significant proportion of the electorate, the vision of Kinnockism loudly rampant most vividly captured at Sheffield, and Majorism quietly defiant most arrestingly caught at Luton, helped to make up or confirm in the minds of these voters that it was not a role reversal they wanted to make after all. Nor was Paddy Ashdown going to get the chance to decide for them. The LibDem leader's election result was, in some senses, a victim of his campaign success.

Travelling 25,000 miles and yomping through 60 walkabouts, by jet plane, hovercraft, catamaran and bus, the LibDem leader left no Scottish sheep nor Cornish seal unwooed. Officer Commanding the Special Vote Squadron stormed across the Channel to France for one headline-catching wheeze before going on to canvass the galaxy from Jodrell Bank. Though occasionally bogged down in the more treacherous swamps of hung parliament speculation, the energy and coherence of the Ashdown campaign propelled constitutional and electoral reform higher up the whole campaign agenda than in any previous election and encouraged Labour into its boldest flirtation with proportional representation. But it also finally handed Major the theme he had been looking for to sharpen his attack on Labour and the LibDems, the opportunity to cast Ashdown as the Trojan commando for a Kinnock government, and the means to encourage Tory defectors to the LibDems to come back home. An election in which a plywood box triumphed over £100,000 sound stages is one which may require the re-writing of many of the manuals of successful campaigning.

But working to the old rules, and applying them more ruthlessly than ever before, all the parties strove to purge their voter-unfriendly faces from the TV screens. Several of our leading politicians went missing during the campaign. Labour confined Gerald Kaufman to his constituency for the duration, or sent him to clandestine meetings with small businessmen in Slough. John Prescott was sent on a fact-finding tour of regional bus depots.

There were some more surprising absences. The apparent reluctance early in the campaign of the LibDems to make use of the telegenic talents of Charles Kennedy had people asking: who shot President Kennedy? Before the conspiracy theories got out of hand (there were calls for Des Wilson's arrest), Kennedy was produced to show that he was alive and well. On the Tory side, search parties had to be organised to ascertain that Kenneth Baker and William Waldegrave had not met tragic accidents on the hustings, though when they turned up there were those, and not just at Conservative Central Office, who wished they had fallen victim of a psychopathic voter. Baker's contribution to the electoral reform debate, with his references to the Nazis and description of PR as "a pact with the Devil", combined a misunderstanding of German history with a dodgy grasp of theology. Waldegrave blundered into the War of Jennifer's Ear and just when Labour seemed to have comprehensively lost it, started shooting at his own side. The story of the little girl with the glue ear should have been Robin Cook's finest hour in five years of remorselessly effective attacks on the Tories' stewardship of the NHS. And worth at least an Oscar nomination for best use of a child actress in a party political broadcast. Instead, as it imploded into a row about who leaked the girl's name to whom, Labour's most salient campaign weapon was left badly blunted. It was also one of several occasions when more minor players seized 15 minutes of electoral fame. Julie Hall, the Labour leader's press officer, gave an emotional denial that she had leaked the name and shed tears to prove it. Peter Hitchens, the Daily Express journalist launched by his editor as a Kinnock-seeking missile, suddenly found fellow journalists on his tail.

Others appearing in cameo roles included Sir Nicholas Fairbairn, the Scottish Tory whose most commonly used prefix – eccentric – hardly does him justice. After his warning that a Labour Britain would be swamped with illegitimate immigrants, Sir Nicholas found that Lord Whitelaw and other senior colleagues were dashing to emigrate as far as possible away from his constituency.

In an election most often described as negative, the Natural Law Party accentuated the positive – if only the positively daft – with its promises of national brain-coherence, a nourishing foreign policy and a course of Yogic flying for the economy.

It was arguably a more coherent political programme than the bizarre advice tendered in the deathbed intervention of David Owen. The former leader of the SDP announced that he would be voting LibDem to keep out Labour, but everybody else should vote Tory to secure electoral reform. The parties competed to create the longest line of celebrity cheerleaders, but that sort of endorsement also proved a mixed blessing. When Andrew Lloyd Webber, fresh from disco-mixing Purcell for the Tory campaign anthem, warned that he would leave Britain if the Tories lost, it was the most persuasive reason many voters had heard for voting Labour.

The real stars of the election turned out to be the voters. The parties had designed campaigns in which the public's role was to be either decorative scenery if they were babies or pensioners, or silent spectators to the politicians' stunts. But a healthy number of voters decided to give themselves speaking parts.

One television audience humiliated party leaders without fear or favour, jeering Kinnock for keeping his personal view of PR a secret, hissing Major for refusing to apologise for the poll tax. Ashdown had his closest encounter in a Liverpool tower block. "Hello, friend," he addressed one of the tenants, employing the instant chumminess of the electioneering politician. The man replied: "I'm not your fookin' friend." A warning, that no politician, opinion pollster or pundit should ever forget after this election, that the voters aren't just extras. They write the most important part of the script. And sometimes the ending can be a surprise. ●

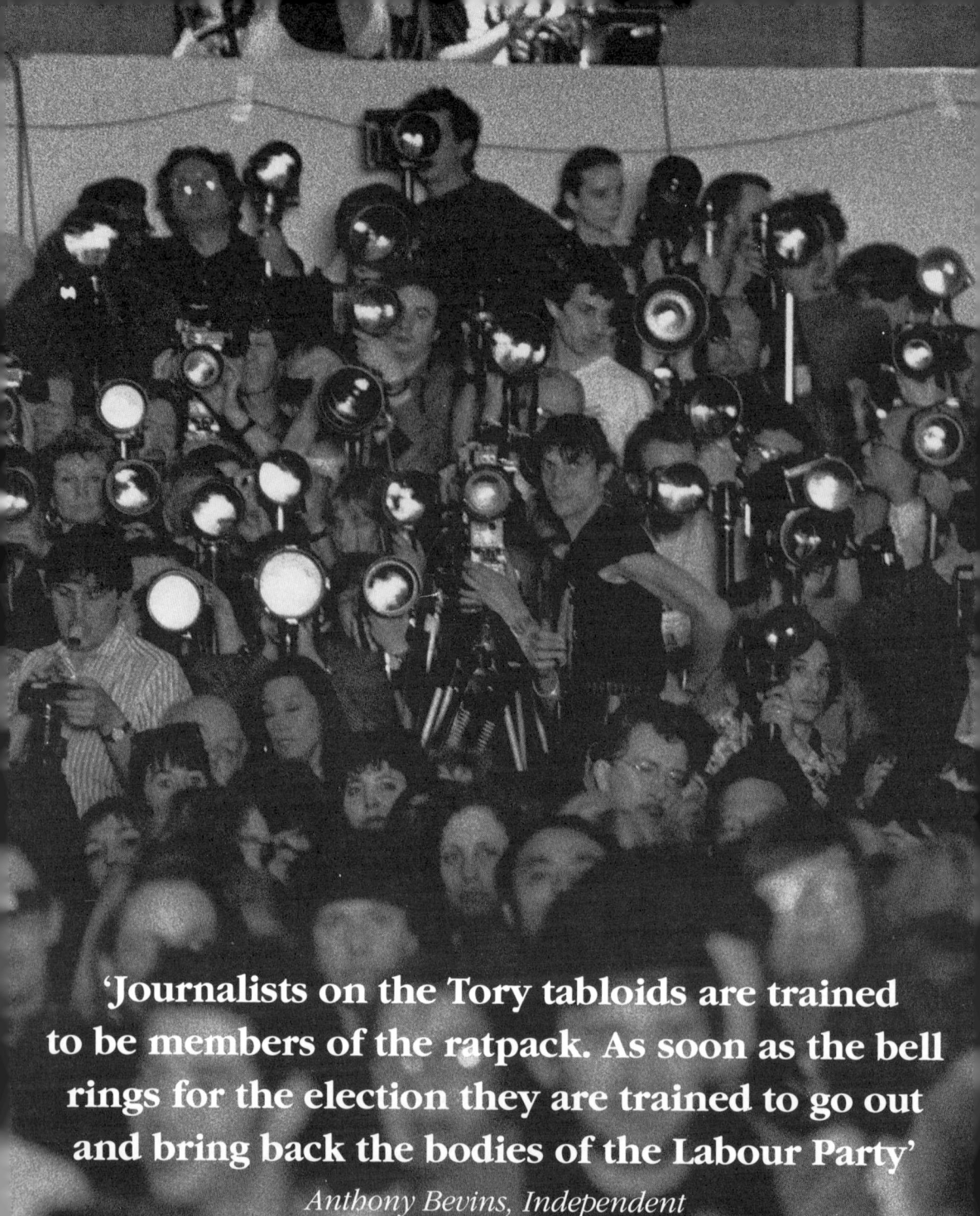

'Journalists on the Tory tabloids are trained to be members of the ratpack. As soon as the bell rings for the election they are trained to go out and bring back the bodies of the Labour Party'

Anthony Bevins, Independent

PRESS-GANGED AT THE POLLS

Martin Linton

Did the tabloids win the election for the Tories? The question has hardly been asked in previous elections. The press has been hostile to the Labour Party for so long that politicians have just accepted it as a part of the landscape, a part of the British way of life. Labour felt it would sound churlish to blame the press for the way people voted. Far better to accept things with good grace, they thought. In any case, hadn't Labour always suffered from this handicap? Hadn't Harold Wilson won several elections in spite of it? And wasn't it true that the majority of Sun readers ignored the paper and voted Labour?

It was almost a taboo subject for politicians until Neil Kinnock, free of the restraints of office, hit back at the press in his resignation speech. "I make and seek no excuses and express no bitterness when I say that the Conservative-supporting press has enabled the Tory Party to win yet again, when the Conservative Party could not have secured victory for itself . . . The relationship between the Conservative Party and those newspapers . . . is a fact of British political life. I did think it would be possible this time to succeed in achieving change in spite of that. Clearly it wasn't."

While this might once have been written off as Labour paranoia, Kinnock was able to quote the assessment of Lord McAlpine, former treasurer of the Tory Party, in the previous day's Sunday Telegraph.

"Those of us close to Smith Square greatly underestimated the influence of the press. The heroes of this campaign were Sir David English, Sir Nicholas Lloyd, Kelvin MacKenzie and the other editors of the grander Tory press. Never in the past nine elections have they come out so strongly in favour of the Conservatives. Never has their attack on the Labour Party been so comprehensive. They exposed, ridiculed and humiliated that party, doing each day in their pages the job that the politicians failed to do from their bright new platforms. This was how the election was won and if the politicians, elated in their hour of victory, are tempted to believe otherwise, they are in very real trouble next time."

If Kinnock wanted an even more candid statement of the role of the Tory tabloids in the election, he could have turned to the Sun a day earlier. "It's The Sun wot won it!" bragged the headline. "Triumphant MPs were queueing yesterday to say 'Thank you my Sun' for helping John Major back in to Number 10", it boasted. David Amess, MP for Basildon, whose early declaration had done so much to dash Labour's hopes, was quoted as saying: "It was your front page that did it. It crystallised all the issues. People in Basildon were so impressed with the Sun's front page that they stuck it in car windows."

A similar view came from Mrs Thatcher via her allies in the Sunday Telegraph. "There is one thing on which Mrs Thatcher and Mr Kinnock agree," the Mandrake column reported. "It is who really won the election . . . I gather that she, too, attributes victory to the press. She has told friends that it was the Tory journalists who won the election and that this should never be forgotten. Men like Mr Paul Johnson and Mr Kelvin MacKenzie. 'You won it,' she said to Sir Nicholas Lloyd, the editor of the Express."

The column added coyly that this was not the sort of thing that Central Office wanted put about and indeed Smith Square and the tabloid editors soon started to play down the press's role in the Tory victory. Three days after boasting "It's The Sun wot won it!" the Sun was reporting: "Bad loser Neil Kinnock stepped down as Labour leader yesterday with one final whinge . . . he blamed his defeat on press coverage." Untroubled by any fetish for consistency, the report carried an official comment from a Sun spokesman: "Neil Kinnock's claim that the press cost him victory is an insult to the intelligence of the 14 million people who voted Conservative."

Sir David English adopted a more subtle line. "To suggest that the Daily Mail single-handedly won the election for the Conservatives and brought about a Labour defeat is very flattering," he wrote, "but it ascribes far more influence to us than we would give ourselves."

Influence is notoriously difficult to measure, but the effect of the press on panels of voters has been measured, most recently by Professor William Miller of Glasgow in the 1987 election. His study showed that there was a much higher swing to Tory among readers of Tory papers in the 12 months leading up to the 1987 election. Among readers of Labour tabloids, such as the Daily Mirror, the swing was 1 per cent. On average it was 5 per cent. Among Express and Mail readers it was 8. Among Sun and Star readers it was 17. On his calculation, the "press effect" was worth a swing of 2 per cent to the Tories (against what would have happened if the Tory tabloid readers had read no paper) and 3 per cent (if they had read pro-Labour papers). In 1992 that would have made the difference between a Tory majority and a hung parliament.

An earlier study by Martin Harrop of Newcastle University drew on panel studies at Nuffield College, Oxford, to show that Tory voters have always been more likely to stay loyal if they read a Tory paper (15 per cent more in 1979, 14 in October 1974, 12 in February 1974). Uncommitted voters have also been more likely to vote Tory if they read a Tory paper (16 per cent more in 1979, 12 in 1970, 18 in 1966).

There has been no panel study this time, but there is plenty of evidence from MORI that suggests, though does not prove, that the press had a similar effect. MORI tracks voting intentions of each paper's readers and the table (right) shows how readers would have voted in the second half of last year, how they actually voted and how a typical group of the same class composition would have voted.

In other words the table measures the swing over what was in effect an extended campaign period between January 1 and April 9 among each paper's readers, which shows that the highest swing was indeed among readers of the Sun (8.5 per cent). But the poll has three drawbacks. Unlike a panel it does not stick with the same voters, so it cannot distinguish between people changing paper and changing opinion. Professor Miller believes this probably understates the influence of the press. It also involves a higher margin of error for small papers. Thirdly, it cannot allow for the influence papers already exert over their readers, which may explain why some of the most committed Tory and Labour papers — the Telegraph, Express, Mail, Mirror – had the least effect during the campaign.

In any case it is difficult to disentangle how far readers chose a paper for its politics or how far they are influenced by its politics. In the quality press, people often choose a paper for its politics. In that case their politics may be reinforced by the paper, but is unlikely to be changed. Tabloid press readers are more likely to be influenced, especially readers of The Sun and The Star. According to research by Professor Miller, Mirror readers are more likely to be committed to a political party (70 per cent), Sun and Star readers less so (41). Mirror readers are interested in politics (75 per cent), Sun and Star readers less so (55). In other words, The Sun and The Star appeal to the uncommitted and the apolitical and their readers are more open to influence.

The Star was nominally independent, but Harrop counts it as a Conservative paper because "the tone of its coverage was consistently hostile to Labour and its election coverage was built around attacks on the Labour Party". On the other hand the Financial Times came out unexpectedly for

NEWSPAPER READERS: HOW THEY SWUNG

ELECTION ADVICE		How they would have voted in Jun-Dec 1991	How far they swung	How they voted on April 9 1992	How they would have voted if they were typical of their social class
Daily Telegraph	Con	72		72	50
(Con)	Lab	13	1>Con	11	27
	LibDem	15		16	20
Daily Express	Con	66		68	45
(Con)	Lab	19	3>Con	15	33
	LibDem	13		15	19
Daily Mail	Con	66		65	45
(Con)	Lab	16	½>Con	14	32
	LibDem	15		18	19
The Times	Con	61		64	51
(Con)	Lab	19	3½>Con	15	25
	LibDem	17		19	20
Today	Con	51		43	43
(Con)	Lab	31	4>Lab	31	36
	LibDem	18		23	18
The Sun	Con	39		45	39
(Con)	Lab	47	8½>Con	36	40
	LibDem	11		15	17
Independent	Con	33		25	55
(Ind)	Lab	39	3>Lab	37	27
	LibDem	25		35	20
The Star	Con	26		32	37
(Ind)	Lab	62	7½>Con	53	39
	LibDem	9		12	17
Daily Mirror	Con	20		20	39
(Lab)	Lab	67	2>Con	63	40
	LibDem	12		14	17
Guardian	Con	12		15	49
(Lab)	Lab	59	3½>Con	55	28
	LibDem	22		25	20

PARTY SUPPORT OF NATIONAL DAILY NEWSPAPERS BY CIRCULATION (PER CENT)

	1945	1950	1951	1955	1959	1964	1966	1970	1974f	1974o	1979	1983	1987	1992
Con	52	50	52	52	54	57	56	55	68	47	66	75	73	70
Lab	35	40	39	40	38	42	43	44	30	29	28	22	25	27
LibDem	12	10	10	9	9	0	4	5	5	5	0	0	3	0
Gap	17	10	13	12	16	15	13	11	38	18	38	53	48	43
Winner	Lab	Lab	Con	Con	Con	Lab	Lab	Con	–	Lab	Con	Con	Con	Con

Updated from Political Communications: The General Election Campaign of 1983 edited by Ivor Crewe and Martin Harrop. The figures do not include Scottish papers or, until 1992, the Financial Times. In that election the nominally independent Star is counted as Conservative and the Finanical Times as Labour. The figures can amount to more than 100 when the papers advise their readers to support more than one party.

Labour on polling day. On this basis he calculates the balance between Conservatiove and Labour supporting newspapers by circulation at 70/27 per cent (see table). This was not quite so bad for Labour as the 1987 election when the balance was 73/25 or the 1983 election when it was 75/22.

But historically the gap is still very wide. It is worth noting that Labour has never won an election when the gap between Conservative and Labour supporting newspapers was more than 18 per cent (see table) and in the last four elections it has averaged over 40 per cent. One could almost say there is a correlation between Labour's electoral success and the size of the Tory-Labour gap in the press.

Certainly the notion that Labour has won a lot of elections against a very hostile press looks questionable. In the only two elections Labour ever won with a double-figure majority – 1945 and 1966 – there were special factors making the press much less partisan than usual.

In 1945 the election came at the end of five years of wartime political truce during which the parties had not attacked one another, campaigned against one another or stood in by-elections against one another. There had been no attacks on Labour in the press, no scares, no reports on party splits. This made it a unique period in British press history.

The truce was abandoned once Churchill called the election at the end of May 1945 and, once unleashed, the Tory press did its worst. It gave full vent to Churchill's "Gestapo" attack on Attlee, in which he claimed that Labour could only introduce its social security proposals by adopting "Gestapo" tactics. The Daily Express attacked Harold Laski, the Labour Party chairman, in a similar vein, calling him "Gauleiter Laski". Foreign correspondents were horrified at the viciousness of the attacks. But seven weeks was too short a period for propaganda to have much effect.

In 1966 the proportion of the press supporting Labour was at its post-war peak of 43 per cent. Even the Times and the Economist failed to support the Conservative cause and among papers loyal to the Tories the tenor of coverage was markedly less hostile. Labour had been in power for 19 months with a majority of five and there was a feeling in the press, as in the country, that "they should be allowed a full innings".

Since 1974 the partisanship of Tory-supporting papers has taken "a more vicious and personal form", according to Martin Harrop, and the proportion of papers supporting Labour has fallen sharply. Tory tabloids have become more openly propagandist during the campaign, like the Daily Mirror, and their journalists more aggressive. As Tony Bevins of the Independent put it: "Journalists on the Tory tabloids are trained to be members of the ratpack. As soon as the bell rings for the election they are trained to go out and bring back the bodies of the Labour Party."

The low point for Labour came in 1983 when the Sun ridiculed Michael Foot ("half ranter, half raver, half baked and half gone") and Jean Rook in the Daily Express went into ecstasies over Mrs Thatcher ("I can feel her vibrating with crusading passion . . . She's . . . superwoman . . . Mrs Big . . . Britain's boss").

The 1992 campaign started out with the tabloids cooler in their support for the Tories than in any recent election. Sir David English even snubbed John Major by failing to welcome him to the Daily Mail Ideal Home Exhibition. But if there was a coolness, it was patched up before the end of the campaign and during the last week the Mail, Express and Sun pulled out all the stops.

There is a little evidence that the tabloids played a role in the late surge to the Tories in the last 48 hours of the campaign. MORI measured a 7.5 per cent swing among Sun readers and a 5 per cent swing among all voters between its last poll on Tuesday and polling day on Thursday. The sample of Sun readers in this last poll is too small to put much weight on, but if the figures were right they could be used to argue that the Sun's influence was decisive.

The Sunday Times Paper Round columnist Brian MacArthur identified 12 constituencies, including Corby and Southampton Test, where the Sun readership was high enough and the Tory majority small enough for a 2 per cent higher swing among Sun readers to have made the difference.

WHAT THE PAPERS SAID . . .

REMEMBER Sarah Pilcher when you cast your vote tomorrow. Seven-year-old Sarah has been waiting nearly two years for an operation to free her from pain . . .
REMEMBER David Tapper and his family when you cast your vote tomorrow. Dave, a 31-year-old bricklayer, has been unemployed for nine months . . .
REMEMBER Roger Thornton-Brown when you cast your vote tomorrow. Roger used to be the kind of small businessman on whose vote the Tories could rely . . .
REMEMBER Mandy Wright when you cast your vote tomorrow. Seven-year-old Mandy was taken ill with a severe tummy bug – thanks for the terrible state of the school's outside toilets. . .
REMEMBER Makala when you vote tomorrow. Makala is 20. For the last three years she has slept rough . . .

PLANNING applications – including loft conversions, home extensions and garages – will have to be approved by gay and lesbian groups in Labour are elected . . .
IF NEIL KINNOCK takes up residence at 10 Downing Street it will be "sudden death" for Britain's fragile housing market, independent experts say . . .
EVEN IF you can afford to buy your home under Labour, bills for gas, water and electricity will soar . . .
RAG trade worker Kelly Simms told yesterday how she will be thrown out of a job by Labour's minimum wage . . .
THIS IS what an ordinary London street looked like 13 years ago. Rats plagued the capital as mountains of rubbish lay about for weeks on end after the binmen went on strike
JIM CALLAGHAN'S last Labour government was ruled with an iron first by tyrant union bosses . . .
BULLDOG Britain will become Europe's poodle as Labour rush to surrender power to the Brussels bureaucrats . . .

There is also the evidence of the ICM recall interviews on the day after the election. A large proportion of comments they quoted from late switchers and late deciders for not voting Labour involved press stories: "I read in the paper about Neil Kinnock having a light bulb in his head and I had strong fears. I also thought Arthur Scargill would raise his ugly head again". "I read two or three articles about Labour's tax plans and the implications they would have on me. I had never before seen them so specifically printed". "I read the Sun, Arthur Scargill, what he was going to do with unions if Labour got in".

This suggests that, quite apart from their numerical superiority, the Tory papers were simply more effective in promoting their party than the ponderous old-fashioned Daily Mirror was in promoting Labour. The light-bulb and the tax tables and Arthur Scargill stories that influenced these voters all appeared in The Sun, the Daily Express and the Daily Mail on the day before polling day, April 8.

The Sun on that day carried a front page editorial headlined "A Question of Trust", which presented the election as a choice between "a solid, dependable man with a cool head" and "a man-with a short fuse who shoots from the lip". It continued with nine pages of "Nightmare on Kinnock Street". The Mirror's front page was far more old-fashioned with a picture of Neil Kinnock and a headline – "It's time for change" – followed by 10 pages to stir the social conscience on the sick, the unemployed, the bankrupt, the homeless and filthy school lavatories.

While the Mirror was talking to the traditional Labour voter of the fifties the Sun was talking to the streetwise voter of the nineties. Where the Mirror was heavy-handed, the Sun was humorous ("We don't want to influence you on your final judgment on who will be Prime Minister! But if it's a bald bloke with wispy red hair and two Ks in his surname, we'll see you at the airport"). Where the Mirror had a two-page interview with Neil Kinnock, the Sun had a Page Three picture of a flab-o-gram girl captioned: "Roly Poly Pat Priestman would be the shape of things to come under a killjoy Labour government."

A study by the marketing consultants EIT (right) measured the impact of about 16 political stories in each paper on April 3 and 7. Stories were classified as positive, neutral or negative towards each party and their impact was evaluated on a scale of 0-100 taking account of length, headline size, prominence and position on the page.

On EIT's assessment the Daily Mail was the most negative towards Labour in its campaign coverage, but it was closely followed by the Sun and the Daily Express. The Daily Mirror was almost as negative towards the Tories. The Daily Express was the most positive towards the Tories, followed by the Mail and the Sun, but the Mirror had less positive impact for Labour.

For the first time in the 1992 election the Tories spent less on press advertising than Labour, taking 39 pages to Labour's 56. In fact they took only one page more than the Natural Law Party. But that was the result of a deliberate decision by Tory chairman Patten to spend more on poster advertising. That may have been the Tory tabloids' own fault for devoting so many pages to what must have looked to Central Office like free advertising. After all, why pay the Sun £33,550 for a full-page advert if the paper will give it for free?

Over the four weeks of the campaign the Sun devoted 76 pages to campaign coverage, the Mirror 84, the Express 117 and the Mail 134. On the basis of EIT's assessment, one could say that a large part of this was effectively free advertising for the political parties – 40 pages of the Sun, 60 pages of the Mirror, 87 pages of the Mail and 94 pages of the Express. If the parties had bought this space commercially, they would have had to pay £1,342,000 to the Sun, £1,788,000 to the Mirror, £1,973,160 to the Mail and £2,233,910 to the Express – more than the combined expenses of all 651 Tory candidates during the campaign.

The very success of the tabloids has brought them on to a stage where they are not only actors, but the spotlight is suddenly on them. Lord McAlpine, Margaret Thatcher and Neil Kinnock all

PRESS-GANGED AT THE POLLS

TRUE POWER OF THE PRESS

APRIL 3

"Kinnock has never had to work for a living. He's only ever been a student. He has never got his hands dirty"

CON	+342
LAB	-383

"Kinnock admits grave errors" "Labour is too soft on crime" "Fear of Labour raising cost of mortgages"

CON	+198
LAB	-384

"My errors of judgment – by Kinnock" "Labour's tax increases would turn recession into slump"

CON	+234
LAB	-538
LIBDEM	-45

"We may lose, admits Blundermouth Baker" "Poll tax bills hit votes" "I'm fit to lead, says Kinnock"

CON	-556

APRIL 7

"Kinnock is jeered on TV show" "Labour want VAT on fuel bills" "Under Neil, Nazi riots if Lab and Lib-Dem share power"

CON	+159
LAB	-672

"Labour will open the floodgates to a wave of immigration" "Neil Kinnock set to sanction the return of the Loony Left"

CON	+481
LAB	-666

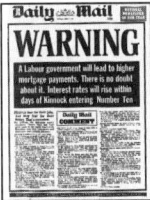

"Interest rates will rise within days of Kinnock entering Number Ten" "Interest rates cut more likely under Labour" – City editor

CON	+359
CON	-44
LAB	-533

"Voters give a TV pasting to Major" "Jobless toll up in all but one seat" "Big slump in new car sales"

CON	-458
LAB	+392

The figures above were arrived at by EIT, who applied "impact evaluation", which is a way of measuring the value of the publicity that a firm gains from a media relations campaign.

The impact of each story is assessed according to an algorithm which takes account of the circulation of the newspaper, the space given to the story, its position on the page, whether it is a left or right hand page and so on. EIT applied this technique to election coverage in the tabloids on two campaign days, April 3 and 7. They classified each story as positive, neutral or negative in its impact on the three main parties and assessed its impact on a scale of 0-100.

On EIT's assessment the Daily Mail had the greatest negative impact on Labour with a score of -1071 over the two days, but the Sun was close on its heels with -1055 and the Daily Express with -1050. The Daily Mirror was almost as negative to the Tory party with a score of -1014.

The Daily Express gave the greatest support to the Tories with a positive score of +679. The Daily Mail was not far behind on +593, though they did have one report that was negative to the Government. The Sun was in third place with a positive score of +501 but the Mirror failed to have the same positive impact for Labour with a score of only +392.

seem to agree that they "won" the election. The implications are only just beginning to sink in.

As Roy Hattersley put it on Channel Four's Hard News after the election: "Of course, in a free society Tory newspapers have an absolute right to support the Tory party, but the way in which the Sun, Mail and Express gave their support over the last three or four months raises real and serious questions about democracy in this country." ●

THE EDITORS THAT WON THE ELECTION

Daily Express

Sir Nicholas Lloyd (born June 9, 1942). Knighted by Thatcher in 1991 for editorial services to the Tory Party. Former editor of the News of the World, he was one of Rupert Murdoch's rising stars until he defected to edit the Express.

Daily Mail

Sir David English (born May 26 1931). Knighted by Thatcher in 1982 for editorial services rendered to the Tory Party. Grand master of the media manipulators, he set the political standard by which all other editors are judged.

The Sun

Kelvin MacKenzie (born Oct 22 1946). Consistently refused knighthoods offered by Thatcher after delivering C2 vote to Tories. Over-the-top style in 1992 election forced News International management to vet coverage.

'It's a very big embarrassment. One possibility was that we were polling in the wrong places'
Nick Moon, NOP political research director

LATE SWINGS, EARLY RESULTS

John Curtice

FORMULATING explanations for the election result is easy. Ascertaining their truth is more difficult. Neither complete proof nor disproof will be offered here, but considerable evidence can be marshalled.

First of all, we need to establish that there was a late swing to the Conservatives. The evidence of three panel surveys in which voters who were interviewed before polling day were re-interviewed afterwards suggests that there was. The lowest estimate of the size of the late swing comes in ICM's recall of the sample it interviewed for the Guardian – just 1 per cent. But MORI's Sunday Times panel recorded a 2.5 per cent swing from Labour to Conservative between the end of the final full week of campaigning and polling day. And the MORI – On The Record panel of floating voters recorded a similar 3 per cent swing.

True, these figures do not suggest that the whole of the difference between the final polls and the eventual swing can be laid at the door of a "late swing" – but that some voters did not behave on polling day as they thought they would as little as the day before seems clear.

If Labour's problems can be laid at the door of its taxation policy, we might expect that Labour should do particularly badly among those who would suffer most: the better paid. Neither the electoral geography nor the opinion polls suggest this was the case.

Take the electoral geography first. Much was made during the campaign that Labour's tax plans would most hurt London and the south-east, where average incomes are highest. Yet in the event, the swing since 1987 in both London and the south was higher than the national average. Across the country as a whole the swing to Labour was 1 per cent higher in those constituencies with the highest household incomes. A similar story is told if we look at those in the pollsters' social grade, AB: professional and managerial workers. ITN's analysis exit poll, which spoke to voters as they left the polling booths, recorded as much as a 9 point increase in Labour support in this group since 1987, equal highest of any of the four social grades. MORI's analysis of all the polls it conducted during the election campaign tell a similar story.

But perhaps the last-minute switch to the Conservatives was among this group? The evidence of the polls is not entirely consistent, but the clear majority failed to find a particularly high late swing among ABs. MORI's Sunday Times panel, for example, records only a 1 per cent swing among ABs in the final week of the campaign. Equally, comparison of the Harris/ITN exit poll's result with that of its final campaign poll reveals just a 2.5 per cent swing among ABs compared with 3.5 per cent in the whole electorate.

But there is an alternative version of the Labour taxation thesis. This is that rather than scaring away those who would have been immediately hit by those tax plans, it put off those who hoped they would be in a position to be affected in the future – the aspirant rich rather than the actually rich. Further, to this was added the impact of the Conservative claim that taxes would rise steeply for all taxpayers under Labour, not just the rich.

The typical taxpayer who hopes to become an atypical taxpayer is supposedly a member of the C2s – the skilled working class. Here the evidence is rather more convincing. The MORI Sunday

Times panel found as much as a 5 per cent swing among the C2s in the final week of the campaign. Comparison of the Harris exit poll with the final Harris campaign poll also finds a 5.5 per cent swing among C2s.

But even so, these findings are not corroborated by the MORI/On The Record panel of floating voters. More generally, in so far as the Conservatives did do relatively well among the C2s in the final week of the campaign, they were catching up on lost ground. As table 1 (opposite) shows, compared with 1987 the swing to Labour in the C2s in the Harris ITN exit poll was unexceptional. MORI's compilation of its polls for the Times points to a similar conclusion.

So pinning Labour's defeat on the behaviour of some particular social group looks like an unproductive business. But this could still mean that fear of Labour's tax policies was an important motivation for switching to the Conservatives.

Here the MORI/On The Record panel is highly revealing. Throughout the campaign its panel asked whether or not people thought Labour would increase the basic rate of tax. A steady and consistent majority of floating voters, around three-quarters, thought that they would. Irrespective of whether or not it cost Labour the election, the party's claim that it would reduce taxation for eight out of every 10 families was clearly a public relations flop.

But intriguingly throughout the campaign, including the final week, beliefs as to whether or not Labour would raise taxes were unrelated to voters' decision whom to vote for. Three-quarters of those making up their minds to vote Conservative thought that Labour would raise their taxes – as did three-quarters of those deciding to vote Labour.

Further, the proportion thinking that Labour would increase income tax did not rise during the last week of the campaign. But other indicators of attitudes towards taxation did change.

What does seem to have changed during the final few days of the campaign was not fear of Labour but faith in the Conservatives. As table 2 shows, there was an 11 point increase in the final week of the campaign in the proportion of floating voters who thought the Conservatives would succeed in cutting taxes. And what was only a 4 point lead for Lamont's tax and spending plans over Smith's in the final week of the campaign turned into a 19 point lead by polling day.

At the same time, as the Tories' taxation profile improved, so fears about what they might do to the public services also seem to have declined. There was, for example, a 15 point drop over the final two weeks of the campaign in the proportion of floating voters who thought the Tories would privatise the health service. And those who switched to the Tories in the final week were also distinguishable from other floating voters in seeing an increase in their confidence in the Conservatives' health and education policies.

So taxation probably did matter – but not simply because the electorate wished to keep the pound in their pocket. After all, 60 per cent of those leaving the polling booths told NOP in the BBC analysis exit poll that they favoured the distribution of income from the better off to the less well off, actually 3 points higher than when the question was asked in last year's British Social Attitudes Survey. Rather, Labour's message that it would keep taxes down lacked credibility. In that context the Conservatives' claims in the final days of the campaign that they would keep taxation down and at the same time maintain adequate levels of public spending were able to strike a chord. Christian democracy from a party able to deliver was preferable to social democracy from a party which could not.

What then might be the short-term explanation for Labour's defeat? One is dislike of Kinnock. It was clear throughout the election campaign, and long before, that Kinnock was not a vote-winner for his party. In the final days of the campaign he may well have become a liability.

Among the MORI/On The Record panel of floating voters, Major's lead as the most capable Prime Minister rose from 19 to 36 points over the final week of the campaign (see table 2). In the MORI/Sunday Times panel of all voters it rose from 9 points to 31. What triggered this movement –

TABLE 1: HOW THE SOCIAL CLASSES SWUNG

AB	Con %	Lab %	Alliance %
1987 General Election	54	13	30
Final Week	51	25	20
1992 General Election	53	22	21

C1			
1987 General Election	47	24	26
Final Week	47	28	22
1992 General Election	48	28	20

C2			
1987 General Election	42	35	21
Final Week	35	46	15
1992 General Election	40	39	18

DE			
1987 General Election	31	46	20
Final Week	26	54	17
1992 General Election	29	52	13

Source: Harris/ITN

TABLE 2: HOW FLOATING VOTERS CHANGED

	Conservative lead over Labour	
	Before Election	After Election
Party best able to handle economy	+18	+41
Most capable Prime Minister	+19	+36
Whose tax and spending plans would make you better off	+4	+19

	% Agree	
	Before Election	After Election
Conservatives will cut level of taxation	37	48
Labour would increase 25p basic rate	76	77

Source: MORI/On the Record panel of floating voters

TABLE 3: UNEMPLOYMENT CHANGE AND SWING
INCREASE IN % UNEMPLOYMENT SINCE MARCH 1990

	Swing to Lab
Less than 1.5%	2.3
More than 3%	3.7
English average	3.1

Based on constituencies in England only

TABLE 4: SEATS AND VOTES

	All UK		excl LibDems and SNP	
	% votes	% seats	% votes	% seats
Con	41.9	51.6	52.2	53.5
Lab	34.2	41.6	42.6	43.2
LibDem	18.3	3.1	–	–
SNP	1.9	0.5	–	–
Plaid Cymru	0.3	0.6	0.4	0.3
Unionists	1.2	2.0	1.5	2.1
SDLP	0.6	0.6	0.7	0.6
Others	2.0	0.0	2.5	0.0

be it Kinnock's rather triumphalist and emotional performance in the Sheffield rally a week before polling day or Conservative and newspaper attacks on his trustworthiness – is impossible to discern. But of the three popular explanations for Labour's defeat, this is perhaps the one for which the evidence is strongest.

But Kinnock cannot shoulder all the blame for Labour's defeat. We also have to examine why Labour was unable to exploit the government's difficulties over the recession.

That the recession cost the government some votes is clear. Only 39 per cent of floating voters thought that the Conservatives had handled the economy well since 1979. The swing to Labour was, as we have already seen, higher in the south where the recession was at its worst. The pro-Tory swing in Scotland is likely to be at least as much a reflection of the relative strength of the economy there as any upsurge in support for Unionism. But even if we confine our attention to England, table 3 shows that the average swing to Labour in those constituencies where the unemployment rate was up by 1.5 per cent or less over the two years before the election was 1.5 points lower than it was in those constituencies where the increase in unemployment had been 3 per cent or more.

But at the same time, the association between local unemployment and the anti-government swing was much weaker than in the 1983 or 1987 elections. And there was no apparent correlation at all between the state of the local housing market and party fortunes. Relative to the severity of the recession, the south protested too little for Labour's good.

Attitudes towards the parties' ability to handle the economy also featured prominently in the last-minute swing from Labour. In the On The Record panel of floating voters the Conservatives' lead on which party could best handle the economy rose from 18 to 41 points over the last week of the campaign (see table 2). And whereas just a week before polling day NOP found that the Conservatives had only a 1 point lead as the best party to handle the recession, in the BBC exit poll they had a 16 point lead on the economy.

So a further crucial weakness in Labour's campaign was its failure to convince the electorate that they could handle Britain's troubled economy more successfully than the Conservatives. Again the evidence suggests that political failure lay at the heart of Labour's problems rather than economic or sociological determinism.

We now turn to why the Conservatives only scraped home with a majority of 21 when they had a vote lead of 7.5 per cent. As anguished Labour supporters pointed out, if just 1,233 voters in 11 constituencies had voted Labour or LibDem rather than Conservative, Major would have lost his overall majority entirely. Yet conventional calculation had suggested that the Conservatives would have been home and dry on a 4 point lead.

Three things worked against the Conservatives. First, the average swing to Labour in marginal constituencies was 3.8 per cent compared with an average swing of 2.5 per cent. In part this reflected the above average swing generally in London and the Midlands in which a large number of marginals were located. But the swing to Labour was generally higher in the marginals in each region than in the country as a whole. At the same time the LibDem vote was squeezed in Conservative/Labour seats, pointing towards anti-government tactical voting by erstwhile LibDem supporters. Such tactical support helped boost the pro-Labour swing in up to a dozen of Labour's 40 gains.

But two other factors were also important. One was that the constituency boundaries became yet further out of date. On average the electorate in those seats which Labour won in 1987 fell by just over 1,000 between 1987 and 1992. In Conservative constituencies, in contrast, the electorate rose by an average of 650. Although the boundary commissioners added an extra (Conservative) seat in Milton Keynes, this did little to assuage the fact that in general the election was fought on boundaries which in England were 16 years old.

In addition there was a marked difference in the turnout in Conservative and Labour strongholds. In Labour-held seats turnout was unchanged on 1987. In Conservative constituencies it rose on average by 3.5 points. This meant that across the country as a whole more Conservative than Labour voters turned out to vote, but in doing so they added to the Conservative national vote total without doing anything to win them parliamentary seats.

The impact of all these pro-Labour biases was profound. One of the key characteristics of the first-past-the-post electoral system is supposed to be that by exaggerating the lead of the largest party over the second party, it ensures the winner has a safe overall majority – thereby avoiding the haggling and instability of a hung parliament. The exaggerative power of the electoral system had already been eroded before 1992 by the widening of the north/south divide. The additional pro-Labour bias in 1992 conspired to remove it entirely. As table 4 shows the Conservatives won 52 per cent of the votes cast for Conservative and Labour – and received 53 per cent of the seats.

Indeed, the only disproportional feature that the electoral system retained was its discrimination against both the LibDems and the SNP. As table 4 shows, if we exclude the votes cast for and seats won by those two parties, the electoral system achieved a degree of proportionality of which any avowedly proportional system would have been proud. Not only did the electoral system fail to produce a winner's bonus, but it also failed to discriminate against most of the smaller parties.

The system was particularly harsh on the SNP, who failed to improve on their 1987 seats total despite a 7 point increase in their support. The mountain they have to climb to challenge Labour's dominance in the central belt remains as steep as ever. There are no seats where they lie within 10 per cent of Labour and only seven where they lie within 20 per cent.

These considerations will no doubt fuel the debate about electoral reform. More immediately, it is clear why the Conservative government needs to ensure that new parliamentary constituencies are in place by the next election. Given the 1992 distribution of the vote, Labour could win an overall majority on a swing of just over 4 per cent – or a lead over the Conservatives of just .5 of a point. The Conservatives, meanwhile, need a 6 point lead for a majority. Far from giving the Conservatives a decisive advantage at the next election, the implementation of the boundary review is essential to avoid them suffering a potentially crippling disadvantage.

And what then of the consequences of this election on the future of the British political system? Far from being a ritualistic irrelevance, its impact could well be profound. We have become used to describing the British political system as one in which the electorate is offered the choice between two parties for government. 1992 was probably the last occasion that choice was offered.

Labour had already begun to contemplate the possibility of embracing electoral reform before the 1992 election. But Kinnock's unwillingness to express his personal views on the subject in the final days of the election campaign was symbolic of the halfway house Labour was occupying. Half the party still believed in the possibility of forming a majority government. The other half was prepared to embrace a more pluralistic conception of government.

But it now seems likely that by 1996, irrespective of what happens to relations between Labour and the LibDems, Labour will embrace some kind of electoral reform. In that case, the choice facing the electorate will be between a continuation of one-party rule or the advent of coalition government. An alternative majority government will not be on offer.

It is impossible to discern which choice the electorate will make. Defeat for Labour may not be inevitable. Equally, neither is victory. But it will mean that the two-party system will be left behind as Britain enters the 21st century. ●

'About as scientific as looking at the entrails of a chicken'

Jim Sillars, on opinion polls with a 3 per cent margin of error

REFORM – THE KEY TO NO.10

Patrick Dunleavy, Helen Margetts and Stuart Weir

SOME overseas corporate analysts classify Britain as a "one-party democracy". If the Conservative Party wins a fifth term on a minority vote in 1996-97 under our first-past-the-post electoral system, that analysis will be a reality.

But need it be so? The prospects for agreement on electoral reform feature centrally in the debates about a Labour/LibDem realignment, but the parties have had little hard evidence on which to base their choice of system.

So how would the 1992 election have turned out under the three leading systems advocated by electoral reformers – the Alternative Vote (AV), the Additional Member System (AMS) and the Single Transferable Vote (STV)?

To find out, we constructed mock election results based on a post-election ICM survey of 9,600 respondents commissioned by the Joseph Rowntree Reform Trust. The size of the poll allowed us to draw a representative sample of opinion in every region. We asked people to fill in ballot papers for AV and STV "elections". From the poll results we have reconstructed what would have happened in every constituency under an AV election and estimated the results in the new constituencies under AMS and STV elections.

The results demonstrate clearly that the AV – which is not a proportional system – only marginally changes the outcome of a first-past-the-post election. Its basic effect was to redistribute a handful of seats from the Tories to the LibDems – mostly in southern England (seven) and Wales (three). The Tories would have lost 11 seats and the LibDems would have gained 10. This would have left a hung parliament in which Major, as leader of the largest party, would have had to rely on the Ulster Unionists to remain in government.

By contrast, both the proportional systems would have allowed Labour and the LibDems to form a coalition government with a comfortable majority over the Conservatives – by 80 seats under AMS and 96 with STV.

Alternative Vote

Under AV, you still vote in a single member constituency, but instead of placing a cross against one name, you can put numbers against all candidates in order of preference. Any candidate who gets more then 50 per cent of the first preference votes is elected. If nobody has 50 per cent, the lowest candidate drops out and their second preference votes are redistributed among the remaining candidates. The process of eliminating the lowest candidate and re-allocating votes continues until one candidate receives more than 50 per cent.

Labour backed AV in 1917 and in 1931, when the MacDonald government passed an AV reform through all stages of the Commons in agreement with the Lloyd George Liberals. A significant body of opinion in the party still prefers this system (Peter Hain, Dale Campbell-Savours and reputedly Neil Kinnock), largely because it does more to preserve a two-party system than PR systems proper and retains single member constituencies.

The simulated result shows, however, that it is also more likely to preserve the Tories' dominance. Labour's share of seats remains virtually unchanged and the Tories lose just ten seats to the LibDems (the SNP gains a further three seats). The Conservatives would still have won, but it would have been a minority government. But with further boundary changes in 1993-95 that favour the Tories, it is entirely feasible that they could continue to win overall majorities in the Commons under AV on a 43 per cent minority vote.

Labour's problem is that in all but two regions – Wales and Greater London – more LibDem second preferences went to the Conservatives than to them; partly because of the clear overall Tory lead, but also because the second preferences of more "progressive" LibDem voters were split between Labour and the Greens (who picked up nearly one-fifth of LibDem second-party votes overall). A large group of voters of all parties would not cast a second-party vote at all – between 15 and 27 per cent – depending on region. These factors hurt Labour badly in some regions: in East Anglia, for example, they lost two (Ipswich and Cambridge) out of three of their current seats. The LibDems did even worse under AV, receiving far fewer seats than their national share of the vote entitled them to.

The conclusion is clear. Unless people were dramatically to change the way they vote, AV would have scarcely any impact on party representation in the Commons. In a pilot study in September 1991, we estimated that 36 seats would change hands. The 1992 result indicates that 25 seats would be re-allocated – just 3.8 per cent of Commons seats.

Additional Member System

Labour has chosen this system for elections to a devolved Scottish parliament and the Germans use a variant of it. A Hansard Society commission, headed by the Conservative peer, Lord Blake, and the Labour think-tank, the Institute for Public Policy Research, have both recommended AMS systems.

Under the variant we tested, existing constituencies would be doubled in size. Half the MPs in the Commons would be elected directly by these enlarged constituencies and half would enter parliament as "top-up" regional MPs, put there by redistributing "wasted" votes to bring the parties' overall share on seats in every region into line with their share of the vote. Parties with less than 5 per cent of the regional vote would get no top-up seats – which is why, on the 1992 share of votes, the Greens, who might otherwise have gained five or six seats, failed to gain one.

All previous research has suggested that AMS elections, on this 50-50 basis, would produce almost an exact fit between the votes cast nationally for each party and their representation in the Commons. Our results confirm this research. Labour performed more strongly in local constituencies in 1992 than in recent elections, so the main change from these studies is that the party would win more local seats and need fewer top-up seats. The LibDems fill almost all their seats with top-up MPs. It is their weakness at constituency level that explains their firm attachment to the multi-member STV system. Yet our results show that with just under 18 per cent of the national vote, they actually gain 14 more seats than under STV – 116 as against 102.

Single Transferable Vote

STV is the most complex and sophisticated of all the three main alternatives to first-past-the-post. It is already in use in the UK – in Euro-elections in Northern Ireland – the Irish Republic and (in simplified form) for elections to the Australian Senate. The Electoral Reform Society is bound by its constitution to adherence to this system.

Voters again mark candidates in order of preference, but as they are voting in far larger, multi-member constituencies, they have many more candidates to choose from. We assumed that most constituencies would return five MPs, with a few electing only four to make our constituencies fit into existing regional boundaries, and gave people ballot papers with 17 candidates on them.

HOW BRITAIN WOULD HAVE VOTED UNDER ALTERNATIVE ELECTORAL SYSTEMS

These tables show how many seats each party would have won under five alternative voting systems.

Alternative Vote (AV)
This system retains the constituency, but voters can number candidates in order of preference. If no candidate wins 50 per cent on first preferences, bottom candidates are eliminated and second preferences reallocated until one candidate reaches 50 per cent.

Single Transferable Vote (STV)
Voters can again number candidates in order of preference, but in four or five-member seats, so each party has several candidates and voters can express an order of preference between their own party's and other parties' candidates.

Additional Member System (AMS)
Half the MPs are elected under the present system and the other 325 are elected as regional "top-up" MPs to bring the parties' shares of MPs into line with their shares of the vote. But parties with less than 5 per cent of the vote in a region would get no seats at all.

Pure Proportional Representation (PR)
Seats are allocated to each party in proportion to their share of the vote. If they get 10 per cent of the vote, they get exactly one-tenth of 651 seats – the first 65 names on their list of candidates.

Modified additional member system
A half-way house similar to the system favoured by Labour for a Scottish parliament, with 500 MPs elected under the present system (in larger constituencies) and 151 as regional "top-up" MPs to make the system more proportional, but only for parties that had already won constituency seats.

The AV, STV and AMS results were simulated by Patrick Dunleavy, Helen Margetts and Stuart Weir on the basis of an ICM survey of 9,600 voters after the election commissioned by the Rowntree Trust. The PR and Modified AMS results were generated by Computer Newspaper Results for the Guardian on the basis of the election results.

	Actual Result	AV	STV	AMS	Pure PR	Modified AMS
Con	336	325	256	269	266	295
Lab	271	270	250	232	227	235
LibDem	20	30	102	116	117	90
SNP	3	6	16	15	15	11
Plaid Cymru	4	3	4	3	3	4
UUP	9	-	-	6	6	7
SDLP	4	-	-	4	4	5
DUP	3	-	-	2	2	3
Sinn Fein	0	-	-	2	2	0
Alliance	0	-	-	1	1	0
Pop U	1	-	-	1	1	1
Others	0	0	6	0	7	0

EAST ANGLIA
20 SEATS

	Actual Result	AV	STV	AMS	Pure PR	Modified AMS
Con	17	19	11	10	10	13
Lab	3	1	5	6	6	4
LibDem	0	0	4	4	4	3

Comparatively few people were unwilling to complete the ballot papers (only 8 per cent of those who voted in the general election).

At least two-fifths of respondents supported candidates of just one party on their STV ballots and voters generally went down the party list of candidates in ballot form order. However, a surprising number picked out the individual candidate – for example, making Cabinet or shadow cabinet members ranked second, third or fourth in the party slate their first-choice candidates. Even comparatively little-known figures in popular terms – Michael Howard, Tom King, Tony Blair – were promoted in this way. "Star" candidates like Gyles Brandreth, Glenda Jackson and Sebastian Coe also performed strongly, as did Winston Churchill in the north-west – where, presumably, quite a few voters believe in resurrection.

Finally, STV supporters will draw encouragement from the fact that over half of voters gave preferences to more than one party, as well as distinguishing between party candidates.

But what is striking about these 1992 STV results is that they are markedly less proportional, though still broadly so, than the AMS results. They give Labour almost as many seats as the Conservatives, though they had 8 per cent fewer 'first preference' votes in 1992.

In our pilot analysis of a previous poll for Rowntree in September 1991, we found that STV gave the LibDems significantly more seats in the Commons (20 per cent of the total) than their share of the vote (then at 14 per cent) entitled them to. LibDems and STV enthusiasts bitterly denounced our findings at the time. They argued that our simulation was at fault, for STV must produce a proportional outcome. In fact, it is simply a product of five-member constituencies.

In 1991, the LibDems picked up the fifth seat across most of Britain simply because, even with just 14 per cent of first preferences, they were the most significant alternative to the two major parties. In 1992, the LibDems underperformed on 18 per cent of the vote, though the same effect held good. The Greens would have won six seats in the south (even though STV system implies a high threshold). Overall, STV would have produced a deviation from proportionality of 5 per cent (as against 16.5 per cent in the actual 1992 General Election). In other words, one in 20 MPs – mostly Labour – in a Commons elected by STV would represent parties that had not won the seat in terms of 'first preference' votes.

Our conclusion remains that STV would produce basically proportional results in Britain, but with four- or five-member constituencies, results in terms of seats can deviate significantly from the national share of first-preference votes. The problem for the LibDems is that only significantly larger constituencies would be sure to provide a proportional result; adopting them would deviate significantly from the electorate's strong preference for small constituencies.

The good news for Labour and the LibDems is that the options for electoral reform, and for possible co-operation, are far narrower than they realised. AV is no longer a starter for Labour, let alone the LibDems, because it hardly dents the Conservatives' electoral strength. Labour must now, at last and too late, bite the bullet and accept that their best prospects for the future lie with coalition politics and a fully proportional electoral system. Only a clear commitment to PR can give them a strong and principled position to defend against the kind of assault the Tories made on electoral reform in the general election.

Equally, Ashdown has to abandon his party's single-minded and sectarian zeal for STV. It is hard to know how far his party really believed in the system anyway; they had done no work on it since the discredited joint Liberal-SDP scheme, which seemed to be designed to secure Liberal seats in north Scotland as much as the campaign cry for "fair votes". Moreover, unlike Labour, the LibDems have conducted no serious analysis of electoral reform for decades and have no formal position on AMS, even though they have accepted it in Scotland. Our analysis shows that they do better under an AMS scheme like ours than they have traditionally believed, and possibly more securely than they might under STV.

EAST MIDLANDS
42 SEATS

	Actual Result	AV	STV	AMS	Pure PR	Modified AMS
Con	28	28	20	20	20	21
Lab	14	14	16	16	15	15
LibDem	0	0	4	6	7	6

GREATER LONDON
84 SEATS

	Actual Result	AV	STV	AMS	Pure PR	Modified AMS
Con	48	47	33	38	38	39
Lab	35	36	30	33	31	32
LibDem	1	1	18	13	13	13
Others	0	0	1	0	2	0

NORTH WEST
73 SEATS

	Actual Result	AV	STV	AMS	Pure PR	Modified AMS
Con	27	29	28	28	28	28
Lab	44	42	37	33	32	34
LibDem	2	2	10	12	12	11
Others	0	0	0	0	1	0

NORTHERN
36 SEATS

	Actual Result	AV	STV	AMS	Pure PR	Modified AMS
Con	6	6	8	12	12	10
Lab	29	29	21	18	18	22
LibDem	1	1	6	6	6	4

SOUTH EAST
109 SEATS

	Actual Result	AV	STV	AMS	Pure PR	Modified AMS
Con	106	103	55	60	59	83
Lab	3	3	29	23	23	13
LibDem	0	3	24	26	26	13
Others	0	0	5	0	1	0

SOUTH WEST
48 SEATS

	Actual Result	AV	STV	AMS	Pure PR	Modified AMS
Con	38	34	24	23	23	29
Lab	4	4	10	10	9	8
LibDem	6	10	11	15	15	11
Others	0	0	0	0	1	0

For both parties, our mock elections show that there is a real prize in co-operating over electoral reform. With either of the two PR systems, they can at least look forward to "shared sovereignty" in Britain. Under the existing "winner-takes-all" electoral system, they are almost certainly condemned to no share in sovereignty at all. That surely will concentrate their minds. ●

Patrick Dunleavy is Professor of Government, Helen Margetts is a researcher in the Government Department at the London School of Economics and Stuart Weir is Senior Research Fellow at the Human Rights Centre, University of Essex. A full account of the research described here is set out in Replaying the 1992 Election: How Britain would have Voted Under Alternative Electoral Systems *(London: Joseph Rowntree Reform Trust and LSE Public Policy Group, June 1992), LSE Papers in Public Policy No.3 (£5 from LSE Department of Government).*

WEST MIDLANDS
58 SEATS

	Actual Result	AV	STV	AMS	Pure PR	Modified AMS
Con	29	31	31	26	26	26
Lab	29	27	27	23	22	23
LibDem	0	0	2	9	9	9
Others	0	0	0	0	1	0

YORKSHIRE AND HUMBERSIDE
54 SEATS

	Actual Result	AV	STV	AMS	Pure PR	Modified AMS
Con	20	20	19	21	20	20
Lab	34	34	26	24	24	26
LibDem	0	0	9	9	10	8

SCOTLAND
72 SEATS

	Actual Result	AV	STV	AMS	Pure PR	Modified AMS
Con	11	5	18	19	18	15
Lab	49	52	31	27	28	38
LibDem	9	9	7	11	10	8
SNP	3	6	16	15	15	11
Others	0	0	0	0	1	0

WALES
38 SEATS

	Actual Result	AV	STV	AMS	Pure PR	Modified AMS
Con	6	3	9	11	11	10
Lab	27	28	18	19	19	20
LibDem	1	4	7	5	5	4
Plaid Cymru	4	3	4	3	3	4

NORTHERN IRELAND
17 SEATS

	Actual Result	AMS	Pure PR	Modified AMS
Con	0	1	1	1
UUP	9	6	6	7
SDLP	4	4	4	5
DUP	3	2	2	3
Sinn Fein	0	2	2	0
Alliance	0	1	1	0
Pop. U	1	1	1	1

'I'm told we won the campaign. Next time I'd like to lose the campaign and win the election'

John Prescott

A TIME FOR CHANGE

David McKie

ONCE THE dust of the election had settled, Paddy Ashdown floated the notion of some kind of anti-Tory co-operation; not in the sense of a formal deal with each party giving the other a free run in some constituencies, but simply in the sense of exploring the common ground that exists (which to judge by the manifestos was quite a lot) to see what might be built on it.

The arithmetic is compelling, but the portents are not encouraging. National pre-electoral pacts are probably no more than a dream. The attempt to create them during the collaboration between the Liberals and the SDP, a party that in a sense was born to work with the Liberals, left many who tried to manage it vowing: never again.

That was one reason why after the 1987 election the Liberal leader David Steel, backed by three of the SDP's founding Gang of Four, resolved to create a single party. To bring together two parties which at the last election saw each other as outright enemies would be fiendishly difficult: then to persuade the party's supporters to change their votes accordingly would be even more perilous.

Proponents of pacts and deals sometimes talk as if voters form large homogeneous blocks that can be shifted around the electoral board by party leaders. The truth is much bleaker. The concept of an anti-Conservative coalition mustering 60 per cent of the vote against the Tories' 40 per cent was always a delusion when opinion polls showed that as many LibDems would prefer Ashdown to work with Major as would like him to side with Kinnock. Fear of a Kinnock government among LibDem supporters helped account for the swing to the Conservatives that clearly occurred at the end of the April campaign. (Had Labour been able to offer a firm guarantee of PR, rather than just heavy hints, things might have been different.)

Local pacts might be easier than national ones. The Liberal/SDP experience was that while in some constituencies the parties resented having to work together, in others they revelled in it. But again, the traditions are different. Even where the parties are working together in local government, the prospects of local electoral deals seem so far almost anorectically slim. A better prospect, since we've seen it working, is the use of the tactical vote. It helped bring about a series of bruising by-election defeats in the 1987-92 Parliament with voters ganging up behind the candidate best equipped to defeat the Conservatives — in Mid-Staffs behind Labour, in Ribble Valley, Eastbourne and Kincardine behind the LibDems. Nor is this practice confined to by-elections. In the 1987 general election the Conservatives suffered from an informal ganging up against them behind Alliance candidates in some seats and Nationalists in others. In their appendix to the 1987 Nuffield study, John Curtice and Michael Steed identified one Labour gain achieved on a tactical vote — Oxford East — but concluded: "every one of the seven Alliance and Nationalist gains was at least in part assisted by tactical voting".

Tactical switching in 1992 seems to have saved Labour from a far more wounding defeat. Most projections of the share of the vote which the parties actually took suggested that it implied a Conservative majority of 60 to 80 seats. In fact it was 21. Part of that is explained by the way regional divergencies worked in Labour's favour, but it also derives from a Labour performance in its target seats which outstripped its performance nationally. The table opposite compares the change in the share of the vote region by region, with the change in those seats in each region which Labour stood to gain on a swing of up to 10 per cent. The pattern is striking. In all regions bar one, the swing to Labour in the target seats was higher than the swing in the region as a whole. In most cases this was coupled with a greater than average drop in the LibDem share of the vote. It should be said, however, that some of this must reflect less tactical voting than a deeper shift in allegiance. The seats with the biggest jump in the Labour share of the vote, and the biggest drop in that of the LibDems as compared with the old Alliance, were often those where the SDP was once a force in the land. Good examples in England (the pattern in Scotland and Wales is complicated by the Nationalist factor) were Norfolk North West (Labour up 16 per cent, LibDem down 18 per cent in a seat once held for the SDP by Christopher Brocklebank-Fowler); Plymouth Devonport (where with David Owen standing down the Labour share of the vote was up by 20 per cent); Plymouth Drake (Labour up 14, LibDem down 18 — again, the fading of the Owen factor); Plymouth Sutton, Erith and Crayford and Southampton Itchen; Labour's most spectacular gain on a 6.6 per cent swing. That this happened in seats where the Conservatives were clearly invulnerable as well as in the marginals underlines the impression that such shifts were more than tactical.

On the LibDem side of the ledger, the seats where the tactical vote failed to operate outnumbered those where it did. There were stray cases like Littleborough and Saddleworth, where Labour's share of the vote was down 6 per cent and the LibDem share up 5 per cent, suggesting that common cause had been made against Geoffrey Dickens. But in many others, like Cheadle and Chelmsford, the LibDem vote fell back in seats they had hoped to win, while Labour, in third place, advanced. A particularly grievous instance for the friends of tactical voting was Falmouth and Camborne in Cornwall, which looked ripe for some ganging up to defeat the Conservative — Sebastian Coe, a non-Cornishman, succeeding a Tory MP, David Mudd, who was more like a Cornish Nationalist. A 4.7 per cent swing to the LibDems would have done it. Instead, the LibDem share of the vote went down 7 points, while Labour, in a hopeless third place, gained 8.3. Thus it was that, with a fearful asymmetry, while former Alliance supporters moving to Labour in crucial seats helped save Labour from crushing defeat, the failure of Labour supporters to gang up behind LibDems' helped to save the Tories' majority. So tactical voting is easy to plot, but hard to deliver. And next time there is an additional complication. Successful tactical voting requires some understanding of which of the parties in a constituency is the main threat to the incumbent. The boundary review, disturbing the old arithmetic and calling for the re-formation of some constituency parties, will wreathe that in confusion. For the moment, then, the one likely response to Ashdown's initiative might be an attempt to replicate for England and Wales the sort of cross-party collaboration that enabled Labour and the LibDems to thrash out a common policy for devolution within the Scottish Convention. Evolutionary cohabitation, not cohabitation by diktat: though even here, it needs to be said that the parties of the convention fell back in Scotland on April 9, while the parties which chose to stay out increased their share of the vote. ●

CHANGES IN PARTY SHARE OF THE VOTE
a) BY REGION
b) IN LABOUR TARGET SEATS IN THE REGION

		Con	Lab	LDem	Nat	Other	swing
GREATER LONDON	(a)	-1.1	+5.6	-6.2	-	+1.7	3.4 to Lab
	(b)	-0.9	+6.5	-6.1	-	+0.3	3.7 to Lab
REST OF SE	(a)	-1.0	+3.9	-3.8	-	-0.9	2.5 to Lab
	(b)	+0.1	+5.4	-8.3	-	0	2.7 to Lab
SOUTH WEST	(a)	-3.0	+3.3	-1.6	-	+1.3	3.2 to Lab
	(b)	-2.4	+7.7	-6.0	-	+0.7	5.1 to Lab
EAST ANGLIA	(a)	-1.1	+6.3	-6.2	-	+1.0	3.7 to Lab
	(b)	-1.0	+7.9	-8.2	-	+1.2	4.5 to Lab
EAST MIDLANDS	(a)	-2.0	+7.4	-5.7	-	+0.3	4.7 to Lab
	(b)	-1.9	+7.9	-6.7	-	+0.6	4.9 to Lab
WEST MIDLANDS	(a)	-0.8	+5.5	-5.8	-	+1.1	3.2 to Lab
	(b)	-1.2	+6.7	-5.9	-	+0.5	4.0 to Lab
NORTH	(a)	+1.1	+4.2	-5.5	-	+0.2	1.6 to Lab
	(b)	+1.9	+6.8	-8.9	-	+0.3	2.5 to Lab
YORKS & H	(a)	+0.5	+3.7	-4.8	-	+0.6	1.6 to Lab
	(b)	+1.5	+4.2	-6.1	-	+0.3	1.4 to Lab
NORTH WEST	(a)	-0.2	+3.7	-4.8	-	+1.3	2.0 to Lab
	(b)	-0.5	+7.1	-7.1	-	+0.6	3.8 to Lab
WALES	(a)	-0.9	+4.4	-5.5	+1.7	+0.3	2.7 to Lab
	(b)	-1.2	+9.6	-9.2	+0.3	+0.6	5.4 to Lab
SCOTLAND	(a)	+1.6	-3.4	-6.1	+7.4	+0.5	2.5 to Con
	(b)	+2.9	+1.7	-8.8	+3.9	+0.3	0.6 to Con
GREAT BRITAIN	(a)	-0.5	+3.7	-4.8	+0.7	+0.9	2.1 to Lab
	(b)	-0.6	+6.8	-7.1	+0.2	+0.6	3.7 to Lab

David McKie

DEBATE

'Secrecy is as old as government itself, and with every good reason. Fortunes can be made by politicians using the inside track of financial knowledge'
John Biffen

THE 1992 general election was dominated by tax rates and the National Health Service. The public had little inkling of the European Communities issue which became the first piece of major legislation in the new Parliament and — surprisingly — little warning of John Major's plans for more "openness" in government. The decision to make public the existence and extent of Cabinet Committees was a significant step in making better known the workings of Whitehall. Inevitably there will be an argument that the reform is more a symbol than substance, but I suspect, in the long run, the consequences will be modest and irreversible.

The growth of Cabinet Committees is a function of the increasing powers of government. Throughout the 20th century there have always been more than 20 people in the Cabinet. It usually meets only once a week. It simply is too large and unwieldy to be an executive body. It has become a deliberative and confirming forum. When an acute issue has risen — such as the Falklands war — the political supervision has been vested in a mere fistful of ministers. The more mundane issues, such as environmental and trade union policy, have been vested, initially, in a Cabinet Committee of relevant ministers with the final say-so resting with the full Cabinet. The Treasury, as far as the budget is concerned, has remained a sovereign Whitehall department whose secrets are kept fast until the Cabinet meeting that takes place in the morning of budget day.

The institutional arrangements have evolved. They are not the product of any one or two reforming Prime Ministers or Cabinet secretaries, but they do bear testimony to the growing burdens of legislation over the past two generations. Even governments determined to deregulate the economy and increase the private sector seem to require an unconscionable amount of legislation. In summary, the role of the Cabinet Committee is to behave like a mini-Cabinet. Its functions include the authorisation and preparation of legislation as well as more general discussion and judgment on political problems. In the nature of politics it combines action and talk. A key number of committees are chosen automatically and this membership is predetermined by ministerial office. The doyen of these are OD (Overseas and Defence) and E (Economic), where the Foreign Office and the Treasury play a dominant role.

There has been growing interest in the ad hoc committees that have proliferated in recent years rather than the long-established bodies such as OD and E. There is a suspicion, fully stated by the media, that these have been used to confirm the dominant role of the Prime Minister. The basis for such an extension of the Cabinet Committee role is wholly valid. There may be problems or legislation covering several departments that require imperative and special ad hoc consideration and which cannot wait upon the normal committee procedure. It is, of course, true that the Prime Minister can select the committee, but in the realities of politics no Prime Minister will prudently disregard the advice of close colleagues, including the Chief Whip.

It is customary to interpret the development of Cabinet Committees in the context of Margaret Thatcher. Two initial points should be made. Decisions to establish committees were not just the high-handed actions of Margaret Thatcher. She could not have proceeded without the sage advice of William Whitelaw. Secondly, the substantial use of Cabinet Committees was not initiated by her. It has proceeded throughout post-war Britain as the powers of government have extended and the cumbersome numbers of full Cabinet have underlined its shortcomings as an executive body. There remains a third point. The Prime Minister is not a part-time, non-executive chairman. In the public mind he or she carries a real personal responsibility for government. This was probably true more than a century ago in the days of Gladstone and Disraeli. It was certainly true in the days of Heath and Callaghan. Therefore, a Prime Minister is entitled to view the cohesion of policy and personalities as a legitimate objective in the choice of Cabinet Committees. A Prime Minister is expected to assert his authority and influence through the selection and management of these bodies.

The decision to make known the existence and membership of Cabinet Committees is welcome since it rationalises the considerable knowledge the media already possesses about their functions. In the circumstances, demystifying will do no harm. There will be proper public interest in the number of such committees, the membership and the chairmanship. Already a media skill is developing which relates the official listings of Cabinet ministers and the status they seem to have from the membership of Cabinet Committees. Thus we are being told that the information on Cabinet Committee membership shows the importance of Michael Heseltine is far greater than just the rating of his ministerial department. I think most of us would have guessed that.

There is no doubt that Cabinet ministers do attach importance to Cabinet Committee responsibilities. When Jim Prior left the Department of Employment for the Northern Ireland Office, part of the reluctant deal was that he would remain a member of E Cabinet Committee. From now onwards every inclusion or absence from Cabinet Committee membership will be studied for the implied prime ministerial favour or frown. Likewise, the actual committee topics will be studied for inferences of government policy. For many it will be news that we have a Cabinet Committee on Eastern Europe. The next stage will be to seek information on its policy objectives and how it is working to fulfil John Major's goal of a European Community "embracing Russia itself".

"Opinion", alas, will lead to frustrated expectations. The smaller numbers in a Cabinet Committee should provide more secure discussion. I hope so. Secrecy is as old as government itself, and for very good reasons. Fortunes can be made by politicians using the inside track of financial knowledge. The Treasury dominance over budgetary plans is well merited. Defence is not a matter for the Whitehall goldfish bowl, as Denis Healey recognised when he took the Chevaline nuclear decision in near secrecy. The challenge for modern government is how to open up these processes, which clearly do not have to be protected by confidentiality. This is particularly true when governments breach the very confidence they impose upon others. In the context the decision to make known formally the topics and membership of Cabinet Committees is a welcome step.

Nonetheless, it is one small step for commonsense rather than a leap forward for the media. ●

> **'These committees are actually the means by which prime ministerial power can be exercised to exclude the Cabinet from knowing what is going on'**
> *Tony Benn*

The Prime Minister's decision to admit, publicly, to the existence of Cabinet Committees, and to publish their membership, has been hailed as a victory for open government and as proof that we need no longer press for a Freedom of Information Act. Such claims are absurd, since the knowledge that such committees exist has been widespread for years, thanks to Dick Crossman, Barbara Castle and myself, who, as Cabinet diarists, had described them in some detail, including their membership, deliberations and conclusions. Lobby correspondents have always known about them too.

What is less well understood is that these committees, which were officially established to lift some of the burden of decision-making from the full Cabinet, are actually the means by which prime ministerial and official power can be exercised to exclude the Cabinet from knowing what is going on. For only the Prime Minister can set up a committee, and this allows the Cabinet to be by-passed on any issue which might cause difficulty.

In 1979, just after Labour left office, I described, in a public lecture on the powers of the Prime Minister, delivered in Bristol, the system as it then was, pointing out that Wilson and Callaghan had set up 23 standing committees and at least 150 ad hoc committees, known as GEN (or General) or MISC (Miscellaneous) committees.

Some of the standing committees were quite straightforward in their remit, covering Defence and Foreign Policy (OPD or DOP), Economic Policy (EY) and so on, and all the Northern Ireland business was conducted by such a committee, which might, or might not, be mentioned in Cabinet. But it was the GENs and the MISCs which were the most significant, for nobody in the Cabinet knew for sure how many there were, or what they did.

I was on GEN 86, which dealt with Industrial Democracy, and then, a few months later, was put on GEN 158, which was set up to handle the industrial problems that arose during the Winter of Discontent, but I had no idea what was being discussed by the 62 different GEN committees that had been set up in between.

Yet we were reminded, in Minutes from the Prime Minister, that the principle of collective Cabinet responsibility applied even to those decisions reached by committees, of whose existence, membership, discussions and conclusions we were totally unaware.

Cabinet Committees, unlike the Cabinet itself, sometimes included senior civil servants who sat alongside ministers and might intervene in discussions, or prepare papers for collective consideration – a process that gives officials a great deal of power.

This power is also exercised through a completely parallel system of Official Committees entirely composed of civil servants whose job it is to discuss the agenda ahead of time and to "steer" the ministerial committees in accordance with the wishes of the Mandarins or even No. 10.

Each Official Committee had the same number as its ministerial counterpart, so that GEN 158 would have been shadowed by GEN 158(0) and EY by EY(0), etc. When the permanent secretaries meet under the chairmanship of the Cabinet secretary, it is sometimes described unofficially as CAB (0).

Moreover, if any Prime Minister wishes to have a matter looked at with a view to getting the decision that he, or she, wants, it will be suggested that the ministerial committee should set up an inter-departmental official committee, which will then go away and deliberate and bring its conclusions back to ministers to be rubber stamped.

The process of winning that clear majority among ministers is also well-established and is undertaken by civil servants using the powerful Whitehall network that they have built up, that includes permanent secretaries and ministerial private secretaries who will be asked to brief their ministers in support of what the Mandarins want, when the matter finally reaches a Cabinet Committee or Cabinet.

Underneath this Cabinet Committee system itself are a number of working groups whose existence may be so highly classified that nobody really knows who they are or what they do. What is at stake, therefore, is not just a question of how ministers conduct public business, but whether it is ministers or the Prime Minister and the civil servants, who are are actually responsible for the decisions that are taken.

The secrecy that has surrounded all this has been maintained by strong civil servants who do not wish the public to know how strong they are, and by weak ministers who do not wish the public to know how weak they are.

Some of the most important decisions ever taken by any government were taken by one or other of these highly secret processes.

Mr Attlee never told the Cabinet, or parliament, that he had ordered the construction of an atomic bomb by Britain, nor was he candid about the agreement under which the United States was able to construct and use more than 100 installations here, and base many thousands of US service personnel in them on a permanent basis, simply announcing that American Air Force planes were here on "Training Missions". Later, the Chevaline nuclear missile was concealed from successive Cabinets and from parliament, having been only known to a handful of people.

All the policies towards Northern Ireland have been similarly decided by a small group of ministers and the Cabinets of which I was a member for 11 years very rarely discussed the matter.

But probably the most important on-going Cabinet Committee is the one that deals with Britain's relations with the European Community, where the Foreign Office is in the key position of power and can, and does, lay down the law to other departments in all matters relating to the Commission and the Council of Ministers.

The strength of the Foreign Office in this key area of policy is buttressed by the fact that it alone is wired into the network of civil service co-operation, all of which is conducted under COREPER (The Committee of Permanent Representatives) in Brussels.

Since the decisions of the Council of Ministers depend upon a great deal of haggling between the member states and the Commission, COREPER is very powerful and laws passed by the Council are enforced in Britain by the British courts and take precedence over our own legislation where the two conflict.

Thus, the Cabinet Committee on Europe is actually making laws that do not require any parliamentary approval and they are doing so by the use of the Crown prerogative of Treaty-making, which is exempt from the requirement that the House of Commons should approve its decisions.

Thus for the first time since 1649, many of the laws of Britain are, in effect, made by the use of Crown Powers, exercised by the Prime Minister, through the agency of a Cabinet Committee, by-passing Cabinet and the Commons.

So it is that by lifting the veil of secrecy surrounding the work of Cabinet Committees a little bit, as the Prime Minister has done, a whole lot of new and relevant questions will need to be answered as people realise how undemocratic our system really is. I hope that it leads to a mounting pressure for real openness and reform. ●

The House of Commons

Seat-by-Seat Guide

HOW TO READ THE GUIDE

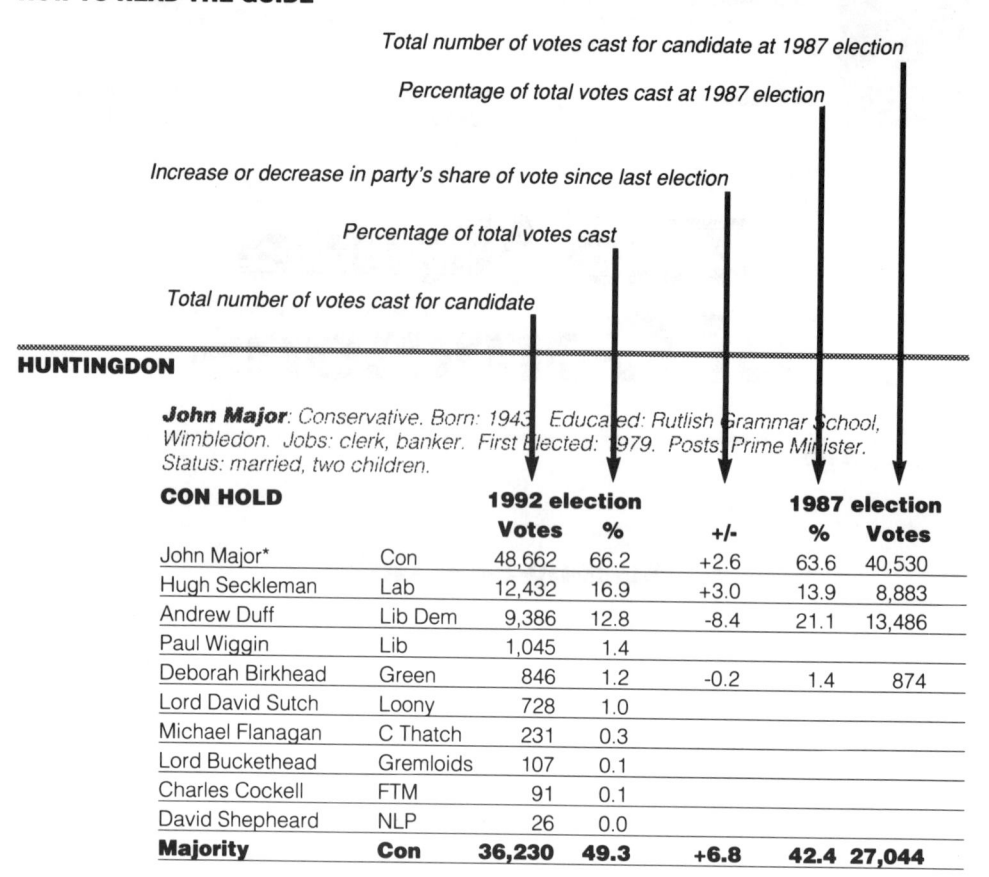

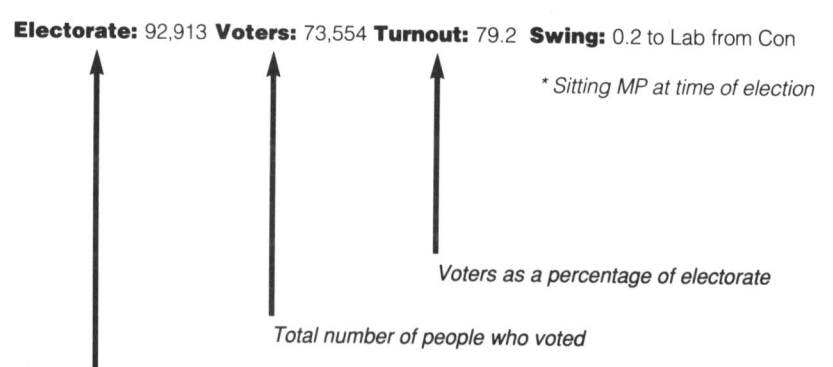

Total number of votes cast for candidate at 1987 election

Percentage of total votes cast at 1987 election

Increase or decrease in party's share of vote since last election

Percentage of total votes cast

Total number of votes cast for candidate

HUNTINGDON

John Major: *Conservative. Born: 1943. Educated: Rutlish Grammar School, Wimbledon. Jobs: clerk, banker. First elected: 1979. Posts: Prime Minister. Status: married, two children.*

CON HOLD		1992 election			1987 election	
		Votes	%	+/-	%	Votes
John Major*	Con	48,662	66.2	+2.6	63.6	40,530
Hugh Seckleman	Lab	12,432	16.9	+3.0	13.9	8,883
Andrew Duff	Lib Dem	9,386	12.8	-8.4	21.1	13,486
Paul Wiggin	Lib	1,045	1.4			
Deborah Birkhead	Green	846	1.2	-0.2	1.4	874
Lord David Sutch	Loony	728	1.0			
Michael Flanagan	C Thatch	231	0.3			
Lord Buckethead	Gremloids	107	0.1			
Charles Cockell	FTM	91	0.1			
David Shepheard	NLP	26	0.0			
Majority	**Con**	**36,230**	**49.3**	**+6.8**	**42.4**	**27,044**

Electorate: 92,913 **Voters:** 73,554 **Turnout:** 79.2 **Swing:** 0.2 to Lab from Con

* Sitting MP at time of election

Voters as a percentage of electorate

Total number of people who voted

Total number of people eligible to vote

ABERAVON

John Morris: Labour. Born: 1931. Educated: University of Aberystwyth; Cambridge. Jobs: barrister. First Elected: 1959. Posts: Shadow Attorney-General. Status: married, three children.

LAB HOLD		1992 election			1987 election	
		Votes	%	+/-	%	Votes
John Morris*	Lab	26,877	67.1	+0.3	66.8	27,126
Hywel Williams	Con	5,567	13.9	-0.5	14.4	5,861
Marilyn Harris	Lib Dem	4,999	12.5	-3.6	16.0	6,517
David Saunders	Plaid Cymru	1,919	4.8	+2.0	2.8	1,124
Capt Beany	Bean Party	707	1.8			
Majority	**Lab**	**21,310**	**53.2**	**+2.5**	**50.7**	**20,609**

Electorate: 51,650 **Voters:** 40,069 **Turnout:** 77.6 **Swing:** 0.4 to Lab from Con

ABERDEEN NORTH

Robert Hughes: Labour. Born: 1932. Educated: Robert Gordon's College, Aberdeen; Pietermaritzburg Technical College, Natal. Jobs: engineering draughtsman. First Elected: 1970. Posts: Chair, Anti-Apartheid Movement; member, Scottish Affairs Select Committee. Status: married, five children.

LAB HOLD		1992 election			1987 election	
		Votes	%	+/-	%	Votes
Robert Hughes*	Lab	18,845	47.0	-7.6	54.7	24,145
James McGugan	SNP	9,608	24.0	+10.8	13.2	5,827
Paul Cook	Con	6,836	17.1	+2.7	14.3	6,330
Martin Ford	Lib Dem	4,772	11.9	-5.9	17.8	7,867
Majority	**Lab**	**9,237**	**23.1**	**-13.8**	**36.9**	**16,278**

Electorate: 60,217 **Voters:** 40,061 **Turnout:** 66.5 **Swing:** 9.2 to SNP from Lab

ABERDEEN SOUTH

Raymond Robertson: Conservative. Born: 1959. Educated: Glasgow University. Jobs: Conservative party official. First Elected: 1992. Posts: member, Scottish Affairs Select Committee.

CON GAIN		1992 election			1987 election	
		Votes	%	+/-	%	Votes
Raymond Robertson	Con	15,808	38.5	+3.6	34.8	14,719
Frank Doran*	Lab	14,291	34.8	-2.9	37.7	15,917
James Davidson	SNP	6,223	15.1	+8.6	6.6	2,776
Irene Keith	Lib Dem	4,767	11.6	-9.3	20.9	8,844
Majority	**Con**	**1,517**	**3.7**	**+6.5**	**2.8**	**1,198**

Electorate: 58,881 **Voters:** 41,089 **Turnout:** 69.8 **Swing:** 3.3 to Con from Lab

ALDERSHOT

Julian Critchley: *Conservative. Born: 1930. Educated: Shrewsbury; Oxford. Jobs: journalist. First Elected: 1959. Status: married, four children.*

CON HOLD		1992 election			1987 election	
		Votes	%	+/-	%	Votes
Julian Critchley*	Con	36,974	57.5	-1.5	59.0	35,272
Adrian Collett	Lib Dem	17,786	27.6	-1.6	29.2	17,488
John Anthony Smith	Lab	8,552	13.3	+1.5	11.8	7,061
David Robinson	Lib	1,038	1.6			
Majority	**Con**	**19,188**	**29.8**	**+0.1**	**29.7**	**17,784**

Electorate: 81,754 **Voters:** 64,350 **Turnout:** 78.7 **Swing:** No Swing

ALDRIDGE-BROWNHILLS

Richard Shepherd: *Conservative. Born: 1942. Educated: London School of Economics. First Elected: 1979.*

CON HOLD		1992 election			1987 election	
		Votes	%	+/-	%	Votes
Richard Shepherd*	Con	28,431	54.3	+1.0	53.3	26,434
Neil Fawcett	Lab	17,407	33.3	+4.9	28.3	14,038
Stewart Reynolds	Lib Dem	6,503	12.4	-5.9	18.3	9,084
Majority	**Con**	**11,024**	**21.1**	**-4.0**	**25.0**	**12,396**

Electorate: 63,404 **Voters:** 52,341 **Turnout:** 82.6 **Swing:** 2.0 to Lab from Con

ALTRINCHAM & SALE

Sir Fergus Montgomery: *Conservative. Born: 1927. Educated: Jarrow Grammar School; Durham University. First Elected: 1959. Posts: Committee of Selection. Status: married*

CON HOLD		1992 election			1987 election	
		Votes	%	+/-	%	Votes
Sir Fergus Montgomery*	Con	29,066	54.7	+1.2	53.5	27,746
Mary Atherton	Lab	12,275	23.1	+2.6	20.5	10,617
John Mulholland	Lib Dem	11,601	21.8	-4.2	26.1	13,518
John Renwick	NLP	212	0.4			
Majority	**Con**	**16,791**	**31.6**	**+4.2**	**27.4**	**14,228**

Electorate: 65,897 **Voters:** 53,154 **Turnout:** 80.7 **Swing:** 0.7 to Lab from Con

CONSTITUENCIES

ALYN & DEESIDE

Barry Jones: Labour. Born: 1938. Educated: Hawarden Grammar School; Bangor College of Education. Jobs: teacher, union official. First Elected: 1970. Status: married, one child

LAB HOLD

		1992 election Votes	%	+/-	1987 election %	Votes
Barry Jones*	Lab	25,206	52.0	+3.5	48.6	22,916
Jeffrey Riley	Con	17,355	35.8	+0.8	35.0	16,533
Bob Britton	Lib Dem	4,687	9.7	-5.7	15.4	7,273
John Rogers	Plaid Cymru	551	1.1	+0.1	1.0	478
Victor Button	Green	433	0.9			
John Cooksey	Ind	200	0.4			
Majority	**Lab**	**7,851**	**16.2**	**+2.7**	**13.5**	**6,383**

Electorate: 60,477 **Voters:** 48,432 **Turnout:** 80.1 **Swing:** 1.3 to Lab from Con

AMBER VALLEY

Phillip Oppenheim: Conservative. Born: 1956. Educated: Harrow; Oxford. First Elected: 1983. Posts: PPS. Status: single

CON HOLD

		1992 election Votes	%	+/-	1987 election %	Votes
Phillip Oppenheim*	Con	27,418	46.1	-5.3	51.4	28,603
John Cooper	Lab	26,706	44.9	+10.6	34.4	19,103
Graham Brocklebank	Lib Dem	5,294	8.9	-5.3	14.2	7,904
Majority	**Con**	**712**	**1.2**	**-15.9**	**17.1**	**9,500**

Electorate: 70,155 **Voters:** 59,418 **Turnout:** 84.7 **Swing:** 7.9 to Lab from Con

ANGUS EAST

Andrew Welsh: Scottish National Party. Born: 1944. Educated: Govan High School; Glasgow University. Jobs: teacher. First Elected: 1974. Posts: member, Scottish Affairs Select Committee. Status: married, one chld.

SNP HOLD

		1992 election Votes	%	+/-	1987 election %	Votes
Andrew Welsh*	SNP	19,006	40.1	-2.3	42.4	19,536
Ronald Harris	Con	18,052	38.1	-0.9	39.0	17,992
Geoffrey Taylor	Lab	5,994	12.6	+1.9	10.8	4,971
Callum McLeod	Lib Dem	3,897	8.2	+0.4	7.8	3,592
Duncan McCabe	Green	449	0.9			
Majority	**SNP**	**954**	**2.0**	**-1.3**	**3.3**	**1,544**

Electorate: 63,170 **Voters:** 47,398 **Turnout:** 75.0 **Swing:** 0.7 to Con from SNP

ANTRIM EAST

Roy Beggs: Ulster Unionist Party. Born: 1936. Educated: Ballyclare High School; Stranmillis Training College. Jobs: teacher. First Elected: 1983. Status: married, four children.

UUP HOLD		1992 election			1987 election	
		Votes	%	+/-	%	Votes
Roy Beggs*	UUP	16,966	43.2	-28.3	71.6	23,942
Nigel Dodds	DUP	9,544	24.3			
Sean Neeson	All	9,132	23.3	-2.4	25.6	8,582
Myrtle Boal	Con	3,359	8.6			
Andrea Palmer	NLP	250	0.6			
Majority	**UUP**	**7,422**	**18.9**	**-27.0**	**45.9**	**15,360**

Electorate: 62,839 **Voters:** 39,251 **Turnout:** 62.5

ANTRIM NORTH

Rev Ian Paisley: Democratic Unionist Party. Born: 1926. Educated: Ballymena Model School; Ballymena Technical High School. Jobs: minister. First Elected: 1970. Posts: Euro MP; Leader of Democratic Unionist Party. Status: married, five children.

DUP HOLD		1992 election			1987 election	
		Votes	%	+/-	%	Votes
Rev Ian Paisley*	DUP	23,152	50.9	-17.8	68.7	28,383
Joe Gaston	UUP	8,216	18.1			
Sean Farren	SDLP	6,512	14.3	+1.8	12.5	5,149
Gareth Williams	All	3,442	7.6	-4.9	12.4	5,140
Richard Sowler	Con	2,263	5.0			
James McGarry	Sinn Fein	1,916	4.2	-2.2	6.4	2,633
Majority	**DUP**	**14,936**	**32.8**	**-23.4**	**56.2**	**23,234**

Electorate: 69,124 **Voters:** 45,501 **Turnout:** 65.8

ANTRIM SOUTH

Clifford Forsythe: Ulster Unionist Party. Born: 1929. Educated: Glengormley Public Elementary School. Jobs: footballer, plumbing contractor. First Elected: 1983. Posts: UUP spokesman on transport and local government; member, Social Security Select Committee.

UUP HOLD		1992 election			1987 election	
		Votes	%	+/-	%	Votes
Clifford Forsythe*	UUP	29,956	70.9	+1.2	69.8	25,395
Donovan McClelland	SDLP	5,397	12.8	+2.9	9.9	3,611
John Blair	All	5,224	12.4	-3.6	16.0	5,808
Henry Cushinan	Sinn Fein	1,220	2.9	-1.5	4.4	1,592
Dino Martin	Loony G	442	1.0			
Majority	**UUP**	**24,559**	**58.1**	**+4.3**	**53.8**	**19,587**

Electorate: 68,013 **Voters:** 42,239 **Turnout:** 62.1 **Swing:** 0.8 to SDLP from UUP

CONSTITUENCIES

ARGYLL & BUTE

Ray Michie: Liberal Democrat. Born: 1934. Educated: Aberdeen High School for girls. Jobs: speech therapist. First Elected: 1987. Posts: LibDem spokeswoman on Scotland and women's issues; member, Scottish Affairs Select Committee. Status: married, three children.

LIBDEM HOLD		1992 election Votes	%	+/-	1987 election %	Votes
Ray Michie*	Lib Dem	12,739	34.9	-2.4	37.3	13,726
John Corrie	Con	10,117	27.7	-5.8	33.5	12,332
Prof Neil MacCormick	SNP	8,689	23.8	+6.7	17.1	6,297
Desmond Browne	Lab	4,946	13.6	+1.5	12.1	4,437
Majority	**Lib Dem**	**2,622**	**7.2**	**+3.4**	**3.8**	**1,394**

Electorate: 47,894 **Voters:** 36,491 **Turnout:** 76.2 **Swing:** 1.7 to LDm from Con

ARUNDEL

Sir Michael Marshall: Conservative. Born: 1930. Educated: Bradfield College; Harvard. Jobs: company chairman. First Elected: 1974. Union: Equity. Status: married

CON HOLD		1992 election Votes	%	+/-	1987 election %	Votes
Sir Michael Marshall*	Con	35,405	58.0	-3.4	61.3	34,356
James Walsh	Lib Dem	15,542	25.5	-2.2	27.6	15,476
Roger Nash	Lab	8,321	13.6	+2.6	11.0	6,177
Denise Renson	Lib	1,103	1.8			
Rob Corbin	Green	693	1.1			
Majority	**Con**	**19,863**	**32.5**	**-1.2**	**33.7**	**18,880**

Electorate: 79,241 **Voters:** 61,064 **Turnout:** 77.1 **Swing:** 0.6 to LDm from Con

ASHFIELD

Geoff Hoon: Labour. Born: 1953. Educated: Cambridge. Jobs: barrister. First Elected: 1992. Posts: Euro MP for Derbyshire and Ashfield. Union: TGWU Status: married, three children

LAB HOLD		1992 election Votes	%	+/-	1987 election %	Votes
Geoff Hoon	Lab	32,018	54.9	+13.2	41.7	22,812
Laurence Robertson	Con	19,031	32.6	-1.0	33.6	18,412
James Turton	Lib Dem	7,291	12.5	-12.2	24.7	13,542
Majority	**Lab**	**12,987**	**22.3**	**+14.2**	**8.0**	**4,400**

Electorate: 75,075 **Voters:** 58,340 **Turnout:** 77.7 **Swing:** 7.1 to Lab from Con

ASHFORD

Sir Keith Speed: Conservative. Born: 1934. Educated: Bedford Modern School; Royal Naval College. Jobs: marketing manager. First Elected: 1968. Posts: delegate, Council of Europe, Western European Union. Status: married, three children.

CON HOLD		1992 election			1987 election	
		Votes	%	+/-	%	Votes
Keith Speed*	Con	31,031	54.6	-1.9	56.5	29,978
Christine Headley	Lib Dem	13,672	24.1	-3.3	27.3	14,490
Doreen Cameron	Lab	11,365	20.0	+5.3	14.7	7,775
Andrew Porter	Green	773	1.4	-0.1	1.5	778
Majority	**Con**	**17,359**	**30.5**	**+1.3**	**29.2**	**15,488**

Electorate: 71,767 **Voters:** 56,841 **Turnout:** 79.2 **Swing:** 0.7 to Con from LDm

ASHTON-UNDER-LYNE

Robert Sheldon: Labour. Born: 1923. Educated: local state schools; London University. Jobs: engineer. First Elected: 1964. Posts: Chairman, Public Accounts Committee. Union: TGWU. Status: married, two children

LAB HOLD		1992 election			1987 election	
		Votes	%	+/-	%	Votes
Robert Sheldon*	Lab	24,550	56.6	+4.8	51.8	22,389
John Pinniger	Con	13,615	31.4	+1.1	30.3	13,103
Charles Turner	Lib Dem	4,005	9.2	-8.7	17.9	7,760
Colin Hall	Lib	907	2.1			
John Brannigan	NLP	289	0.7			
Majority	**Lab**	**10,935**	**25.2**	**+3.7**	**21.5**	**9,286**

Electorate: 58,701 **Voters:** 43,366 **Turnout:** 73.9 **Swing:** 1.9 to Lab from Con

AYLESBURY

David Lidington: Conservative. Born: 1956. Educated: Cambridge. Jobs: political adviser. First Elected: 1992. Status: married

CON HOLD		1992 election			1987 election	
		Votes	%	+/-	%	Votes
David Lidington	Con	36,500	57.4	-0.1	57.5	32,970
Sharon Bowles	Lib Dem	17,640	27.7	-0.9	28.6	16,412
Roger Priest	Lab	8,517	13.4	-0.5	13.8	7,936
Nigel Foster	Green	702	1.1			
Bruno D'Arcy	NLP	239	0.4			
Majority	**Con**	**18,860**	**29.7**	**+0.8**	**28.9**	**16,558**

Electorate: 79,208 **Voters:** 63,598 **Turnout:** 80.3 **Swing:** 0.4 to Con from LDm

CONSTITUENCIES

AYR

Phil Gallie: Conservative. Born: 1939. Educated: Dunfermline High School. Jobs: electrical engineer, power industry manager. First Elected: 1992. Posts: member, Scottish Affairs Select Committee. Status: married, two children

CON HOLD		1992 election			1987 election	
		Votes	%	+/-	%	Votes
Phil Gallie	Con	22,172	40.8	+1.3	39.4	20,942
Alastair Osborne	Lab	22,087	40.6	+1.5	39.1	20,760
Barbara Mullin	SNP	5,949	10.9	+4.3	6.7	3,548
John Boss	Lib Dem	4,067	7.5	-7.3	14.8	7,859
Richard Scott	NLP	132	0.2			
Majority	**Con**	**85**	**0.2**	**-0.2**	**0.3**	**182**

Electorate: 65,481 **Voters:** 54,407 **Turnout:** 83.1 **Swing:** No Swing

BANBURY

Tony Baldry: Conservative. Born: 1950. Educated: Leighton Park; Sussex University. Jobs: barrister. First Elected: 1983. Posts: junior minister, Department of the Environment. Status: married, two children

CON HOLD		1992 election			1987 election	
		Votes	%	+/-	%	Votes
Tony Baldry*	Con	32,215	55.0	-1.2	56.2	29,716
Angela Billingham	Lab	15,495	26.5	+6.1	20.4	10,789
Geoffrey Fisher	Lib Dem	10,602	18.1	-5.3	23.4	12,386
Robin Ticciati	NLP	250	0.4			
Majority	**Con**	**16,720**	**28.6**	**-4.2**	**32.8**	**17,330**

Electorate: 71,840 **Voters:** 58,562 **Turnout:** 81.5 **Swing:** 3.6 to Lab from Con

BANFF & BUCHAN

Alex Salmond: Scottish National Party. Born: 1954. Educated: Linlithgow Academy; St Andrew's University. Jobs: economist. First Elected: 1987. Posts: National convener of SNP, Treasury spokesman. Status: married.

SNP HOLD		1992 election			1987 election	
		Votes	%	+/-	%	Votes
Alex Salmond*	SNP	21,954	47.5	+3.3	44.3	19,462
Sandy Manson	Con	17,846	38.6	-0.1	38.7	17,021
Brian Balcombe	Lab	3,803	8.2	+0.8	7.5	3,281
Rhona Kemp	Lib Dem	2,588	5.6	-4.0	9.6	4,211
Majority	**SNP**	**4,108**	**8.9**	**+3.3**	**5.6**	**2,441**

Electorate: 64,873 **Voters:** 46,191 **Turnout:** 71.2 **Swing:** 1.7 to SNP from Con

BARKING

Jo Richardson: *Labour. Born: 1923. Educated: local state schools. First Elected: 1974. Union: GMB, MSF. Status: single*

LAB HOLD

		1992 election			1987 election	
		Votes	%	+/-	%	Votes
Jo Richardson*	Lab	18,224	51.6	+7.3	44.3	15,307
John Kennedy	Con	11,956	33.9	-0.6	34.4	11,898
Stephen Churchman	Lib Dem	5,133	14.5	-6.7	21.2	7,336
Majority	**Lab**	**6,268**	**17.7**	**+7.9**	**9.9**	**3,409**

Electorate: 50,454 **Voters:** 35,313 **Turnout:** 70.0 **Swing:** 3.9 to Lab from Con

BARNSLEY CENTRAL

Eric Illsley: *Labour. Born: 1955. Educated: Leeds University. Jobs: union official. First Elected: 1987. Posts: Labour Whip. Status: married, two children*

LAB HOLD

		1992 election			1987 election	
		Votes	%	+/-	%	Votes
Eric Illsley*	Lab	27,048	69.3	+2.5	66.8	26,139
David Senior	Con	7,687	19.7	+1.6	18.1	7,088
Stephen Cowton	Lib Dem	4,321	11.1	-4.1	15.1	5,928
Majority	**Lab**	**19,361**	**49.6**	**+0.9**	**48.7**	**19,051**

Electorate: 55,373 **Voters:** 39,056 **Turnout:** 70.5 **Swing:** 0.5 to Lab from Con

BARNSLEY EAST

Terry Patchett: *Labour. Born: 1940. Educated: local state schools. Jobs: miner First Elected: 1983. Union: NUM. Status: married, three children*

LAB HOLD

		1992 election			1987 election	
		Votes	%	+/-	%	Votes
Terry Patchett*	Lab	30,346	77.2	+2.7	74.5	28,948
John Procter	Con	5,569	14.2	+0.2	14.0	5,437
Sylvia Anginotti	Lib Dem	3,399	8.6	-2.9	11.5	4,482
Majority	**Lab**	**24,777**	**63.0**	**+2.5**	**60.5**	**23,511**

Electorate: 54,051 **Voters:** 39,314 **Turnout:** 72.7 **Swing:** 1.3 to Lab from Con

BARNSLEY WEST & PENISTONE

Michael Clapham: Labour. Born: 1943. Educated: Leeds Polytechnic. Jobs: miner, college lecturer. First Elected: 1992. Union: NUM. Status: married, two children.

LAB HOLD		1992 election Votes	%	+/-	1987 election %	Votes
Michael Clapham	Lab	27,965	58.3	+0.9	57.3	26,498
Graham Sawyer	Con	13,461	28.0	+1.4	26.6	12,307
Ian Nicolson	Lib Dem	5,610	11.7	-4.3	16.0	7,409
Don Jones	Green	970	2.0			
Majority	**Lab**	**14,504**	**30.2**	**-0.5**	**30.7**	**14,191**

Electorate: 63,374 **Voters:** 48,006 **Turnout:** 75.8 **Swing:** 0.2 to Con from Lab

BARROW & FURNESS

John Hutton: Labour. Born: 1955. Educated: Oxford. Jobs: lecturer. First Elected: 1992. Status: married, four children.

LAB GAIN		1992 election Votes	%	+/-	1987 election %	Votes
John Hutton	Lab	26,568	47.7	+8.5	39.3	21,504
Cecil Franks*	Con	22,990	41.3	-5.1	46.5	25,432
Clive Crane	Lib Dem	6,089	10.9	-3.3	14.2	7,799
Majority	**Lab**	**3,578**	**6.4**	**+13.6**	**7.2**	**3,928**

Electorate: 67,764 **Voters:** 55,647 **Turnout:** 82.1 **Swing:** 6.8 to Lab from Con

BASILDON

David Amess: Conservative. Born: 1952. Educated: St. Bonaventure's primary school. Jobs: teacher, accountant. First Elected: 1983. Posts: PPS. Status: married, five children.

CON HOLD		1992 election Votes	%	+/-	1987 election %	Votes
David Amess*	Con	24,159	44.9	+1.4	43.5	21,858
John Potter	Lab	22,679	42.2	+3.9	38.3	19,209
Geoff Williams	Lib Dem	6,967	12.9	-5.3	18.2	9,139
Majority	**Con**	**1,480**	**2.8**	**-2.5**	**5.3**	**2,649**

Electorate: 67,585 **Voters:** 53,805 **Turnout:** 79.6 **Swing:** 1.3 to Lab from Con

BASINGSTOKE

Andrew Hunter: Conservative. Born: 1943. Educated: St. George's School, Harpenden; Durham and Cambridge Universities. Jobs: teacher. First Elected: 1983. Status: married, two children.

CON HOLD

		1992 election Votes	%	+/-	1987 election %	Votes
Andrew Hunter*	Con	37,521	54.6	-1.4	56.0	33,657
David Bull	Lab	16,323	23.8	+6.1	17.7	10,632
Chris Curtis	Lib Dem	14,119	20.6	-5.7	26.3	15,764
Valerie Oldaker	Green	714	1.0			
Majority	**Con**	**21,198**	**30.9**	**+1.1**	**29.8**	**17,893**

Electorate: 82,952 **Voters:** 68,677 **Turnout:** 82.8 **Swing:** 3.7 to Lab from Con

BASSETLAW

Joe Ashton: Labour. Born: 1933. Educated: High Storrs Grammar School; Sheffield Technical College. Jobs: engineer, journalist. First Elected: 1968. Posts: member, National Heritage Select Committee. Status: married, one child.

LAB HOLD

		1992 election Votes	%	+/-	1987 election %	Votes
Joe Ashton*	Lab	29,061	53.4	+5.3	48.1	25,385
Caroline Spelman	Con	19,064	35.0	-2.5	37.5	19,772
Mike Reynolds	Lib Dem	6,340	11.6	-2.8	14.4	7,616
Majority	**Lab**	**9,997**	**18.4**	**+7.7**	**10.6**	**5,613**

Electorate: 69,375 **Voters:** 54,465 **Turnout:** 78.5 **Swing:** 3.9 to Lab from Con

BATH

Don Foster: Liberal Democrat. Born: 1947. Educated: Keele University. Jobs: teacher, management consultant. First Elected: 1992. Posts: Lib Dem spokesman on education and training. Status: married, two children

LIBDEM GAIN

		1992 election Votes	%	+/-	1987 election %	Votes
Don Foster	Lib Dem	25,718	48.9	+6.3	42.7	22,103
Chris Patten*	Con	21,950	41.8	-3.6	45.4	23,515
Pam Richards	Lab	4,102	7.8	-2.8	10.6	5,507
Duncan McCanlis	Green	433	0.8	-0.5	1.3	687
May Barker	Lib	172	0.3			
Alan Sked	Anti Fed	117	0.2			
John Rumming	Ind	79	0.2			
Majority	**Lib Dem**	**3,768**	**7.2**	**+9.9**	**2.7**	**1,412**

Electorate: 63,689 **Voters:** 52,571 **Turnout:** 82.5 **Swing:** 4.9 to LDm from Con

BATLEY & SPEN

Mrs Elizabeth Peacock: Conservative. Born: 1937. Educated: St. Monica's Convent, Skipton. First Elected: 1983. Posts: PPS. Status: married, two children.

CON HOLD		1992 election			1987 election	
		Votes	%	+/-	%	Votes
Elizabeth Peacock*	Con	27,629	45.4	+2.0	43.4	25,512
Eunice Durkin	Lab	26,221	43.1	+2.0	41.1	24,150
Gordon Beever	Lib Dem	6,380	10.5	-3.8	14.3	8,372
Clive Lord	Green	628	1.0			
Majority	**Con**	**1,408**	**2.3**	**-0.0**	**2.3**	**1,362**

Electorate: 76,417 **Voters:** 60,858 **Turnout:** 79.6 **Swing:** No Swing

BATTERSEA

John Bowis: Conservative. Born: 1945. Educated: Tonbridge School; Oxford. Jobs: party official. First Elected: 1987. Posts: PPS; vice-president, Conservative Trade Unionists. Status: married, three children

CON HOLD		1992 election			1987 election	
		Votes	%	+/-	%	Votes
John Bowis*	Con	26,390	50.5	+6.2	44.2	20,945
Alf Dubs	Lab	21,550	41.2	-1.2	42.4	20,088
Roger O'Brien	Lib Dem	3,659	7.0	-4.9	11.9	5,634
Ian Wingrove	Green	584	1.1	-0.1	1.2	559
Bill Stevens	NLP	98	0.2			
Majority	**Con**	**4,840**	**9.3**	**+7.4**	**1.8**	**857**

Electorate: 68,218 **Voters:** 52,281 **Turnout:** 76.6 **Swing:** 3.7 to Con from Lab

BEACONSFIELD

Timothy Smith: Conservative. Born: 1947. Educated: Harrow; Oxford. Jobs: accountant. First Elected: 1977. Posts: vice chairman, Conservative Party. Status: married, two children.

CON HOLD		1992 election			1987 election	
		Votes	%	+/-	%	Votes
Timothy Smith*	Con	33,817	64.0	-2.0	66.0	33,324
Anne Purse	Lib Dem	10,220	19.3	-4.4	23.7	11,985
Graham Smith	Lab	7,163	13.5	+3.2	10.3	5,203
William Foulds	Ind C	1,317	2.5			
Andrew Foss	NLP	196	0.4			
Joan Martin	ERIP	166	0.3			
Majority	**Con**	**23,597**	**44.6**	**+2.4**	**42.2**	**21,339**

Electorate: 64,268 **Voters:** 52,879 **Turnout:** 82.3 **Swing:** 1.2 to Con from LDm

BECKENHAM

Piers Merchant: *Conservative. Born: 1951. Educated: Durham University. Jobs: journalist, advertising. First Elected: 1983. Posts: PPS. Status: married, two children.*

CON HOLD		1992 election			1987 election	
		Votes	%	+/-	%	Votes
Piers Merchant	Con	26,323	56.9	+0.6	56.3	24,903
Kenneth Ritchie	Lab	11,038	23.8	+6.0	17.8	7,888
Mary Williams	Lib Dem	8,038	17.4	-8.5	25.9	11,439
Gerry Williams	Lib	643	1.4			
Patrick Shaw	NLP	243	0.5			
Majority	**Con**	**15,285**	**33.0**	**+2.6**	**30.4**	**13,464**

Electorate: 59,440 **Voters:** 46,285 **Turnout:** 77.9 **Swing:** 2.7 to Lab from Con

BEDFORDSHIRE MID

Sir Nicholas Lyell: *Conservative. Born: 1938. Educated: Stowe; Oxford. Jobs: barrister. First Elected: 1979. Posts: Attorney-General. Status: married, four children.*

CON HOLD		1992 election			1987 election	
		Votes	%	+/-	%	Votes
Sir Nicholas Lyell*	Con	40,230	58.2	-0.8	59.0	37,411
Richard Clayton	Lab	15,092	21.8	+3.8	18.1	11,463
Nick Hills	Lib Dem	11,957	17.3	-5.7	23.0	14,560
Phil Cottier	Lib	1,582	2.3			
Marek Lorys	NLP	279	0.4			
Majority	**Con**	**25,138**	**36.4**	**+0.3**	**36.0**	**22,851**

Electorate: 81,864 **Voters:** 69,140 **Turnout:** 84.5 **Swing:** 2.3 to Lab from Con

BEDFORDSHIRE NORTH

Sir Trevor Skeet: *Conservative. Born: 1918. Educated: Kings College, Auckland University, New Zealand. Jobs: barrister. First Elected: 1959. Posts: member, Science and Technology Select Committee. Status: married, two children.*

CON HOLD		1992 election			1987 election	
		Votes	%	+/-	%	Votes
Sir Trevor Skeet*	Con	29,920	50.7	-1.9	52.6	29,845
Patrick Hall	Lab	18,302	31.0	+7.8	23.2	13,140
Michael Smithson	Lib Dem	10,014	17.0	-6.5	23.5	13,340
Louise Smith	Green	643	1.1			
Bernard Bench	NLP	178	0.3			
Majority	**Con**	**11,618**	**19.7**	**-9.4**	**29.1**	**16,505**

Electorate: 73,789 **Voters:** 59,057 **Turnout:** 80.0 **Swing:** 4.9 to Lab from Con

CONSTITUENCIES

BEDFORDSHIRE SOUTH WEST

David Madel: Conservative. Born: 1938. Educated: Uppingham; Oxford. Jobs: advertising executive. First Elected: 1970. Posts: member, European Legislation Select Committee. Status: married, two children.

CON HOLD

		1992 election			1987 election	
		Votes	%	+/-	%	Votes
David Madel*	Con	37,498	57.1	-1.0	58.2	36,140
Barry Elliott	Lab	16,225	24.7	+6.5	18.3	11,352
Mark Freeman	Lib Dem	10,988	16.7	-5.5	22.3	13,835
Peter Rollings	Green	689	1.0	-0.3	1.3	822
Dobie Gilmour	NLP	239	0.4			
Majority	**Con**	**21,273**	**32.4**	**-3.5**	**35.9**	**22,305**

Electorate: 79,662 **Voters:** 65,639 **Turnout:** 82.4 **Swing:** 3.7 to Lab from Con

BELFAST EAST

Peter Robinson: Democratic Unionist Party. Born: 1948. Educated: Annadale Grammar School; Castlereagh College of Further Education. First Elected: 1979. Status: married, three children.

DUP HOLD

		1992 election			1987 election	
		Votes	%	+/-	%	Votes
Peter Robinson*	DUP	18,437	51.5	-10.4	61.9	20,372
John Alderdice	All	10,650	29.8	-2.4	32.1	10,574
David Greene	Con	3,314	9.3			
Dorothy Dunlop	Ind U	2,256	6.3			
Joe O'Donnell	Sinn Fein	679	1.9	-0.1	2.0	649
Joe Bell	WP	327	0.9	-3.1	4.0	1,314
Guy Redden	NLP	128	0.4			
Majority	**DUP**	**7,787**	**21.8**	**-8.0**	**29.8**	**9,798**

Electorate: 52,833 **Voters:** 35,791 **Turnout:** 67.7 **Swing:** 4.0 to All from DUP

BELFAST NORTH

Cecil Walker: United Ulster Unionist Party. Born: 1924. Educated: Methodist College, Belfast. Jobs: timber executive. First Elected: 1983. Status: married, two children.

UUP HOLD

		1992 election			1987 election	
		Votes	%	+/-	%	Votes
Cecil Walker*	UUP	17,240	48.0	+9.0	39.0	14,355
Alban Maginness	SDLP	7,615	21.2	+5.5	15.7	5,795
Paddy McManus	Sinn Fein	4,693	13.1	-0.7	13.7	5,062
Tom Campbell	All	2,246	6.3	-1.5	7.8	2,871
Margaret Redpath	Con	2,107	5.9			
Seamus Lynch	NA	1,386	3.9			
Margaret Smith	WP	419	1.2	-7.2	8.3	3,062
Daniel O'Leary	NLP	208	0.6			
Majority	**UUP**	**9,625**	**26.8**	**+3.5**	**23.3**	**8,560**

Electorate: 55,062 **Voters:** 35,914 **Turnout:** 65.2 **Swing:** 1.8 to UUP from SDLP

BELFAST SOUTH

Rev Martin Smyth: Ulster Unionist Party. Born: 1931. Educated: Methodist College, Belfast, Londonderry. Jobs: minister. First Elected: 1982. Posts: member, Health Select Committee. Status: married, two children.

UUP HOLD		1992 election			1987 election	
		Votes	%	+/-	%	Votes
Rev Martin Smyth*	UUP	16,336	48.6	-9.2	57.8	18,917
Alasdair McDonnell	SDLP	6,266	18.7	+5.6	13.0	4,268
John Montgomery	All	5,054	15.0	-6.2	21.3	6,963
Leonard Fee	Con	3,356	10.0			
Sean Hayes	Sinn Fein	1,123	3.3	+0.2	3.1	1,030
Peter Hadden	LTU	875	2.6			
Patrick Lynn	WP	362	1.1	-3.6	4.7	1,528
Teresa Mullan	NLP	212	0.6			
Majority	**UUP**	**10,070**	**30.0**	**-6.6**	**36.5**	**11,954**

Electorate: 52,032 **Voters:** 33,584 **Turnout:** 64.5 **Swing:** 7.4 to SDLP from UUP

BELFAST WEST

Dr Joe Hendron: Social Democratic and Labour Party. Born: 1932. Educated: St Malachy's College, Queen's University, Belfast. Jobs: doctor. First Elected: 1992. Status: married, four children.

SDLP GAIN		1992 election			1987 election	
		Votes	%	+/-	%	Votes
Joe Hendron	SDLP	17,415	43.6	+7.8	35.7	14,641
Gerry Adams*	Sinn Fein	16,826	42.1	+0.9	41.2	16,862
Fred Cobain	UUP	4,766	11.9	-6.7	18.7	7,646
John Lowry	WP	750	1.9	-2.6	4.4	1,819
Michael Kennedy	NLP	213	0.5			
Majority	**SDLP**	**589**	**1.5**	**+6.9**	**5.4**	**2,221**

Electorate: 54,609 **Voters:** 39,970 **Turnout:** 73.2 **Swing:** 3.4 to SDLP from Sinn Fein

BERKSHIRE EAST

Andrew Mackay: Conservative. Born: 1949. Educated: Solihull School. Jobs: consultant. First Elected: 1983. Status: married, two children.

CON HOLD		1992 election			1987 election	
		Votes	%	+/-	%	Votes
Andrew Mackay*	Con	43,898	59.7	-0.6	60.3	39,094
Linda Murray	LibDem	15,218	20.7	-4.7	25.4	16,468
Keith Dibble	Lab	14,458	19.7	+5.3	14.3	9,287
Majority	**Con**	**28,680**	**39.0**	**+4.1**	**34.9**	**22,626**

Electorate: 90,365 **Voters:** 73,574 **Turnout:** 81.4 **Swing:** 2.0 to Con from LDm

CONSTITUENCIES

BERWICK-UPON-TWEED

Alan Beith: Liberal Democrat. Born: 1943. Educated: King's School, Macclesfield; Oxford. Jobs: lecturer. First Elected: 1973. Posts: LibDem Treasury Spokesman; member, House of Commons Commission, Treasury and Civil Service Select Committee. Status: married, two children.

LIBDEM HOLD		1992 election			1987 election	
		Votes	%	+/-	%	Votes
Alan Beith*	Lib Dem	19,283	44.4	-7.7	52.1	21,903
Anthony Henfrey	Con	14,240	32.8	+3.3	29.5	12,400
Gordon Adam	Lab	9,933	22.9	+5.4	17.5	7,360
Majority	**Lib Dem**	**5,043**	**11.6**	**-11.0**	**22.6**	**9,503**

Electorate: 54,919 **Voters:** 43,456 **Turnout:** 79.1 **Swing:** 5.5 to Con from LDm

BETHNAL GREEN & STEPNEY

Peter Shore: Labour. Born: 1924. Educated: Quarry Bank Grammar School, Liverpool; Cambridge. Jobs: party research director. First Elected: 1964. Union: TGWU. Posts: member, Foreign Affairs Select Committee. Status: married, three children.

LAB HOLD		1992 election			1987 election	
		Votes	%	+/-	%	Votes
Peter Shore*	Lab	20,350	55.8	+7.6	48.2	15,490
Jeremy Shaw	Lib Dem	8,120	22.3	-9.5	31.8	10,206
Jane Emmerson	Con	6,507	17.9	-1.4	19.2	6,176
Richard Edmonds	BNP	1,310	3.6			
Stanley Kelsey	Comm GB	156	0.4			
Majority	**Lab**	**12,230**	**33.6**	**+17.1**	**16.5**	**5,284**

Electorate: 55,675 **Voters:** 36,443 **Turnout:** 65.5 **Swing:** 8.6 to Lab from LDm

BEVERLEY

James Cran: Conservative. Born: 1944. Educated: Ruthrieston School; Aberdeen and Heriot Watt Universities. Jobs: party researcher. First Elected: 1987. Status: married, one child.

CON HOLD		1992 election			1987 election	
		Votes	%	+/-	%	Votes
James Cran*	Con	34,503	53.3	+1.1	52.2	31,459
Arthur Collinge	Lib Dem	17,986	27.8	-3.5	31.3	18,864
Colin Challen	Lab	12,026	18.6	+2.1	16.4	9,901
David Hetherington	NLP	199	0.3			
Majority	**Con**	**16,517**	**25.5**	**+4.6**	**20.9**	**12,595**

Electorate: 81,198 **Voters:** 64,714 **Turnout:** 79.7 **Swing:** 2.3 to Con from LDm

BEXHILL & BATTLE

Charles Wardle: *Conservative. Born: 1939. Educated: Tonbridge School; Oxford. Jobs: merchant banker. First Elected: 1983. Status: married, one child.*

CON HOLD		1992 election			1987 election	
		Votes	%	+/-	%	Votes
Charles Wardle*	Con	31,330	60.2	-6.2	66.4	33,570
Susan Prochak	Lib Dem	15,023	28.9	+3.0	25.8	13,051
Frank Taylor	Lab	4,883	9.4	+1.7	7.7	3,903
Jonathan Prus	Green	594	1.1			
Mary Smith	CSP	190	0.4			
Majority	**Con**	**16,307**	**31.3**	**-9.3**	**40.6**	**20,519**

Electorate: 65,850 **Voters:** 52,020 **Turnout:** 79.0 **Swing:** 4.6 to LDm from Con

BEXLEYHEATH

Cyril Townsend: *Conservative. Born: 1937. Educated: Bradfield College; Sandhurst. Jobs: Army officer. First Elected: 1974. Posts: joint chairman, Council for the Advancement of Arab British Understanding. Status: married, two children.*

CON HOLD		1992 election			1987 election	
		Votes	%	+/-	%	Votes
Cyril Townsend*	Con	25,606	54.0	+0.3	53.7	24,866
John Browning	Lab	11,520	24.3	+6.5	17.8	8,218
Wendy Chaplin	Lib Dem	10,107	21.3	-7.2	28.5	13,179
Roger Cundy	Ind	170	0.4			
Majority	**Con**	**14,086**	**29.7**	**+4.5**	**25.3**	**11,687**

Electorate: 57,684 **Voters:** 47,403 **Turnout:** 82.2 **Swing:** 3.1 to Lab from Con

BILLERICAY

Teresa Gorman: *Conservative. Born: 1931. Educated: Fulham County School; London University. Jobs: teacher, company manager. First Elected: 1987. Status: married.*

CON HOLD		1992 election			1987 election	
		Votes	%	+/-	%	Votes
Teresa Gorman*	Con	37,406	56.5	+1.6	54.9	33,741
Frank Bellard	Lib Dem	14,912	22.5	-3.1	25.6	15,725
Alison Miller	Lab	13,880	21.0	+1.5	19.4	11,942
Majority	**Con**	**22,494**	**34.0**	**+4.6**	**29.3**	**18,016**

Electorate: 80,388 **Voters:** 66,198 **Turnout:** 82.3 **Swing:** 2.3 to Con from LDm

BIRKENHEAD

Frank Field: Labour. Born: 1942. Educated: St. Clement Danes Grammar School; Hull University. Jobs: director, Low Pay Unit. First Elected: 1979. Posts: chairman, Social Security Select Committee. Union: TGWU. Status: single.

LAB HOLD		1992 election			1987 election	
		Votes	%	+/-	%	Votes
Frank Field*	Lab	29,098	63.6	+4.9	58.7	27,883
Robert Hughes	Con	11,485	25.1	-1.2	26.3	12,511
Pat Williams	Lib Dem	4,417	9.7	-5.3	14.9	7,095
Tina Fox	Green	543	1.2			
Bridget Griffiths	NLP	190	0.4			
Majority	**Lab**	**17,613**	**38.5**	**+6.1**	**32.4**	**15,372**

Electorate: 62,682 **Voters:** 45,733 **Turnout:** 73.0 **Swing:** 3.1 to Lab from Con

BIRMINGHAM, EDGBASTON

Dame Jill Knight: Conservative. Born: 1927. Educated: King Edward Grammar School, Birmingham. Jobs: company director. First Elected: 1966. Posts: executive member, 1922 Committee. Status: widow, two children.

CON HOLD		1992 election			1987 election	
		Votes	%	+/-	%	Votes
Dame Jill Knight*	Con	18,529	49.0	-0.8	49.8	18,595
John Wilton	Lab	14,222	37.6	+10.8	26.8	10,014
Iain Robertson-Steel	Lib Dem	4,419	11.7	-9.3	21.0	7,843
Phil Simpson	Green	643	1.7	+0.2	1.5	559
Majority	**Con**	**4,307**	**11.4**	**-11.6**	**23.0**	**8,581**

Electorate: 53,041 **Voters:** 37,813 **Turnout:** 71.3 **Swing:** 5.8 to Lab from Con

BIRMINGHAM, ERDINGTON

Robin Corbett: Labour. Born: 1933. Educated: Holly Lodge Grammar School, Smethwick. Jobs: journalist. First Elected: 1974. Posts: Labour spokesman on national heritage. Status: married, three children.

LAB HOLD		1992 election			1987 election	
		Votes	%	+/-	%	Votes
Robin Corbett*	Lab	18,549	50.5	+4.6	45.9	17,037
Stanley Hope	Con	13,814	37.6	-1.7	39.2	14,570
John Campbell	Lib Dem	4,398	12.0	-2.9	14.9	5,530
Majority	**Lab**	**4,735**	**12.9**	**+6.2**	**6.6**	**2,467**

Electorate: 52,398 **Voters:** 36,761 **Turnout:** 70.2 **Swing:** 3.1 to Lab from Con

BIRMINGHAM, HALL GREEN

Andrew Hargreaves: Conservative. Born: 1955. Educated: Eton; Oxford. Jobs: auctioneer. First Elected: 1987. Status: married, two children.

CON HOLD		1992 election			1987 election	
		Votes	%	+/-	%	Votes
Andrew Hargreaves*	Con	21,649	46.1	+1.2	44.9	20,478
Jane Slowey	Lab	17,984	38.3	+10.1	28.2	12,857
David McGrath	Lib Dem	7,342	15.6	-11.4	27.0	12,323
Majority	**Con**	**3,665**	**7.8**	**-8.9**	**16.7**	**7,621**

Electorate: 60,091 **Voters**: 46,975 **Turnout**: 78.2 **Swing**: 4.4 to Lab from Con

BIRMINGHAM, HODGE HILL

Terry Davis: Labour. Born: 1938. Educated: King Edward VI Grammar School, Stourbridge; London University. Jobs: motor industry manager. First Elected: 1971. Posts: member, Public Accounts Committee. Union: MSF. Status: married, two children.

LAB HOLD		1992 election			1987 election	
		Votes	%	+/-	%	Votes
Terry Davis*	Lab	21,895	53.6	+4.9	48.7	19,872
Elizabeth Gibson	Con	14,827	36.3	-0.6	36.9	15,083
Sean Hagan	Lib Dem	3,740	9.2	-5.2	14.4	5,868
Eddy Whicker	NF	370	0.9			
Majority	**Lab**	**7,068**	**17.3**	**+5.6**	**11.7**	**4,789**

Electorate: 57,651 **Voters**: 40,832 **Turnout**: 70.8 **Swing**: 2.8 to Lab from Con

BIRMINGHAM, LADYWOOD

Clare Short: Labour. Born: 1946. Educated: Leeds University. Jobs: director of voluntary organisations. First Elected: 1983. Posts: Labour spokeswoman on environmental protection; member, National Executive. Status: married.

LAB HOLD		1992 election			1987 election	
		Votes	%	+/-	%	Votes
Clare Short*	Lab	24,887	66.3	+8.6	57.7	21,971
Barbara Ashford	Con	9,604	25.6	-5.8	31.3	11,943
Brian Worth	Lib Dem	3,068	8.2	-1.1	9.3	3,532
Majority	**Lab**	**15,283**	**40.7**	**+14.4**	**26.3**	**10,028**

Electorate: 56,970 **Voters**: 37,559 **Turnout**: 65.9 **Swing**: 7.2 to Lab from Con

CONSTITUENCIES

BIRMINGHAM, NORTHFIELD

Richard Burden: Labour. Born 1954. Educated: local state schools; Warwick University. Jobs: trade union offficial. First Elected: 1992. Status: single.

LAB GAIN

		1992 election			1987 election	
		Votes	%	+/-	%	Votes
Richard Burden	Lab	24,433	45.5	+6.3	39.2	20,889
Roger King*	Con	23,803	44.4	-0.8	45.1	24,024
David Cropp	Lib Dem	5,431	10.1	-5.5	15.6	8,319
Majority	**Lab**	**630**	**1.2**	**+7.1**	**5.9**	**3,135**

Electorate: 70,533 **Voters:** 53,667 **Turnout:** 76.1 **Swing:** 3.5 to Lab from Con

BIRMINGHAM, PERRY BARR

Jeff Rooker: Labour. Born: 1941. Educated: Handsworth Technical School; Aston University. Jobs: lecturer. First Elected: 1974. Posts: Labour spokesman on education. Union: MSF. Status: married.

LAB HOLD

		1992 election			1987 election	
		Votes	%	+/-	%	Votes
Jeff Rooker*	Lab	27,507	53.2	+2.8	50.4	25,894
Graham Green	Con	18,917	36.6	-0.3	36.9	18,961
Toby Philpott	Lib Dem	5,261	10.2	-2.5	12.7	6,514
Majority	**Lab**	**8,590**	**16.6**	**+3.1**	**13.5**	**6,933**

Electorate: 72,161 **Voters:** 51,685 **Turnout:** 71.6 **Swing:** 1.6 to Lab from Con

BIRMINGHAM, SELLY OAK

Lynne Jones: Labour. Born: 1951. Educated: Birmingham University. Jobs: housing manager. First Elected: 1992. Union: MSF. Status: married, two children

LAB GAIN

		1992 election			1987 election	
		Votes	%	+/-	%	Votes
Lynne Jones	Lab	25,430	46.0	+6.7	39.3	20,721
A. Beaumont-Dark*	Con	23,370	42.3	-1.9	44.2	23,305
David Osborne	Lib Dem	5,679	10.3	-5.1	15.4	8,128
Paul Slatter	Green	535	1.0	-0.2	1.2	611
Christopher Barwood	NLP	178	0.3			
Kenan Malik	Rev Comm	84	0.2			
Majority	**Lab**	**2,060**	**3.7**	**+8.6**	**4.9**	**2,584**

Electorate: 72,150 **Voters:** 55,276 **Turnout:** 76.6 **Swing:** 4.3 to Lab from Con

BIRMINGHAM, SMALL HEATH

Roger Godsiff: Labour. Born: 1946. Educated: local state schools. Jobs: trade union official. First Elected: 1992. Union: GMB. Status: married, two children.

LAB HOLD		1992 election			1987 election	
		Votes	%	+/-	%	Votes
Roger Godsiff	Lab	22,675	65.2	-1.1	66.3	22,787
Qayyum Chaudhary	Con	8,686	25.0	+3.8	21.1	7,266
Haydn Thomas	Lib Dem	2,575	7.4	-3.1	10.5	3,600
Hazel Clawley	Green	824	2.4	+0.7	1.6	559
Majority	**Lab**	**13,989**	**40.2**	**-4.9**	**45.2**	**15,521**

Electorate: 55,213 **Voters:** 34,760 **Turnout:** 63.0 **Swing:** 2.5 to Con from Lab

BIRMINGHAM, SPARKBROOK

Roy Hattersley: Labour. Born: 1932. Educated: Sheffield City Grammar School; Hull University. Jobs: journalist. First Elected: 1964. Status: married.

LAB HOLD		1992 election			1987 election	
		Votes	%	+/-	%	Votes
Roy Hattersley*	Lab	22,116	64.1	+3.2	60.8	20,513
Mohammed Khamisa	Con	8,544	24.8	-0.9	25.7	8,654
David Parry	Lib Dem	3,028	8.8	-2.5	11.3	3,803
Charles Alldrick	Green	833	2.4	+0.9	1.6	526
Majority	**Lab**	**13,572**	**39.3**	**+4.2**	**35.2**	**11,859**

Electorate: 51,677 **Voters:** 34,521 **Turnout:** 66.8 **Swing:** 2.1 to Lab from Con

BIRMINGHAM, YARDLEY

Estelle Morris: Labour. Born: 1952. Educated: Coventry College of Education; University of Warwick. Jobs: teacher. First Elected: 1992. Status: single.

LAB GAIN		1992 election			1987 election	
		Votes	%	+/-	%	Votes
Estelle Morris	Lab	14,884	34.9	-1.8	36.6	15,409
David Gilroy Bevan*	Con	14,722	34.5	-8.1	42.6	17,931
John Hemming	Lib Dem	12,899	30.2	+9.5	20.8	8,734
Pauline Read	NF	192	0.4			
Majority	**Lab**	**162**	**0.4**	**+6.4**	**6.0**	**2,522**

Electorate: 54,749 **Voters:** 42,697 **Turnout:** 78.0 **Swing:** 3.2 to Lab from Con

BISHOP AUCKLAND

Derek Foster: Labour. Born: 1937. Educated: Bede Grammar School Sunderland; Oxford. Jobs: teacher, education director. First Elected: 1979. Posts: Labour Chief Whip. Status: married, four children.

LAB HOLD		1992 election			1987 election	
		Votes	%	+/-	%	Votes
Derek Foster*	Lab	27,763	50.0	+2.0	48.0	25,648
David Williamson	Con	17,676	31.8	-3.0	34.8	18,613
William Wade	Lib Dem	10,099	18.2	+1.0	17.2	9,195
Majority	**Lab**	**10,087**	**18.2**	**+5.0**	**13.2**	**7,035**

Electorate: 72,572 **Voters:** 55,538 **Turnout:** 76.5 **Swing:** 2.5 to Lab from Con

BLABY

Andrew Robathan: Conservative. Born: 1951. Educated: Merchant Taylors; Oxford, Sandhurst. Jobs: army officer. First Elected: 1992. Posts: member, Employment Select Committee. Status: married.

CON HOLD		1992 election			1987 election	
		Votes	%	+/-	%	Votes
Andrew Robathan	Con	39,498	57.9	-2.6	60.5	37,732
Ethel Ranson	Lab	14,151	20.7	+6.2	14.5	9,046
Margery Lewin	Lib Dem	13,780	20.2	-4.8	25.0	15,556
John Peacock	BNP	521	0.8			
Sue Lincoln	NLP	260	0.4			
Majority	**Con**	**25,347**	**37.2**	**+1.6**	**35.6**	**22,176**

Electorate: 81,790 **Voters:** 68,210 **Turnout:** 83.4 **Swing:** 4.4 to Lab from Con

BLACKBURN

Jack Straw: Labour. Born: 1946. Educated: Brentwood School; Leeds University. Jobs: barrister, journalist, political adviser. First Elected: 1979. Posts: Shadow Environment Secretary (Local Government). Status: married, two children.

LAB HOLD		1992 election			1987 election	
		Votes	%	+/-	%	Votes
Jack Straw*	Lab	26,633	48.4	-1.5	49.9	27,965
Ross Coates	Con	20,606	37.5	-2.6	40.1	22,468
Derek Mann	Lib Dem	6,332	11.5	+1.5	10.0	5,602
Robin Field	Green	878	1.6			
Margo Grimshaw	LP	334	0.6			
William Ayliffe	NLP	195	0.4			
Majority	**Lab**	**6,027**	**11.0**	**+1.2**	**9.8**	**5,497**

Electorate: 73,251 **Voters:** 54,978 **Turnout:** 75.1 **Swing:** 0.6 to Lab from Con

BLACKPOOL NORTH

Harold Elletson: Conservative. Born: 1960. Educated: Eton; Exeter University. Jobs: marketing consultant. First Elected: 1992. Status: married, one child.

CON HOLD		1992 election			1987 election	
		Votes	%	+/-	%	Votes
Harold Elletson	Con	21,501	47.7	-0.3	48.0	20,680
Eric Kirton	Lab	18,461	41.0	+10.0	31.0	13,359
Andre Lahiff	Lib Dem	4,786	10.6	-10.3	21.0	9,032
Sir Guy Francis	Loony	178	0.4			
Hugh Walker	NLP	125	0.3			
Majority	**Con**	**3,040**	**6.7**	**-10.2**	**17.0**	**7,321**

Electorate: 58,087 **Voters:** 45,051 **Turnout:** 77.6 **Swing:** 5.1 to Lab from Con

BLACKPOOL SOUTH

Nicholas Hawkins: Conservative. Born: 1957. Educated: Bedford Modern Grammar; Oxford. Jobs: barrister. First Elected: 1992. Status: married, three children.

CON HOLD		1992 election			1987 election	
		Votes	%	+/-	%	Votes
Nicholas Hawkins	Con	19,880	45.2	-2.8	48.0	20,312
Gordon Marsden	Lab	18,213	41.4	+9.4	32.1	13,568
Robert Wynne	Lib Dem	5,675	12.9	-7.0	19.9	8,405
Douglas Henning	NLP	173	0.4			
Majority	**Con**	**1,667**	**3.8**	**-12.2**	**15.9**	**6,744**

Electorate: 56,801 **Voters:** 43,941 **Turnout:** 77.4 **Swing:** 6.1 to Lab from Con

BLAENAU GWENT

Llewellyn Smith: Labour. Born: 1944. Educated: Greenfield Secondary Modern School; University of Wales. Jobs: factory labourer, computer operator. First Elected: 1992. Posts: Euro MP. Union: TGWU. Status: married, three children.

LAB HOLD		1992 election			1987 election	
		Votes	%	+/-	%	Votes
Llewellyn Smith	Lab	34,333	79.0	+3.1	75.9	32,820
David Melding	Con	4,266	9.8	-1.7	11.5	4,959
Alastair Burns	Lib Dem	2,774	6.4	-2.5	8.9	3,847
Alun Davies	Plaid Cymru	2,099	4.8	+1.1	3.7	1,621
Majority	**Lab**	**30,067**	**69.2**	**+4.7**	**64.4**	**27,861**

Electorate: 55,638 **Voters:** 43,472 **Turnout:** 78.1 **Swing:** 2.4 to Lab from Con

BLAYDON

John McWilliam: Labour. Born: 1941. Educated: Leith Academy; Heriot Watt College. First Elected: 1979. Posts: member, Defence Select Committee, chairmen's panel. Union: NCU. Status: married, two children.

LAB HOLD

		1992 election Votes	%	+/-	1987 election %	Votes
John McWilliam*	Lab	27,028	52.7	+2.3	50.3	25,277
Peter Pescod	Con	13,685	26.7	+2.5	24.2	12,147
Paul Nunn	Lib Dem	10,602	20.7	-4.8	25.5	12,789
Majority	**Lab**	**13,343**	**26.0**	**+1.1**	**24.9**	**12,488**

Electorate: 66,044 **Voters:** 51,315 **Turnout:** 77.7 **Swing:** No Swing

BLYTH VALLEY

Ronnie Campbell: Labour. Born: 1943. Educated: local state schools. Jobs: miner. First Elected: 1987. Posts: member, Parliamentary Commissioner Select Committee. Union: NUM. Status: married, six children.

LAB HOLD

		1992 election Votes	%	+/-	1987 election %	Votes
Ronnie Campbell*	Lab	24,542	49.9	+7.4	42.5	19,604
Peter Tracey	Lib Dem	16,498	33.5	-7.1	40.6	18,751
Michael Revell	Con	7,691	15.6	-1.3	16.9	7,823
Steve Tyley	Green	470	1.0			
Majority	**Lab**	**8,044**	**16.3**	**+14.5**	**1.8**	**853**

Electorate: 60,913 **Voters:** 49,201 **Turnout:** 80.8 **Swing:** 7.3 to Lab from LDm

BOLSOVER

Dennis Skinner: Labour. Born: 1932. Educated: Tupton Hall Grammar School; Ruskin College, Oxford. Jobs: miner. First Elected: 1970. Posts: Labour National Executive. Union: NUM. Status: married, three children.

LAB HOLD

		1992 election Votes	%	+/-	1987 election %	Votes
Dennis Skinner*	Lab	33,973	64.5	+8.3	56.2	28,453
Timothy James	Con	13,313	25.3	-3.0	28.3	14,333
Susan Barber	Lib Dem	5,363	10.2	-5.3	15.5	7,836
Majority	**Lab**	**20,660**	**39.2**	**+11.3**	**27.9**	**14,120**

Electorate: 66,693 **Voters:** 52,649 **Turnout:** 78.9 **Swing:** 5.7 to Lab from Con

BOLTON NORTH EAST

Peter Thurnham: Conservative. Born: 1938. Educated: Oundle; Cambridge. Jobs: engineer. First Elected: 1983. Posts: PPS. Status: married, five children.

CON HOLD		1992 election			1987 election	
		Votes	%	+/-	%	Votes
Peter Thurnham*	Con	21,644	44.9	+0.5	44.4	20,742
David Crausby	Lab	21,459	44.5	+1.8	42.6	19,929
Brian Dunning	Lib Dem	4,971	10.3	-2.7	13.0	6,060
Peter Tong	NLP	181	0.4			
Majority	**Con**	**185**	**0.4**	**-1.4**	**1.7**	**813**

Electorate: 58,659 **Voters:** 48,255 **Turnout:** 82.3 **Swing:** 0.7 to Lab from Con

BOLTON SOUTH EAST

David Young: Labour. Born: 1930. Educated: Greenock Academy; Glasgow University. First Elected: 1974. Posts: member, Employment Select Committee, Public Accounts Commission. Status: married.

LAB HOLD		1992 election			1987 election	
		Votes	%	+/-	%	Votes
David Young*	Lab	26,906	54.3	+0.0	54.3	26,791
Nicholas Wood-Dow	Con	14,215	28.7	-2.5	31.2	15,410
Dennis Lee	Lib Dem	5,243	10.6	-3.9	14.5	7,161
William Hardman	Ind Lab	2,894	5.8			
Lewis Walch	NLP	290	0.6			
Majority	**Lab**	**12,691**	**25.6**	**+2.6**	**23.1**	**11,381**

Electorate: 65,600 **Voters:** 49,548 **Turnout:** 75.5 **Swing:** 1.3 to Lab from Con

BOLTON WEST

Tom Sackville: Conservative. Born: 1950. Educated: Eton; Oxford. Jobs: bullion broker. First Elected: 1983. Posts: Health minister. Status: married, two children.

CON HOLD		1992 election			1987 election	
		Votes	%	+/-	%	Votes
Tom Sackville*	Con	26,452	44.4	+0.1	44.3	24,779
Clifford Morris	Lab	25,373	42.6	+6.5	36.1	20,186
Barbara Ronson	Lib Dem	7,529	12.6	-6.9	19.6	10,936
Jacqueline Phillips	NLP	240	0.4			
Majority	**Con**	**1,079**	**1.8**	**-6.4**	**8.2**	**4,593**

Electorate: 71,344 **Voters:** 59,594 **Turnout:** 83.5 **Swing:** 3.2 to Lab from Con

CONSTITUENCIES

BOOTHFERRY

David Davis: Conservative. Born: 1948. Educated: Bec Grammar School; Warwick University. Jobs: manager. First Elected: 1987. Posts: Government Whip. Status: married, three children.

CON HOLD		1992 election Votes	%	+/-	1987 election %	Votes
David Davis*	Con	35,266	54.8	-0.9	55.7	31,716
Louise Coubrough	Lab	17,731	27.5	+5.6	21.9	12,498
John Goss	Lib Dem	11,388	17.7	-4.7	22.4	12,746
Majority	**Con**	**17,535**	**27.2**	**-6.1**	**33.3**	**18,970**

Electorate: 80,747 **Voters:** 64,385 **Turnout:** 79.7 **Swing:** 3.3 to Lab from Con

BOOTLE

Joe Benton: Labour. Born: 1933. Educated: St Monica's School; Bootle Technical College. Jobs: personnel manager. First Elected: 1990. Status: married, four children.

LAB HOLD		1992 election Votes	%	+/-	1987 election %	Votes
Joe Benton*	Lab	37,464	74.6	+7.7	66.9	34,975
Christopher Varley	Con	8,022	16.0	-4.1	20.1	10,498
John Cunningham	Lib Dem	3,301	6.6	-6.5	13.0	6,820
Medina Hall	Lib	1,174	2.3			
Thomas Haynes	NLP	264	0.5			
Majority	**Lab**	**29,442**	**58.6**	**+11.8**	**46.8**	**24,477**

Electorate: 69,308 **Voters:** 50,225 **Turnout:** 72.5 **Swing:** 5.9 to Lab from Con

BY-ELECTION November 1990: LAB HOLD. J. Benton (Lab) 22,052 (78.4%), J. Clappison (Con) 2,587 (9.2%), J. Cunningham (Lib Dem) 2,216 (7.9%), Lab majority 19,465 (69.2%), SWING 11.2% to Lab from Con

BOSWORTH

David Tredinnick: Conservative. Born: 1950. Educated: Eton; Oxford. Jobs: sales manager. First Elected: 1987. Posts: PPS. Status: married, two children.

CON HOLD		1992 election Votes	%	+/-	1987 election %	Votes
David Tredinnick*	Con	36,618	54.2	-0.2	54.4	34,145
David Everitt	Lab	17,524	26.0	+8.8	17.2	10,787
Gregory Drozdz	Lib Dem	12,643	18.7	-8.6	27.3	17,129
Brian Fewster	Green	716	1.1	+0.0	1.1	660
Majority	**Con**	**19,094**	**28.3**	**+1.2**	**27.1**	**17,016**

Electorate: 80,234 **Voters:** 67,501 **Turnout:** 84.1 **Swing:** 4.5 to Lab from Con

BOURNEMOUTH EAST

David Atkinson: *Conservative. Born: 1940. Educated: St George's College, Weybridge; Southend College of Technology. First Elected: 1977. Posts: delegate, Council of Europe. Status: married, two children.*

CON HOLD

		1992 election Votes	%	+/-	1987 election %	Votes
David Atkinson*	Con	30,820	56.4	-1.9	58.3	30,925
Neil Russell	Lib Dem	15,997	29.3	-1.4	30.6	16,242
Peter Brushett	Lab	7,541	13.8	+2.7	11.1	5,885
Susan Holmes	NLP	329	0.6			
Majority	**Con**	**14,823**	**27.1**	**-0.6**	**27.7**	**14,683**

Electorate: 75,089 **Voters:** 54,687 **Turnout:** 72.8 **Swing:** 0.3 to LDm from Con

BOURNEMOUTH WEST

John Butterfill: *Conservative. Born: 1941. Educated: Caterham School; College of Estate Management. Jobs: chartered surveyor, company director. First Elected: 1983. Posts: PPS; member, Trade and Industry Select Committee. Status: married, four children.*

CON HOLD

		1992 election Votes	%	+/-	1987 election %	Votes
John Butterfill*	Con	29,820	52.7	-2.5	55.2	30,117
Janet Dover	Lib Dem	17,117	30.2	-1.7	32.0	17,466
Ben Grower	Lab	9,423	16.7	+3.8	12.9	7,018
Alexander Springham	NLP	232	0.4			
Majority	**Con**	**12,703**	**22.4**	**-0.7**	**23.2**	**12,651**

Electorate: 74,738 **Voters:** 56,592 **Turnout:** 75.7 **Swing:** 0.4 to LDm from Con

BOW & POPLAR

Mildred Gordon: *Labour. Born: 1923. Educated: local state schools, Forest Teacher Training College. Jobs: teacher. First Elected: 1987. Posts: member, Education Select Committee. Status: married, one child.*

LAB HOLD

		1992 election Votes	%	+/-	1987 election %	Votes
Mildred Gordon*	Lab	18,487	49.5	+3.1	46.4	15,746
Peter Hughes	Lib Dem	10,083	27.0	-5.7	32.7	11,115
Simon Pearce	Con	6,876	18.4	-1.6	20.1	6,810
John Tyndall	BNP	1,107	3.0			
Steve Petter	Green	612	1.6			
William Hite	NLP	158	0.4			
Majority	**Lab**	**8,404**	**22.5**	**+8.9**	**13.6**	**4,631**

Electorate: 56,685 **Voters:** 37,323 **Turnout:** 65.8 **Swing:** 4.4 to Lab from LDm

BRADFORD NORTH

Terry Rooney: Labour. Born: 1950. Educated: local state schools; Bradford College. Jobs: welfare rights worker. First Elected: 1990. Status: married, three children.

LAB HOLD		1992 election			1987 election	
		Votes	%	+/-	%	Votes
Terry Rooney*	Lab	23,420	47.8	+5.0	42.8	21,009
Mohammed Riaz	Con	15,756	32.2	-7.3	39.5	19,376
David Ward	Lib Dem	9,133	18.7	+1.0	17.7	8,656
Willy Beckett	Loony	350	0.7			
Hani Nasr	Islamic	304	0.6			
Majority	**Lab**	**7,664**	**15.7**	**+12.3**	**3.3**	**1,633**

Electorate: 66,719 **Voters:** 48,963 **Turnout:** 73.4 **Swing:** 6.2 to Lab from Con

BY-ELECTION November 1990: LAB HOLD. T. Rooney (Lab) 18,619 (51.7%), D. Ward (Lib Dem) 9,105 (25.3%), J. Atkin (Con) 6,048 (16.8%), Lab majority 9,514 (26.4%), SWING 15.8% to Lab from Con

BRADFORD SOUTH

Bob Cryer: Labour. Born: 1934. Educated: local state schools; Hull University. Jobs: lecturer; Euro MP. First Elected: 1974. Posts: chairman, Statutory Instruments Select Committee. Status: married, two children.

LAB HOLD		1992 election			1987 election	
		Votes	%	+/-	%	Votes
Bob Cryer*	Lab	25,185	47.6	+6.2	41.4	21,230
Andrew Popat	Con	20,283	38.4	-2.4	40.8	20,921
Brian Boulton	Lib Dem	7,243	13.7	-4.1	17.8	9,109
Mohammad Naseem	Islamic	156	0.3			
Majority	**Lab**	**4,902**	**9.3**	**+8.7**	**0.6**	**309**

Electorate: 69,914 **Voters:** 52,867 **Turnout:** 75.6 **Swing:** 4.3 to Lab from Con

BRADFORD WEST

Max Madden: Labour. Born: 1941. Educated: Pinner Grammar School. Jobs: journalist, party official. First Elected: 1974. Union: TGWU. Status: married.

LAB HOLD		1992 election			1987 election	
		Votes	%	+/-	%	Votes
Max Madden*	Lab	26,046	53.2	+1.3	51.9	25,775
Andrew Ashworth	Con	16,544	33.8	-2.9	36.7	18,224
Alun Griffiths	Lib Dem	5,150	10.5	-0.9	11.4	5,657
Peter Braham	Green	735	1.5			
David Pidcock	Islamic	471	1.0			
Majority	**Lab**	**9,502**	**19.4**	**+4.2**	**15.2**	**7,551**

Electorate: 70,016 **Voters:** 48,946 **Turnout:** 69.9 **Swing:** 2.1 to Lab from Con

BRAINTREE

Tony Newton: *Conservative. Born: 1937. Educated: Friends' School, Saffron Walden; Oxford. Jobs: party researcher. First Elected: 1974. Posts: Lord President and Leader of the Commons. Status: married, two children.*

CON HOLD		1992 election			1987 election	
		Votes	%	+/-	%	Votes
Tony Newton*	Con	34,415	52.3	-1.9	54.2	32,978
Ian Willmore	Lab	16,921	25.7	+6.4	19.3	11,764
Diana Wallis	Lib Dem	13,603	20.7	-5.8	26.5	16,121
James Abbott	Green	855	1.3			
Majority	**Con**	**17,494**	**26.6**	**-1.1**	**27.7**	**16,857**

Electorate: 78,880 **Voters:** 65,794 **Turnout:** 83.4 **Swing:** 4.1 to Lab from Con

BRECON & RADNOR

Jonathan Evans: *Conservative. Born: 1950. Educated: Lewis Grammar School; Pengam. Jobs: solicitor. First Elected: 1992. Posts: member, Welsh Affairs Select Committee. Status: married, three children.*

CON GAIN		1992 election			1987 election	
		Votes	%	+/-	%	Votes
Jonathan Evans	Con	15,977	36.1	+1.4	34.7	14,453
Richard Livsey*	Lib Dem	15,847	35.8	+1.0	34.8	14,509
Chris Mann	Lab	11,634	26.3	-2.9	29.2	12,180
Sian Meredudd	Plaid Cymru	418	0.9	-0.3	1.3	535
Hugh Richards	Green	393	0.9			
Majority	**Con**	**130**	**0.3**	**+0.4**	**0.1**	**56**

Electorate: 51,509 **Voters:** 44,269 **Turnout:** 85.9 **Swing:** 0.2 to Con from LDm

BRENT EAST

Ken Livingstone: *Labour. Born: 1945. Educated: local state schools; Fawcett Teacher Training College. Jobs: cancer research worker. First Elected: 1987. Status: divorced.*

LAB HOLD		1992 election			1987 election	
		Votes	%	+/-	%	Votes
Ken Livingstone*	Lab	19,387	52.8	+10.2	42.6	16,772
Damian Green	Con	13,416	36.6	-1.9	38.4	15,119
Mark Cummins	Lib Dem	3,249	8.9	-5.7	14.5	5,710
Theresa Dean	Green	548	1.5	-0.3	1.8	716
Anne Murphy	Comm GB	96	0.3			
Majority	**Lab**	**5,971**	**16.3**	**+12.1**	**4.2**	**1,653**

Electorate: 53,319 **Voters:** 36,696 **Turnout:** 68.8 **Swing:** 6.0 to Lab from Con

CONSTITUENCIES

BRENT NORTH

Sir Rhodes Boyson: Conservative. Born: 1925. Educated: Haslingden Grammar School; Universities of Wales, Manchester and Cambridge. Jobs: head teacher. First Elected: 1974. Status: married.

CON HOLD		1992 election Votes	%	+/-	1987 election %	Votes
Sir Rhodes Boyson*	Con	23,445	56.4	-3.5	59.9	26,823
Jim Moher	Lab	13,314	32.0	+7.2	24.8	11,103
Paul Lorber	Lib Dem	4,149	10.0	-5.4	15.3	6,868
Thakore Vipul	Ind	356	0.9			
Tony Davids	NLP	318	0.8			
Majority	**Con**	**10,131**	**24.4**	**-10.7**	**35.1**	**15,720**

Electorate: 58,917 **Voters:** 41,582 **Turnout:** 70.6 **Swing:** 5.4 to Lab from Con

BRENT SOUTH

Paul Boateng: Labour. Born: 1951. Educated: Ghana International School; Apsley Grammar School; Bristol University. Jobs: barrister. First Elected: 1987. Posts: Labour spokesman for Lord Chancellor's department. Status: married, five children.

LAB HOLD		1992 election Votes	%	+/-	1987 election %	Votes
Paul Boateng*	Lab	20,662	57.5	+5.6	51.9	21,140
Robert Blackman	Con	10,957	30.5	-1.9	32.4	13,209
Mike Harskin	Lib Dem	3,658	10.2	-5.5	15.7	6,375
Darren Johnson	Green	479	1.3			
Chandrakant Jani	NLP	166	0.5			
Majority	**Lab**	**9,705**	**27.0**	**+7.5**	**19.5**	**7,931**

Electorate: 56,034 **Voters:** 35,922 **Turnout:** 64.1 **Swing:** 3.8 to Lab from Con

BRENTFORD & ISLEWORTH

Niranjan Deva: Conservative. Born: 1948. Educated: Loughborough University. Jobs: businessman. First Elected: 1992. Posts: member, National Consumer Council. Status: married.

CON HOLD		1992 election Votes	%	+/-	1987 election %	Votes
Niranjan Deva	Con	24,752	45.8	-1.9	47.7	26,230
Ann Keen	Lab	22,666	42.0	+8.7	33.2	18,277
Janet Salmon	Lib Dem	5,683	10.5	-7.0	17.5	9,626
John Bradley	Green	927	1.7	+0.2	1.5	849
Majority	**Con**	**2,086**	**3.9**	**-10.6**	**14.5**	**7,953**

Electorate: 70,880 **Voters:** 54,028 **Turnout:** 76.2 **Swing:** 5.3 to Lab from Con

BRENTWOOD & ONGAR

Eric Pickles: Conservative. Born: 1952. Educated: Leeds Polytechnic. Jobs: employment consultant. Posts: member, Environment Select Committee. First Elected: 1992. Status: married.

CON HOLD

		1992 election Votes	%	+/-	1987 election %	Votes
Eric Pickles	Con	32,145	57.6	-2.8	60.5	32,258
Elizabeth Bottomley	Lib Dem	17,000	30.5	+5.5	25.0	13,337
Francis Keohane	Lab	6,080	10.9	-2.3	13.2	7,042
Carolyn Bartley	Green	535	1.0	-0.3	1.3	686
Majority	**Con**	**15,145**	**27.2**	**-8.3**	**35.5**	**18,921**

Electorate: 65,830 **Voters:** 55,760 **Turnout:** 84.7 **Swing:** 4.2 to LDm from Con

BRIDGEND

Win Griffiths: Labour. Born: 1943. Educated: University College, Cardiff. Jobs: teacher, Euro MP. First Elected: 1987. Posts: Labour spokesman on education. Union: TGWU. Status: married, two children.

LAB HOLD

		1992 election Votes	%	+/-	1987 election %	Votes
Win Griffiths*	Lab	24,143	51.3	+3.7	47.5	21,893
David Unwin	Con	16,817	35.7	-2.3	38.0	17,513
David Mills	Lib Dem	4,827	10.3	-1.9	12.1	5,590
Alun Lloyd Jones	Plaid Cymru	1,301	2.8	+0.5	2.3	1,065
Majority	**Lab**	**7,326**	**15.6**	**+6.0**	**9.5**	**4,380**

Electorate: 58,531 **Voters:** 47,088 **Turnout:** 80.4 **Swing:** 3.0 to Lab from Con

BRIDGWATER

Tom King: Conservative. Born: 1933. Educated: Rugby; Cambridge. Jobs: manager. First Elected: 1970. Status: married, two children.

CON HOLD

		1992 election Votes	%	+/-	1987 election %	Votes
Tom King*	Con	26,610	46.8	-4.8	51.5	27,177
Bill Revans	Lib Dem	16,894	29.7	-0.6	30.3	15,982
Peter James	Lab	12,365	21.7	+3.5	18.2	9,594
Graham Dummett	Green	746	1.3			
Alan Body	Ind	183	0.3			
Gillian Sanson	NLP	112	0.2			
Majority	**Con**	**9,716**	**17.1**	**-4.1**	**21.2**	**11,195**

Electorate: 71,567 **Voters:** 56,910 **Turnout:** 79.5 **Swing:** 2.1 to LDm from Con

BRIDLINGTON

John Townend: *Conservative. Born: 1934. Educated: Hymers College, Hull. Jobs: wine merchant and chartered accountant. First Elected: 1979. Status: married, four children.*

CON HOLD		1992 election			1987 election	
		Votes	%	+/-	%	Votes
John Townend*	Con	33,604	50.8	-4.0	54.8	32,351
John Leeman	Lib Dem	17,246	26.1	+0.6	25.5	15,030
Steven Hatfield	Lab	15,263	23.1	+5.0	18.1	10,653
Majority	**Con**	**16,358**	**24.7**	**-4.6**	**29.3**	**17,321**

Electorate: 84,829 **Voters:** 66,113 **Turnout:** 77.9 **Swing:** 2.3 to LDm from Con

BRIGG & CLEETHORPES

Michael Brown: *Conservative. Born: 1951. Educated: secondary modern school; Littlehampton; York University. First Elected: 1979. Posts: PPS. Status: single.*

CON HOLD		1992 election			1987 election	
		Votes	%	+/-	%	Votes
Michael Brown*	Con	31,673	49.3	+0.6	48.7	29,725
Ian Cawsey	Lab	22,404	34.9	+12.2	22.7	13,876
Margaret Cockbill	Lib Dem	9,374	14.6	-14.0	28.6	17,475
Neil Jacques	Green	790	1.2			
Majority	**Con**	**9,269**	**14.4**	**-5.6**	**20.1**	**12,250**

Electorate: 82,377 **Voters:** 64,241 **Turnout:** 78.0 **Swing:** 5.8 to Lab from Con

BRIGHTON, KEMPTOWN

Andrew Bowden: *Conservative. Born: 1930. Educated: Ardingly College. Jobs: barrister, lecturer. First Elected: 1970. Posts: delegate, Council of Europe, Western European Union. Status: married, two children.*

CON HOLD		1992 election			1987 election	
		Votes	%	+/-	%	Votes
Andrew Bowden*	Con	21,129	48.1	-5.4	53.5	24,031
Gill Haynes	Lab	18,073	41.2	+8.3	32.9	14,771
Paul Scott	Lib Dem	4,461	10.2	-3.4	13.5	6,080
Elizabeth Overall	NLP	230	0.5			
Majority	**Con**	**3,056**	**7.0**	**-13.7**	**20.6**	**9,260**

Electorate: 57,646 **Voters:** 43,893 **Turnout:** 76.1 **Swing:** 6.8 to Lab from Con

BRIGHTON, PAVILION

Sir Derek Spencer: *Conservative. Born: 1936. Educated: Clitheroe Grammar School; Oxford. Jobs: barrister. First Elected: 1983. Posts: Solicitor-General. Status: married, children.*

CON HOLD		1992 election Votes	%	+/-	1987 election %	Votes
Derek Spencer	Con	20,630	46.6	-4.2	50.8	22,056
David Lepper	Lab	16,955	38.3	+8.6	29.7	12,914
Tom Pearce	Lib Dem	5,606	12.7	-6.8	19.5	8,459
Iain Brodie	Green	963	2.2			
Eileen Turner	NLP	103	0.2			
Majority	**Con**	**3,675**	**8.3**	**-12.7**	**21.1**	**9,142**

Electorate: 57,616 **Voters:** 44,257 **Turnout:** 76.8 **Swing:** 6.4 to Lab from Con

BRISTOL EAST

Jean Corston: *Labour. Born: 1942. Educated: Yeovil Girls' High School; London School of Economics. Jobs: party organiser, barrister. First Elected: 1992. Status: married, two children.*

LAB GAIN		1992 election Votes	%	+/-	1987 election %	Votes
Jean Corston	Lab	22,418	44.6	+9.1	35.4	17,783
Jonathan Sayeed*	Con	19,726	39.2	-4.4	43.6	21,906
John Kiely	Lib Dem	7,903	15.7	-4.7	20.4	10,247
Ian Anderson	NF	270	0.5			
Majority	**Lab**	**2,692**	**5.4**	**+13.6**	**8.2**	**4,123**

Electorate: 62,577 **Voters:** 50,317 **Turnout:** 80.4 **Swing:** 6.8 to Lab from Con

BRISTOL NORTH WEST

Michael Stern: *Conservative. Born: 1942. Educated: Christ's College, Finchley. Jobs: accountant. First Elected: 1983. Posts: member, Public Accounts Committee. Status: married, one child.*

CON HOLD		1992 election Votes	%	+/-	1987 election %	Votes
Michael Stern*	Con	25,354	42.3	-4.3	46.6	26,953
Doug Naysmith	Lab	25,309	42.3	+7.7	34.6	20,001
John Taylor	Lib Dem	8,498	14.2	-4.6	18.8	10,885
Hilary Long	Soc Dem	729	1.2			
Majority	**Con**	**45**	**0.1**	**-11.9**	**12.0**	**6,952**

Electorate: 72,726 **Voters:** 59,890 **Turnout:** 82.4 **Swing:** 6.0 to Lab from Con

BRISTOL SOUTH

Dawn Primarolo: Labour. Born: 1954. Educated: Bristol Polytechnic. Job: secretary. First Elected: 1987. Posts: Labour spokeswoman on health. Union: MSF. Status: divorced, one child.

LAB HOLD		1992 election			1987 election	
		Votes	%	+/-	%	Votes
Dawn Primarolo*	Lab	25,164	50.1	+9.3	40.9	20,798
John Bercow	Con	16,245	32.4	-5.7	38.1	19,394
Paul Crossley	Lib Dem	7,892	15.7	-3.8	19.6	9,952
John Boxall	Green	756	1.5	+0.3	1.2	600
Neil Phillips	NLP	136	0.3			
Majority	**Lab**	**8,919**	**17.8**	**+15.0**	**2.8**	**1,404**

Electorate: 64,309 **Voters:** 50,193 **Turnout:** 78.0 **Swing:** 7.5 to Lab from Con

BRISTOL WEST

William Waldegrave: Conservative. Born: 1946. Educated: Eton; Oxford. Jobs: political researcher. First Elected: 1979. Posts: Chancellor of the Duchy of Lancaster. Status: married, four children.

CON HOLD		1992 election			1987 election	
		Votes	%	+/-	%	Votes
William Waldegrave*	Con	22,169	42.2	-3.3	45.5	24,695
Charles Boney	Lib Dem	16,098	30.7	-0.7	31.3	16,992
Headley Bashforth	Lab	12,992	24.8	+3.9	20.9	11,337
Alastair Sawday	Green	906	1.7	-0.3	2.0	1,096
David Cross	NLP	104	0.2			
Ben Brent	Rev Comm	92	0.2			
Philip Hammond	SOADDA	87	0.2			
Tim Hedges	Anti Fed	42	0.1			
Majority	**Con**	**6,071**	**11.6**	**-2.6**	**14.2**	**7,703**

Electorate: 70,579 **Voters:** 52,490 **Turnout:** 74.4 **Swing:** 1.3 to LDm from Con

BROMSGROVE

Roy Thomason: Conservative. Born: 1944. Educated: Cheney School Oxford; London University. Jobs: solicitor. First Elected: 1992. Posts: member, Environment Select Committee. Status: married, four children.

CON HOLD		1992 election			1987 election	
		Votes	%	+/-	%	Votes
Roy Thomason	Con	31,709	54.1	-0.7	54.7	29,051
Catherine Mole	Lab	18,007	30.7	+7.4	23.3	12,366
Alexis Cassin	Lib Dem	8,090	13.8	-8.2	22.0	11,663
John Churchman	Green	856	1.5			
Majority	**Con**	**13,702**	**23.4**	**-8.1**	**31.4**	**16,685**

Electorate: 71,111 **Voters:** 58,662 **Turnout:** 82.5 **Swing:** 4.0 to Lab from Con

BROXBOURNE

Marion Roe: Conservative. Born: 1936. Educated: Croydon High School. First Elected: 1983. Posts: chairwoman, Health Select Committee. Status: married, three children.

CON HOLD		1992 election			1987 election	
		Votes	%	+/-	%	Votes
Marion Roe*	Con	36,094	62.6	-0.6	63.2	33,567
Martin Hudson	Lab	12,124	21.0	+4.1	16.9	8,984
Julia Davies	Lib Dem	9,244	16.0	-3.9	19.9	10,572
George Woolhouse	NLP	198	0.3			
Majority	**Con**	**23,970**	**41.6**	**-1.7**	**43.3**	**22,995**

Electorate: 72,116 **Voters:** 57,660 **Turnout:** 80.0 **Swing:** 2.4 to Lab from Con

BROXTOWE

Jim Lester: Conservative. Born: 1932. Educated: Nottingham High School. First Elected: 1974. Posts: member, Foreign Affairs Select Committee. Status: married, two children.

CON HOLD		1992 election			1987 election	
		Votes	%	+/-	%	Votes
Jim Lester*	Con	31,096	51.0	-2.6	53.6	30,462
James Walker	Lab	21,205	34.8	+10.5	24.3	13,811
John Ross	Lib Dem	8,395	13.8	-8.3	22.1	12,562
David Lukehurst	NLP	293	0.5			
Majority	**Con**	**9,891**	**16.2**	**-13.1**	**29.3**	**16,651**

Electorate: 73,123 **Voters:** 60,989 **Turnout:** 83.4 **Swing:** 6.5 to Lab from Con

BUCKINGHAM

George Walden: Conservative. Born: 1939. Educated: Latymer Upper School; Cambridge. Jobs: diplomat. First Elected: 1983. Status: married, three children.

CON HOLD		1992 election			1987 election	
		Votes	%	+/-	%	Votes
George Walden*	Con	29,496	62.5	+3.8	58.6	32,162
Tudor Jones	Lib Dem	9,705	20.6	-4.3	24.9	13,636
Keith White	Lab	7,662	16.2	-0.3	16.5	9,053
Lawrence Sheaff	NLP	353	0.7			
Majority	**Con**	**19,791**	**41.9**	**+8.1**	**33.8**	**18,526**

Electorate: 56,063 **Voters:** 47,216 **Turnout:** 84.2 **Swing:** 4.1 to Con from LDm

BURNLEY

Peter Pike: Labour. Born: 1937. Educated: secondary school. Jobs: bank clerk, factory worker, party organiser. First Elected: 1983. Posts: Labour spokesman on environment (local government). Status: married, two children.

LAB HOLD		1992 election			1987 election	
		Votes	%	+/-	%	Votes
Peter Pike*	Lab	27,184	53.0	+4.6	48.4	25,140
Brenda Binge	Con	15,693	30.6	-3.2	33.8	17,583
Gordon Birtwistle	Lib Dem	8,414	16.4	-1.4	17.8	9,241
Majority	**Lab**	**11,491**	**22.4**	**+7.9**	**14.5**	**7,557**

Electorate: 68,952 **Voters:** 51,291 **Turnout:** 74.4 **Swing:** 3.9 to Lab from Con

BURTON

Sir Ivan Lawrence: Conservative. Born: 1936. Educated: grammar School; Brighton, Oxford. Jobs: barrister. First Elected: 1974. Posts: chairman, Home Affairs Select Committee. Status: married, one child.

CON HOLD		1992 election			1987 election	
		Votes	%	+/-	%	Votes
Ivan Lawrence*	Con	30,845	49.7	-1.0	50.7	29,160
Patricia Muddyman	Lab	24,849	40.0	+6.4	33.6	19,330
Rob Renold	Lib Dem	6,375	10.3	-5.5	15.7	9,046
Majority	**Con**	**5,996**	**9.7**	**-7.4**	**17.1**	**9,830**

Electorate: 75,292 **Voters:** 62,069 **Turnout:** 82.4 **Swing:** 3.7 to Lab from Con

BURY NORTH

Alistair Burt: Conservative. Born: 1955. Educated: Bury Grammar School; Oxford. Jobs: solicitor. First Elected: 1983. Status: married, two children.

CON HOLD		1992 election			1987 election	
		Votes	%	+/-	%	Votes
Alistair Burt*	Con	29,266	49.7	-0.5	50.1	28,097
Jim Dobbin	Lab	24,502	41.6	+3.8	37.8	21,168
Colin McGrath	Lib Dem	5,010	8.5	-3.6	12.1	6,804
Mike Sullivan	NLP	163	0.3			
Majority	**Con**	**4,764**	**8.1**	**-4.3**	**12.4**	**6,929**

Electorate: 69,529 **Voters:** 58,941 **Turnout:** 84.8 **Swing:** 2.1 to Lab from Con

BURY SOUTH

David Sumberg: Conservative. Born: 1941. Educated: Tettenhall College, Wolverhampton. Jobs: solicitor. First Elected: 1983. Posts: member, Foreign Affairs Select Committee. Status: married, two children.

CON HOLD		1992 election			1987 election	
		Votes	%	+/-	%	Votes
David Sumberg*	Con	24,873	46.0	+0.0	46.1	23,878
Hazel Blears	Lab	24,085	44.6	+3.7	40.9	21,199
Adrian Cruden	Lib Dem	4,832	8.9	-4.1	13.1	6,772
Norma Sullivan	NLP	228	0.4			
Majority	**Con**	**788**	**1.5**	**-3.7**	**5.2**	**2,679**

Electorate: 65,793 **Voters:** 54,018 **Turnout:** 82.1 **Swing:** 1.9 to Lab from Con

BURY ST EDMUNDS

Richard Spring: Conservative. Born: 1946. Educated: Rondesbosch; Cambridge. Jobs: managing director. First Elected: 1992. Posts: member, Employment Select Committee. Status: married, two children.

CON HOLD		1992 election			1987 election	
		Votes	%	+/-	%	Votes
Richard Spring	Con	33,554	53.5	-5.8	59.3	33,672
Tommy Sheppard	Lab	14,767	23.6	+6.2	17.3	9,841
John Williams	Lib Dem	13,814	22.0	+0.5	21.5	12,214
Joanna Lillis	NLP	550	0.9			
Majority	**Con**	**18,787**	**30.0**	**-7.8**	**37.8**	**21,458**

Electorate: 79,967 **Voters:** 62,685 **Turnout:** 78.4 **Swing:** 6.0 to Lab from Con

CAERNARFON

Dafydd Wigley: Plaid Cymru. Born: 1943. Educated: Caernarfon Grammar School, Manchester University. Jobs: accountant, executive. First Elected: 1974. Posts: president of Plaid Cymru. Status: married, two children.

PLAID CYMRU HOLD		1992 election			1987 election	
		Votes	%	+/-	%	Votes
Dafydd Wigley*	Plaid Cymru	21,439	59.0	+1.9	57.1	20,338
Peter Fowler	Con	6,963	19.2	-2.0	21.1	7,526
Sharon Mainwaring	Lab	5,641	15.5	-0.3	15.9	5,652
Robert Arwel Williams	Lib Dem	2,101	5.8	-0.1	5.9	2,103
Gwyndaf Evans	NLP	173	0.5			
Majority	**Plaid Cymru**	**14,476**	**39.9**	**+3.9**	**36.0**	**12,812**

Electorate: 46,468 **Voters:** 36,317 **Turnout:** 78.2 **Swing:** 1.9 to PC from Con

CONSTITUENCIES

CAERPHILLY

Ron Davies: Labour. Born: 1946. Educated: Portsmouth Polytechnic; University College of Wales. Jobs: teacher. First Elected: 1983. Posts: Shadow minister for food, agriculture and rural affairs. Status: married, one child.

LAB HOLD		1992 election			1987 election	
		Votes	%	+/-	%	Votes
Ron Davies*	Lab	31,713	63.7	+5.2	58.4	28,698
Howard Philpott	Con	9,041	18.1	-1.3	19.4	9,531
Lindsay Whittle	Plaid Cymru	4,821	9.7	+1.6	8.1	3,955
Stan Wilson	Lib Dem	4,247	8.5	-5.6	14.1	6,923
Majority	**Lab**	**22,672**	**45.5**	**+6.5**	**39.0**	**19,167**

Electorate: 64,529 **Voters:** 49,822 **Turnout:** 77.2 **Swing:** 3.2 to Lab from Con

CAITHNESS & SUTHERLAND

Robert Maclennan: Liberal Democrat. Born: 1936. Educated: Glasgow Academy; Oxford. Jobs: barrister. First Elected: 1966. Posts: Lib Dem spokesman on home affairs; member, Public Accounts Committee. Status: married, two children.

LIBDEM HOLD		1992 election			1987 election	
		Votes	%	+/-	%	Votes
Robert Maclennan*	Lib Dem	10,032	45.1	-8.5	53.6	12,338
George Bruce	Con	4,667	21.0	+4.3	16.7	3,844
Kerr MacGregor	SNP	4,049	18.2	+7.9	10.3	2,371
Michael Coyne	Lab	3,483	15.7	+0.7	14.9	3,437
Majority	**Lib Dem**	**5,365**	**24.1**	**-12.8**	**36.9**	**8,494**

Electorate: 30,905 **Voters:** 22,231 **Turnout:** 71.9 **Swing:** 6.4 to Con from LDm

CALDER VALLEY

Sir Donald Thompson: Conservative. Born: 1931. Educated: Hipperholme Grammar School. Jobs: farmer. First Elected: 1979. Posts: delegate to Council of Europe, Western European Union. Status: married, two children.

CON HOLD		1992 election			1987 election	
		Votes	%	+/-	%	Votes
Sir Donald Thompson*	Con	27,753	45.4	+1.9	43.5	25,892
David Chaytor	Lab	22,875	37.4	+4.1	33.4	19,847
Stephen Pearson	Lib Dem	9,842	16.1	-7.0	23.1	13,761
Vivienne Smith	Green	622	1.0			
Majority	**Con**	**4,878**	**8.0**	**-2.2**	**10.2**	**6,045**

Electorate: 74,417 **Voters:** 61,092 **Turnout:** 82.1 **Swing:** 1.1 to Lab from Con

CAMBRIDGE

Anne Campbell: Labour. Born: 1940. Educated: Cambridge. Jobs: statistician. First Elected: 1992. Union: MSF. Posts: member, Science and Technology Select Committee. Status: married, three children.

LAB GAIN

		1992 election			1987 election	
		Votes	%	+/-	%	Votes
Anne Campbell	Lab	20,039	39.7	+11.4	28.3	15,319
Mark Bishop	Con	19,459	38.5	-1.4	40.0	21,624
David Howarth	Lib Dem	10,037	19.9	-10.7	30.6	16,564
Tim Cooper	Green	720	1.4	+0.3	1.1	597
Dick Winnington	Loony	175	0.3			
Roger Chalmers	NLP	83	0.2			
Majority	**Lab**	**580**	**1.1**	**+12.8**	**9.4**	**5,060**

Electorate: 69,022 **Voters:** 50,513 **Turnout:** 73.2 **Swing:** 6.4 to Lab from Con

CAMBRIDGESHIRE NE

Malcolm Moss: Conservative. Born: 1943. Educated: Audenshaw Grammar School; Cambridge. Jobs: teacher, insurance consultant. First Elected: 1987. Posts: PPS. Status: married, two children.

CON HOLD

		1992 election			1987 election	
		Votes	%	+/-	%	Votes
Malcolm Moss*	Con	34,288	54.0	+7.1	47.0	26,983
Maurice Leeke	Lib Dem	19,195	30.3	-14.2	44.5	25,555
Ronald Harris	Lab	8,746	13.8	+5.3	8.5	4,891
Chris Ash	Lib	998	1.6			
Marion Chalmers	NLP	227	0.4			
Majority	**Con**	**15,093**	**23.8**	**+21.3**	**2.5**	**1,428**

Electorate: 79,935 **Voters:** 63,454 **Turnout:** 79.4 **Swing:** 10.6 to Con from LDm

CAMBRIDGESHIRE SE

Jim Paice: Conservative. Born: 1949. Educated: Framlingham College; Writtle Agricultural College. Jobs: farmer. First Elected: 1987. Posts: PPS. Status: married, two children.

CON HOLD

		1992 election			1987 election	
		Votes	%	+/-	%	Votes
Jim Paice*	Con	36,693	57.9	-0.8	58.8	32,901
Ron Wotherspoon	Lib Dem	12,883	20.3	-7.2	27.5	15,399
Murray Jones	Lab	12,688	20.0	+6.3	13.7	7,694
John Marsh	Green	836	1.3			
Bridget Langridge	NLP	231	0.4			
Majority	**Con**	**23,810**	**37.6**	**+6.3**	**31.3**	**17,502**

Electorate: 78,600 **Voters:** 63,331 **Turnout:** 80.6 **Swing:** 3.2 to Con from LDm

CAMBRIDGESHIRE SW

Sir Anthony Grant: *Conservative. Born: 1925. Educated: St. Paul's School; , Oxford. Jobs: solicitor. First Elected: 1964. Posts: Chairman, Association of Conservative Clubs; member, Trade and Industry Select Committee. Status: married, two children.*

CON HOLD		1992 election		+/-	1987 election	
		Votes	%		%	Votes
Sir Anthony Grant*	Con	38,902	56.8	-0.9	57.7	36,622
Sue Sutton	Lib Dem	19,265	28.1	-0.8	29.0	18,371
Kevin Price	Lab	9,378	13.7	+0.4	13.3	8,434
Linda Whitebread	Green	699	1.0			
Francis Chalmers	NLP	225	0.3			
Majority	**Con**	**19,637**	**28.7**	**-0.1**	**28.8**	**18,251**

Electorate: 84,418 **Voters:** 68,469 **Turnout:** 81.1 **Swing:** No Swing

CANNOCK & BURNTWOOD

Tony Wright: *Labour. Born: 1948. Educated: Kettering Grammar School; London School of Economics. Jobs: lecturer. First Elected: 1992. Status: married, three children.*

LAB GAIN		1992 election		+/-	1987 election	
		Votes	%		%	Votes
Tony Wright	Lab	28,139	46.0	+6.5	39.5	21,497
Gerald Howarth*	Con	26,633	43.6	-0.9	44.5	24,186
Peter Treasaden	Lib Dem	5,899	9.6	-6.3	16.0	8,698
M Hartshorne	Loony	469	0.8			
Majority	**Lab**	**1,506**	**2.5**	**+7.4**	**4.9**	**2,689**

Electorate: 72,600 **Voters:** 61,140 **Turnout:** 84.2 **Swing:** 3.7 to Lab from Con

CANTERBURY

Julian Brazier: *Conservative. Born: 1953. Educated: Wellington College; Oxford. Jobs: company executive. First Elected: 1987. Posts: PPS. Status: married.*

CON HOLD		1992 election		+/-	1987 election	
		Votes	%		%	Votes
Julian Brazier*	Con	29,827	50.8	-3.0	53.8	30,273
Martin Vye	Lib Dem	19,022	32.4	+5.0	27.3	15,382
Malcolm Whitemore	Lab	8,936	15.2	-1.7	16.9	9,494
Wendy Arnall	Green	747	1.3	-0.4	1.7	947
Sally Curphey	NLP	203	0.3			
Majority	**Con**	**10,805**	**18.4**	**-8.1**	**26.5**	**14,891**

Electorate: 75,181 **Voters:** 58,735 **Turnout:** 78.1 **Swing:** 4.0 to LDm from Con

CARDIFF CENTRAL

Jon Owen Jones: Labour. Born: 1954. Educated: Ysgol Gyfun Rhydyfelin; University of East Anglia, University College Cardiff. Jobs: teacher. First Elected: 1992. Posts: member, Welsh Affairs Select Committee. Status: married, one child.

LAB GAIN		1992 election			1987 election	
		Votes	%	+/-	%	Votes
Jon Owen Jones	Lab	18,014	42.0	+9.7	32.3	13,255
Ian Grist*	Con	14,549	33.9	-3.2	37.1	15,241
Jenny Randerson	Lib Dem	9,170	21.4	-8.0	29.4	12,062
Huw Marshall	Plaid Cymru	748	1.7	+0.4	1.3	535
Chris von Ruhland	Green	330	0.8			
Brian Francis	NLP	105	0.2			
Majority	**Lab**	**3,465**	**8.1**	**+12.9**	**4.8**	**1,986**

Electorate: 57,716 **Voters:** 42,916 **Turnout:** 74.4 **Swing:** 6.5 to Lab from Con

CARDIFF NORTH

Gwilym Jones: Conservative. Born: 1947. Educated: London and South Wales. Jobs: insurance broker. First Elected: 1983. Posts: PPS. Status: married, two children.

CON HOLD		1992 election			1987 election	
		Votes	%	+/-	%	Votes
Gwilym Jones*	Con	21,547	45.1	-0.1	45.3	20,061
Julie Morgan	Lab	18,578	38.9	+12.2	26.7	11,827
Eve Warlow	Lib Dem	6,487	13.6	-12.9	26.5	11,725
Eluned Bush	Plaid Cymru	916	1.9	+0.4	1.6	692
John Morse	BNP	121	0.3			
David Palmer	NLP	86	0.2			
Majority	**Con**	**2,969**	**6.2**	**-12.4**	**18.6**	**8,234**

Electorate: 56,721 **Voters:** 47,735 **Turnout:** 84.2 **Swing:** 6.2 to Lab from Con

CARDIFF SOUTH & PENARTH

Alun Michael: Labour. Born: 1943. Educated: Colwyn Bay Grammar School; Keele University. Jobs: journalist, youth worker. First Elected: 1987. Posts: Labour spokesman on home affairs. Status: married, five children.

LAB HOLD		1992 election			1987 election	
		Votes	%	+/-	%	Votes
Alun Michael*	Lab	26,383	55.5	+8.8	46.7	20,956
Thomas Hunter Jarvie	Con	15,958	33.6	-2.9	36.5	16,382
Peter Verma	Lib Dem	3,707	7.8	-7.6	15.4	6,900
Barbara Anglezarke	Plaid Cymru	776	1.6	+0.3	1.3	599
Lester Davey	Green	676	1.4			
Majority	**Lab**	**10,425**	**21.9**	**+11.7**	**10.2**	**4,574**

Electorate: 61,484 **Voters:** 47,500 **Turnout:** 77.3 **Swing:** 5.9 to Lab from Con

CARDIFF WEST

Rhodri Morgan: Labour. Born: 1939. Educated: Whitchurch Grammar School, Cardiff; Oxford. Jobs: tutor, researcher. First Elected: 1987. Posts: Labour spokesman on Welsh affairs. Status: married, three children.

LAB HOLD		1992 election			1987 election	
		Votes	%	+/-	%	Votes
Rhodri Morgan*	Lab	24,306	53.2	+7.7	45.5	20,329
Michael Prior	Con	15,015	32.9	-3.6	36.5	16,284
Jacqui Gasson	Lib Dem	5,002	10.9	-5.4	16.3	7,300
Penni Bestic	Plaid Cymru	1,177	2.6	+0.9	1.6	736
Andrew Harding	NLP	184	0.4			
Majority	**Lab**	**9,291**	**20.3**	**+11.3**	**9.1**	**4,045**

Electorate: 58,898 **Voters:** 45,684 **Turnout:** 77.6 **Swing:** 5.6 to Lab from Con

CARLISLE

Eric Martlew: Labour. Born: 1949. Educated: local state schools; Carlisle Technical College. Jobs: laboratory technician, personnel manager. First Elected: 1987. Posts: Labour spokesman on defence and disarmament; member, Agriculture Select Committee. Union: TGWU. Status: married.

LAB HOLD		1992 election			1987 election	
		Votes	%	+/-	%	Votes
Eric Martlew*	Lab	20,479	46.8	+4.5	42.2	18,311
Clive Condie	Con	17,371	39.7	-0.4	40.1	17,395
Ralph Aldersey	Lib Dem	5,740	13.1	-4.5	17.7	7,655
Nina Robinson	NLP	190	0.4			
Majority	**Lab**	**3,108**	**7.1**	**+5.0**	**2.1**	**916**

Electorate: 55,140 **Voters:** 43,780 **Turnout:** 79.4 **Swing:** 2.5 to Lab from Con

CARMARTHEN

Dr Alan Wynne Williams: Labour. Born: 1945. Educated: Carmarthen Grammar School; Oxford. Jobs: lecturer. First Elected: 1987. Posts: member, Science and Technology Select Committee. Status: married.

LAB HOLD		1992 election			1987 election	
		Votes	%	+/-	%	Votes
Alan Wynne Williams*	Lab	20,879	36.6	+1.3	35.4	19,128
Rhodri Glyn Thomas	Plaid Cymru	17,957	31.5	+8.5	23.0	12,457
Stephen Cavenagh	Con	12,782	22.4	-5.0	27.4	14,811
Juliana Hughes	Lib Dem	5,353	9.4	-3.9	13.3	7,203
Majority	**Lab**	**2,922**	**5.1**	**-2.9**	**8.0**	**4,317**

Electorate: 68,887 **Voters:** 56,971 **Turnout:** 82.7 **Swing:** 3.6 to PC from Lab

CARRICK, CUMNOCK & DOON

George Foulkes: Labour. Born: 1942. Educated: Keith Grammar School; Edinburgh University. Jobs: director of voluntary bodies. First Elected: 1979. Posts: Labour spokesman on defence and disarmament. Union: GMB-APEX. Status: married, three children.

LAB HOLD

		1992 election Votes	%	+/-	1987 election %	Votes
George Foulkes*	Lab	25,142	59.1	-1.0	60.1	25,669
James Boswell	Con	8,516	20.0	-0.7	20.7	8,867
Charles Douglas	SNP	6,910	16.2	+6.7	9.6	4,094
Mary Paris	Lib Dem	2,005	4.7	-4.9	9.6	4,106
Majority	**Lab**	**16,626**	**39.1**	**-0.3**	**39.3**	**16,802**

Electorate: 55,330 **Voters:** 42,573 **Turnout:** 76.9 **Swing:** 0.1 to Con from Lab

CARSHALTON & WALLINGTON

Nigel Forman: Conservative. Born: 1943. Educated: Shrewsbury School; Oxford. Jobs: political researcher. First Elected: 1976. Posts: junior minister, Department of Education.

CON HOLD

		1992 election Votes	%	+/-	1987 election %	Votes
Nigel Forman*	Con	26,243	49.7	-4.2	54.0	27,984
Thomas Brake	Lib Dem	16,300	30.9	+4.7	26.2	13,575
Margaret Moran	Lab	9,333	17.7	-0.5	18.2	9,440
Bob Steel	Green	614	1.2	-0.5	1.6	843
Danny Bamford	Loony G	266	0.5			
Majority	**Con**	**9,943**	**18.8**	**-8.9**	**27.8**	**14,409**

Electorate: 65,179 **Voters:** 52,756 **Turnout:** 80.9 **Swing:** 4.5 to LDm from Con

CASTLE POINT

Dr Robert Spink: Conservative. Born: 1948. Jobs: management consultant. First Elected: 1992. Posts: member, Education Select Committee. Status: married, four children.

CON HOLD

		1992 election Votes	%	+/-	1987 election %	Votes
Robert Spink	Con	29,629	55.6	-4.3	59.9	29,681
David Flack	Lab	12,799	24.0	+5.0	19.0	9,422
Allan Petchey	Lib Dem	10,208	19.1	-1.9	21.1	10,433
Irene Willis	Green	683	1.3			
Majority	**Con**	**16,830**	**31.6**	**-7.3**	**38.9**	**19,248**

Electorate: 66,229 **Voters:** 53,319 **Turnout:** 80.5 **Swing:** 4.7 to Lab from Con

CEREDIGION & N PEMBROKE

Cynog Dafis: Plaid Cymru. Born: 1938. Educated: Neath Grammar School; University College, Aberystwyth. Jobs: teacher. First Elected: 1992.

PLAID CYMRU GAIN

		1992 election Votes	%	+/-	1987 election %	Votes
Cynog Dafis	Plaid Cymru	16,020	31.3	+15.0	16.2	7,848
Geraint Howells*	Lib Dem	12,827	25.1	-11.6	36.6	17,683
John Williams	Con	12,718	24.8	-2.0	26.9	12,983
John Davies	Lab	9,637	18.8	+0.3	18.6	8,965
Majority	**Plaid Cymru**	**3,193**	**6.2**	**+26.6**	**9.7**	**4,700**

Electorate: 66,180 **Voters:** 51,202 **Turnout:** 77.4 **Swing:** 13.3 to PC from LDm

CHEADLE

Stephen Day: Conservative. Born: 1948. Educated: Otley Secondary Modern School; Leeds Polytechnic. Jobs: sales manager. First Elected: 1987. Posts: member, Social Security Select Committee. Status: married, one child.

CON HOLD

		1992 election Votes	%	+/-	1987 election %	Votes
Stephen Day*	Con	32,504	58.2	+3.2	55.1	30,484
Patsy Calton	Lib Dem	16,726	30.0	-5.9	35.9	19,853
Sandy Broadhurst	Lab	6,442	11.5	+2.4	9.1	5,037
Philippa Whittle	NLP	168	0.3			
Majority	**Con**	**15,778**	**28.3**	**+9.1**	**19.2**	**10,631**

Electorate: 66,131 **Voters:** 55,840 **Turnout:** 84.4 **Swing:** 4.5 to Con from LDm

CHELMSFORD

Simon Burns: Conservative. Born: 1952. Educated: Christ the King School, Accra; Oxford. Jobs: conference organiser. First Elected: 1987. Posts: PPS. Status: married, one child.

CON HOLD

		1992 election Votes	%	+/-	1987 election %	Votes
Simon Burns*	Con	39,043	55.3	+3.4	51.9	35,231
Hugh Nicholson	Lib Dem	20,783	29.4	-11.1	40.5	27,470
Roy Chad	Lab	10,010	14.2	+7.3	6.8	4,642
Eleanor Burgess	Green	769	1.1	+0.4	0.7	486
Majority	**Con**	**18,260**	**25.9**	**+14.4**	**11.4**	**7,761**

Electorate: 83,441 **Voters:** 70,605 **Turnout:** 84.6 **Swing:** 7.2 to Con from LDm

CHELSEA

Nicholas Scott: Conservative. Born: 1933. Educated: Clapham College. First Elected: 1966. Posts: Minister for Social Security and Disabled People. Status: married, five children.

CON HOLD		1992 election			1987 election	
		Votes	%	+/-	%	Votes
Nicholas Scott*	Con	17,471	65.1	+0.5	64.6	18,443
Rima Horton	Lab	4,682	17.5	+2.0	15.4	4,406
Susan Broidy	Lib Dem	4,101	15.3	-2.7	17.9	5,124
Niki Kortvelyessy	Green	485	1.8	-0.2	2.1	587
Douglas Armstrong	Anti Fed	88	0.3			
Majority	**Con**	**12,789**	**47.7**	**+1.0**	**46.6**	**13,319**

Electorate: 42,371 **Voters:** 26,827 **Turnout:** 63.3 **Swing:** 0.7 to Lab from Con

CHELTENHAM

Nigel Jones: Liberal Democrat. Born: 1948. Educated: Prince Henry's Grammar; Evesham. Jobs: computer consultant. First Elected: 1992. Posts: LibDem spokesman on local government and housing. Status: married, three children.

LIBDEM GAIN		1992 election			1987 election	
		Votes	%	+/-	%	Votes
Nigel Jones	Lib Dem	30,351	47.3	+5.0	42.3	26,475
John Taylor	Con	28,683	44.7	-5.4	50.2	31,371
Pam Tatlow	Lab	4,077	6.4	-1.2	7.5	4,701
Mervyn Rendall	AFE	665	1.0			
Henry Brighouse	NLP	169	0.3			
Mark Bruce-Smith	Ind	162	0.3			
Majority	**Lib Dem**	**1,668**	**2.6**	**+10.4**	**7.8**	**4,896**

Electorate: 79,808 **Voters:** 64,107 **Turnout:** 80.3 **Swing:** 5.2 to LDm from Con

CHERTSEY & WALTON

Sir Geoffrey Pattie: Conservative. Born: 1936. Educated: Durham School; Cambridge. Jobs: barrister, company director. First Elected: 1974. Posts: vice-chairman, Conservative Party. Status: married, one child.

CON HOLD		1992 election			1987 election	
		Votes	%	+/-	%	Votes
Sir Geoffrey Pattie*	Con	34,164	60.2	+0.7	59.5	32,119
Anthony Kremer	Lib Dem	11,344	20.0	-7.2	27.2	14,650
Irene Hamilton	Lab	10,793	19.0	+5.7	13.3	7,185
Stephanie Bennell	NLP	444	0.8			
Majority	**Con**	**22,820**	**40.2**	**+7.8**	**32.4**	**17,469**

Electorate: 70,465 **Voters:** 56,745 **Turnout:** 80.5 **Swing:** 3.9 to Con from LDm

CHESHAM & AMERSHAM

Cheryl Gillan: Conservative. Born: 1952. Educated: Cheltenham Ladies College. Jobs: marketing director. First Elected: 1992. Posts: member, Science and Technology Select Committee. Status: married.

CON HOLD		1992 election			1987 election	
		Votes	%	+/-	%	Votes
Cheryl Gillan	Con	36,273	63.3	+1.2	62.2	34,504
Andrew Ketteringham	Lib Dem	14,053	24.5	-2.6	27.1	15,064
Candy Atherton	Lab	5,931	10.4	+1.0	9.3	5,170
Christine Strickland	Green	753	1.3	-0.1	1.4	760
Tom Griffith-Jones	NLP	255	0.4			
Majority	**Con**	**22,220**	**38.8**	**+3.8**	**35.0**	**19,440**

Electorate: 69,895 **Voters:** 57,265 **Turnout:** 81.9 **Swing:** 1.9 to Con from LDm

CHESTER, CITY OF

Gyles Brandreth: Conservative. Born: 1948. Educated: Bedales; Oxford. Jobs: journalist, broadcaster. First Elected: 1992. Posts: member, National Heritage Select Committee. Status: married, three children.

CON HOLD		1992 election			1987 election	
		Votes	%	+/-	%	Votes
Gyles Brandreth	Con	23,411	44.1	-0.8	44.9	23,582
David Robinson	Lab	22,310	42.0	+6.4	35.6	18,727
Gordon Smith	Lib Dem	6,867	12.9	-6.6	19.5	10,262
Tom Barker	Green	448	0.8			
Stephen Cross	NLP	98	0.2			
Majority	**Con**	**1,101**	**2.1**	**-7.2**	**9.2**	**4,855**

Electorate: 63,370 **Voters:** 53,134 **Turnout:** 83.8 **Swing:** 3.6 to Lab from Con

CHESTERFIELD

Tony Benn: Labour. Born: 1925. Educated: Westminster; Oxford. Jobs: broadcaster. First Elected: 1950. Posts: member, Labour National Executive. Union: TGWU. Status: married, four children.

LAB HOLD		1992 election			1987 election	
		Votes	%	+/-	%	Votes
Tony Benn*	Lab	26,461	47.3	+1.8	45.5	24,532
Tony Rogers	Lib Dem	20,047	35.8	+6.2	29.6	15,955
Peter Lewis	Con	9,473	16.9	-8.0	25.0	13,472
Majority	**Lab**	**6,414**	**11.5**	**-4.4**	**15.9**	**8,577**

Electorate: 71,783 **Voters:** 55,981 **Turnout:** 78.0 **Swing:** 2.2 to LDm from Lab

CHICHESTER

Anthony Nelson: Conservative. Born: 1948. Educated: Harrow; Cambridge. Jobs: merchant banker. First Elected: 1974. Posts: Economic Secretary to the Treasury. Status: married, two children.

CON HOLD		1992 election Votes	%	+/-	1987 election %	Votes
Anthony Nelson*	Con	37,906	59.3	-2.5	61.8	37,274
Peter Gardiner	Lib Dem	17,019	26.6	-1.7	28.3	17,097
Diane Andrewes	Lab	7,192	11.3	+3.4	7.9	4,751
Eric Paine	Green	876	1.4	-0.6	2.0	1,196
Jennifer Weights	Lib	643	1.0			
Jean Jackson	NLP	238	0.4			
Majority	**Con**	**20,887**	**32.7**	**-0.8**	**33.5**	**20,177**

Electorate: 82,124 **Voters:** 63,874 **Turnout:** 77.8 **Swing:** 0.4 to LDm from Con

CHINGFORD

Iain Duncan-Smith: Conservative. Born: 1954. Educated: Dunchurch College of Management; Sandhurst. Jobs: army officer, company executive. First Elected: 1992. Status: married, three children.

CON HOLD		1992 election Votes	%	+/-	1987 election %	Votes
Iain Duncan-Smith	Con	25,730	59.2	-3.0	62.3	27,110
Peter Dawe	Lab	10,792	24.8	+9.6	15.3	6,650
Simon Banks	Lib Dem	5,705	13.1	-7.9	21.0	9,155
David Green	Lib	602	1.4			
John Baguley	Green	575	1.3	-0.1	1.5	634
Rev Christine John	Ind	41	0.1			
Majority	**Con**	**14,938**	**34.4**	**-6.8**	**41.2**	**17,955**

Electorate: 55,401 **Voters:** 43,445 **Turnout:** 78.4 **Swing:** 6.3 to Lab from Con

CHIPPING BARNET

Sydney Chapman: Conservative. Born: 1935. Educated: Rugby; Manchester University. Jobs: architect, planner. First Elected: 1970. Posts: Government Whip. Status: married, three children.

CON HOLD		1992 election Votes	%	+/-	1987 election %	Votes
Sydney Chapman*	Con	25,589	57.0	-0.9	57.9	24,686
Alan Williams	Lab	11,638	25.9	+6.9	19.0	8,115
David Smith	Lib Dem	7,247	16.1	-6.9	23.0	9,815
Diane Derksen	NLP	222	0.5			
Christopher Johnson	Fun	213	0.5			
Majority	**Con**	**13,951**	**31.1**	**-3.8**	**34.9**	**14,871**

Electorate: 57,153 **Voters:** 44,909 **Turnout:** 78.6 **Swing:** 3.9 to Lab from Con

CHISLEHURST

Roger Sims: *Conservative. Born: 1930. Educated: City Boys' Grammar School; Leicester. Jobs: export manager. First Elected: 1974. Posts: member, Health Select Committee. Status: married, three children.*

CON HOLD		1992 election			1987 election	
		Votes	%	+/-	%	Votes
Roger Sims*	Con	24,761	58.4	+0.7	57.6	24,165
Ian Wingfield	Lab	9,485	22.4	+3.0	19.3	8,115
Bill Hawthorne	Lib Dem	6,683	15.8	-7.3	23.0	9,658
Ian Richmond	Lib	849	2.0			
Frances Speed	Green	652	1.5			
Majority	**Con**	**15,276**	**36.0**	**+1.4**	**34.6**	**14,507**

Electorate: 53,782 **Voters:** 42,430 **Turnout:** 78.9 **Swing:** 1.1 to Lab from Con

CHORLEY

Den Dover: *Conservative. Born: 1938. Educated: Manchester Grammar School; Manchester University. Jobs: civil engineer, builder. First Elected: 1974. Status: married, two children.*

CON HOLD		1992 election			1987 election	
		Votes	%	+/-	%	Votes
Den Dover*	Con	30,715	47.2	-0.8	48.0	29,015
Ray McManus	Lab	26,469	40.7	+6.0	34.7	20,958
Janet Ross-Mills	Lib Dem	7,452	11.5	-4.6	16.1	9,706
Peter Leadbetter	NLP	402	0.6			
Majority	**Con**	**4,246**	**6.5**	**-6.8**	**13.3**	**8,057**

Electorate: 78,531 **Voters:** 65,038 **Turnout:** 82.8 **Swing:** 3.4 to Lab from Con

CHRISTCHURCH

Robert Adley: *Conservative. Born: 1935. Educated: Uppingham. Jobs: marketing consultant. First Elected: 1970. Posts: chairman, All Party Railways Group; chairman, Transport Select Committee. Status: married, two children.*

CON HOLD		1992 election			1987 election	
		Votes	%	+/-	%	Votes
Robert Adley*	Con	36,627	63.5	-2.4	65.9	35,656
Rev Dennis Bussey	Lib Dem	13,612	23.6	-0.9	24.5	13,282
Alan Lloyd	Lab	6,997	12.1	+2.6	9.6	5,174
James Barratt	NLP	243	0.4			
Adrian Wareham	CRA	175	0.3			
Majority	**Con**	**23,015**	**39.9**	**-1.4**	**41.3**	**22,374**

Electorate: 71,438 **Voters:** 57,654 **Turnout:** 80.7 **Swing:** 0.7 to LDm from Con

CIRENCESTER & TEWKESBURY

Geoffrey Clifton-Brown: *Conservative. Born: 1953. Educated: Eton; Royal Agricultural College, Cirencester. Jobs: chartered surveyor, farmer. First Elected: 1992. Posts: member, Environment Select Committee. Status: married, two children.*

CON HOLD		1992 election			1987 election	
		Votes	%	+/-	%	Votes
Geoffrey Clifton-Brown	Con	40,258	55.6	+0.2	55.4	36,272
Edward Weston	Lib Dem	24,200	33.4	-2.6	36.0	23,610
Trevor Page	Lab	7,262	10.0	+1.9	8.2	5,342
Rodney Clayton	NLP	449	0.6			
Patrick Trice-Rolph	Ind	287	0.4			
Majority	**Con**	**16,058**	**22.2**	**+2.8**	**19.3**	**12,662**

Electorate: 88,299 **Voters:** 72,456 **Turnout:** 82.1 **Swing:** 1.4 to Con from LDm

CITY OF LONDON & WESTMINSTER SOUTH

Peter Brooke: *Conservative. Born: 1934. Educated: Marlborough; Oxford. Jobs: management consultant. First Elected: 1977. Status: married, three children.*

CON HOLD		1992 election			1987 election	
		Votes	%	+/-	%	Votes
Peter Brooke*	Con	20,938	60.3	+2.5	57.8	19,333
Charlie Smith	Lab	7,569	21.8	+1.4	20.4	6,821
Jane Smithard	Lib Dem	5,392	15.5	-6.3	21.8	7,299
Guy Herbert	Green	458	1.3			
Peter Stockton	Loony	147	0.4			
Alex Farrell	IFM	107	0.3			
Richard Johnson	NLP	101	0.3			
Majority	**Con**	**13,369**	**38.5**	**+2.5**	**36.0**	**12,034**

Electorate: 55,021 **Voters:** 34,712 **Turnout:** 63.1 **Swing:** 0.6 to Con from Lab

CLACKMANNAN

Martin O'Neill: *Labour. Born: 1945. Educated: Trinity Academy; Heriot Watt University. Jobs: insurance clerk. First Elected: 1979. Posts: Labour spokesman on energy. Union: Graphical Print Media Union. Status: married, two children.*

LAB HOLD		1992 election			1987 election	
		Votes	%	+/-	%	Votes
Martin O'Neill*	Lab	18,829	49.1	-4.6	53.7	20,317
Andrew Brophy	SNP	10,326	26.9	+6.0	20.9	7,916
James Mackie	Con	6,638	17.3	+2.4	14.9	5,620
Ann Watters	Lib Dem	2,567	6.7	-3.8	10.5	3,961
Majority	**Lab**	**8,503**	**22.2**	**-10.6**	**32.8**	**12,401**

Electorate: 48,963 **Voters:** 38,360 **Turnout:** 78.3 **Swing:** 5.3 to SNP from Lab

CLWYD NORTH WEST

Rod Richards: Conservative. Born: 1947. Educated: Llandovery College, University of Wales. Jobs: hotel owner, broadcaster. First Elected: 1992. Posts: member, Welsh Affairs Select Committee. Status: married, three children.

CON HOLD		1992 election			1987 election	
		Votes	%	+/-	%	Votes
Rod Richards	Con	24,488	46.2	-2.3	48.5	24,116
Christopher Ruane	Lab	18,438	34.8	+10.0	24.8	12,335
Robert Ingham	Lib Dem	7,999	15.1	-7.6	22.7	11,279
Taylor Neil	Plaid Cymru	1,888	3.6	-0.4	4.0	1,966
Mary Swift	NLP	158	0.3			
Majority	**Con**	**6,050**	**11.4**	**-12.3**	**23.7**	**11,781**

Electorate: 67,351 **Voters:** 52,971 **Turnout:** 78.6 **Swing:** 6.1 to Lab from Con

CLWYD SOUTH WEST

Martyn Jones: Labour. Born: 1947. Educated: local state schools; Liverpool Polytechnic. Jobs: microbiologist. First Elected: 1987. Posts: member, Agriculture Select Committee. Union: TGWU. Status: married, two children.

LAB HOLD		1992 election			1987 election	
		Votes	%	+/-	%	Votes
Martyn Jones*	Lab	21,490	43.5	+8.1	35.4	16,701
Gwilym Owen	Con	16,549	33.5	+0.2	33.2	15,673
Gwyn Williams	Lib Dem	6,027	12.2	-10.7	22.9	10,778
Eifion Lloyd Jones	Plaid Cymru	4,835	9.8	+1.3	8.5	3,987
Nigel Worth	Green	351	0.7			
Jean Leadbetter	NLP	155	0.3			
Majority	**Lab**	**4,941**	**10.0**	**+7.8**	**2.2**	**1,028**

Electorate: 60,607 **Voters:** 49,407 **Turnout:** 81.5 **Swing:** 3.9 to Lab from Con

CLYDEBANK & MILNGAVIE

Tony Worthington: Labour. Born: 1941. Educated: City School, Lincoln; London School of Economics, York and Durham Universities. Jobs: lecturer. First Elected: 1987. Posts: Labour spokesman on development and co-operation. Status: married, two children.

LAB HOLD		1992 election			1987 election	
		Votes	%	+/-	%	Votes
Tony Worthington*	Lab	19,637	53.3	-3.6	56.9	22,528
Gordon Hughes	SNP	7,207	19.6	+7.1	12.5	4,935
William Harvey	Con	6,654	18.1	+2.3	15.7	6,224
Alistair Tough	Lib Dem	3,216	8.7	-6.2	14.9	5,891
Joan Barrie	NLP	112	0.3			
Majority	**Lab**	**12,430**	**33.8**	**-7.4**	**41.2**	**16,304**

Electorate: 47,337 **Voters:** 36,826 **Turnout:** 77.8 **Swing:** 5.3 to SNP from Lab

CLYDESDALE

James Hood:Labour. Born: 1948. Educated: local state schools; Nottingham University. Jobs: miner, engineer. First Elected: 1987. Union: NUM. Posts: chairman, European Legislation Select Committee. Status: married, two children.

LAB HOLD		1992 election			1987 election	
		Votes	%	+/-	%	Votes
James Hood*	Lab	21,418	44.6	-0.7	45.3	21,826
Carol Goodwin	Con	11,231	23.4	-0.1	23.5	11,324
Iain Gray	SNP	11,084	23.1	+8.3	14.8	7,125
Elspeth Buchanan	Lib Dem	3,957	8.2	-8.2	16.4	7,909
Stephen Cartwright	BNP	342	0.7			
Majority	**Lab**	**10,187**	**21.2**	**-0.6**	**21.8**	**10,502**

Electorate: 61,878 **Voters:** 48,032 **Turnout:** 77.6 **Swing:** 0.3 to Con from Lab

COLCHESTER NORTH

Bernard Jenkin: Conservative. Born: 1959. Educated: Highgate School; Cambridge. Jobs: political adviser. First Elected: 1992. Status: married, two children.

CON HOLD		1992 election			1987 election	
		Votes	%	+/-	%	Votes
Bernard Jenkin	Con	35,213	51.5	-0.8	52.3	32,747
James Raven	Lib Dem	18,721	27.4	-3.2	30.5	19,124
Dave Lee	Lab	13,870	20.3	+3.1	17.2	10,768
Muhammed Shabbeer	Green	372	0.5			
Michael Mears	NLP	238	0.3			
Majority	**Con**	**16,492**	**24.1**	**+2.4**	**21.7**	**13,623**

Electorate: 86,479 **Voters:** 68,414 **Turnout:** 79.1 **Swing:** 1.2 to Con from LDm

COLCHESTER SOUTH & MALDON

John Whittingdale:Conservative. Born: 1959. Educated: Winchester College; London University. Jobs: political adviser. First Elected: 1992. Status: married.

CON HOLD		1992 election			1987 election	
		Votes	%	+/-	%	Votes
John Whittingdale	Con	37,548	54.8	-0.1	54.9	34,894
Ian Thorn	Lib Dem	15,727	23.0	-7.6	30.6	19,411
Chris Pearson	Lab	14,158	20.7	+6.2	14.5	9,229
Matthew Patterson	Green	1,028	1.5			
Majority	**Con**	**21,821**	**31.9**	**+7.5**	**24.4**	**15,483**

Electorate: 86,410 **Voters:** 68,461 **Turnout:** 79.2 **Swing:** 3.8 to Con from LDm

COLNE VALLEY

Graham Riddick: Conservative. Born: 1955. Educated: Stowe; Warwick University. Jobs: sales manager. First Elected: 1987. Posts: PPS. Status: married, one child.

CON HOLD		1992 election			1987 election	
		Votes	%	+/-	%	Votes
Graham Riddick*	Con	24,804	42.0	+5.6	36.4	20,457
John Harman	Lab	17,579	29.8	+0.7	29.1	16,353
Nigel Priestley	Lib Dem	15,953	27.0	-6.4	33.4	18,780
Robin Stewart	Green	443	0.8	-0.3	1.1	614
Melody Staniforth	Loony	160	0.3			
John Hasty	Ind	73	0.1			
James Tattersall	NLP	44	0.1			
Majority	**Con**	**7,225**	**12.2**	**+9.3**	**3.0**	**1,677**

Electorate: 72,043 **Voters:** 59,056 **Turnout:** 82.0 **Swing:** 2.5 to Con from Lab

CONGLETON

Ann Winterton: Conservative. Born: 1941. Educated: Erdington Grammar School. First Elected: 1983. Posts: member, Agriculture Select Committee; chairman, All Party Pro-life group. Status: married, three children.

CON HOLD		1992 election			1987 election	
		Votes	%	+/-	%	Votes
Ann Winterton*	Con	29,163	49.0	+0.7	48.3	26,513
Iain Brodie-Browne	Lib Dem	18,043	30.3	-3.5	33.8	18,544
Matthew Finnegan	Lab	11,927	20.0	+2.2	17.9	9,810
Peter Brown	NLP	399	0.7			
Majority	**Con**	**11,120**	**18.7**	**+4.2**	**14.5**	**7,969**

Electorate: 70,477 **Voters:** 59,532 **Turnout:** 84.5 **Swing:** 2.1 to Con from LDm

CONWY

Sir Wyn Roberts: Conservative. Born: 1930. Educated: Beaumaris Grammar School; Harrow; Oxford. Jobs: journalist, broadcaster. First Elected: 1970. Posts: Minister of State Welsh Office. Status: married, three children.

CON HOLD		1992 election			1987 election	
		Votes	%	+/-	%	Votes
Sir Wyn Roberts*	Con	14,250	33.7	-5.0	38.7	15,730
Rev Roger Roberts	Lib Dem	13,255	31.4	+0.1	31.2	12,706
Elizabeth Williams	Lab	10,883	25.8	+3.5	22.3	9,049
Rhodri Davies	Plaid Cymru	3,108	7.4	-0.5	7.8	3,177
Owen Wainwright	Ind C	637	1.5			
David Hughes	NLP	114	0.3			
Majority	**Con**	**995**	**2.4**	**-5.1**	**7.4**	**3,024**

Electorate: 53,576 **Voters:** 42,247 **Turnout:** 78.9 **Swing:** 2.5 to LDm from Con

COPELAND

Dr Jack Cunningham: Labour. Born: 1939. Educated: Jarrow Grammar School; Durham University. Jobs: research scientist, union official. First Elected: 1970. Posts: Shadow Foreign Secretary. Status: married, three children.

LAB HOLD		1992 election			1987 election	
		Votes	%	+/-	%	Votes
Jack Cunningham*	Lab	22,328	48.7	+1.5	47.2	20,999
Philip Davies	Con	19,889	43.4	+0.4	43.0	19,105
Roger Putnam	Lib Dem	3,508	7.6	-1.5	9.1	4,052
James Sinton	NLP	148	0.3			
Majority	**Lab**	**2,439**	**5.3**	**+1.1**	**4.3**	**1,894**

Electorate: 54,911 **Voters:** 45,873 **Turnout:** 83.5 **Swing:** 0.5 to Lab from Con

CORBY

William Powell: Conservative. Born: 1948. Educated: Lancing College; Cambridge. Jobs: barrister, researcher. First Elected: 1983. Posts: PPS; member, Science and Technology Select Committee. Status: married, three children.

CON HOLD		1992 election			1987 election	
		Votes	%	+/-	%	Votes
William Powell*	Con	25,203	44.5	+0.2	44.3	23,323
Sandy Feather	Lab	24,861	43.9	+3.0	40.9	21,518
Melvyn Rosse	Lib Dem	5,792	10.2	-4.6	14.8	7,805
Judith Wood	Lib	784	1.4			
Majority	**Con**	**342**	**0.6**	**-2.8**	**3.4**	**1,805**

Electorate: 68,333 **Voters:** 56,640 **Turnout:** 82.9 **Swing:** 1.4 to Lab from Con

CORNWALL NORTH

Paul Tyler: Liberal Democrat. Born: 1941. Educated: Sherborne, Oxford. Jobs: public relations consultant. First Elected: 1974. Posts: LibDem agriculture spokesman. Status: married, two children.

LIBDEM GAIN		1992 election			1987 election	
		Votes	%	+/-	%	Votes
Paul Tyler	Lib Dem	29,696	47.4	+5.5	41.9	24,180
Sir Gerry Neale*	Con	27,775	44.3	-7.4	51.7	29,862
Frank Jordan	Lab	4,103	6.6	+0.1	6.4	3,719
Phillip Andrews	Lib	678	1.1			
Geoffrey Rowe	Ind	276	0.4			
Helen Treadwell	NLP	112	0.2			
Majority	**Lib Dem**	**1,921**	**3.1**	**+12.9**	**9.8**	**5,682**

Electorate: 76,844 **Voters:** 62,640 **Turnout:** 81.5 **Swing:** 6.5 to LDm from Con

CONSTITUENCIES

CORNWALL SOUTH EAST

Robert Hicks: *Conservative. Born: 1938. Educated: Queen Elizabeth Grammar School, Crediton; London University. Jobs: lecturer. First Elected: 1970. Posts: member, European Legislation Select Committee, chairmen's panel. Status: divorced, two children.*

CON HOLD		1992 election			1987 election	
		Votes	%	+/-	%	Votes
Robert Hicks*	Con	30,565	51.0	-0.6	51.6	28,818
Robin Teverson	Lib Dem	22,861	38.1	-1.6	39.8	22,211
Linda Gilroy	Lab	5,536	9.2	+0.6	8.7	4,847
Maureen Cook	Lib	644	1.1			
Anthony Quick	Anti Fed	227	0.4			
Rosaleen Allen	NLP	155	0.3			
Majority	**Con**	**7,704**	**12.8**	**+1.0**	**11.8**	**6,607**

Electorate: 73,027 **Voters:** 59,988 **Turnout:** 82.1 **Swing:** 0.5 to Con from LDm

COVENTRY NORTH EAST

Robert Ainsworth: *Labour. Born: 1952. Educated: local state schools. Jobs: sheet metal worker. First Elected: 1992. Union: MSF. Status: married, two children.*

LAB HOLD		1992 election			1987 election	
		Votes	%	+/-	%	Votes
Robert Ainsworth	Lab	24,896	52.5	-1.8	54.3	25,832
Keith Perrin	Con	13,220	27.9	-1.5	29.3	13,965
Vincent McKee	Lib Dem	5,306	11.2	-4.6	15.8	7,502
John Hughes*	Ind Lab	4,008	8.5			
Majority	**Lab**	**11,676**	**24.6**	**-0.3**	**24.9**	**11,867**

Electorate: 64,787 **Voters:** 47,430 **Turnout:** 73.2 **Swing:** 0.2 to Con from Lab

COVENTRY NORTH WEST

Geoffrey Robinson: *Labour. Born: 1938. Educated: Emmanuel School, London; Cambridge. Jobs: company director, political researcher. First Elected: 1976. Status: married, two children.*

LAB HOLD		1992 election			1987 election	
		Votes	%	+/-	%	Votes
Geoffrey Robinson*	Lab	20,349	51.7	+2.7	49.0	19,450
Agnes Hill	Con	13,917	35.4	+0.6	34.7	13,787
Ann Simpson	Lib Dem	5,070	12.9	-3.4	16.3	6,455
Majority	**Lab**	**6,432**	**16.4**	**+2.1**	**14.3**	**5,663**

Electorate: 50,670 **Voters:** 39,336 **Turnout:** 77.6 **Swing:** 1.0 to Lab from Con

COVENTRY SOUTH EAST

Jim Cunningham: Labour. Born: 1941. Jobs: engineer. First Elected: 1992. Union: MSF. Status: married, two children.

LAB HOLD

		1992 election			1987 election	
		Votes	%	+/-	%	Votes
Jim Cunningham	Lab	11,902	32.6	-14.9	47.5	17,969
Martine Hyams	Con	10,591	29.0	-0.9	29.9	11,316
Dave Nellist*	Ind Lab	10,551	28.9			
Tony Armstrong	Lib Dem	3,318	9.1	-12.3	21.4	8,095
Norman Tompkinson	NF	173	0.5			
Majority	**Lab**	**1,311**	**3.6**	**-14.0**	**17.6**	**6,653**

Electorate: 48,796 **Voters**: 36,535 **Turnout**: 74.9 **Swing**: 7.0 to Con from Lab

COVENTRY SOUTH WEST

John Butcher: Conservative. Born: 1946. Educated: Huntingdon Grammar School; Birmingham University. Jobs: company director. First Elected: 1979. Status: married, three children.

CON HOLD

		1992 election			1987 election	
		Votes	%	+/-	%	Votes
John Butcher*	Con	23,225	45.7	+2.4	43.3	22,318
Bob Slater	Lab	21,789	42.8	+5.8	37.0	19,108
Geoffrey Sewards	Lib Dem	4,666	9.2	-10.5	19.7	10,166
Rob Wheway	Lib	989	1.9			
David Morris	NLP	204	0.4			
Majority	**Con**	**1,436**	**2.8**	**-3.4**	**6.2**	**3,210**

Electorate: 63,474 **Voters**: 50,873 **Turnout**: 80.1 **Swing**: 1.7 to Lab from Con

CRAWLEY

Nicholas Soames: Conservative. Born: 1948. Educated: Eton. Jobs: equerry, stockbroker. First Elected: 1983. Posts: Junior Minister for Agriculture. Status: married, one child.

CON HOLD

		1992 election			1987 election	
		Votes	%	+/-	%	Votes
Nicholas Soames*	Con	30,204	48.7	-0.8	49.5	29,259
Laura Moffatt	Lab	22,439	36.2	+7.2	29.0	17,121
Gordon Seekings	Lib Dem	8,558	13.8	-7.7	21.5	12,674
Mark Wilson	Green	766	1.2			
Majority	**Con**	**7,765**	**12.5**	**-8.0**	**20.6**	**12,138**

Electorate: 78,277 **Voters**: 61,967 **Turnout**: 79.2 **Swing**: 4.0 to Lab from Con

CREWE & NANTWICH

Gwyneth Dunwoody: *Labour. Born: 1930. Educated: Fulham Secondary School. First Elected: 1966. Posts: member, Transport Select Committee, chairmen's panel. Status: divorced, three children.*

LAB HOLD		1992 election Votes	%	+/-	1987 election %	Votes
Gwyneth Dunwoody*	Lab	28,065	45.7	+1.7	44.0	25,457
Brian Silvester	Con	25,370	41.3	-0.8	42.1	24,365
Gwyn Griffiths	Lib Dem	7,315	11.9	-2.0	13.9	8,022
Natalie Wilkinson	Green	651	1.1			
Majority	**Lab**	**2,695**	**4.4**	**+2.5**	**1.9**	**1,092**

Electorate: 74,993 **Voters:** 61,401 **Turnout:** 81.9 **Swing:** 1.3 to Lab from Con

CROSBY

Sir Malcolm Thornton: *Conservative. Born: 1939. Educated: Wallasey Grammar School; Liverpool Nautical College. Jobs: river pilot. First Elected: 1979. Posts: chairman, Education Select Committee. Status: married.*

CON HOLD		1992 election Votes	%	+/-	1987 election %	Votes
Malcolm Thornton*	Con	32,267	47.4	+1.3	46.2	30,842
Maria Eagle	Lab	17,461	25.7	+7.7	17.9	11,992
Flo Clucas	Lib Dem	16,562	24.3	-11.6	35.9	23,989
John Marks	Lib	1,052	1.5			
Sean Brady	Green	559	0.8			
Neil Paterson	NLP	152	0.2			
Majority	**Con**	**14,806**	**21.8**	**+11.5**	**10.3**	**6,853**

Electorate: 82,537 **Voters:** 68,053 **Turnout:** 82.5 **Swing:** 3.2 to Lab from Con

CROYDON CENTRAL

Sir Paul Beresford: *Conservative. Born: 1946. Educated: Otago University, New Zealand. Jobs: dental surgeon. First Elected: 1992. Posts: member, Education Select Committee. Status: married, three children.*

CON HOLD		1992 election Votes	%	+/-	1987 election %	Votes
Sir Paul Beresford	Con	22,168	55.4	-1.2	56.6	22,133
Geraint Davies	Lab	12,518	31.3	+6.9	24.3	9,516
Deborah Richardson	Lib Dem	5,342	13.3	-5.7	19.0	7,435
Majority	**Con**	**9,650**	**24.1**	**-8.2**	**32.3**	**12,617**

Electorate: 55,798 **Voters:** 40,028 **Turnout:** 71.7 **Swing:** 4.1 to Lab from Con

CROYDON NORTH EAST

David Congdon: *Conservative. Born: 1949. Educated: Alleyn's School; Thames Polytechnic. Jobs: computer consultant. First Elected: 1992. Posts: member, Health Select Committee. Status: married, one child.*

CON HOLD

		1992 election			1987 election	
		Votes	%	+/-	%	Votes
David Congdon	Con	23,835	51.4	-3.6	55.0	24,188
Mary Walker	Lab	16,362	35.3	+8.7	26.5	11,669
John Fraser	Lib Dem	6,186	13.3	-5.1	18.5	8,128
Majority	**Con**	**7,473**	**16.1**	**-12.4**	**28.5**	**12,519**

Electorate: 64,405 **Voters:** 46,383 **Turnout:** 72.0 **Swing:** 6.2 to Lab from Con

CROYDON NORTH WEST

Malcolm Wicks: *Labour. Born: 1947. Educated: Elizabeth College, Guernsey; London School of Economics. Jobs: director of welfare agency. First Elected: 1992. Status: married, three children.*

LAB GAIN

		1992 election			1987 election	
		Votes	%	+/-	%	Votes
Malcolm Wicks	Lab	19,152	47.3	+10.3	37.0	14,677
Humfrey Malins*	Con	17,626	43.5	-3.5	47.0	18,665
Linda Hawkins	Lib Dem	3,728	9.2	-6.8	16.0	6,363
Majority	**Lab**	**1,526**	**3.8**	**+13.8**	**10.0**	**3,988**

Electorate: 57,241 **Voters:** 40,506 **Turnout:** 70.8 **Swing:** 6.9 to Lab from Con

CROYDON SOUTH

Richard Ottaway: *Conservative. Born: 1945. Educated: Royal Naval College, Dartmouth; Bristol University. Jobs: solicitor. First Elected: 1983. Posts: PPS. Status: married.*

CON HOLD

		1992 election			1987 election	
		Votes	%	+/-	%	Votes
Richard Ottaway	Con	31,993	63.7	-0.4	64.1	30,732
Peter Billenness	Lib Dem	11,568	23.0	-1.3	24.3	11,669
Helen Salmon	Lab	6,444	12.8	+3.1	9.8	4,679
Mark Samuel	Choice	239	0.5			
Majority	**Con**	**20,425**	**40.7**	**+0.9**	**39.7**	**19,063**

Electorate: 64,768 **Voters:** 50,244 **Turnout:** 77.6 **Swing:** 0.5 to Con from LDm

CUMBERNAULD & KILSYTH

Norman Hogg: Labour. Born: 1938. Educated: local state schools. Jobs: trade union official. First Elected: 1979. Union: TGWU. Posts: member, chairmen's panel. Status: married.

LAB HOLD

		1992 election Votes	%	+/-	1987 election %	Votes
Norman Hogg*	Lab	19,855	54.0	-6.0	60.0	21,385
Tom Johnston	SNP	10,640	28.9	+9.4	19.6	6,982
Iain Mitchell	Con	4,143	11.3	+2.2	9.1	3,227
Jean Haddow	Lib Dem	2,118	5.8	-5.6	11.4	4,059
Majority	**Lab**	**9,215**	**25.1**	**-15.3**	**40.4**	**14,403**

Electorate: 46,489 **Voters:** 36,756 **Turnout:** 79.1 **Swing:** 7.7 to SNP from Lab

---

CUNNINGHAME NORTH

Brian Wilson: Labour. Born: 1948. Educated: Dundee University. Jobs: journalist. First Elected: 1987. Posts: Labour spokesman on Citizen's charter and women. Status: married, one child.

LAB HOLD

		1992 election Votes	%	+/-	1987 election %	Votes
Brian Wilson*	Lab	17,564	41.0	-3.4	44.4	19,016
Edith Clarkson	Con	14,625	34.1	+0.1	34.0	14,594
David Crossan	SNP	7,813	18.2	+8.7	9.5	4,076
Douglas Herbison	Lib Dem	2,864	6.7	-5.4	12.1	5,185
Majority	**Lab**	**2,939**	**6.9**	**-3.5**	**10.3**	**4,422**

Electorate: 54,803 **Voters:** 42,866 **Turnout:** 78.2 **Swing:** 1.7 to Con from Lab

---

CUNNINGHAME SOUTH

Brian Donohue: Labour. Born: 1948. Educated: Irvine Royal Academy; Kilmarnock Technical College. Jobs: trade union official. First Elected: 1992. Status: married, two children.

LAB HOLD

		1992 election Votes	%	+/-	1987 election %	Votes
Brian Donohue	Lab	19,687	52.9	-7.9	60.8	22,728
Ricky Bell	SNP	9,007	24.2	+13.2	11.0	4,115
Sebastian Leslie	Con	6,070	16.3	+0.0	16.3	6,095
Brian Ashley	Lib Dem	2,299	6.2	-5.7	11.8	4,426
Bill Jackson	NLP	128	0.3			
Majority	**Lab**	**10,680**	**28.7**	**-15.8**	**44.5**	**16,633**

Electorate: 49,010 **Voters:** 37,191 **Turnout:** 75.9 **Swing:** 10.5 to SNP from Lab

CYNON VALLEY

Ann Clwyd: Labour. Born: 1937. Educated: Holywell Grammar School; University College, Bangor. Jobs: journalist, Euro MP. First Elected: 1984. Posts: Shadow Welsh Secretary. Union: TGWU. Status: married.

LAB HOLD

		1992 election Votes	%	+/-	1987 election %	Votes
Ann Clwyd*	Lab	26,254	69.1	+0.2	68.9	26,222
Andrew Smith	Con	4,890	12.9	+0.7	12.2	4,638
Terry Benney	Plaid Cymru	4,186	11.0	+4.3	6.7	2,549
Marcello Verma	Lib Dem	2,667	7.0	-5.2	12.2	4,651
Majority	**Lab**	**21,364**	**56.2**	**-0.5**	**56.7**	**21,571**

Electorate: 49,695 **Voters:** 37,997 **Turnout:** 76.5 **Swing:** 0.2 to Con from Lab

DAGENHAM

Bryan Gould: Labour. Born: 1939. Educated: schools in New Zealand; Victoria and Auckland Universities, Oxford. Jobs: lecturer, journalist, diplomat. First Elected: 1974. Posts: Shadow National Heritage Secretary. Status: married, two children.

LAB HOLD

		1992 election Votes	%	+/-	1987 election %	Votes
Bryan Gould*	Lab	22,027	52.3	+7.8	44.4	18,454
Don Rossiter	Con	15,294	36.3	-2.2	38.5	15,985
Charles Marquand	Lib Dem	4,824	11.4	-5.6	17.1	7,088
Majority	**Lab**	**6,733**	**16.0**	**+10.0**	**5.9**	**2,469**

Electorate: 59,645 **Voters:** 42,145 **Turnout:** 70.7 **Swing:** 5.0 to Lab from Con

DARLINGTON

Alan Milburn: Labour. Born: 1958. Educated: Lancaster University. Jobs: business development officer. First Elected: 1992. Union: MSF. Status: divorced, one child.

LAB GAIN

		1992 election Votes	%	+/-	1987 election %	Votes
Alan Milburn	Lab	26,556	48.1	+6.5	41.6	22,170
Michael Fallon*	Con	23,758	43.0	-3.6	46.6	24,831
Peter Bergg	Lib Dem	4,586	8.3	-3.5	11.8	6,289
Donald Clarke	BNP	355	0.6			
Majority	**Lab**	**2,798**	**5.1**	**+10.1**	**5.0**	**2,661**

Electorate: 66,094 **Voters:** 55,255 **Turnout:** 83.6 **Swing:** 5.0 to Lab from Con

DARTFORD

Bob Dunn: Conservative. Born: 1946. Educated: Manchester Polytechnic; Salford University. Jobs: buyer. First Elected: 1979. Posts: executive member, 1922 Committee. Status: married, two children.

CON HOLD		1992 election Votes	%	+/-	1987 election %	Votes
Bob Dunn*	Con	31,194	51.8	-1.6	53.5	30,685
Howard Stoate	Lab	20,880	34.7	+7.2	27.5	15,756
Peter Bryden	Lib Dem	7,584	12.6	-5.6	18.2	10,439
Alan Munro	FDP	262	0.4	-0.4	0.9	491
Angela Holland	NLP	247	0.4			
Majority	**Con**	**10,314**	**17.1**	**-8.9**	**26.0**	**14,929**

Electorate: 72,366 **Voters:** 60,167 **Turnout:** 83.1 **Swing:** 4.4 to Lab from Con

DAVENTRY

Timothy Boswell: Conservative. Born: 1942. Educated: Marlborough College; Oxford. Jobs: political researcher. First Elected: 1987. Posts: Government Whip. Status: married, three children.

CON HOLD		1992 election Votes	%	+/-	1987 election %	Votes
Timothy Boswell*	Con	34,734	58.4	+0.5	57.9	31,353
Lesley Koumi	Lab	14,460	24.3	+3.8	20.5	11,097
Tony Rounthwaite	Lib Dem	9,820	16.5	-5.0	21.6	11,663
Russell France	NLP	422	0.7			
Majority	**Con**	**20,274**	**34.1**	**-2.3**	**36.4**	**19,690**

Electorate: 71,824 **Voters:** 59,436 **Turnout:** 82.8 **Swing:** 1.7 to Lab from Con

DAVYHULME

Winston Churchill: Conservative. Born: 1940. Educated: Eton; Oxford. First Elected: 1970. Posts: member, Defence Select Committee. Status: married, four children.

CON HOLD		1992 election Votes	%	+/-	1987 election %	Votes
Winston Churchill*	Con	24,216	48.0	+1.4	46.6	23,633
Barry Brotherton	Lab	19,790	39.2	+8.8	30.4	15,434
Jacqueline Pearcey	Lib Dem	5,797	11.5	-11.5	23.0	11,637
Terence Brotheridge	NLP	665	1.3			
Majority	**Con**	**4,426**	**8.8**	**-7.4**	**16.2**	**8,199**

Electorate: 61,679 **Voters:** 50,468 **Turnout:** 81.8 **Swing:** 3.7 to Lab from Con

DELYN

David Hanson: Labour. Born: 1957. Educated: local state schools; Hull University. Jobs: charity officer. First Elected: 1992. Union: MSF. Posts: member, Welsh Affairs Select Committee. Status: married, three children.

LAB GAIN

		1992 election Votes	%	+/-	1987 election %	Votes
David Hanson	Lab	24,979	45.0	+4.9	39.1	20,504
Mike Whitby	Con	22,940	41.3	-1.2	41.4	21,728
Ray Dodd	Lib Dem	6,208	11.2	-6.2	17.0	8,913
Ashley Drake	Plaid Cymru	1,414	2.5	-0.0	2.6	1,339
Majority	**Lab**	**2,039**	**3.7**	**+6.1**	**2.4**	**1,224**

Electorate: 66,591 **Voters:** 55,541 **Turnout:** 83.4 **Swing:** 3.0 to Lab from Con

DENTON & REDDISH

Andrew Bennett: Labour. Born: 1939. Educated: Birmingham University. Jobs: teacher. First Elected: 1974. Posts: member, Environment Select Committee, Statutory Instruments Select Committee. Status: married, three children.

LAB HOLD

		1992 election Votes	%	+/-	1987 election %	Votes
Andrew Bennett*	Lab	29,021	55.2	+5.6	49.6	26,023
Jeffrey Horswell	Con	16,937	32.2	-1.6	33.9	17,773
Fred Ridley	Lib Dem	4,953	9.4	-7.1	16.6	8,697
Martin Powell	Lib	1,296	2.5			
John Fuller	NLP	354	0.7			
Majority	**Lab**	**12,084**	**23.0**	**+7.3**	**15.7**	**8,250**

Electorate: 68,463 **Voters:** 52,561 **Turnout:** 76.8 **Swing:** 3.6 to Lab from Con

DERBY NORTH

Greg Knight: Conservative. Born: 1949. Educated: Alderman Newton's grammar school, Leicester. Jobs: solicitor. First Elected: 1983. Posts: Government Whip. Status: single.

CON HOLD

		1992 election Votes	%	+/-	1987 election %	Votes
Greg Knight*	Con	28,574	48.4	-0.4	48.8	26,516
Bob Laxton	Lab	24,121	40.9	+3.6	37.3	20,236
Bob Charlesworth	Lib Dem	5,638	9.6	-3.8	13.4	7,268
Eric Wall	Green	383	0.6	+0.1	0.5	291
Peter Hart	NF	245	0.4			
Nicholas Onley	NLP	58	0.1			
Majority	**Con**	**4,453**	**7.5**	**-4.0**	**11.6**	**6,280**

Electorate: 73,176 **Voters:** 59,019 **Turnout:** 80.7 **Swing:** 2.0 to Lab from Con

DERBY SOUTH

Margaret Beckett: Labour. Born: 1943. Educated: Notre Dame High School, Norwich; Manchester College of Science and Technology. Jobs: metallurgist, political researcher. First Elected: 1974. Posts: Shadow Leader of the House; Deputy Leader of the Labour Party. Union: TGWU. Status: married

LAB HOLD		1992 election			1987 election	
		Votes	%	+/-	%	Votes
Margaret Beckett*	Lab	25,917	51.7	+8.1	43.7	21,003
Nicholas Brown	Con	18,981	37.9	-2.6	40.5	19,487
Simon Hartropp	Lib Dem	5,198	10.4	-5.4	15.8	7,608
Majority	**Lab**	**6,936**	**13.8**	**+10.7**	**3.2**	**1,516**

Electorate: 66,328 **Voters:** 50,096 **Turnout:** 75.5 **Swing:** 5.3 to Lab from Con

DERBYSHIRE NORTH EAST

Harry Barnes: Labour. Born: 1936. Educated: Easington Colliery school; Hull University. Jobs: railway clerk. First Elected: 1987. Posts: member, European Legislation Select Committee. Union: MSF. Status: married, two children.

LAB HOLD		1992 election			1987 election	
		Votes	%	+/-	%	Votes
Harry Barnes*	Lab	28,860	48.8	+4.4	44.4	24,747
John Hayes	Con	22,590	38.2	+0.5	37.7	21,027
David Stone	Lib Dem	7,675	13.0	-4.9	17.9	9,985
Majority	**Lab**	**6,270**	**10.6**	**+3.9**	**6.7**	**3,720**

Electorate: 70,707 **Voters:** 59,125 **Turnout:** 83.6 **Swing:** 2.0 to Lab from Con

DERBYSHIRE SOUTH

Edwina Currie: Conservative. Born: 1946. Educated: Liverpool Institute for Girls; Oxford. Jobs: teacher, lecturer. First Elected: 1983. Status: married, two children.

CON HOLD		1992 election			1987 election	
		Votes	%	+/-	%	Votes
Edwina Currie*	Con	34,266	48.7	-0.4	49.1	31,927
Mark Todd	Lab	29,608	42.1	+8.8	33.2	21,616
Diana Brass	Lib Dem	6,236	8.9	-8.8	17.7	11,509
Titus Mercer	NLP	291	0.4			
Majority	**Con**	**4,658**	**6.6**	**-9.2**	**15.9**	**10,311**

Electorate: 82,342 **Voters:** 70,401 **Turnout:** 85.5 **Swing:** 4.6 to Lab from Con

DERBYSHIRE WEST

Patrick McLoughlin: *Conservative. Born: 1957. Educated: Cardinal Griffin Roman Catholic School. Jobs: agricultural worker, Coal Board worker. Posts: Under-Secretary, Department of Employment. First Elected: 1986. Status: married, two children.*

CON HOLD		1992 election Votes	%	+/-	1987 election %	Votes
Patrick McLoughlin*	Con	32,879	54.3	+1.2	53.1	31,224
Richard Fearn	Lib Dem	14,110	23.3	-11.9	35.2	20,697
Stephen Clamp	Lab	13,528	22.4	+10.7	11.7	6,875
Majority	**Con**	**18,769**	**31.0**	**+13.1**	**17.9**	**10,527**

Electorate: 71,201 **Voters:** 60,517 **Turnout:** 85.0 **Swing:** 6.6 to Con from LDm

DEVIZES

Michael Ancram: *Conservative. Born: 1945. Educated: Ampleforth College; Oxford University. Jobs: barrister, company director. Posts: member, Public Accounts Committee. First Elected: 1979. Status: married, two children.*

CON HOLD		1992 election Votes	%	+/-	1987 election %	Votes
Michael Ancram	Con	39,090	53.3	-1.4	54.8	36,372
Jane Mactaggart	Lib Dem	19,378	26.4	-1.5	27.9	18,542
Rosemary Berry	Lab	13,060	17.8	+0.5	17.3	11,487
Stuart Coles	Lib	962	1.3			
David Ripley	Green	808	1.1			
Majority	**Con**	**19,712**	**26.9**	**+0.0**	**26.9**	**17,830**

Electorate: 89,745 **Voters:** 73,298 **Turnout:** 81.7 **Swing:** No Swing

DEVON NORTH

Nick Harvey: *Liberal Democrat. Born: 1961. Educated: Queen's College, Taunton, Middlesex Polytechnic. Jobs: political adviser. First Elected: 1992. Posts: LibDem transport spokesman. Status: single.*

LIBDEM GAIN		1992 election Votes	%	+/-	1987 election %	Votes
Nick Harvey	Lib Dem	27,414	47.1	+4.3	42.8	23,602
Tony Speller*	Con	26,620	45.7	-5.2	50.9	28,071
Paul Donner	Lab	3,410	5.9	-0.4	6.3	3,467
Cathrine Simmons	Green	658	1.1			
Gray Treadwell	NLP	107	0.2			
Majority	**Lib Dem**	**794**	**1.4**	**+9.5**	**8.1**	**4,469**

Electorate: 68,998 **Voters:** 58,209 **Turnout:** 84.4 **Swing:** 4.7 to LDm from Con

DEVON WEST & TORRIDGE

Emma Nicholson: Conservative. Born: 1941. Educated: St Mary's School, Wantage; Royal Academy of Music. Jobs: director of voluntary organisation. First Elected: 1987. Status: married.

CON HOLD		1992 election			1987 election	
		Votes	%	+/-	%	Votes
Emma Nicholson*	Con	29,627	47.3	-3.0	50.3	29,484
David McBride	Lib Dem	26,013	41.5	+2.3	39.2	23,016
David Brenton	Lab	5,997	9.6	+1.1	8.5	4,990
Frank Williamson	Green	898	1.4	-0.6	2.0	1,168
David Collins	NLP	141	0.2			
Majority	**Con**	**3,614**	**5.8**	**-5.3**	**11.0**	**6,468**

Electorate: 76,933 **Voters:** 62,676 **Turnout:** 81.5 **Swing:** 2.6 to LDm from Con

DEWSBURY

Ann Taylor: Labour. Born: 1947. Educated: Bolton School, Bradford and Sheffield Universities. Jobs: teacher. First Elected: 1974. Posts: Shadow Education Secretary. Union: GMB. Status: married, two children.

LAB HOLD		1992 election			1987 election	
		Votes	%	+/-	%	Votes
Ann Taylor*	Lab	25,596	43.8	+1.4	42.4	23,668
John Whitfield	Con	24,962	42.7	+1.1	41.6	23,223
Robert Meadowcroft	Lib Dem	6,570	11.2	-4.7	16.0	8,907
Lady Jane Birdwood	BNP	660	1.1			
Neil Denby	Green	471	0.8			
Janet Marsden	NLP	146	0.2			
Majority	**Lab**	**634**	**1.1**	**+0.3**	**0.8**	**445**

Electorate: 72,839 **Voters:** 58,405 **Turnout:** 80.2 **Swing:** 0.1 to Lab from Con

DONCASTER CENTRAL

Harold Walker: Labour. Born: 1927. Educated: Manchester College of Technology. Jobs: toolmaker, tutor. First Elected: 1964. Status: married, one child.

LAB HOLD		1992 election			1987 election	
		Votes	%	+/-	%	Votes
Harold Walker*	Lab	27,795	54.3	+3.2	51.2	26,266
William Glossop	Con	17,113	33.5	-1.7	35.2	18,070
Cliff Hampson	Lib Dem	6,057	11.8	-1.8	13.6	7,004
Michael Driver	WRP	184	0.4			
Majority	**Lab**	**10,682**	**20.9**	**+4.9**	**16.0**	**8,196**

Electorate: 68,890 **Voters:** 51,149 **Turnout:** 74.2 **Swing:** 2.5 to Lab from Con

DONCASTER NORTH

Kevin Hughes: Labour. Born: 1952. Educated: local state schools; Sheffield University. Jobs: miner. First Elected: 1992. Union: NUM. Status: married, two children.

LAB HOLD		1992 election			1987 election	
		Votes	%	+/-	%	Votes
Kevin Hughes	Lab	34,135	61.8	+0.0	61.8	32,953
Robert Light	Con	14,322	25.9	+1.5	24.4	13,015
Steve Whiting	Lib Dem	6,787	12.3	-1.6	13.9	7,394
Majority	**Lab**	**19,813**	**35.9**	**-1.5**	**37.4**	**19,938**

Electorate: 74,732 **Voters:** 55,244 **Turnout:** 73.9 **Swing:** 0.7 to Con from Lab

DON VALLEY

Martin Redmond: Labour. Born: 1937. Educated: Woodlands RC School; Sheffield University. Jobs: HGV driver. First Elected: 1983. Union: NUM. Posts: delegate, Council of Europe, Western European Union. Status: single

LAB HOLD		1992 election			1987 election	
		Votes	%	+/-	%	Votes
Martin Redmond*	Lab	32,008	55.0	+1.9	53.1	29,200
Nicholas Paget-Brown	Con	18,474	31.7	-0.5	32.3	17,733
Malcolm Jevons	Lib Dem	6,920	11.9	-2.7	14.6	8,027
Stephen Platt	Green	803	1.4			
Majority	**Lab**	**13,534**	**23.3**	**+2.4**	**20.9**	**11,467**

Electorate: 76,327 **Voters:** 58,205 **Turnout:** 76.3 **Swing:** 1.2 to Lab from Con

DORSET NORTH

Nicholas Baker: Conservative. Born: 1938. Educated: St Neot's School, Hants; Oxford. Jobs: solicitor. First Elected: 1979. Posts: Government Whip. Status: married, two children.

CON HOLD		1992 election			1987 election	
		Votes	%	+/-	%	Votes
Nicholas Baker*	Con	34,234	54.6	-2.5	57.0	32,854
Linda Siegle	Lib Dem	24,154	38.5	+2.1	36.4	20,947
John Fitzmaurice	Lab	4,360	6.9	+0.3	6.6	3,819
Majority	**Con**	**10,080**	**16.1**	**-4.6**	**20.7**	**11,907**

Electorate: 76,718 **Voters:** 62,748 **Turnout:** 81.8 **Swing:** 2.3 to LDm from Con

DORSET SOUTH

Ian Bruce: *Conservative. Born: 1947. Educated: Mid Essex Technical College; Bradford University. Jobs: work study engineer, consultant. First Elected: 1987. Posts: member, Employment Select Committee. Status: married, four children.*

CON HOLD		1992 election			1987 election	
		Votes	%	+/-	%	Votes
Ian Bruce*	Con	29,319	50.3	-4.5	54.8	30,184
Brian Ellis	Lib Dem	15,811	27.1	-0.3	27.5	15,117
Alan Chedzoy	Lab	12,298	21.1	+3.8	17.2	9,494
J Nager	Ind	673	1.2	+0.7	0.4	244
Mark Griffiths	NLP	191	0.3			
Majority	**Con**	**13,508**	**23.2**	**-4.2**	**27.4**	**15,067**

Electorate: 75,788 **Voters:** 58,292 **Turnout:** 76.9 **Swing:** 2.1 to LDm from Con

DORSET WEST

Sir James Spicer: *Conservative. Born: 1925. Educated: Latymer Upper School. Jobs: farmer, company director. First Elected: 1974. Posts: vice-chairman, Conservative Party. Status: married, two children.*

CON HOLD		1992 election			1987 election	
		Votes	%	+/-	%	Votes
Sir James Spicer*	Con	27,766	50.8	-5.3	56.2	28,305
Robin Legg	Lib Dem	19,756	36.2	+4.5	31.6	15,941
Joe Mann	Lab	7,082	13.0	+0.8	12.2	6,123
Majority	**Con**	**8,010**	**14.7**	**-9.9**	**24.5**	**12,364**

Electorate: 67,256 **Voters:** 54,604 **Turnout:** 81.2 **Swing:** 4.9 to LDm from Con

DOVER

David Shaw: *Conservative. Born: 1950. Educated: King's College, Wimbledon; City of London Polytechnic. Jobs: company director. First Elected: 1987. Posts: member, Social Security Select Committee. Status: married.*

CON HOLD		1992 election			1987 election	
		Votes	%	+/-	%	Votes
David Shaw*	Con	25,395	44.1	-1.9	46.0	25,343
Gwyn Prosser	Lab	24,562	42.6	+8.5	34.1	18,802
Mike Sole	Lib Dem	6,212	10.8	-9.1	19.9	10,942
Adrian Sullivan	Green	637	1.1			
Peter Sherred	Ind	407	0.7			
Brian Philp	Ind C	250	0.4			
Colin Percy	NLP	127	0.2			
Majority	**Con**	**833**	**1.4**	**-10.4**	**11.9**	**6,541**

Electorate: 68,962 **Voters:** 57,590 **Turnout:** 83.5 **Swing:** 5.2 to Lab from Con

DOWN NORTH

Sir James Kilfedder: Ulster Popular Unionist. Born: 1928. Educated: Portora Royal School; Trinity College Dublin. Jobs: barrister. Posts: member, chairmen's panel. First Elected: 1964.

POP U HOLD		1992 election			1987 election	
		Votes	%	+/-	%	Votes
James Kilfedder*	Pop U	19,305	42.9	-2.2	45.1	18,420
Laurence Kennedy	Con	14,371	32.0			
Addie Morrow	All	6,611	14.7	-4.7	19.4	7,932
Denny Vitty	DUP	4,414	9.8			
Andrew Wilmot	NLP	255	0.6			
Majority	**Pop U**	**4,934**	**11.0**	**+1.3**	**9.7**	**3,953**

Electorate: 68,662 **Voters:** 44,956 **Turnout:** 65.5

DOWN SOUTH

Eddie McGrady: Social Democratic and Labour Party. Born: 1935. Educated: St Patrick's High School, Downpatrick; Belfast College of Technology. Jobs: accountant. First Elected: 1987. Posts: SDLP Whip; housing spokesman. Status: married, three children.

SDLP HOLD		1992 election			1987 election	
		Votes	%	+/-	%	Votes
Eddie McGrady*	SDLP	31,523	51.2	+4.2	47.0	26,579
Drew Nelson	UUP	25,181	40.9	-4.8	45.7	25,848
Sean Fitzpatrick	Sinn Fein	1,843	3.0	-1.2	4.2	2,363
Michael Healey	All	1,542	2.5	+0.6	1.9	1,069
Stephanie McKenzie	Con	1,488	2.4			
Majority	**SDLP**	**6,342**	**10.3**	**+9.0**	**1.3**	**731**

Electorate: 76,093 **Voters:** 61,577 **Turnout:** 80.9 **Swing:** 4.5 to SDLP from UUP

DUDLEY EAST

Dr John Gilbert: Labour. Born: 1927. Educated: Merchant Taylors; Oxford. Jobs: accountant. First Elected: 1974. Union: GMB. Status: married, two children.

LAB HOLD		1992 election			1987 election	
		Votes	%	+/-	%	Votes
John Gilbert*	Lab	29,806	52.8	+6.9	45.9	24,942
James Holland	Con	20,606	36.5	-3.0	39.5	21,469
Ian Jenkins	Lib Dem	5,400	9.6	-5.1	14.6	7,965
George Cartwright	NF	675	1.2			
Majority	**Lab**	**9,200**	**16.3**	**+9.9**	**6.4**	**3,473**

Electorate: 75,355 **Voters:** 56,487 **Turnout:** 75.0 **Swing:** 4.9 to Lab from Con

DUDLEY WEST

Dr John Blackburn: Conservative. Born: 1933. Educated: Liverpool Collegiate School; Liverpool University. Jobs: soldier, policeman, sales manager. First Elected: 1979. Posts: member, National Heritage Select Committee. Status: married, two children.

CON HOLD		1992 election			1987 election	
		Votes	%	+/-	%	Votes
John Blackburn*	Con	34,729	48.8	-1.0	49.8	32,224
Kevin Lomax	Lab	28,940	40.7	+6.7	34.0	21,980
Gerry Lewis	Lib Dem	7,446	10.5	-5.7	16.2	10,477
Majority	**Con**	**5,789**	**8.1**	**-7.7**	**15.8**	**10,244**

Electorate: 86,632 **Voters:** 71,115 **Turnout:** 82.1 **Swing:** 3.8 to Lab from Con

DULWICH

Tessa Jowell: Labour. Born: 1947. Educated: St Margaret's School, Aberdeen; Edinburgh University. Jobs: director of voluntary organisation. First Elected: 1992. Union: MSF. Posts: member, Social Security Select Committee. Status: married, two children.

LAB GAIN		1992 election			1987 election	
		Votes	%	+/-	%	Votes
Tessa Jowell	Lab	17,714	47.3	+5.3	42.0	16,383
Gerry Bowden*	Con	15,658	41.8	-0.6	42.4	16,563
Alex Goldie	Lib Dem	4,078	10.9	-3.6	14.5	5,664
Majority	**Lab**	**2,056**	**5.5**	**+6.0**	**0.5**	**180**

Electorate: 55,141 **Voters:** 37,450 **Turnout:** 67.9 **Swing:** 3.0 to Lab from Con

DUMBARTON

John McFall: Labour. Born: 1944. Educated: Paisley College of Technology; Strathclyde University. Jobs: teacher. First Elected: 1987. Posts: Labour spokesman on Scottish affairs; member, Transport Select Committee. Union: GMB. Status: married, four children.

LAB HOLD		1992 election			1987 election	
		Votes	%	+/-	%	Votes
John McFall*	Lab	19,255	43.6	+0.6	43.0	19,778
Tom Begg	Con	13,126	29.7	-1.9	31.7	14,556
Bill McKechnie	SNP	8,127	18.4	+6.3	12.1	5,564
John Morrison	Lib Dem	3,425	7.8	-5.4	13.2	6,060
Diana Krass	NLP	192	0.4			
Majority	**Lab**	**6,129**	**13.9**	**+2.5**	**11.4**	**5,222**

Electorate: 57,222 **Voters:** 44,125 **Turnout:** 77.1 **Swing:** 1.3 to Lab from Con

DUMFRIES

Sir Hector Monro: Conservative. Born: 1922. Educated: Canford; Cambridge. First Elected: 1964. Posts: Scottish Office Minister. Status: married, two children.

CON HOLD

		1992 election Votes	%	+/-	1987 election %	Votes
Sir Hector Monro*	Con	21,089	43.1	+1.3	41.9	18,785
Peter Rennie	Lab	14,674	30.0	+4.8	25.2	11,292
Alasdair Morgan	SNP	6,971	14.3	+0.0	14.2	6,391
Neil Wallace	Lib Dem	5,749	11.8	-6.2	18.0	8,064
Graham McLeod	Ind Green	312	0.6			
Thomas Barlow	NLP	107	0.2			
Majority	**Con**	**6,415**	**13.1**	**-3.6**	**16.7**	**7,493**

Electorate: 61,145 **Voters:** 48,902 **Turnout:** 80.0 **Swing:** 1.8 to Lab from Con

DUNDEE EAST

John McAllion: Labour. Born: 1948. Educated: St Augustine's Secondary School, Glasgow; St. Andrew's University. Jobs: teacher, political researcher. First Elected: 1987. Union: GMB. Status: married, two children.

LAB HOLD

		1992 election Votes	%	+/-	1987 election %	Votes
John McAllion*	Lab	18,761	44.1	+1.8	42.3	19,539
David Coutts	SNP	14,197	33.4	-6.8	40.1	18,524
Stephen Blackwood	Con	7,549	17.8	+4.9	12.9	5,938
Ian Yuill	Lib Dem	1,725	4.1	-0.6	4.6	2,143
Shiona Baird	Green	205	0.5			
Ronald Baxter	NLP	77	0.2			
Majority	**Lab**	**4,564**	**10.7**	**+8.5**	**2.2**	**1,015**

Electorate: 58,959 **Voters:** 42,514 **Turnout:** 72.1 **Swing:** 4.3 to Lab from SNP

DUNDEE WEST

Ernie Ross: Labour. Born: 1942. Educated: St John's Secondary School. Jobs: quality control engineer. First Elected: 1979. Posts: member, Employment Select Committee. Union: MSF. Status: married, three children.

LAB HOLD

		1992 election Votes	%	+/-	1987 election %	Votes
Ernie Ross*	Lab	20,498	49.0	-4.4	53.4	24,916
Keith Brown	SNP	9,894	23.6	+8.3	15.3	7,164
Andrew Spearman	Con	7,746	18.5	+0.5	18.0	8,390
Elizabeth Dick	Lib Dem	3,132	7.5	-5.2	12.7	5,922
Elly Hood	Green	432	1.0			
Donald Arnold	NLP	159	0.4			
Majority	**Lab**	**10,604**	**25.3**	**-10.1**	**35.4**	**16,526**

Electorate: 59,953 **Voters:** 41,861 **Turnout:** 69.8 **Swing:** 6.3 to SNP from Lab

DUNFERMLINE EAST

Gordon Brown: Labour. Born: 1951. Educated: Kirkcaldy High School; Edinburgh University. Jobs: lecturer, journalist. First Elected: 1983. Posts: Shadow Chancellor. Status: single.

LAB HOLD		**1992 election**			**1987 election**	
		Votes	%	+/-	%	Votes
Gordon Brown*	Lab	23,692	62.4	-2.3	64.8	25,381
Mark Tennant	Con	6,248	16.5	+1.7	14.8	5,792
John Lloyd	SNP	5,746	15.1	+5.2	10.0	3,901
Teresa Little	Lib Dem	2,262	6.0	-4.6	10.5	4,122
Majority	**Lab**	**17,444**	**46.0**	**-4.0**	**50.0**	**19,589**

Electorate: 50,179 **Voters:** 37,948 **Turnout:** 75.6 **Swing:** 2.0 to Con from Lab

DUNFERMLINE WEST

Rachel Squire: Labour. Born: 1954. Educated: Godolphin and Latymer; Durham University. Jobs: trade union official. First Elected: 1992. Union: NUPE. Status: married

LAB HOLD		**1992 election**			**1987 election**	
		Votes	%	+/-	%	Votes
Rachel Squire	Lab	16,374	42.0	-5.0	47.0	18,493
Mike Scott-Hayward	Con	8,890	22.8	-0.3	23.1	9,091
Jay Smith	SNP	7,563	19.4	+10.7	8.7	3,435
Elizabeth Harris	Lib Dem	6,122	15.7	-5.4	21.1	8,288
Majority	**Lab**	**7,484**	**19.2**	**-4.7**	**23.9**	**9,402**

Electorate: 50,948 **Voters:** 38,949 **Turnout:** 76.4 **Swing:** 2.4 to Con from Lab

DURHAM, CITY OF

Gerry Steinberg: Labour. Born: 1945. Educated: Whinney Hill Secondary School; Durham Johnston School; Sheffield College of Education; Newcastle Polytechnic. Jobs: teacher. First Elected: 1987. Posts: member, Education Select Committee. Union: TGWU. Status: married, two children.

LAB HOLD		**1992 election**			**1987 election**	
		Votes	%	+/-	%	Votes
Gerry Steinberg*	Lab	27,095	53.3	+8.3	44.9	23,382
Martin Woodroofe	Con	12,037	23.7	+1.7	21.9	11,408
Nigel Martin	Lib Dem	10,915	21.5	-11.7	33.2	17,257
Sarah Jane Banks	Green	812	1.6			
Majority	**Lab**	**15,058**	**29.6**	**+17.8**	**11.8**	**6,125**

Electorate: 68,165 **Voters:** 50,859 **Turnout:** 74.6 **Swing:** 3.3 to Lab from Con

DURHAM NORTH

Giles Radice: Labour. Born: 1936. Educated: Winchester; Oxford. Jobs: trade union researcher. First Elected: 1973. Posts: member, Treasury Select Committee. Union: GMB. Status: married, five children.

LAB HOLD		1992 election Votes	%	+/-	1987 election %	Votes
Giles Radice*	Lab	33,567	59.9	+3.7	56.2	30,798
Elizabeth Sibley	Con	13,930	24.8	+3.6	21.2	11,627
Philip Appleby	Lib Dem	8,572	15.3	-7.3	22.6	12,365
Majority	**Lab**	**19,637**	**35.0**	**+1.4**	**33.6**	**18,433**

Electorate: 73,694 **Voters:** 56,069 **Turnout:** 76.1 **Swing:** No Swing

DURHAM NORTH WEST

Hilary Armstrong: Labour. Born: 1945. Educated: West Ham College of Technology. Jobs: social worker, community worker. First Elected: 1987. Union: MSF. Status: single.

LAB HOLD		1992 election Votes	%	+/-	1987 election %	Votes
Hilary Armstrong*	Lab	26,734	57.9	+7.0	50.9	22,947
Theresa May	Con	12,747	27.6	-0.8	28.4	12,785
Tim Farron	Lib Dem	6,728	14.6	-6.2	20.7	9,349
Majority	**Lab**	**13,987**	**30.3**	**+7.7**	**22.5**	**10,162**

Electorate: 61,139 **Voters:** 46,209 **Turnout:** 75.6 **Swing:** 3.9 to Lab from Con

EALING, ACTON

Sir George Young: Conservative. Born: 1941. Educated: Eton; Oxford. Jobs: economic adviser, housing worker. First Elected: 1974. Posts: Minister for Housing and Planning. Status: married, four children.

CON HOLD		1992 election Votes	%	+/-	1987 election %	Votes
Sir George Young*	Con	22,579	50.6	-2.8	53.4	25,499
Yvonne Johnson	Lab	15,572	34.9	+7.1	27.8	13,266
Leslie Rowe	Lib Dem	5,487	12.3	-6.5	18.8	8,973
Astra Seibe	Green	554	1.2			
Tom Pitt-Aikens	Ind C	432	1.0			
Majority	**Con**	**7,007**	**15.7**	**-9.9**	**25.6**	**12,233**

Electorate: 58,687 **Voters:** 44,624 **Turnout:** 76.0 **Swing:** 5.0 to Lab from Con

EALING NORTH

Harry Greenway: *Conservative. Born: 1934. Educated: Warwick School; College of St Mark & St John, London. Jobs: deputy headmaster. First Elected: 1979. Posts: chairman, All Party Education Committee. Status: married, three children.*

CON HOLD		1992 election			1987 election	
		Votes	%	+/-	%	Votes
Harry Greenway*	Con	24,898	49.7	-6.3	56.0	30,147
Martin Stears	Lab	18,932	37.8	+10.0	27.8	14,947
Peter Hankinson	Lib Dem	5,247	10.5	-4.7	15.2	8,149
Douglas Earl	Green	554	1.1	+0.0	1.1	577
Christopher Hill	NF	277	0.6			
Randall Davis	CD	180	0.4			
Majority	**Con**	**5,966**	**11.9**	**-16.3**	**28.2**	**15,1200**

Electorate: 63,528 **Voters:** 50,088 **Turnout:** 78.8 **Swing:** 8.1 to Lab from Con

EALING, SOUTHALL

Piara Khabra: *Labour. Born: 1924. Educated: Punjab University. Jobs: voluntary worker. First Elected: 1992. Union: MSF. Status: married, one child.*

LAB HOLD		1992 election			1987 election	
		Votes	%	+/-	%	Votes
Piara Khabra	Lab	23,476	47.4	-3.3	50.7	26,480
Philip Treleaven	Con	16,610	33.6	-1.9	35.5	18,503
Sydney Bidwell*	True Lab	4,665	9.4			
Pash Nandhra	Lib Dem	3,790	7.7	-5.7	13.3	6,947
Nick Goodwin	Green	964	1.9			
Majority	**Lab**	**6,866**	**13.9**	**-1.4**	**15.3**	**7,977**

Electorate: 65,574 **Voters:** 49,505 **Turnout:** 75.5 **Swing:** 0.7 to Con from Lab

EASINGTON

John Cummings: *Labour. Born: 1943. Educated: local state schools; Easington Technical College. Jobs: miner. First Elected: 1987. Union: NUM. Status: single.*

LAB HOLD		1992 election			1987 election	
		Votes	%	+/-	%	Votes
John Cummings*	Lab	34,269	72.7	+4.6	68.1	32,396
William Perry	Con	7,879	16.7	+0.4	16.3	7,757
Peter Freitag	Lib Dem	5,001	10.6	-5.0	15.6	7,447
Majority	**Lab**	**26,390**	**56.0**	**+4.2**	**51.8**	**24,639**

Electorate: 65,061 **Voters:** 47,149 **Turnout:** 72.5 **Swing:** 2.1 to Lab from Con

EASTBOURNE

Nigel Waterson: Conservative. Born: 1950. Educated: Leeds Grammar School; University. Jobs: solicitor. First Elected: 1992. Status: married.

CON REGAIN		1992 election			1987 election	
		Votes	%	+/-	%	Votes
Nigel Waterson	Con	31,792	51.6	-8.3	59.9	33,587
David Bellotti*	Lib Dem	26,311	42.7	+13.0	29.7	16,664
Ivan Gibbons	Lab	2,834	4.6	-4.2	8.8	4,928
David Aherne	Green	391	0.6	-0.9	1.5	867
Theresia Williamson	Lib	296	0.5			
Majority	**Con**	**5,481**	**8.9**	**-21.3**	**30.2**	**16,923**

Electorate: 76,103 **Voters:** 61,624 **Turnout:** 81.0 **Swing:** 10.7 to LDm from Con

BY-ELECTION October 1990: LIB DEM GAIN. D. Bellotti (Lib Dem) 23,415 (50.8%), R. Hickmet (Con) 18,865 (40.9%), C. Atkins (Lab) 2,308 (5.0%), Lib Dem majority 4,550 (9.9%), SWING 20.1% to Lib Dem from Con

EAST KILBRIDE

Adam Ingram: Labour. Born: 1947. Educated: Cranhill Secondary School, Glasgow. Jobs: trade union official. First Elected: 1987. Union: TGWU. Posts: member, Trade and Industry Select Committee. Status: married.

LAB HOLD		1992 election			1987 election	
		Votes	%	+/-	%	Votes
Adam Ingram*	Lab	24,055	46.9	-2.1	49.0	24,491
Kathleen McAlorum	SNP	12,063	23.5	+11.0	12.6	6,275
Gordon Lind	Con	9,781	19.1	+4.4	14.7	7,344
Sandra Grieve	Lib Dem	5,377	10.5	-13.3	23.7	11,867
Majority	**Lab**	**11,992**	**23.4**	**-1.9**	**25.3**	**12,624**

Electorate: 64,080 **Voters:** 51,276 **Turnout:** 80.0 **Swing:** 6.5 to SNP from Lab

EASTLEIGH

Stephen Milligan: Conservative. Born: 1948. Educated: Bradfield College; Oxford. Jobs: broadcaster, journalist. First Elected: 1992. Status: single.

CON HOLD		1992 election			1987 election	
		Votes	%	+/-	%	Votes
Stephen Milligan	Con	38,998	51.3	+0.0	51.3	35,584
David Chidgey	Lib Dem	21,296	28.0	-4.0	32.0	22,229
Johanna Sugrue	Lab	15,768	20.7	+4.0	16.7	11,599
Majority	**Con**	**17,702**	**23.3**	**+4.0**	**19.2**	**13,355**

Electorate: 91,736 **Voters:** 76,062 **Turnout:** 82.9 **Swing:** 2.0 to Con from LDm

EAST LOTHIAN

John Home Robertson: Labour. Born: 1948. Educated: Ampleforth. Jobs: farmer. First Elected: 1978. Posts: member, Defence Select Committee. Union: TSSA. Status: married, two children.

LAB HOLD		1992 election Votes	%	+/-	1987 election %	Votes
John Home Robertson*	Lab	25,537	46.5	-1.6	48.0	24,583
James Hepburne Scott	Con	15,501	28.2	-0.1	28.3	14,478
George Thomson	SNP	7,776	14.2	+6.9	7.3	3,727
Tim McKay	Lib Dem	6,126	11.2	-4.3	15.5	7,929
Majority	**Lab**	**10,036**	**18.3**	**-1.5**	**19.7**	**10,105**

Electorate: 66,699 **Voters:** 54,940 **Turnout:** 82.4 **Swing:** 0.7 to Con from Lab

EASTWOOD

Allan Stewart: Conservative. Born: 1942. Educated: Bell Baxter High School, Cupar; St Andrew's University. Jobs: lecturer. First Elected: 1983. Posts: Scottish Office minister. Status: married, two children.

CON HOLD		1992 election Votes	%	+/-	1987 election %	Votes
Allan Stewart*	Con	24,124	46.8	+7.3	39.5	19,388
Peter Grant-Hutchison	Lab	12,436	24.1	-0.9	25.1	12,305
Moira Craig	Lib Dem	8,493	16.5	-10.8	27.2	13,374
Paul Scott	SNP	6,372	12.4	+4.1	8.2	4,033
Lee Fergusson	NLP	146	0.3			
Majority	**Con**	**11,688**	**22.7**	**+10.4**	**12.2**	**6,014**

Electorate: 63,685 **Voters:** 51,571 **Turnout:** 81.0 **Swing:** 4.1 to Con from Lab

ECCLES

Joan Lestor: Labour. Born: 1931. Educated: Blaenavon School; London University. Jobs: teacher. First Elected: 1966. Union: GMB. Status: single with two adopted children.

LAB HOLD		1992 election Votes	%	+/-	1987 election %	Votes
Joan Lestor*	Lab	27,357	56.9	+6.1	50.8	25,346
Gary Ling	Con	14,131	29.4	-2.0	31.3	15,647
Geoff Reid	Lib Dem	5,835	12.1	-5.8	17.9	8,924
Richard Duriez	Green	521	1.1			
Joan Garner	NLP	270	0.6			
Majority	**Lab**	**13,226**	**27.5**	**+8.1**	**19.4**	**9,699**

Electorate: 64,910 **Voters:** 48,114 **Turnout:** 74.1 **Swing:** 4.0 to Lab from Con

EDDISBURY

Alistair Goodlad: Conservative. Born: 1943. Educated: Marlborough College; Cambridge. Jobs: company director First Elected: 1974. Posts: Minister of State, Foreign Office. Status: married, two children.

CON HOLD		1992 election Votes	%	+/-	1987 election %	Votes
Alistair Goodlad*	Con	31,625	51.0	-0.1	51.1	29,474
Norma Edwards	Lab	18,928	30.5	+7.0	23.5	13,574
Derrick Lyon	Lib Dem	10,543	17.0	-6.6	23.7	13,639
Andrew Basden	Green	783	1.3	-0.4	1.7	976
Nigel Pollard	NLP	107	0.2			
Majority	**Con**	**12,697**	**20.5**	**-7.0**	**27.5**	**15,835**

Electorate: 75,089 **Voters:** 61,986 **Turnout:** 82.6 **Swing:** 3.5 to Lab from Con

EDINBURGH CENTRAL

Alistair Darling: Labour. Born: 1953. Educated: Aberdeen University. Jobs: solicitor. First Elected: 1987. Posts: Shadow Financial Secretary to the Treasury. Union: GMB. Status: married, two children.

LAB HOLD		1992 election Votes	%	+/-	1987 election %	Votes
Alistair Darling*	Lab	15,189	38.8	-1.4	40.2	16,502
Paul Martin	Con	13,063	33.4	-1.3	34.7	14,240
Lynne Devine	SNP	5,539	14.1	+7.9	6.2	2,559
Andrew Myles	Lib Dem	4,500	11.5	-6.4	17.9	7,333
Robin Harper	Green	630	1.6	+0.5	1.1	438
Dick Wilson	Lib	235	0.6			
Majority	**Lab**	**2,126**	**5.4**	**-0.1**	**5.5**	**2,262**

Electorate: 56,527 **Voters:** 39,156 **Turnout:** 69.3 **Swing:** No Swing

EDINBURGH EAST

Dr Gavin Strang: Labour. Born: 1943. Educated: Morrison's Academy, Perthshire; Edinburgh University. Jobs: scientist. First Elected: 1970. Union: TGWU. Posts: member, Science and Technology Select Committee. Status: married, one child.

LAB HOLD		1992 election Votes	%	+/-	1987 election %	Votes
Gavin Strang*	Lab	15,446	45.7	-4.6	50.4	18,257
Kenneth Ward	Con	8,235	24.4	-0.3	24.7	8,962
Donald McKinney	SNP	6,225	18.4	+9.0	9.5	3,434
Devin Scobie	Lib Dem	3,432	10.2	-5.3	15.4	5,592
Graham Farmer	Green	424	1.3			
Majority	**Lab**	**7,211**	**21.4**	**-4.3**	**25.6**	**9,295**

Electorate: 45,687 **Voters:** 33,762 **Turnout:** 73.9 **Swing:** 2.1 to Con from Lab

EDINBURGH, LEITH

Malcolm Chisholm: Labour. Born: 1949. Educated: Edinburgh University. Jobs: teacher. First Elected: 1992. Status: married, three children.

LAB HOLD		1992 election			1987 election	
		Votes	%	+/-	%	Votes
Malcolm Chisholm	Lab	13,790	34.2	-15.1	49.3	21,104
Fiona Hyslop	SNP	8,805	21.8	+12.4	9.5	4,045
Bin Ashiq Rizvi	Con	8,496	21.1	-1.8	22.9	9,777
Hilary Campbell	Lib Dem	4,975	12.3	-6.0	18.3	7,843
Ron Brown*	Ind Lab	4,142	10.3			
Alan Swan	NLP	96	0.2			
Majority	**Lab**	**4,985**	**12.4**	**-14.1**	**26.5**	**11,327**

Electorate: 56,520 **Voters:** 40,304 **Turnout:** 71.3 **Swing:** 13.8 to SNP from Lab

EDINBURGH, PENTLANDS

Malcolm Rifkind: Conservative. Born: 1946. Educated: George Watson's College; Edinburgh University. Jobs: barrister. First Elected: 1974. Posts: Defence Secretary. Status: married, two children.

CON HOLD		1992 election			1987 election	
		Votes	%	+/-	%	Votes
Malcolm Rifkind*	Con	18,128	40.7	+2.4	38.3	17,278
Mark Lazarowicz	Lab	13,838	31.1	+1.1	30.0	13,533
Kathleen Caskie	SNP	6,882	15.4	+8.2	7.2	3,264
Keith Smith	Lib Dem	5,597	12.6	-12.0	24.5	11,072
David Rae	NLP	111	0.2			
Majority	**Con**	**4,290**	**9.6**	**+1.3**	**8.3**	**3,745**

Electorate: 55,567 **Voters:** 44,556 **Turnout:** 80.2 **Swing:** 0.7 to Con from Lab

EDINBURGH SOUTH

Nigel Griffiths: Labour. Born: 1955. Educated: Edinburgh University. Jobs: welfare rights officer. First Elected: 1987. Posts: Labour spokesman on consumer affairs. Union: USDAW. Status: married.

LAB HOLD		1992 election			1987 election	
		Votes	%	+/-	%	Votes
Nigel Griffiths*	Lab	18,485	41.5	+3.8	37.7	18,211
Struan Stevenson	Con	14,309	32.1	-1.7	33.8	16,352
Bob McCreadie	Lib Dem	5,961	13.4	-9.2	22.5	10,900
Roger Knox	SNP	5,727	12.8	+7.8	5.1	2,455
George Manclark	NLP	108	0.2			
Majority	**Lab**	**4,176**	**9.4**	**+5.5**	**3.8**	**1,859**

Electorate: 61,355 **Voters:** 44,590 **Turnout:** 72.7 **Swing:** 2.8 to Lab from Con

EDINBURGH WEST

Lord James Douglas-Hamilton: *Conservative. Born: 1942. Educated: Eton; Oxford. Jobs: barrister. First Elected: 1974. Posts: Scottish Office minister. Status: married, four children.*

CON HOLD

		1992 election Votes	%	+/-	1987 election %	Votes
Lord James Douglas-Hamilton*	Con	18,071	37.0	-0.3	37.4	18,450
Donald Gorrie	Lib Dem	17,192	35.2	+0.4	34.9	17,216
Irene Kitson	Lab	8,759	18.0	-4.2	22.2	10,957
Graham Sutherland	SNP	4,117	8.4	+2.8	5.6	2,774
Alan Fleming	Lib	272	0.6			
Linda Hendry	Green	234	0.5			
David Bruce	BNP	133	0.3			
Majority	**Con**	**879**	**1.8**	**-0.7**	**2.5**	**1,234**

Electorate: 58,998 **Voters:** 48,778 **Turnout:** 82.7 **Swing:** 0.3 to LDm from Con

EDMONTON

Dr Ian Twinn: *Conservative. Born: 1950. Educated: Netherhall Secondary Modern School, Cambridge; Cambridge Grammar School; University College of Wales. Jobs: lecturer. First Elected: 1983. Posts: PPS. Status: married, two children.*

CON HOLD

		1992 election Votes	%	+/-	1987 election %	Votes
Ian Twinn*	Con	22,076	46.3	-4.9	51.2	24,556
Andy Love	Lab	21,483	45.0	+9.0	36.0	17,270
Elwyn Jones	Lib Dem	3,940	8.3	-4.5	12.8	6,115
Elizabeth Solley	NLP	207	0.4			
Majority	**Con**	**593**	**1.2**	**-14.0**	**15.2**	**7,286**

Electorate: 63,052 **Voters:** 47,706 **Turnout:** 75.7 **Swing:** 7.0 to Lab from Con

ELLESMERE PORT & NESTON

Andrew Miller: *Labour. Born: 1949. Educated: London School of Economics. Jobs: trade union official. First Elected: 1992. Union: MSF. Status: married, three children.*

LAB GAIN

		1992 election Votes	%	+/-	1987 election %	Votes
Andrew Miller	Lab	27,782	46.1	+4.9	41.2	23,811
Andrew Pearce	Con	25,793	42.8	-1.6	44.4	25,664
Elizabeth Jewkes	Lib Dem	5,944	9.9	-4.2	14.1	8,143
Mike Money	Green	589	1.0			
Alan Rae	NLP	105	0.2			
Majority	**Lab**	**1,989**	**3.3**	**+6.5**	**3.2**	**1,853**

Electorate: 71,572 **Voters:** 60,213 **Turnout:** 84.1 **Swing:** 3.3 to Lab from Con

ELMET

Spencer Batiste: Conservative. Born: 1945. Educated: Sorbonne; Cambridge. Jobs: solicitor. First Elected: 1983. Posts: president, Conservative Trade Unionists; member, Trade and Industry Select Committee. Status: married, two children.

CON HOLD		1992 election			1987 election	
		Votes	%	+/-	%	Votes
Spencer Batiste*	Con	27,677	47.5	+0.6	46.9	25,658
Colin Burgon	Lab	24,416	41.9	+4.8	37.1	20,302
Ann Beck	Lib Dem	6,144	10.5	-5.5	16.0	8,755
Majority	**Con**	**3,261**	**5.6**	**-4.2**	**9.8**	**5,356**

Electorate: 70,558 **Voters:** 58,237 **Turnout:** 82.5 **Swing:** 2.1 to Lab from Con

ELTHAM

Peter Bottomley: Conservative. Born: 1944. Educated: Westminster; Cambridge. Jobs: industrial relations. First Elected: 1975. Posts: member, Transport Select Committee. Status: married, three children.

CON HOLD		1992 election			1987 election	
		Votes	%	+/-	%	Votes
Peter Bottomley*	Con	18,813	46.0	-1.5	47.5	19,752
Clive Efford	Lab	17,147	41.9	+9.9	32.0	13,292
Chris McGinty	Lib Dem	4,804	11.7	-8.8	20.5	8,542
Andrew Graham	Ind C	165	0.4			
Majority	**Con**	**1,666**	**4.1**	**-11.5**	**15.5**	**6,460**

Electorate: 51,989 **Voters:** 40,929 **Turnout:** 78.7 **Swing:** 5.7 to Lab from Con

ENFIELD NORTH

Tim Eggar: Conservative. Born: 1951. Educated: Winchester College; Cambridge. Jobs: merchant banker. First Elected: 1979. Posts: Minister for Energy. Status: married, two children.

CON HOLD		1992 election			1987 election	
		Votes	%	+/-	%	Votes
Tim Eggar*	Con	27,789	52.9	-2.6	55.5	28,758
Martin Upham	Lab	18,359	34.9	+6.5	28.5	14,743
Sarah Tustin	Lib Dem	5,817	11.1	-3.7	14.7	7,633
John Markham	NLP	565	1.1			
Majority	**Con**	**9,430**	**18.0**	**-9.1**	**27.1**	**14,015**

Electorate: 67,421 **Voters:** 52,530 **Turnout:** 77.9 **Swing:** 4.6 to Lab from Con

ENFIELD, SOUTHGATE

Michael Portillo: Conservative. Born: 1953. Educated: Harrow County Boys' School; Cambridge. Jobs: political researcher. First Elected: 1984. Posts: Chief Secretary to the Treasury. Status: married.

CON HOLD

		1992 election Votes	%	+/-	1987 election %	Votes
Michael Portillo*	Con	28,422	57.9	-0.9	58.8	28,445
Karen Livney	Lab	12,859	26.2	+7.4	18.8	9,114
Kevin Keane	Lib Dem	7,080	14.4	-6.5	20.9	10,100
Marghanita Hollands	Green	696	1.4	+0.0	1.4	696
Majority	**Con**	**15,563**	**31.7**	**-6.2**	**37.9**	**18,345**

Electorate: 64,311 **Voters:** 49,057 **Turnout:** 76.3 **Swing:** 4.1 to Lab from Con

EPPING FOREST

Steve Norris: Conservative. Born: 1945. Educated: Liverpool Institute High School; Oxford. Jobs: car sales company director. First Elected: 1983. Posts: Minister for Transport in London. Status: married, two children.

CON HOLD

		1992 election Votes	%	+/-	1987 election %	Votes
Steve Norris*	Con	32,407	59.5	-1.4	60.9	31,536
Stephen Murray	Lab	12,219	22.4	+4.1	18.4	9,499
Beryl Austen	Lib Dem	9,265	17.0	-2.3	19.4	10,023
Andrew O'Brien	Epping	552	1.0			
Majority	**Con**	**20,188**	**37.1**	**-4.5**	**41.6**	**21,513**

Electorate: 67,585 **Voters:** 54,443 **Turnout:** 80.6 **Swing:** 2.8 to Lab from Con

BY-ELECTION December 1988: CON HOLD. S. Norris (Con) 13,183 (39.5%), A. Thompson (Lib Dem) 8,679 (26.0%), S. Murray (Lab) 6,261 (18.7%), Con majority 4,504 (13.5%)

EPSOM & EWELL

Archie Hamilton: Conservative. Born: 1941. Educated: Eton. Jobs: farmer. First Elected: 1978. Posts: Minister for the Armed Forces. Status: married, three children.

CON HOLD

		1992 election Votes	%	+/-	1987 election %	Votes
Archie Hamilton*	Con	32,861	60.2	-2.0	62.2	33,145
Martin Emerson	Lib Dem	12,840	23.5	+0.3	23.2	12,384
Richard Warren	Lab	8,577	15.7	+1.2	14.5	7,751
Guy Hatchard	NLP	334	0.6			
Majority	**Con**	**20,021**	**36.7**	**-2.3**	**39.0**	**20,761**

Electorate: 68,138 **Voters:** 54,612 **Turnout:** 80.1 **Swing:** 1.2 to LDm from Con

EREWASH

Angela Knight: Conservative. Born: 1950. Educated: Penrhos Girls' College; Bristol University. Jobs: engineering company director. First Elected: 1992. Posts: member, Education Select Committee. Status: married, two children.

CON HOLD		1992 election			1987 election	
		Votes	%	+/-	%	Votes
Angela Knight	Con	29,907	47.2	-1.4	48.6	28,775
Sean Stafford	Lab	24,204	38.2	+6.1	32.1	19,021
Philip Tuck	Lib Dem	8,606	13.6	-5.7	19.3	11,442
Laurence Johnson	BNP	645	1.0			
Majority	**Con**	**5,703**	**9.0**	**-7.5**	**16.5**	**9,754**

Electorate: 75,627 **Voters:** 63,362 **Turnout:** 83.8 **Swing:** 3.7 to Lab from Con

ERITH & CRAYFORD

David Evennett: Conservative. Born: 1949. Educated: Buckhurst Hill High School; London School of Economics. Jobs: teacher, insurance broker. First Elected: 1983. Status: married, two children.

CON HOLD		1992 election			1987 election	
		Votes	%	+/-	%	Votes
David Evennett*	Con	21,926	46.5	+1.3	45.2	20,203
Nigel Beard	Lab	19,587	41.5	+12.0	29.5	13,209
Florence Jamieson	Lib Dem	5,657	12.0	-13.3	25.3	11,300
Majority	**Con**	**2,339**	**5.0**	**-10.7**	**15.6**	**6,994**

Electorate: 59,213 **Voters:** 47,170 **Turnout:** 79.7 **Swing:** 5.3 to Lab from Con

ESHER

Ian Taylor: Conservative. Born: 1945. Educated: Whitley Abbey School, Coventry; Keele University. Jobs: investment analyst. First Elected: 1987. Posts: PPS. Status: married, two children.

CON HOLD		1992 election			1987 election	
		Votes	%	+/-	%	Votes
Ian Taylor*	Con	31,115	65.4	-0.1	65.6	31,334
John Richling	Lib Dem	10,744	22.6	-3.1	25.7	12,266
Julie Reay	Lab	5,685	12.0	+3.2	8.8	4,197
Majority	**Con**	**20,371**	**42.8**	**+3.0**	**39.9**	**19,068**

Electorate: 58,840 **Voters:** 47,544 **Turnout:** 80.8 **Swing:** 1.5 to Con from LDm

EXETER

Sir John Hannam: Conservative. Born: 1929. Educated: Yeovil Grammar School. Jobs: hotelier. First Elected: 1970. Status: married, two children.

CON HOLD		1992 election			1987 election	
		Votes	%	+/-	%	Votes
Sir John Hannam*	Con	25,543	41.1	-3.3	44.4	26,922
John Lloyd	Lab	22,498	36.2	+13.7	22.5	13,643
Graham Oakes	Lib Dem	12,059	19.4	-12.4	31.8	19,266
Alison Micklem	Lib	1,119	1.8			
Tim Brenan	Green	764	1.2	+0.2	1.0	597
Michael Turnbull	NLP	98	0.2			
Majority	**Con**	**3,045**	**4.9**	**-7.7**	**12.6**	**7,656**

Electorate: 76,723 **Voters:** 62,081 **Turnout:** 80.9 **Swing:** 8.5 to Lab from Con

FALKIRK EAST

Michael Connarty: Labour. Born: 1947. Educated: Glasgow University. Jobs: teacher. First Elected: 1992. Union: TGWU. Status: married, two children.

LAB HOLD		1992 election			1987 election	
		Votes	%	+/-	%	Votes
Michael Connarty	Lab	18,423	46.1	-8.1	54.2	21,379
Ron Halliday	SNP	10,454	26.2	+10.8	15.4	6,056
Keith Harding	Con	8,279	20.7	+2.1	18.7	7,356
Debra Storr	Lib Dem	2,775	6.9	-4.8	11.7	4,624
Majority	**Lab**	**7,969**	**20.0**	**-15.6**	**35.6**	**14,023**

Electorate: 51,918 **Voters:** 39,931 **Turnout:** 76.9 **Swing:** 9.5 to SNP from Lab

FALKIRK WEST

Dennis Canavan: Labour. Born: 1942. Educated: St Columba's High School, Cowdenbeath; Edinburgh University. Jobs: teacher. First Elected: 1974. Union: COHSE. Posts: member, Foreign Affairs Select Committee. Status: married, four children.

LAB HOLD		1992 election			1987 election	
		Votes	%	+/-	%	Votes
Dennis Canavan*	Lab	19,162	49.8	-3.4	53.2	20,256
Bill Houston	SNP	9,350	24.3	+7.8	16.5	6,296
Michael Macdonald	Con	7,558	19.6	+2.0	17.6	6,704
Martin Reilly	Lib Dem	2,414	6.3	-6.4	12.7	4,841
Majority	**Lab**	**9,812**	**25.5**	**-10.1**	**35.6**	**13,552**

Electorate: 50,126 **Voters:** 38,484 **Turnout:** 76.8 **Swing:** 5.6 to SNP from Lab

FALMOUTH & CAMBORNE

Sebastian Coe: *Conservative. Born: 1956. Educated: Loughborough University. Jobs: company director, athlete. First Elected: 1992. Posts: member, Employment Select Committee. Status: married.*

CON HOLD		1992 election			1987 election	
		Votes	%	+/-	%	Votes
Sebastian Coe	Con	21,150	36.9	-7.0	43.9	23,725
Terrye Jones	Lib Dem	17,883	31.2	-3.4	34.6	18,686
John Cosgrove	Lab	16,732	29.2	+8.3	20.9	11,271
Paul Holmes	Lib	730	1.3			
Kevin Saunders	Green	466	0.8			
Freddie Zapp	Loony	327	0.6	-0.1	0.7	373
Andrew Pringle	NLP	56	0.1			
Majority	**Con**	**3,267**	**5.7**	**-3.6**	**9.3**	**5,039**

Electorate: 70,702 **Voters:** 57,344 **Turnout:** 81.1 **Swing:** 1.8 to LDm from Con

FAREHAM

Peter Lloyd: *Conservative. Born: 1937. Educated: Tonbridge School; Cambridge. Jobs: marketing manager. First Elected: 1979. Posts: Minister of State, Home Office. Status: married, two children.*

CON HOLD		1992 election			1987 election	
		Votes	%	+/-	%	Votes
Peter Lloyd*	Con	40,482	61.0	-0.1	61.1	36,781
John Thompson	Lib Dem	16,341	24.6	-5.3	29.9	17,986
Elizabeth Weston	Lab	8,766	13.2	+4.1	9.1	5,451
Malcolm Brimecome	Green	818	1.2			
Majority	**Con**	**24,141**	**36.4**	**+5.1**	**31.2**	**18,795**

Electorate: 81,124 **Voters:** 66,407 **Turnout:** 81.9 **Swing:** 2.6 to Con from LDm

FAVERSHAM

Roger Moate: *Conservative. Born: 1938. Educated: Latymer Upper School. Jobs: insurance broker. First Elected: 1970. Status: married, three children.*

CON HOLD		1992 election			1987 election	
		Votes	%	+/-	%	Votes
Roger Moate*	Con	32,755	50.1	-1.0	51.1	31,074
Helen Brinton	Lab	16,404	25.1	+4.3	20.8	12,616
Roger Truelove	Lib Dem	15,896	24.3	-3.8	28.1	17,096
Robin Bradshaw	NLP	294	0.4			
Majority	**Con**	**16,351**	**25.0**	**+2.0**	**23.0**	**13,978**

Electorate: 81,977 **Voters:** 65,349 **Turnout:** 79.7 **Swing:** 2.7 to Lab from Con

FELTHAM & HESTON

Alan Keen: Labour. Born: 1937. Educated: Sir William Turners, Redcar. Jobs: fire protection consultant. First Elected: 1992. Union: GMB. Status: married, two children.

LAB GAIN		1992 election			1987 election	
		Votes	%	+/-	%	Votes
Alan Keen	Lab	27,660	46.1	+8.7	37.4	22,325
Patrick Ground*	Con	25,665	42.8	-3.7	46.5	27,755
Michael Hoban	Lib Dem	6,700	11.2	-5.0	16.1	9,623
Majority	**Lab**	**1,995**	**3.3**	**+12.4**	**9.1**	**5,430**

Electorate: 81,221 **Voters:** 60,025 **Turnout:** 73.9 **Swing:** 6.2 to Lab from Con

FERMANAGH & SOUTH TYRONE

Ken Maginnis: Ulster Unionist Party. Born: 1938. Educated: Royal School, Dungannon; Stranmillis College, Belfast. Jobs: teacher. First Elected: 1983. Status: married, four children.

UUP HOLD		1992 election			1987 election	
		Votes	%	+/-	%	Votes
Ken Maginnis*	UUP	26,923	48.8	-0.7	49.6	27,446
Tommy Gallagher	SDLP	12,810	23.2	+4.1	19.1	10,581
Francie Molloy	Sinn Fein	12,604	22.9	-3.5	26.4	14,623
Davy Kettyles	Prog Soc	1,094	2.0			
Eric Bullick	All	950	1.7	+0.0	1.7	941
Gerry Cullen	NA	747	1.4			
Majority	**UUP**	**14,113**	**25.6**	**+2.4**	**23.2**	**12,823**

Electorate: 70,192 **Voters:** 55,128 **Turnout:** 78.5 **Swing:** 2.4 to SDLP from UUP

FIFE CENTRAL

Henry McLeish: Labour. Born: 1948. Educated: Buckhaven High School; Heriot Watt University. Jobs: local government officer. First Elected: 1987. Posts: Labour spokesman on Scottish affairs. Status: married, two children.

LAB HOLD		1992 election			1987 election	
		Votes	%	+/-	%	Votes
Henry McLeish*	Lab	21,036	50.4	-3.0	53.4	22,827
Tricia Marwick	SNP	10,458	25.1	+10.3	14.7	6,296
Carol Cender	Con	7,353	17.6	+1.0	16.7	7,118
Craig Harrow	Lib Dem	2,892	6.9	-8.3	15.2	6,487
Majority	**Lab**	**10,578**	**25.3**	**-11.4**	**36.8**	**15,709**

Electorate: 56,152 **Voters:** 41,739 **Turnout:** 74.3 **Swing:** 6.7 to SNP from Lab

CONSTITUENCIES

FIFE NORTH EAST

Menzies Campbell: *Liberal Democrat. Born: 1941. Educated: Hillhead High School; Glasgow University. Jobs: barrister. First Elected: 1987. Posts: LibDem spokesman on defence, sport; member, Defence Select Committee. Status: married.*

LIBDEM HOLD		1992 election Votes	%	+/-	1987 election %	Votes
Menzies Campbell*	Lib Dem	19,430	46.4	+1.6	44.8	17,868
Mary Scanlon	Con	16,122	38.5	-2.7	41.2	16,421
David Roche	SNP	3,589	8.6	+2.0	6.6	2,616
Lynda Clark	Lab	2,319	5.5	-1.9	7.4	2,947
Tim Flynn	Green	294	0.7			
David Senior	Lib	85	0.2			
Majority	**Lib Dem**	**3,308**	**7.9**	**+4.3**	**3.6**	**1,447**

Electorate: 53,747 **Voters:** 41,839 **Turnout:** 77.8 **Swing:** 2.1 to LDm from Con

FINCHLEY

Hartley Booth: *Conservative. Born: 1946. Educated: Bristol and Cambridge Universities. Jobs: barrister. First Elected: 1992. Posts: member, European Legislation Select Committee; Home Affairs Select Committee. Status: married, three children.*

CON HOLD		1992 election Votes	%	+/-	1987 election %	Votes
Hartley Booth	Con	21,039	51.2	-2.7	53.9	21,603
Ann Marjoram	Lab	14,651	35.7	+4.0	31.7	12,690
Hilary Leighter	Lib Dem	4,568	11.1	-2.8	13.9	5,580
Ashley Gunstock	Green	564	1.4			
Sally Johnson	Loony	130	0.3			
James Macrae	NLP	129	0.3			
Majority	**Con**	**6,388**	**15.5**	**-6.7**	**22.2**	**8,913**

Electorate: 52,907 **Voters:** 41,081 **Turnout:** 77.6 **Swing:** 3.3 to Lab from Con

FOLKESTONE & HYTHE

Michael Howard: *Conservative. Born: 1941. Educated: Llanelli Grammar School; Cambridge. Jobs: barrister. First Elected: 1983. Posts: Environment Secretary. Status: married, three children.*

CON HOLD		1992 election Votes	%	+/-	1987 election %	Votes
Michael Howard*	Con	27,437	52.3	-3.0	55.4	27,915
Linda Cufley	Lib Dem	18,527	35.3	-1.9	37.3	18,789
Peter Doherty	Lab	6,347	12.1	+4.7	7.4	3,720
Anthony Hobbs	NLP	123	0.2			
Majority	**Con**	**8,910**	**17.0**	**-1.1**	**18.1**	**9,126**

Electorate: 65,856 **Voters:** 52,434 **Turnout:** 79.6 **Swing:** 0.6 to LDm from Con

FOYLE

John Hume: Social Democratic and Labour Party. Born: 1937. Educated: St Columb's College, Derry; St. Patrick's College, Maynooth; National University of Ireland. Jobs: lecturer. First Elected: 1983. Posts: leader of SDLP. Status: married, five children.

SDLP HOLD		1992 election		+/-	1987 election	
		Votes	%		%	Votes
John Hume*	SDLP	26,710	51.5	+2.7	48.8	23,743
Gregor Campbell	DUP	13,705	26.4	-2.1	28.5	13,883
Martin McGuinness	Sinn Fein	9,149	17.6	-0.3	17.9	8,707
Lara McIlroy	All	1,390	2.7	+0.1	2.6	1,276
Gordon McKenzie	WP	514	1.0	-1.1	2.1	1,022
John Burns	NLP	422	0.8			
Majority	**SDLP**	**13,005**	**25.1**	**+4.8**	**20.3**	**9,860**

Electorate: 74,585 **Voters:** 51,890 **Turnout:** 69.6 **Swing:** 2.4 to SDLP from DUP

FULHAM

Matthew Carrington: Conservative. Born: 1947. Educated: French Lycée, London University. Jobs: banker. First Elected: 1987. Posts: PPS. Status: married, one child.

CON HOLD		1992 election		+/-	1987 election	
		Votes	%		%	Votes
Matthew Carrington*	Con	21,438	53.4	+1.6	51.8	21,752
Nick Moore	Lab	14,859	37.0	+0.3	36.7	15,430
Peter Crystal	Lib Dem	3,339	8.3	-2.1	10.4	4,365
Elizabeth Streeter	Green	443	1.1	+0.0	1.1	465
John Darby	NLP	91	0.2			
Majority	**Con**	**6,579**	**16.4**	**+1.3**	**15.0**	**6,322**

Electorate: 52,740 **Voters:** 40,170 **Turnout:** 76.2 **Swing:** 0.7 to Con from Lab

FYLDE

Michael Jack: Conservative. Born: 1946. Educated: Bradford Grammar School; Leicester University. Jobs: company executive. First Elected: 1987. Posts: Minister of State, Home Office. Status: married, two children.

CON HOLD		1992 election		+/-	1987 election	
		Votes	%		%	Votes
Michael Jack*	Con	30,639	61.4	+0.7	60.7	29,559
Nigel Cryer	Lib Dem	9,648	19.3	-4.9	24.2	11,787
Carol Hughes	Lab	9,382	18.8	+4.5	14.3	6,955
Peter Leadbetter	NLP	239	0.5			
Majority	**Con**	**20,991**	**42.1**	**+5.6**	**36.5**	**17,772**

Electorate: 63,573 **Voters:** 49,908 **Turnout:** 78.5 **Swing:** 2.8 to Con from LDm

GAINSBOROUGH & HORNCASTLE

Edward Leigh: Conservative. Born: 1950. Educated: French Lycée; Durham University. Jobs: barrister. First Elected: 1983. Posts: Trade and Industry minister. Status: married, four children.

CON HOLD

		1992 election Votes	%	+/-	1987 election %	Votes
Edward Leigh*	Con	31,444	54.0	+0.6	53.3	28,621
Neil Taylor	Lib Dem	15,199	26.1	-9.1	35.2	18,898
Fiona Jones	Lab	11,619	19.9	+8.5	11.5	6,156
Majority	**Con**	**16,245**	**27.9**	**+9.8**	**18.1**	**9,723**

Electorate: 72,038 **Voters:** 58,262 **Turnout:** 80.9 **Swing:** 4.9 to Con from LDm

GALLOWAY & UPPER NITHSDALE

Ian Lang: Conservative. Born: 1940. Educated: Rugby; Cambridge. First Elected: 1979. Posts: Scottish Secretary. Status: married, two children.

CON HOLD

		1992 election Votes	%	+/-	1987 election %	Votes
Ian Lang*	Con	18,681	42.0	+1.6	40.4	16,592
Matt Brown	SNP	16,213	36.4	+5.0	31.5	12,919
John Dowson	Lab	5,766	13.0	+0.1	12.9	5,298
John McKerchar	Lib Dem	3,826	8.6	-6.0	14.6	6,001
Majority	**Con**	**2,468**	**5.5**	**-3.4**	**8.9**	**3,673**

Electorate: 54,474 **Voters:** 44,486 **Turnout:** 81.7 **Swing:** 1.7 to SNP from Con

GATESHEAD EAST

Joyce Quin: Labour. Born: 1944. Educated: local state schools; Newcastle University. Jobs: political researcher, lecturer. First Elected: 1987. Posts: Labour spokeswoman on employment. Status: single.

LAB HOLD

		1992 election Votes	%	+/-	1987 election %	Votes
Joyce Quin*	Lab	30,100	63.5	+4.3	59.2	28,895
Martin Callanan	Con	11,570	24.4	+0.5	23.9	11,667
Ron Beadle	Lib Dem	5,720	12.1	-4.8	16.9	8,231
Majority	**Lab**	**18,530**	**39.1**	**+3.8**	**35.3**	**17,228**

Electorate: 64,355 **Voters:** 47,390 **Turnout:** 73.6 **Swing:** 1.9 to Lab from Con

GEDLING

Andrew Mitchell: Conservative. Born: 1956. Educated: Rugby; Cambridge. Jobs: finance consultant. First Elected: 1987. Posts: PPS; vice-chairman, Conservative Party. Status: married, two children.

CON HOLD		1992 election Votes	%	+/-	1987 election %	Votes
Andrew Mitchell*	Con	30,191	53.2	-1.3	54.5	29,492
Vernon Coaker	Lab	19,554	34.4	+10.5	23.9	12,953
David George	Lib Dem	6,863	12.1	-9.5	21.6	11,684
Anna Miszeweka	NLP	168	0.3			
Majority	**Con**	**10,637**	**18.7**	**-11.8**	**30.6**	**16,539**

Electorate: 68,953 **Voters:** 56,776 **Turnout:** 82.3 **Swing:** 5.9 to Lab from Con

GILLINGHAM

James Couchman: Conservative. Born: 1942. Educated: Cranleigh School; King's College, Newcastle; Durham University. Jobs: manager. First Elected: 1983. Posts: member, Public Accounts Committee. Status: married, two children.

CON HOLD		1992 election Votes	%	+/-	1987 election %	Votes
James Couchman*	Con	30,201	52.3	-0.7	53.1	28,711
Paul Clark	Lab	13,563	23.5	+6.4	17.1	9,230
Mark Wallbank	Lib Dem	13,509	23.4	-6.5	29.9	16,162
Craig MacKinlay	Ind	248	0.4			
Daniel Jolicoeur	NLP	190	0.3			
Majority	**Con**	**16,638**	**28.8**	**+5.6**	**23.2**	**12,549**

Electorate: 71,851 **Voters:** 57,711 **Turnout:** 80.3 **Swing:** 3.6 to Lab from Con

GLANFORD & SCUNTHORPE

Elliot Morley: Labour. Born: 1952. Educated: St Margaret's High School, Liverpool. Jobs: teacher. First Elected: 1987. Posts: Labour spokesman on food and agriculture. Status: married, two children.

LAB HOLD		1992 election Votes	%	+/-	1987 election %	Votes
Elliot Morley*	Lab	30,623	52.8	+9.3	43.5	24,733
Andrew Saywood	Con	22,211	38.3	-4.3	42.6	24,221
Wesley Paxton	Lib Dem	4,172	7.2	-6.5	13.7	7,762
Cyril Nottingham	Soc Dem	982	1.7			
Majority	**Lab**	**8,412**	**14.5**	**+13.6**	**0.9**	**512**

Electorate: 73,479 **Voters:** 57,988 **Turnout:** 78.9 **Swing:** 6.8 to Lab from Con

GLASGOW, CATHCART

John Maxton: *Labour. Born: 1936. Educated: Lord Williams Grammar School, Thame; Oxford University. Jobs: lecturer. First Elected: 1979. Posts: member, National Heritage Select Committee. Status: married, three children.*

LAB HOLD		1992 election			1987 election	
		Votes	%	+/-	%	Votes
John Maxton*	Lab	16,265	48.3	-3.8	52.1	19,623
John Young	Con	8,264	24.5	+2.2	22.4	8,420
William Steven	SNP	6,107	18.1	+7.8	10.3	3,883
George Dick	Lib Dem	2,614	7.8	-7.4	15.2	5,722
Kay Allan	Green	441	1.3			
Majority	**Lab**	**8,001**	**23.7**	**-6.0**	**29.8**	**11,203**

Electorate: 44,689 **Voters:** 33,691 **Turnout:** 75.4 **Swing:** 3.0 to Con from Lab

GLASGOW CENTRAL

Mike Watson: *Labour. Born: 1949. Educated: Dundee High School; Heriot Watt University. Jobs: trade union official. First Elected: 1989. Union: MSF. Status: married.*

LAB HOLD		1992 election			1987 election	
		Votes	%	+/-	%	Votes
Mike Watson*	Lab	17,341	57.2	-7.3	64.5	21,619
Brendan O'Hara	SNP	6,322	20.8	+10.9	10.0	3,339
Ewen Stewart	Con	4,208	13.9	+0.9	13.0	4,366
Alan Rennie	Lib Dem	1,921	6.3	-4.2	10.5	3,528
Irene Brandt	Green	435	1.4	+0.6	0.9	290
Tam Burn	Comm GB	106	0.3			
Majority	**Lab**	**11,019**	**36.3**	**-15.1**	**51.5**	**17,253**

Electorate: 48,107 **Voters:** 30,333 **Turnout:** 63.1 **Swing:** 9.1 to SNP from Lab
BY-ELECTION June 1989: LAB HOLD. M. Watson (Lab) 14,480 (54.6%), A. Neil (SNP) 8,018 (30.2%), A. Hogarth (Con) 2,028 (7.6%), Lab majority 6,462 (24.4%), SWING 15.1% to SNP from Lab

GLASGOW, GARSCADDEN

Donald Dewar: *Labour. Born: 1937. Educated: Glasgow Academy; Glasgow University. Jobs: solicitor. First Elected: 1966. Posts: Shadow Social Security Secretary. Status: divorced, two children.*

LAB HOLD		1992 election			1987 election	
		Votes	%	+/-	%	Votes
Donald Dewar*	Lab	18,920	64.4	-3.3	67.7	23,178
Dick Douglas*	SNP	5,580	19.0	+6.7	12.3	4,201
Jim Scott	Con	3,385	11.5	+0.8	10.7	3,660
Charles Brodie	Lib Dem	1,425	4.9	-4.5	9.4	3,211
William Orr	NLP	61	0.2			
Majority	**Lab**	**13,340**	**45.4**	**-10.0**	**55.4**	**18,977**

Electorate: 41,289 **Voters:** 29,371 **Turnout:** 71.1 **Swing:** 5.0 to SNP from Lab

GLASGOW, GOVAN

Ian Davidson: Labour. Born: 1950. Educated: Galashiels Academy; Edinburgh. Jobs: voluntary services consultant. First Elected: 1992. Union: MSF. Status: married, two children.

LAB REGAIN

		1992 election			1987 election	
		Votes	%	+/-	%	Votes
Ian Davidson	Lab	17,051	48.9	-15.9	64.8	24,071
Jim Sillars*	SNP	12,926	37.1	+26.7	10.4	3,851
James Donnelly	Con	3,458	9.9	-2.0	11.9	4,411
Robert Stewart	Lib Dem	1,227	3.5	-8.8	12.3	4,562
David Spaven	Green	181	0.5			
Majority	**Lab**	**4,125**	**11.8**	**-40.7**	**52.5**	**19,509**

Electorate: 45,822 **Voters**: 34,843 **Turnout**: 76.0 **Swing**: 21.3 to SNP from Lab

BY-ELECTION November 1988: SNP GAIN. J. Sillars (SNP) 14,677 (48.8%), R. Gillespie (Lab) 11,123 (37.0%), G. Hamilton (Con) 2,207 (7.3%), SNP majority 3,554 (11.8%), SWING 33.1% to SNP from Lab

GLASGOW, HILLHEAD

George Galloway: Labour. Born: 1954. Educated: Harris Academy, Dundee. Jobs: director of voluntary organisation, party agent. First Elected: 1987. Union: TGWU. Status: married, one child.

LAB HOLD

		1992 election			1987 election	
		Votes	%	+/-	%	Votes
George Galloway*	Lab	15,148	38.5	-4.4	42.9	17,958
Christopher Mason	Lib Dem	10,322	26.2	-8.9	35.1	14,707
Aileen Bates	Con	6,728	17.1	+2.6	14.4	6,048
Sandra White	SNP	6,484	16.5	+10.0	6.5	2,713
Lizbeth Collie	Green	558	1.4	+0.4	1.1	443
Helen Gold	Rev Comm	73	0.2			
Duncan Patterson	NLP	60	0.2			
Majority	**Lab**	**4,826**	**12.3**	**+4.5**	**7.8**	**3,251**

Electorate: 57,223 **Voters**: 39,373 **Turnout**: 68.8 **Swing**: 2.2 to Lab from LDm

GLASGOW, MARYHILL

Maria Fyfe: Labour. Born: 1938. Educated: Notre Dame High School, Glasgow, University of Strathclyde. Jobs: lecturer. First Elected: 1987. Posts: Labour spokeswoman on Scottish affairs. Union: TGWU. Status: widow, two children.

LAB HOLD

		1992 election			1987 election	
		Votes	%	+/-	%	Votes
Maria Fyfe*	Lab	19,452	61.6	-4.8	66.4	23,482
Clifford Williamson	SNP	6,033	19.1	+8.1	11.0	3,895
John Godfrey	Con	3,248	10.3	+0.9	9.4	3,307
Jim Alexander	Lib Dem	2,215	7.0	-4.6	11.7	4,118
Phil O'Brien	Green	530	1.7	+0.2	1.5	539
Michael Henderson	NLP	78	0.2			
Majority	**Lab**	**13,419**	**42.5**	**-12.3**	**54.8**	**19,364**

Electorate: 48,426 **Voters**: 31,556 **Turnout**: 65.2 **Swing**: 6.4 to SNP from Lab

GLASGOW, POLLOK

James Dunnachie: Labour. Born: 1930. Educated: local state schools. First Elected: 1987. Union: AEU. Status: married.

LAB HOLD		1992 election			1987 election	
		Votes	%	+/-	%	Votes
James Dunnachie*	Lab	14,170	43.4	-19.7	63.1	23,239
Tommy Sheridan	SML	6,287	19.3			
Russell Gray	Con	5,147	15.8	+1.5	14.3	5,256
George Leslie	SNP	5,107	15.6	+6.1	9.6	3,528
David Jago	Lib Dem	1,932	5.9	-6.2	12.1	4,445
Majority	**Lab**	**7,883**	**24.1**	**-24.7**	**48.8**	**17,983**

Electorate: 46,139 **Voters:** 32,643 **Turnout:** 70.7

GLASGOW, PROVAN

Jimmy Wray: Labour. Born: 1938. Educated: St Bonaventure's, Gorbals. Jobs: HGV driver, party agent. First Elected: 1987. Union: TGWU. Posts: member, European Legislation Select Committee. Status: married, three children.

LAB HOLD		1992 election			1987 election	
		Votes	%	+/-	%	Votes
Jimmy Wray*	Lab	15,885	66.5	-6.4	72.9	22,032
Alexandra MacRae	SNP	5,182	21.7	+9.6	12.1	3,660
Andrew Rosindell	Con	1,865	7.8	+0.1	7.7	2,336
Charles Bell	Lib Dem	948	4.0	-3.3	7.2	2,189
Majority	**Lab**	**10,703**	**44.8**	**-16.0**	**60.8**	**18,372**

Electorate: 36,560 **Voters:** 23,880 **Turnout:** 65.3 **Swing:** 8.0 to SNP from Lab

GLASGOW, RUTHERGLEN

Tommy McAvoy: Labour. Born: 1943. Educated: St Columbkilles, Rutherglen. First Elected: 1987. Posts: Labour Whip. Union: AEU. Status: married, four children.

LAB HOLD		1992 election			1987 election	
		Votes	%	+/-	%	Votes
Tommy McAvoy*	Lab	21,962	55.4	-0.6	56.0	24,790
Brian Cooklin	Con	6,692	16.9	+5.4	11.5	5,088
John Higgins	SNP	6,470	16.3	+8.2	8.1	3,584
David Baillie	Lib Dem	4,470	11.3	-13.1	24.4	10,795
Barbara Slaughter	Int Comm	62	0.2			
Majority	**Lab**	**15,270**	**38.5**	**+6.9**	**31.6**	**13,995**

Electorate: 52,709 **Voters:** 39,656 **Turnout:** 75.2 **Swing:** 3.0 to Con from Lab

GLASGOW, SHETTLESTON

David Marshall: Labour. Born: 1941. Educated: Woodside Senior Secondary, Glasgow. Jobs: farm worker, tram conductor. First Elected: 1979. Posts: chairman, Transport Select Committee. Union: TGWU. Status: married, three children.

LAB HOLD

		1992 election Votes	%	+/-	1987 election %	Votes
David Marshall*	Lab	21,665	60.6	-3.0	63.6	23,991
Nichola Sturgeon	SNP	6,831	19.1	+6.4	12.7	4,807
Norman Mortimer	Con	5,396	15.1	+1.8	13.3	5,010
Joan Orskov	Lib Dem	1,881	5.3	-5.2	10.4	3,942
Majority	**Lab**	**14,834**	**41.5**	**-8.8**	**50.3**	**18,981**

Electorate: 51,910 **Voters:** 35,773 **Turnout:** 68.9 **Swing:** 4.7 to SNP from Lab

GLASGOW, SPRINGBURN

Michael Martin: Labour. Born: 1945. Educated: St Patrick's School, Glasgow. Jobs: sheet metal worker, shop steward. First Elected: 1979. Union: MSF. Posts: member, chairmen's panel. Status: married, two children.

LAB HOLD

		1992 election Votes	%	+/-	1987 election %	Votes
Michael Martin*	Lab	20,369	67.7	-6.0	73.6	25,617
Stuart Miller	SNP	5,863	19.5	+9.3	10.2	3,554
Andrew Barnett	Con	2,625	8.7	+0.5	8.3	2,870
Rod Ackland	Lib Dem	1,242	4.1	-3.8	7.9	2,746
Majority	**Lab**	**14,506**	**48.2**	**-15.2**	**63.4**	**22,063**

Electorate: 45,842 **Voters:** 30,099 **Turnout:** 65.7 **Swing:** 7.6 to SNP from Lab

GLOUCESTER

Douglas French: Conservative. Born: 1944. Educated: Glyn Grammar School, Epsom; Cambridge. Jobs: barrister, political researcher. First Elected: 1987. Posts: Chairman, Bow Group. Status: married, three children.

CON HOLD

		1992 election Votes	%	+/-	1987 election %	Votes
Douglas French*	Con	29,870	46.2	-3.5	49.7	29,826
Kevin Stephens	Lab	23,812	36.8	+7.2	29.6	17,791
John Sewell	Lib Dem	10,978	17.0	-3.7	20.7	12,417
Majority	**Con**	**6,058**	**9.4**	**-10.7**	**20.0**	**12,035**

Electorate: 80,578 **Voters:** 64,660 **Turnout:** 80.2 **Swing:** 5.3 to Lab from Con

GLOUCESTERSHIRE WEST

Paul Marland: *Conservative. Born: 1940. Educated: Gordonstoun; Trinity College, Dublin. Jobs: farmer. First Elected: 1979. Posts: member, Agriculture Select Committee. Status: married, three children.*

CON HOLD		1992 election			1987 election	
		Votes	%	+/-	%	Votes
Paul Marland*	Con	29,232	43.6	-2.7	46.2	29,257
Diana Organ	Lab	24,274	36.2	+8.4	27.8	17,578
Liz Boait	Lib Dem	13,366	19.9	-6.1	26.0	16,440
Anthony Reeve	Brit Ind	172	0.3			
Colin Palmer	Century	75	0.1			
Majority	**Con**	**4,958**	**7.4**	**-11.1**	**18.5**	**11,679**

Electorate: 80,007 **Voters:** 67,119 **Turnout:** 83.9 **Swing:** 5.5 to Lab from Con

GORDON

Malcolm Bruce: *Liberal Democrat. Born: 1944. Educated: Wrekin College; St Andrews and Strathclyde Universities. Jobs: journalist, industry. First Elected: 1983. Posts: leader of Scottish Liberal Democrats; member, Science and Technology Select Committee; LibDem spokesman on trade and industry. Status: married, two children.*

LIB DEM HOLD		1992 election			1987 election	
		Votes	%	+/-	%	Votes
Malcolm Bruce*	Lib Dem	22,158	37.4	-12.0	49.5	26,770
John Porter	Con	21,884	37.0	+5.1	31.9	17,251
Brian Adam	SNP	8,445	14.3	+7.1	7.2	3,876
Peter Morrell	Lab	6,682	11.3	-0.2	11.5	6,228
Majority	**Lib Dem**	**274**	**0.5**	**-17.1**	**17.6**	**9,519**

Electorate: 80,103 **Voters:** 59,169 **Turnout:** 73.9 **Swing:** 8.6 to Con from LDm

GOSPORT

Peter Viggers: *Conservative. Born: 1938. Educated: Portsmouth Grammar School; Cambridge. Jobs: company director. First Elected: 1974. Posts: member, Defence Select Committee. Status: married, three children.*

CON HOLD		1992 election			1987 election	
		Votes	%	+/-	%	Votes
Peter Viggers*	Con	31,094	58.1	-0.4	58.5	29,804
Michael Russell	Lib Dem	14,776	27.6	-3.9	31.6	16,081
Marilyn Angus	Lab	7,275	13.6	+3.7	9.9	5,053
Patrick Ettie	Pensioners	332	0.6			
Majority	**Con**	**16,318**	**30.5**	**+3.6**	**26.9**	**13,723**

Electorate: 69,638 **Voters:** 53,477 **Turnout:** 76.8 **Swing:** 1.8 to Con from LDm

GOWER

Gareth Wardell: Labour. Born: 1944. Educated: Gwendraeth Grammar School; London School of Economics. Jobs: lecturer. First Elected: 1982. Posts: chairman, Welsh Select Committee. Union: GMB-APEX. Status: married, one child.

LAB HOLD		**1992 election**			**1987 election**	
		Votes	%	+/-	%	Votes
Gareth Wardell*	Lab	23,455	50.1	+3.5	46.6	22,138
Anthony Donnelly	Con	16,437	35.1	+0.6	34.5	16,374
Christopher Davies	Lib Dem	4,655	9.9	-6.2	16.1	7,645
Adam Price	Plaid Cymru	1,658	3.5	+0.7	2.8	1,341
Brian Kingzett	Green	448	1.0			
Gerry Egan	Loony G	114	0.2			
Michael Beresford	NLP	74	0.2			
Majority	**Lab**	**7,018**	**15.0**	**+2.8**	**12.1**	**5,764**

Electorate: 57,231 **Voters:** 46,841 **Turnout:** 81.8 **Swing:** 1.4 to Lab from Con

GRANTHAM

Douglas Hogg: Conservative. Born: 1945. Educated: Eton; Oxford. Jobs: barrister. First Elected: 1979. Posts: Minister of State, Foreign Office. Status: married, two children.

CON HOLD		**1992 election**			**1987 election**	
		Votes	%	+/-	%	Votes
Douglas Hogg*	Con	37,194	56.2	-0.9	57.1	33,988
Steven Taggart	Lab	17,606	26.6	+6.1	20.5	12,197
James Heppell	Lib Dem	9,882	14.9	-6.4	21.3	12,685
John Hiley	Lib	1,500	2.3			
Majority	**Con**	**19,588**	**29.6**	**-6.2**	**35.8**	**21,303**

Electorate: 83,463 **Voters:** 66,182 **Turnout:** 79.3 **Swing:** 3.5 to Lab from Con

GRAVESHAM

Jacques Arnold: Conservative. Born: 1947. Educated: Brazil; London School of Economics. Jobs: banker. First Elected: 1987. Status: married, three children.

CON HOLD		**1992 election**			**1987 election**	
		Votes	%	+/-	%	Votes
Jacques Arnold*	Con	29,322	49.7	-0.4	50.1	28,891
Graham Green	Lab	23,829	40.4	+5.5	34.8	20,099
Derek Deedman	Lib Dem	5,269	8.9	-6.2	15.1	8,724
Andrew Bunstone	Ind	273	0.5			
Rhoderick Boulding	ILP	187	0.3			
Barrie Buxton	Socialist	174	0.3			
Majority	**Con**	**5,493**	**9.3**	**-5.9**	**15.2**	**8,792**

Electorate: 70,740 **Voters:** 59,054 **Turnout:** 83.5 **Swing:** 3.0 to Lab from Con

GREAT GRIMSBY

Austin Mitchell: Labour. Born: 1934. Educated: Bingley Grammar; Manchester University. Jobs: broadcaster. First Elected: 1977. Union: GMB. Status: married, two children.

LAB HOLD		1992 election			1987 election	
		Votes	%	+/-	%	Votes
Austin Mitchell*	Lab	25,895	51.0	+5.5	45.5	23,463
Philip Jackson	Con	18,391	36.2	+7.8	28.4	14,679
Pat Frankish	Lib Dem	6,475	12.8	-13.3	26.1	13,457
Majority	**Lab**	**7,504**	**14.8**	**-2.2**	**17.0**	**8,784**

Electorate: 67,427 **Voters:** 50,761 **Turnout:** 75.3 **Swing:** 1.1 to Con from Lab

GREAT YARMOUTH

Michael Carttiss: Conservative. Born: 1938. Educated: Great Yarmouth Technical High School; London University. Jobs: teacher, party agent. First Elected: 1983. Status: single.

CON HOLD		1992 election			1987 election	
		Votes	%	+/-	%	Votes
Michael Carttiss*	Con	25,505	47.9	-3.8	51.7	25,336
Barbara Baughan	Lab	20,196	38.0	+6.8	31.1	15,253
Malcolm Scott	Lib Dem	7,225	13.6	-3.5	17.1	8,387
Philomena Larkin	NLP	284	0.5			
Majority	**Con**	**5,309**	**10.0**	**-10.6**	**20.6**	**10,083**

Electorate: 68,263 **Voters:** 53,210 **Turnout:** 77.9 **Swing:** 5.3 to Lab from Con

GREENOCK & PORT GLASGOW

Dr Norman Godman: Labour. Born: 1938. Educated: Hull University. Jobs: teacher. First Elected: 1983. Union: TGWU. Posts: member, European Legislation Select Committee. Status: married.

LAB HOLD		1992 election			1987 election	
		Votes	%	+/-	%	Votes
Norman Godman*	Lab	22,258	58.0	-5.9	63.9	27,848
Ian Black	SNP	7,279	19.0	+10.4	8.5	3,721
John McCullough	Con	4,479	11.7	+2.0	9.6	4,199
Christopher Lambert	Lib Dem	4,359	11.4	-6.5	17.9	7,793
Majority	**Lab**	**14,979**	**39.0**	**-7.0**	**46.0**	**20,055**

Electorate: 52,053 **Voters:** 38,375 **Turnout:** 73.7 **Swing:** 8.2 to SNP from Lab

GREENWICH

Nick Raynsford: Labour. Born: 1945. Educated: Repton Scool; Cambridge. Jobs: housing consultant. First Elected: 1986. Union: TGWU. Posts: member, Environment Select Committee. Status: married, three children.

LAB GAIN

		1992 election			1987 election	
		Votes	%	+/-	%	Votes
Nick Raynsford	Lab	14,630	41.0	+6.2	34.9	13,008
Rosie Barnes*	Soc Dem	13,273	37.2	-3.4	40.6	15,149
Alison McNair	Con	6,960	19.5	-3.8	23.3	8,695
Robert McCracken	Green	483	1.4	+0.4	0.9	346
Ronald Mallone	Fellowship	147	0.4	+0.3	0.2	59
Malcolm Hardee	UTCHAP	103	0.3			
John Small	NLP	70	0.2			
Majority	**Lab**	**1,357**	**3.8**	**+9.6**	**5.7**	**2,141**

Electorate: 47,789 **Voters:** 35,666 **Turnout:** 74.6 **Swing:** 4.8 to Lab from SDP

GUILDFORD

David Howell: Conservative. Born: 1936. Educated: Eton; Cambridge. Jobs: political researcher, journalist. First Elected: 1966. Posts: chairman, Foreign Affairs Select Committee. Status: married, three children.

CON HOLD

		1992 election			1987 election	
		Votes	%	+/-	%	Votes
David Howell*	Con	33,516	55.3	-0.2	55.5	32,504
Margaret Sharp	Lib Dem	20,112	33.2	-0.8	33.9	19,897
Howard Mann	Lab	6,781	11.2	+0.6	10.6	6,216
Alarick Law	NLP	234	0.4			
Majority	**Con**	**13,404**	**22.1**	**+0.6**	**21.5**	**12,607**

Electorate: 77,265 **Voters:** 60,643 **Turnout:** 78.5 **Swing:** 0.3 to Con from LDm

HACKNEY NORTH & STOKE NEWINGTON

Diane Abbott: Labour. Born: 1953. Educated: Harrow County Grammar School; Cambridge. Jobs: local government worker, broadcaster. First Elected: 1987. Posts: member, Treasury Select Committee. Union: BECTU.

LAB HOLD

		1992 election			1987 election	
		Votes	%	+/-	%	Votes
Diane Abbott*	Lab	20,083	57.8	+9.1	48.7	18,912
Cole Manson	Con	9,356	26.9	-2.0	28.9	11,234
Keith Fitchett	Lib Dem	3,996	11.5	-7.7	19.2	7,446
Heather Hunt	Green	1,111	3.2	+0.6	2.6	997
John Windsor	NLP	178	0.5			
Majority	**Lab**	**10,727**	**30.9**	**+11.1**	**19.8**	**7,678**

Electorate: 54,655 **Voters:** 34,724 **Turnout:** 63.5 **Swing:** 5.6 to Lab from Con

CONSTITUENCIES

HACKNEY SOUTH & SHOREDITCH

Brian Sedgemore: Labour. Born: 1937. Educated: Heles School, Exeter; Oxford. Jobs: barrister. First Elected: 1974. Posts: member, Treasury Select Committee. Status: divorced, one child.

LAB HOLD		1992 election			1987 election	
		Votes	%	+/-	%	Votes
Brian Sedgemore*	Lab	19,730	53.4	+5.5	47.8	18,799
Andrew Turner	Con	10,714	29.0	+0.3	28.7	11,277
George Wintle	Lib Dem	5,533	15.0	-7.5	22.4	8,812
Len Lucas	Green	772	2.1			
Geraldine Norman	NLP	226	0.6			
Majority	**Lab**	**9,016**	**24.4**	**+5.2**	**19.1**	**7,522**

Electorate: 57,935 **Voters:** 36,975 **Turnout:** 63.8 **Swing:** 2.6 to Lab from Con

HALESOWEN & STOURBRIDGE

Warren Hawksley: Conservative. Born: 1943. Educated: Mill Mead, Shrewsbury; Denstone College, Staffs. Jobs: bank official, hotelier. First Elected: 1979. Status: married, two children.

CON HOLD		1992 election			1987 election	
		Votes	%	+/-	%	Votes
Warren Hawksley	Con	32,312	50.6	+0.5	50.1	31,037
Alan Hankon	Lab	22,730	35.6	+7.8	27.8	17,229
Vinod Sharma	Lib Dem	7,941	12.4	-9.6	22.1	13,658
Timothy Weller	Green	908	1.4			
Majority	**Con**	**9,582**	**15.0**	**-7.3**	**22.3**	**13,808**

Electorate: 77,644 **Voters:** 63,891 **Turnout:** 82.3 **Swing:** 3.7 to Lab from Con

HALIFAX

Alice Mahon: Labour. Born: 1937. Educated: local grammar school; Bradford University. Jobs: nursing auxiliary. First Elected: 1987. Union: NUPE. Posts: member, Health Select Committee. Status: married, two children.

LAB HOLD		1992 election			1987 election	
		Votes	%	+/-	%	Votes
Alice Mahon*	Lab	25,115	43.5	+0.1	43.4	24,741
Terence Martin	Con	24,637	42.7	+1.4	41.3	23,529
Ian Howell	Lib Dem	7,364	12.7	-2.6	15.4	8,758
Raymond Pearson	Nat	649	1.1			
Majority	**Lab**	**478**	**0.8**	**-1.3**	**2.1**	**1,212**

Electorate: 73,401 **Voters:** 57,765 **Turnout:** 78.7 **Swing:** 0.6 to Con from Lab

HALTON

Gordon Oakes: Labour. Born: 1931. Educated: Wade Deacon Grammar School; Widnes; Liverpool University. Jobs: solicitor. First Elected: 1964. Status: married, three children.

LAB HOLD		1992 election			1987 election	
		Votes	%	+/-	%	Votes
Gordon Oakes*	Lab	35,025	59.7	+4.2	55.5	32,065
Grant Mercer	Con	16,821	28.7	-1.6	30.2	17,487
David Reaper	Lib Dem	6,104	10.4	-3.9	14.3	8,272
Stephen Herley	Loony	398	0.7			
Nichola Collins	NLP	338	0.6			
Majority	**Lab**	**18,204**	**31.0**	**+5.8**	**25.2**	**14,578**

Electorate: 74,906 **Voters:** 58,686 **Turnout:** 78.3 **Swing:** 2.9 to Lab from Con

HAMILTON

George Robertson: Labour. Born: 1946. Educated: Dunoon Grammar School; Dundee University. Jobs: trade union official. First Elected: 1978. Posts: Labour spokesman on foreign and commonwealth affairs. Status: married, three children.

LAB HOLD		1992 election			1987 election	
		Votes	%	+/-	%	Votes
George Robertson*	Lab	25,849	55.2	-4.5	59.7	28,563
Billy Morrison	SNP	9,246	19.7	+7.0	12.7	6,093
Margaret Mitchell	Con	8,250	17.6	+3.2	14.4	6,901
John Oswald	Lib Dem	3,515	7.5	-5.7	13.2	6,302
Majority	**Lab**	**16,603**	**35.4**	**-9.8**	**45.3**	**21,662**

Electorate: 61,531 **Voters:** 46,860 **Turnout:** 76.2 **Swing:** 5.8 to SNP from Lab

HAMMERSMITH

Clive Soley: Labour. Born: 1939. Educated: Downshall Secondary Modern School; Ilford; Strathclyde University. Jobs: probation officer. First Elected: 1979. Status: divorced

LAB HOLD		1992 election			1987 election	
		Votes	%	+/-	%	Votes
Clive Soley*	Lab	17,329	51.0	+6.0	45.0	15,811
Tony Hennessy	Con	12,575	37.0	-1.1	38.1	13,396
John Bates	Lib Dem	3,380	10.0	-5.0	14.9	5,241
Roger Crosskey	Green	546	1.6	+0.3	1.3	453
Kevin Turner	NLP	89	0.3			
Helen Szamuely	Anti Fed	41	0.1			
Majority	**Lab**	**4,754**	**14.0**	**+7.1**	**6.9**	**2,415**

Electorate: 47,229 **Voters:** 33,960 **Turnout:** 71.9 **Swing:** 3.6 to Lab from Con

HAMPSHIRE EAST

Michael Mates: *Conservative. Born: 1934. Educated: Blundell's School; Cambridge. Jobs: army officer. First Elected: 1974. Posts: Minister of State, Northern Ireland. Posts: member, Social Security Select Committee. Status: married, five children.*

CON HOLD		1992 election			1987 election	
		Votes	%	+/-	%	Votes
Michael Mates*	Con	47,541	64.2	-0.3	64.5	43,093
Susan Baring	Lib Dem	18,376	24.8	-4.1	28.9	19,307
James Phillips	Lab	6,840	9.2	+2.6	6.6	4,443
Ian Foster	Green	1,113	1.5			
Stanley Hale	RCC	165	0.2			
Majority	**Con**	**29,165**	**39.4**	**+3.8**	**35.6**	**23,786**

Electorate: 92,139 **Voters:** 74,035 **Turnout:** 80.4 **Swing:** 1.9 to Con from LDm

HAMPSHIRE NORTH WEST

Sir David Mitchell: *Conservative. Born: 1928. Educated: Aldenham School. Jobs: farmer, wine shipper. First Elected: 1964. Status: separated, three children.*

CON HOLD		1992 election			1987 election	
		Votes	%	+/-	%	Votes
Sir David Mitchell*	Con	34,310	58.1	+0.4	57.8	31,470
Mike Simpson	Lib Dem	16,462	27.9	-5.2	33.1	18,033
Michael Stockwell	Lab	7,433	12.6	+3.5	9.1	4,980
Doreen Ashley	Green	825	1.4			
Majority	**Con**	**17,848**	**30.2**	**+5.6**	**24.7**	**13,437**

Electorate: 73,101 **Voters:** 59,030 **Turnout:** 80.8 **Swing:** 2.8 to Con from LDm

HAMPSTEAD & HIGHGATE

Glenda Jackson: *Labour. Born: 1936. Educated: West Kirkby Grammar School. Jobs: actress. First Elected: 1992. Union: Equity, sponsored by ASLEF. Status: one child.*

LAB GAIN		1992 election			1987 election	
		Votes	%	+/-	%	Votes
Glenda Jackson	Lab	19,193	45.1	+7.6	37.6	17,015
Oliver Letwin	Con	17,753	41.8	-0.7	42.5	19,236
David Wrede	Lib Dem	4,765	11.2	-8.1	19.3	8,744
Steven Games	Green	594	1.4			
Richard Prosser	NLP	86	0.2			
Anna Hall	Raver	44	0.1			
Charles Wilson	Scalliwag	44	0.1			
Captain Rizz	Rizz	33	0.1			
Majority	**Lab**	**1,440**	**3.4**	**+8.3**	**4.9**	**2,221**

Electorate: 58,203 **Voters:** 42,512 **Turnout:** 73.0 **Swing:** 4.1 to Lab from Con

HARBOROUGH

Edward Garnier: Conservative. Born: 1952. Educated: Wellington College; Oxford. Jobs: barrister. First Elected: 1992. Posts: member, Home Affairs Select Committee, Statutory Instruments Select Committee. Status: married, three children.

CON HOLD		1992 election			1987 election	
		Votes	%	+/-	%	Votes
Edward Garnier	Con	34,280	54.6	-4.9	59.4	35,216
Mark Cox	Lib Dem	20,737	33.0	+5.3	27.7	16,406
Cynthia Mackay	Lab	7,483	11.9	-1.0	12.9	7,646
Andrew Irwin	NLP	328	0.5			
Majority	**Con**	**13,543**	**21.6**	**-10.2**	**31.7**	**18,810**

Electorate: 76,514 **Voters:** 62,828 **Turnout:** 82.1 **Swing:** 5.1 to LDm from Con

HARLOW

Jerry Hayes: Conservative. Born: 1953. Educated: Oratory School; London University. Jobs: barrister. First Elected: 1983. Status: married, two children.

CON HOLD		1992 election			1987 election	
		Votes	%	+/-	%	Votes
Jerry Hayes*	Con	26,608	47.0	-0.3	47.2	26,017
Bill Rammell	Lab	23,668	41.8	+5.2	36.6	20,140
Lorna Spenceley	Lib Dem	6,375	11.3	-4.9	16.2	8,915
Majority	**Con**	**2,940**	**5.2**	**-5.5**	**10.7**	**5,877**

Electorate: 68,615 **Voters:** 56,651 **Turnout:** 82.6 **Swing:** 2.7 to Lab from Con

HARROGATE

Robert Banks: Conservative. Born: 1937. Educated: Haileybury. Jobs: company director. First Elected: 1974. Status: married, five children.

CON HOLD		1992 election			1987 election	
		Votes	%	+/-	%	Votes
Robert Banks*	Con	32,023	53.9	-1.7	55.6	31,167
Tim Hurren	Lib Dem	19,434	32.7	-1.7	34.3	19,265
Andy Wright	Lab	7,230	12.2	+2.0	10.1	5,671
Arnold Warneken	Green	780	1.3			
Majority	**Con**	**12,589**	**21.2**	**-0.0**	**21.2**	**11,902**

Electorate: 76,250 **Voters:** 59,467 **Turnout:** 78.0 **Swing:** No Swing

CONSTITUENCIES

HARROW EAST

Hugh Dykes: Conservative. Born: 1939. Educated: Weston-super-Mare Grammar School; Cambridge. Jobs: stockbroker. First Elected: 1970. Posts: member, European Legislation Select Committee; chairman, European Movement. Status: married, three children.

CON HOLD		1992 election			1987 election	
		Votes	%	+/-	%	Votes
Hugh Dykes*	Con	30,752	52.9	-1.3	54.2	32,302
Tony McNulty	Lab	19,654	33.8	+10.2	23.5	14,029
Veronica Chamberlain	Lib Dem	6,360	10.9	-11.3	22.2	13,251
Peter Burrows	Lib	1,142	2.0			
Susan Hamza	NLP	212	0.4			
Jan Lester	Anti Fed	49	0.1			
Majority	**Con**	**11,098**	**19.1**	**-11.6**	**30.7**	**18,273**

Electorate: 74,733 **Voters:** 58,169 **Turnout:** 77.8 **Swing:** 5.8 to Lab from Con

HARROW WEST

Robert Hughes: Conservative. Born: 1951. Educated: Spring Grove Grammar School; Harrow College of Technology. Jobs: broadcaster. First Elected: 1987. Posts: Government Whip. Status: married, three children.

CON HOLD		1992 election			1987 election	
		Votes	%	+/-	%	Votes
Robert Hughes*	Con	30,240	55.2	+0.0	55.2	30,456
Claude Moraes	Lab	12,343	22.5	+5.0	17.5	9,665
Christopher Noyce	Lib Dem	11,050	20.2	-7.1	27.2	15,012
Gabriel Aitman	Lib	845	1.5			
Jacqueline Argyle	NLP	306	0.6			
Majority	**Con**	**17,897**	**32.7**	**+4.7**	**28.0**	**15,444**

Electorate: 69,616 **Voters:** 54,784 **Turnout:** 78.7 **Swing:** 2.5 to Lab from Con

HARTLEPOOL

Peter Mandelson: Labour. Born: 1953. Educated: Hendon Senior High School; Oxford. Jobs: broadcaster, party official. First Elected: 1992. Union: GMB. Status: single

LAB HOLD		1992 election			1987 election	
		Votes	%	+/-	%	Votes
Peter Mandelson	Lab	26,816	51.9	+3.4	48.5	24,296
Graham Robb	Con	18,034	34.9	+1.0	33.9	17,007
Ian Cameron	Lib Dem	6,860	13.3	-0.8	14.1	7,047
Majority	**Lab**	**8,782**	**17.0**	**+2.4**	**14.5**	**7,289**

Electorate: 67,968 **Voters:** 51,710 **Turnout:** 76.1 **Swing:** 1.2 to Lab from Con

HARWICH

Iain Sproat: *Conservative. Born: 1938. Educated: Winchester College; Oxford. Jobs: industrial adviser, company director. First Elected: 1970. Status: married.*

CON HOLD		1992 election			1987 election	
		Votes	%	+/-	%	Votes
Iain Sproat	Con	32,369	51.9	+0.1	51.8	29,344
Pauline Bevan	Lib Dem	15,210	24.4	-6.1	30.5	17,262
Ralph Knight	Lab	14,511	23.3	+5.8	17.5	9,920
Eileen McGrath	NLP	279	0.4			
Majority	**Con**	**17,159**	**27.5**	**+6.2**	**21.3**	**12,082**

Electorate: 80,260 **Voters:** 62,369 **Turnout:** 77.7 **Swing:** 3.1 to Con from LDm

HASTINGS & RYE

Jacqui Lait: *Conservative. Born: 1947. Educated: Paisley Grammar School; Strathclyde University. Jobs: parliamentary consultant. First Elected: 1992. Posts: member, Health Select Committee. Status: married.*

CON HOLD		1992 election			1987 election	
		Votes	%	+/-	%	Votes
Jacqui Lait	Con	25,573	47.6	-2.5	50.1	26,163
Monroe Palmer	Lib Dem	18,939	35.2	-0.8	36.0	18,816
Richard Stevens	Lab	8,458	15.7	+2.7	13.1	6,825
Sally Phillips	Green	640	1.2			
Tiverton Howell	Loony	168	0.3	-0.2	0.5	242
Majority	**Con**	**6,634**	**12.3**	**-1.7**	**14.1**	**7,347**

Electorate: 71,838 **Voters:** 53,778 **Turnout:** 74.9 **Swing:** 0.9 to LDm from Con

HAVANT

David Willetts: *Conservative. Born: 1956. Educated: King Edward's School, Birmingham; Oxford. Jobs: political adviser. First Elected: 1992. Posts: member, Social Security Select Committee. Status: married, one child.*

CON HOLD		1992 election			1987 election	
		Votes	%	+/-	%	Votes
David Willetts	Con	32,233	55.0	-2.2	57.1	32,527
Steve van Hagen	Lib Dem	14,649	25.0	-3.1	28.1	16,017
Graham Morris	Lab	10,968	18.7	+4.6	14.1	8,030
Terry Mitchell	Green	793	1.4			
Majority	**Con**	**17,584**	**30.0**	**+1.0**	**29.0**	**16,510**

Electorate: 74,217 **Voters:** 58,643 **Turnout:** 79.0 **Swing:** 0.5 to Con from LDm

CONSTITUENCIES

HAYES & HARLINGTON

Terry Dicks: *Conservative. Born: 1937. Educated: London School of Economics, Oxford. Jobs: clerk, local government officer. First Elected: 1983. Posts: member, Transport Select Committee. Status: married, three children.*

CON HOLD		1992 election			1987 election	
		Votes	%	+/-	%	Votes
Terry Dicks*	Con	19,489	44.9	-4.3	49.2	21,355
John McDonnell	Lab	19,436	44.8	+9.3	35.5	15,390
Tony Little	Lib Dem	4,472	10.3	-5.0	15.3	6,641
Majority	**Con**	**53**	**0.1**	**-13.6**	**13.7**	**5,965**

Electorate: 54,449 **Voters:** 43,397 **Turnout:** 79.7 **Swing:** 6.8 to Lab from Con

HAZEL GROVE

Sir Tom Arnold: *Conservative. Born: 1947. Educated: Bedales; Oxford. Jobs: theatre producer. First Elected: 1974. Posts: vice-chairman, Conservative Party. Posts: member, Treasury Select Committee. Status: married, one child.*

CON HOLD		1992 election			1987 election	
		Votes	%	+/-	%	Votes
Sir Tom Arnold*	Con	24,479	44.8	-0.7	45.5	24,396
Andrew Stunell	Lib Dem	23,550	43.1	+1.1	42.0	22,556
Colin McAllister	Lab	6,390	11.7	-0.1	11.8	6,354
Mike Penn	NLP	204	0.4			
Majority	**Con**	**929**	**1.7**	**-1.7**	**3.4**	**1,840**

Electorate: 64,302 **Voters:** 54,623 **Turnout:** 84.9 **Swing:** 0.9 to LDm from Con

HEMSWORTH

Derek Enright: *Labour. Born: 1935. Educated: St Michael's College, Leeds; Oxford. Jobs: consultant, Euro MP. First Elected: 1991. Posts: member, European Legislation Select Committee. Status: married, four children.*

LAB HOLD		1992 election			1987 election	
		Votes	%	+/-	%	Votes
Derek Enright*	Lab	29,942	70.8	+3.8	67.0	27,859
Garnet Harrison	Con	7,867	18.6	+1.4	17.2	7,159
Valerie Megson	Lib Dem	4,459	10.5	-5.2	15.8	6,568
Majority	**Lab**	**22,075**	**52.2**	**+2.4**	**49.8**	**20,700**

Electorate: 55,679 **Voters:** 42,268 **Turnout:** 75.9 **Swing:** 1.2 to Lab from Con

BY-ELECTION November 1991: LAB GAIN. D. Enright (Lab) 15,895 (66.3%), V. Megson (LibDem) 4,808 (20.1%), G. Harrison (Con) 2,512 (10.5%), Lab majority 11,087 (46.3%), SWING 2.5% to LibDem from Lab

HENDON NORTH

John Gorst: Conservative. Born: 1928. Educated: Ardingly College, Sussex; Cambridge. Jobs: public relations, advertising. First Elected: 1970. Posts: member, National Heritage Select Committee; vice-chairman, All Party War Crimes Committee. Status: married, five children.

CON HOLD		1992 election			1987 election	
		Votes	%	+/-	%	Votes
John Gorst*	Con	20,569	53.2	-2.4	55.6	20,155
David Hill	Lab	13,447	34.8	+9.3	25.5	9,223
Peter Kemp	Lib Dem	4,136	10.7	-8.2	18.9	6,859
Patricia Duncan	Green	430	1.1			
Patricia Orr	NLP	95	0.2			
Majority	**Con**	**7,122**	**18.4**	**-11.8**	**30.2**	**10,932**

Electorate: 51,513 **Voters:** 38,677 **Turnout:** 75.1 **Swing:** 5.9 to Lab from Con

HENDON SOUTH

John Marshall: Conservative. Born: 1940. Educated: Harris Academy, Dundee; St Andrew's University. Jobs: stockbroker, Euro MP. First Elected: 1987. Posts: PPS. Status: married, two children.

CON HOLD		1992 election			1987 election	
		Votes	%	+/-	%	Votes
John Marshall*	Con	20,593	58.8	+3.2	55.5	19,341
Leonora Lloyd	Lab	8,546	24.4	+3.5	20.9	7,261
Jack Cohen	Lib Dem	5,609	16.0	-7.6	23.6	8,217
Jonathan Leslie	NLP	289	0.8			
Majority	**Con**	**12,047**	**34.4**	**+2.4**	**31.9**	**11,124**

Electorate: 48,401 **Voters:** 35,037 **Turnout:** 72.4 **Swing:** 0.2 to Lab from Con

HENLEY

Michael Heseltine: Conservative. Born: 1933. Educated: Shrewsbury School; Oxford. Jobs: company director. First Elected: 1966. Posts: President of the Board of Trade. Status: married, three children.

CON HOLD		1992 election			1987 election	
		Votes	%	+/-	%	Votes
Michael Heseltine*	Con	30,835	59.7	-1.4	61.1	29,978
David Turner	Lib Dem	12,443	24.1	-2.2	26.3	12,896
Ivan Russell-Swinnerton	Lab	7,676	14.9	+2.3	12.6	6,173
Alan Plane	Anti H	431	0.8			
Sara Banerji	NLP	274	0.5			
Majority	**Con**	**18,392**	**35.6**	**+0.8**	**34.8**	**17,082**

Electorate: 64,702 **Voters:** 51,659 **Turnout:** 79.8 **Swing:** 0.4 to Con from LDm

CONSTITUENCIES

HEREFORD

Colin Shepherd: *Conservative. Born: 1938. Educated: Oundle; Cambridge. Jobs: company director. First Elected: 1974. Posts: chairman, Commons Catering Sub-committee. Status: married, three children.*

CON HOLD		1992 election			1987 election	
		Votes	%	+/-	%	Votes
Colin Shepherd*	Con	26,727	47.2	-0.3	47.5	24,865
Gwynoro Jones	Lib Dem	23,314	41.2	-3.6	44.8	23,452
Josephine Kelly	Lab	6,005	10.6	+2.9	7.7	4,031
Chris Mattingly	Green	596	1.1			
Majority	**Con**	**3,413**	**6.0**	**+3.3**	**2.7**	**1,413**

Electorate: 69,676 **Voters:** 56,642 **Turnout:** 81.3 **Swing:** 1.7 to Con from LDm

HERTFORD & STORTFORD

Bowen Wells: *Conservative. Born: 1935. Educated: St Paul's School; Exeter University. Jobs: teacher, company director. First Elected: 1979. Posts: PPS. Status: married, two children.*

CON HOLD		1992 election			1987 election	
		Votes	%	+/-	%	Votes
Bowen Wells*	Con	35,716	57.5	+0.0	57.5	33,763
Chris White	Lib Dem	15,506	25.0	-3.4	28.3	16,623
Alasdair Bovaird	Lab	10,125	16.3	+3.5	12.8	7,494
Jamie Goth	Green	780	1.3	-0.1	1.4	814
Majority	**Con**	**20,210**	**32.5**	**+3.3**	**29.2**	**17,140**

Electorate: 76,654 **Voters:** 62,127 **Turnout:** 81.0 **Swing:** 1.7 to Con from LDm

HERTFORDSHIRE NORTH

Oliver Heald: *Conservative. Born: 1954. Educated: Reading School; Cambridge. Jobs: barrister. First Elected: 1992. Posts: member, Employment Select Committee. Status: married, three children.*

CON HOLD		1992 election			1987 election	
		Votes	%	+/-	%	Votes
Oliver Heald	Con	33,679	49.8	+0.1	49.7	31,750
Roger Liddle	Lib Dem	17,148	25.4	-6.4	31.8	20,308
Sarah Bissett Johnson	Lab	16,449	24.3	+5.9	18.5	11,782
Bryan Irving	NLP	339	0.5			
Majority	**Con**	**16,531**	**24.4**	**+6.5**	**17.9**	**11,442**

Electorate: 80,066 **Voters:** 67,615 **Turnout:** 84.4 **Swing:** 3.3 to Con from LDm

HERTFORDSHIRE SOUTH WEST

Richard Page: Conservative. Born: 1941. Educated: Hurstpierpoint College, Sussex; Luton Technical College. First Elected: 1976. Posts: member, Public Accounts Committee. Status: married, two children.

CON HOLD		1992 election			1987 election	
		Votes	%	+/-	%	Votes
Richard Page*	Con	33,825	57.0	+1.2	55.8	32,791
Ann Shaw	Lib Dem	13,718	23.1	-5.8	28.9	17,007
Andrew Gale	Lab	11,512	19.4	+4.1	15.3	8,966
Chris Adamson	NLP	281	0.5			
Majority	**Con**	**20,107**	**33.9**	**+7.0**	**26.9**	**15,784**

Electorate: 70,836 **Voters:** 59,336 **Turnout:** 83.8 **Swing:** 3.5 to Con from LDm

HERTFORDSHIRE WEST

Robert Jones: Conservative. Born: 1950. Educated: Merchant Taylors; St Andrew's University. Jobs: housing policy adviser. First Elected: 1983. Posts: chairman, Environment Select Committee. Status: married.

CON HOLD		1992 election			1987 election	
		Votes	%	+/-	%	Votes
Robert Jones*	Con	33,340	51.5	+1.8	49.7	31,760
Eryl McNally	Lab	19,400	30.0	+6.0	24.0	15,317
Martin Trevett	Lib Dem	10,464	16.2	-10.2	26.3	16,836
James Hannaway	Green	674	1.0			
John McAuley	NF	665	1.0			
Guy Harvey	NLP	175	0.3			
Majority	**Con**	**13,940**	**21.5**	**-1.8**	**23.4**	**14,924**

Electorate: 78,573 **Voters:** 64,718 **Turnout:** 82.4 **Swing:** 2.1 to Lab from Con

HERTSMERE

James Clappison: Conservative. Born: 1956. Educated: St. Patrick's School, York; Oxford. Jobs: barrister. First Elected: 1992. Posts: member, Health Select Committee. Status: married, three children.

CON HOLD		1992 election			1987 election	
		Votes	%	+/-	%	Votes
James Clappison	Con	32,133	56.8	+0.2	56.6	31,278
David Souter	Lab	13,398	23.7	+4.1	19.6	10,835
Zerbanoo Gifford	Lib Dem	10,681	18.9	-4.9	23.8	13,172
Diana Harding	NLP	373	0.7			
Majority	**Con**	**18,735**	**33.1**	**+0.4**	**32.8**	**18,106**

Electorate: 69,951 **Voters:** 56,585 **Turnout:** 80.9 **Swing:** 1.9 to Lab from Con

CONSTITUENCIES

HEXHAM

Peter Atkinson: Conservative. Born: 1943. Educated: Cheltenham College. Jobs: journalist, company director. First Elected: 1992. Posts: member, Scottish Affairs Select Committee. Status: married, two children.

CON HOLD		1992 election			1987 election	
		Votes	%	+/-	%	Votes
Peter Atkinson	Con	24,967	52.4	+2.8	49.6	22,370
Ian Swithenbank	Lab	11,529	24.2	+6.2	18.0	8,103
Jonathan Wallace	Lib Dem	10,344	21.7	-10.0	31.7	14,304
John Hartshorne	Green	781	1.6	+0.9	0.7	336
Majority	**Con**	**13,438**	**28.2**	**+10.3**	**17.9**	**8,066**

Electorate: 57,812 **Voters:** 47,621 **Turnout:** 82.4 **Swing:** 1.7 to Lab from Con

HEYWOOD & MIDDLETON

Jim Callaghan: Labour. Born: 1927. Educated: Manchester and London Universities. Jobs: art lecturer. First Elected: 1983. Posts: member, National Heritage Select Committee, chairmen's panel. Status: single

LAB HOLD		1992 election			1987 election	
		Votes	%	+/-	%	Votes
Jim Callaghan*	Lab	22,380	52.2	+2.4	49.9	21,900
Eric Ollerenshaw	Con	14,306	33.4	-0.9	34.3	15,052
Michael Taylor	Lib Dem	5,262	12.3	-3.6	15.8	6,953
Phil Burke	Lib	757	1.8			
Anne Marie Scott	NLP	134	0.3			
Majority	**Lab**	**8,074**	**18.8**	**+3.3**	**15.6**	**6,848**

Electorate: 57,176 **Voters:** 42,839 **Turnout:** 74.9 **Swing:** 1.6 to Lab from Con

HIGH PEAK

Charles Hendry: Conservative. Born: 1959. Educated: Rugby; Edinburgh University. Jobs: political adviser, public relations. First Elected: 1992. Posts: member, National Heritage Select Committee, chairmen's panel. Status: single

CON HOLD		1992 election			1987 election	
		Votes	%	+/-	%	Votes
Charles Hendry	Con	27,538	46.0	+0.3	45.7	25,715
Tom Levitt	Lab	22,719	37.9	+9.1	28.8	16,199
Simon Molloy	Lib Dem	8,861	14.8	-10.8	25.6	14,389
Roger Floyd	Green	794	1.3			
Majority	**Con**	**4,819**	**8.0**	**-8.9**	**16.9**	**9,516**

Electorate: 70,793 **Voters:** 59,912 **Turnout:** 84.6 **Swing:** 4.4 to Lab from Con

HOLBORN & ST PANCRAS

Frank Dobson: Labour. Born: 1940. Educated: Archbishop Holgate Grammar School, York; London School of Economics. Jobs: electricity industry. First Elected: 1979. Posts: Shadow Employment Secretary. Union: RMT. Status: married, three children.

LAB HOLD		1992 election			1987 election	
		Votes	%	+/-	%	Votes
Frank Dobson*	Lab	22,243	54.8	+4.1	50.6	22,966
Andrew McHallam	Con	11,419	28.1	-3.0	31.1	14,113
J. Horne-Roberts	Lib Dem	5,476	13.5	-4.1	17.6	7,994
Paul Wolf-Light	Green	959	2.4			
Mark Hersey	NLP	212	0.5			
Richard Headicar	Socialist	175	0.4			
Nigel Lewis	WAR	133	0.3			
Majority	**Lab**	**10,824**	**26.6**	**+7.1**	**19.5**	**8,853**

Electorate: 64,480 **Voters:** 40,617 **Turnout:** 63.0 **Swing:** 3.5 to Lab from Con

HOLLAND WITH BOSTON

Sir Richard Body: Conservative. Born: 1927. Educated: Reading School. Jobs: barrister. First Elected: 1955. Status: married, two children.

CON HOLD		1992 election			1987 election	
		Votes	%	+/-	%	Votes
Sir Richard Body*	Con	29,159	55.1	-2.8	57.9	27,412
John Hough	Lab	15,328	29.0	+8.4	20.5	9,734
Nigel Ley	Lib Dem	8,434	15.9	-4.8	20.7	9,817
Majority	**Con**	**13,831**	**26.1**	**-11.0**	**37.1**	**17,595**

Electorate: 67,900 **Voters:** 52,921 **Turnout:** 77.9 **Swing:** 5.6 to Lab from Con

HONITON

Sir Peter Emery: Conservative. Born: 1926. Educated: USA; Oxford. Jobs: company director. First Elected: 1959. Posts: chairman, Procedure Select Committee. Status: married, four children.

CON HOLD		1992 election			1987 election	
		Votes	%	+/-	%	Votes
Sir Peter Emery*	Con	33,533	52.4	-6.7	59.2	34,931
Jennifer Sharratt	Lib Dem	17,022	26.6	-4.5	31.1	18,369
Ray Davison	Lab	8,142	12.7	+4.3	8.4	4,988
David Owen	Ind C	2,175	3.4			
Stuart Hughes	Loony G	1,442	2.3			
Geoff Halliwell	Lib	1,005	1.6			
Alan Tootill	Green	650	1.0			
Majority	**Con**	**16,511**	**25.8**	**-2.2**	**28.1**	**16,562**

Electorate: 79,223 **Voters:** 63,969 **Turnout:** 80.7 **Swing:** 1.1 to LDm from Con

HORNCHURCH

Robin Squire: *Conservative. Born: 1944. Educated: Tiffin School, Kingston. Jobs: accountant. First Elected: 1979. Posts: Environment minister. Status: married, two children.*

CON HOLD		1992 election			1987 election	
		Votes	%	+/-	%	Votes
Robin Squire*	Con	25,817	53.5	+2.3	51.2	24,039
Leonie Cooper	Lab	16,652	34.5	+6.1	28.4	13,345
Barry Oddy	Lib Dem	5,366	11.1	-9.3	20.4	9,609
Terrence Matthews	Soc Dem	453	0.9			
Majority	**Con**	**9,165**	**19.0**	**-3.8**	**22.8**	**10,694**

Electorate: 60,522 **Voters:** 48,288 **Turnout:** 79.8 **Swing:** 1.9 to Lab from Con

HORNSEY & WOOD GREEN

Barbara Roche: *Labour. Born: 1954. Educated: Oxford. Jobs: barrister. First Elected: 1992. Posts: member, Home Affairs Select Committee. Status: married, one child.*

LAB GAIN		1992 election			1987 election	
		Votes	%	+/-	%	Votes
Barbara Roche	Lab	27,020	48.5	+8.5	40.0	23,618
Andrew Boff	Con	21,843	39.2	-3.8	43.0	25,397
Peter Dunphy	Lib Dem	5,547	10.0	-5.2	15.1	8,928
Liz Crosbie	Green	1,051	1.9	-0.1	2.0	1,154
Peter Davies	NLP	197	0.4			
Wystan Massey	Rev Comm	89	0.2			
Majority	**Lab**	**5,177**	**9.3**	**+12.3**	**3.0**	**1,779**

Electorate: 73,491 **Voters:** 55,747 **Turnout:** 75.9 **Swing:** 6.1 to Lab from Con

HORSHAM

Sir Peter Hordern: *Conservative. Born: 1929. Educated: Australia; Oxford. Jobs: stockbroker, company director. First Elected: 1964. Posts: chairman, Public Accounts Commission. Status: married, three children.*

CON HOLD		1992 election			1987 election	
		Votes	%	+/-	%	Votes
Sir Peter Hordern*	Con	42,210	61.7	-2.0	63.7	39,775
Julie Stainton	Lib Dem	17,138	25.1	-0.3	25.4	15,868
Stephen Uwins	Lab	6,745	9.9	+1.2	8.7	5,435
Judith Elliott	Lib	1,281	1.9			
Trevor King	Green	692	1.0	-1.2	2.2	1,383
Jim Duggan	PPP	332	0.5			
Majority	**Con**	**25,072**	**36.7**	**-1.6**	**38.3**	**23,907**

Electorate: 84,158 **Voters:** 68,398 **Turnout:** 81.3 **Swing:** 0.8 to LDm from Con

HOUGHTON & WASHINGTON

Roland Boyes: Labour. Born: 1937. Educated: Bradford University. Jobs: teacher, Euro MP. First Elected: 1983. Union: GMB. Posts: member, Health Select Committee. Status: married, two children.

LAB HOLD		1992 election			1987 election	
		Votes	%	+/-	%	Votes
Roland Boyes*	Lab	34,733	62.0	+2.9	59.1	32,805
Andrew Tyrie	Con	13,925	24.9	+2.1	22.7	12,612
Owen Dumpleton	Lib Dem	7,346	13.1	-5.1	18.2	10,090
Majority	**Lab**	**20,808**	**37.2**	**+0.8**	**36.4**	**20,193**

Electorate: 79,325 **Voters:** 56,004 **Turnout:** 70.6 **Swing:** 0.4 to Lab from Con

HOVE

Timothy Sainsbury: Conservative. Born: 1932. Educated: Eton; Oxford. Jobs: company director. First Elected: 1973. Posts: Minister for Industry. Status: married, four children.

CON HOLD		1992 election			1987 election	
		Votes	%	+/-	%	Votes
Timothy Sainsbury*	Con	24,525	49.0	-9.9	58.8	28,952
Don Turner	Lab	12,257	24.5	+6.2	18.3	9,010
Anne Jones	Lib Dem	9,709	19.4	-2.4	21.8	10,734
Nigel Furness	Hove C	2,658	5.3			
Gordon Sinclair	Green	814	1.6			
John Morilly	NLP	126	0.3			
Majority	**Con**	**12,268**	**24.5**	**-12.5**	**37.0**	**18,218**

Electorate: 67,450 **Voters:** 50,089 **Turnout:** 74.3 **Swing:** 8.0 to Lab from Con

HUDDERSFIELD

Barry Sheerman: Labour. Born: 1940. Educated: Hampton Grammar School; London School of Economics. Jobs: lecturer. First Elected: 1983. Posts: Labour spokesman on disabled people's rights. Union: MSF. Status: married, four children.

LAB HOLD		1992 election			1987 election	
		Votes	%	+/-	%	Votes
Barry Sheerman*	Lab	23,832	48.7	+2.9	45.9	23,019
Jane Kenyon	Con	16,574	33.9	+2.5	31.4	15,741
Ann Denham	Lib Dem	7,777	15.9	-5.6	21.5	10,773
Nick Harvey	Green	576	1.2	-0.1	1.3	638
Michael Cran	NLP	135	0.3			
Majority	**Lab**	**7,258**	**14.8**	**+0.3**	**14.5**	**7,278**

Electorate: 67,604 **Voters:** 48,894 **Turnout:** 72.3 **Swing:** 0.2 to Lab from Con

CONSTITUENCIES

HULL EAST

John Prescott: *Labour. Born: 1938. Educated: Grange Secondary Modern, Ellesmere Port; Ruskin College, Oxford; Hull University. Jobs: merchant navy steward, trade union official. First Elected: 1970. Posts: Shadow Transport Secretary. Union: RMT. Status: married, two children.*

LAB HOLD		1992 election Votes	%	+/-	1987 election %	Votes
John Prescott*	Lab	30,092	62.9	+6.6	56.3	27,287
John Fareham	Con	11,373	23.8	-2.2	26.0	12,598
Jim Wastling	Lib Dem	6,050	12.6	-5.0	17.7	8,572
Cliff Kinzell	NLP	323	0.7			
Majority	**Lab**	**18,719**	**39.1**	**+8.8**	**30.3**	**14,689**

Electorate: 69,036 **Voters:** 47,838 **Turnout:** 69.3 **Swing:** 4.4 to Lab from Con

HULL NORTH

Kevin McNamara: *Labour. Born: 1934. Educated: St Mary's College, Crosby; Hull University. Jobs: lecturer. First Elected: 1966. Posts: Shadow Northern Ireland Secretary. Union: TGWU. Status: married, five children.*

LAB HOLD		1992 election Votes	%	+/-	1987 election %	Votes
Kevin McNamara*	Lab	26,619	55.9	+4.7	51.2	26,123
Barry Coleman	Con	11,235	23.6	-3.7	27.3	13,954
Andrew Meadowcroft	Lib Dem	9,504	20.0	-1.5	21.5	10,962
Gregory Richardson	NLP	253	0.5			
Majority	**Lab**	**15,384**	**32.3**	**+8.5**	**23.8**	**12,169**

Electorate: 71,363 **Voters:** 47,611 **Turnout:** 66.7 **Swing:** 4.2 to Lab from Con

HULL WEST

Stuart Randall: *Labour. Born: 1938. Educated: University College, Cardiff. Jobs: systems engineer, manager. First Elected: 1983. Union: EETPU. Status: married, three children.*

LAB HOLD		1992 election Votes	%	+/-	1987 election %	Votes
Stuart Randall*	Lab	21,139	57.3	+5.4	51.9	19,527
Donald Stewart	Con	10,554	28.6	-1.7	30.3	11,397
Robert Tress	Lib Dem	4,867	13.2	-4.5	17.7	6,669
Barry Franklin	NLP	308	0.8			
Majority	**Lab**	**10,585**	**28.7**	**+7.1**	**21.6**	**8,130**

Electorate: 56,111 **Voters:** 36,868 **Turnout:** 65.7 **Swing:** 3.5 to Lab from Con

HUNTINGDON

John Major: Conservative. Born: 1943. Educated: Rutlish Grammar School; Wimbledon. Jobs: clerk, bank official. First Elected: 1979. Posts: Prime Minister. Status: married, two children.

CON HOLD

		1992 election			1987 election	
		Votes	%	+/-	%	Votes
John Major*	Con	48,662	66.2	+2.6	63.6	40,530
Hugh Seckleman	Lab	12,432	16.9	+3.0	13.9	8,883
Andrew Duff	Lib Dem	9,386	12.8	-8.4	21.1	13,486
Paul Wiggin	Lib	1,045	1.4			
Deborah Birkhead	Green	846	1.2	-0.2	1.4	874
Lord David Sutch	Loony	728	1.0			
Michael Flanagan	C Thatch	231	0.3			
Lord Buckethead	Gremloids	107	0.1			
Charles Cockell	FTM	91	0.1			
David Shepheard	NLP	26	0.0			
Majority	**Con**	**36,230**	**49.3**	**+6.8**	**42.4**	**27,044**

Electorate: 92,913 **Voters**: 73,554 **Turnout**: 79.2 **Swing**: 0.2 to Lab from Con

HYNDBURN

Greg Pope: Labour. Born: 1960. Educated: local state schools, Hull University. Jobs: local government officer. First Elected: 1992. Status: married, two children.

LAB GAIN

		1992 election			1987 election	
		Votes	%	+/-	%	Votes
Greg Pope	Lab	23,042	46.9	+7.1	39.8	19,386
Kenneth Hargreaves*	Con	21,082	42.9	-1.5	44.4	21,606
Yvonne Stars	Lib Dem	4,886	9.9	-5.3	15.2	7,423
Stephen Whittle	NLP	150	0.3			
Majority	**Lab**	**1,960**	**4.0**	**+8.6**	**4.6**	**2,220**

Electorate: 58,539 **Voters**: 49,160 **Turnout**: 84.0 **Swing**: 4.3 to Lab from Con

ILFORD NORTH

Vivian Bendall: Conservative. Born: 1938. Educated: Broad Green College. Jobs: estate agent. First Elected: 1978. Status: divorced

CON HOLD

		1992 election			1987 election	
		Votes	%	+/-	%	Votes
Vivian Bendall*	Con	24,698	54.0	-1.0	54.9	24,110
Lesley Hilton	Lab	15,627	34.2	+6.8	27.4	12,020
Ralph Scott	Lib Dem	5,430	11.9	-5.8	17.7	7,757
Majority	**Con**	**9,071**	**19.8**	**-7.7**	**27.5**	**12,090**

Electorate: 58,670 **Voters**: 45,755 **Turnout**: 78.0 **Swing**: 3.9 to Lab from Con

ILFORD SOUTH

Mike Gapes: Labour. Born: 1952. Educated: Cambridge. Jobs: political researcher. First Elected: 1992. Posts: member, Foreign Affairs Select Committee. Status: single.

LAB GAIN		1992 election			1987 election	
		Votes	%	+/-	%	Votes
Mike Gapes	Lab	19,418	45.3	+7.8	37.5	15,779
Neil Thorne*	Con	19,016	44.4	-4.0	48.4	20,351
George Hogarth	Lib Dem	4,126	9.6	-4.5	14.1	5,928
N. Bramachari	NLP	269	0.6			
Majority	**Lab**	**402**	**0.9**	**+11.8**	**10.9**	**4,572**

Electorate: 55,741 **Voters:** 42,829 **Turnout:** 76.8 **Swing:** 5.9 to Lab from Con

INVERNESS, NAIRN & LOCHABER

Sir Russell Johnston: Liberal Democrat. Born: 1932. Educated: Portree Secondary High, Skye; Edinburgh University. Jobs: teacher. First Elected: 1964. Posts: LibDem spokesman on Europe, delegate, Council of Europe, Western European Union. Status: married, four children.

LIBDEM HOLD		1992 election			1987 election	
		Votes	%	+/-	%	Votes
Sir Russell Johnston*	Lib Dem	13,258	26.0	-10.8	36.8	17,422
David Stewart	Lab	12,800	25.1	-0.2	25.3	11,991
Fergus Ewing	SNP	12,562	24.7	+9.9	14.8	7,001
John Scott	Con	11,517	22.6	-0.4	23.0	10,901
John Martin	Green	766	1.5			
Majority	**Lib Dem**	**458**	**0.9**	**-10.6**	**11.5**	**5,431**

Electorate: 69,468 **Voters:** 50,903 **Turnout:** 73.3 **Swing:** 5.3 to Lab from LDm

IPSWICH

Jamie Cann: Labour. Born: 1946. Educated: Barton on Humber Grammar School; Kesteven College of Education. Jobs: teacher. First Elected: 1992. Status: married, two children.

LAB GAIN		1992 election			1987 election	
		Votes	%	+/-	%	Votes
Jamie Cann	Lab	23,680	43.8	+1.1	42.7	22,454
Michael Irvine*	Con	23,415	43.3	-1.1	44.4	23,328
Joe White	Lib Dem	6,159	11.4	-1.2	12.6	6,596
Jane Scott	Green	591	1.1			
Eric Kaplan	NLP	181	0.3			
Majority	**Lab**	**265**	**0.5**	**+2.2**	**1.7**	**874**

Electorate: 67,261 **Voters:** 54,026 **Turnout:** 80.3 **Swing:** 1.1 to Lab from Con

ISLE OF WIGHT

Barry Field: *Conservative. Born: 1946. Educated: Mitcham Grammar School. Jobs: crematorium director. First Elected: 1987. Posts: member, Environment Select Committee. Status: married, two children.*

CON HOLD		1992 election			1987 election	
		Votes	%	+/-	%	Votes
Barry Field*	Con	38,163	47.9	-3.2	51.2	40,175
Peter Brand	Lib Dem	36,336	45.6	+2.7	43.0	33,733
Kenn Pearson	Lab	4,784	6.0	+0.1	5.9	4,626
Clive Daly	NLP	350	0.4			
Majority	**Con**	**1,827**	**2.3**	**-5.9**	**8.2**	**6,442**

Electorate: 99,838 **Voters:** 79,633 **Turnout:** 79.8 **Swing:** 3.0 to LDm from Con

ISLINGTON NORTH

Jeremy Corbyn: *Labour. Born: 1949. Educated: Adams Grammar School; Newport, Salop. Jobs: trade union official. First Elected: 1983. Posts: member, Social Security Select Committee. Union: NUPE.*

LAB HOLD		1992 election			1987 election	
		Votes	%	+/-	%	Votes
Jeremy Corbyn*	Lab	21,742	57.4	+7.5	50.0	19,577
Lurline Champagnie	Con	8,958	23.7	-1.6	25.3	9,920
Sarah Ludford	Lib Dem	5,732	15.1	-6.7	21.8	8,560
Chris Ashby	Green	1,420	3.8	+0.9	2.9	1,131
Majority	**Lab**	**12,784**	**33.8**	**+9.1**	**24.6**	**9,657**

Electorate: 56,270 **Voters:** 37,852 **Turnout:** 67.3 **Swing:** 4.6 to Lab from Con

ISLINGTON SOUTH & FINSBURY

Chris Smith: *Labour. Born: 1951. Educated: George Watson's College, Edinburgh; Cambridge University. Jobs: housing worker. First Elected: 1983. Posts: Shadow minister for environment protection. Union: MSF. Status: single*

LAB HOLD		1992 election			1987 election	
		Votes	%	+/-	%	Votes
Chris Smith*	Lab	20,586	51.1	+11.0	40.1	16,511
Mark Jones	Con	9,934	24.7	+4.1	20.6	8,482
Christopher Pryce	Lib Dem	9,387	23.3	-14.8	38.1	15,706
Rhona Hersey	JBR	149	0.4			
Maria Avino	Loony	142	0.4			
Michael Spinks	NLP	83	0.2			
Majority	**Lab**	**10,652**	**26.4**	**+24.5**	**2.0**	**805**

Electorate: 55,541 **Voters:** 40,281 **Turnout:** 72.5 **Swing:** 3.5 to Lab from Con

ISLWYN

Neil Kinnock: Labour. Born: 1942. Educated: Lewis Grammar School; Pengam; University College, Cardiff. Jobs: tutor organiser. First Elected: 1970. Union: TGWU. Status: married, two children.

LAB HOLD		1992 election			1987 election	
		Votes	%	+/-	%	Votes
Neil Kinnock*	Lab	30,908	74.3	+3.0	71.3	28,901
Peter Bone	Con	6,180	14.8	+0.2	14.7	5,954
Michael Symonds	Lib Dem	2,352	5.7	-3.6	9.2	3,746
Helen Jones	Plaid Cymru	1,636	3.9	-0.8	4.8	1,932
Lord Sutch	Loony	547	1.3			
Majority	**Lab**	**24,728**	**59.4**	**+2.8**	**56.6**	**22,947**

Electorate: 51,079 **Voters:** 41,623 **Turnout:** 81.5 **Swing:** 1.4 to Lab from Con

JARROW

Don Dixon: Labour. Born: 1929. Educated: local state schools. Jobs: shipyard worker. First Elected: 1979. Posts: Labour deputy chief whip. Union: GMB. Status: married, two children.

LAB HOLD		1992 election			1987 election	
		Votes	%	+/-	%	Votes
Don Dixon*	Lab	28,956	62.1	-1.3	63.4	29,651
Terence Ward	Con	11,049	23.7	+0.5	23.2	10,856
Keith Orrell	Lib Dem	6,608	14.2	+0.8	13.3	6,230
Majority	**Lab**	**17,907**	**38.4**	**-1.8**	**40.2**	**18,795**

Electorate: 62,611 **Voters:** 46,613 **Turnout:** 74.4 **Swing:** 0.9 to Con from Lab

KEIGHLEY

Gary Waller: Conservative. Born: 1945. Educated: Rugby; Lancaster University. Jobs: journalist. First Elected: 1979. Status: single

CON HOLD		1992 election			1987 election	
		Votes	%	+/-	%	Votes
Gary Waller*	Con	25,983	47.4	+1.7	45.8	23,903
Tommy Flanagan	Lab	22,387	40.8	+5.8	35.0	18,297
Ian Simpson	Lib Dem	5,793	10.6	-8.7	19.2	10,041
Mike Crowson	Green	642	1.2			
Majority	**Con**	**3,596**	**6.6**	**-4.2**	**10.7**	**5,606**

Electorate: 66,358 **Voters:** 54,805 **Turnout:** 82.6 **Swing:** 2.1 to Lab from Con

KENSINGTON

Dudley Fishburn: *Conservative. Born: 1946. Educated: Eton; Harvard. Jobs: journalist. First Elected: 1988. Posts: PPS. Status: married, four children.*

CON HOLD		1992 election			1987 election	
		Votes	%	+/-	%	Votes
Dudley Fishburn*	Con	15,540	50.3	+2.8	47.5	14,818
Ann Holmes	Lab	11,992	38.8	+5.6	33.2	10,371
Chris Shirley	Lib Dem	2,770	9.0	-8.3	17.2	5,379
Ajay Burlington-Johnson	Green	415	1.3	-0.3	1.7	528
Anthony Hardy	NLP	90	0.3			
Anne Bulloch	Anti Fed	71	0.2			
Majority	**Con**	**3,548**	**11.5**	**-2.8**	**14.3**	**4,447**

Electorate: 42,129 **Voters:** 30,878 **Turnout:** 73.3 **Swing:** 1.4 to Lab from Con

BY-ELECTION July 1988: CON HOLD. D. Fishburn (Con) 9,829 (41.6%), A. Holmes (Lab) 9,014 (38.2%), W. Goodhart (LibDem) 2,546 (10.8%), Con majority 815 (3.4%), SWING 5.4% to Lab from Con

KENT MID

Andrew Rowe: *Conservative. Born: 1935. Educated: Eton; Oxford. Jobs: teacher, civil servant. First Elected: 1983. Posts: delegate, Council of Europe, Western European Union. Status: married, three children.*

CON HOLD		1992 election			1987 election	
		Votes	%	+/-	%	Votes
Andrew Rowe*	Con	33,633	56.7	+1.6	55.1	28,719
Tim Robson	Lab	13,984	23.6	+5.5	18.1	9,420
Graham Colley	Lib Dem	11,476	19.3	-7.4	26.8	13,951
Gerard Valente	NLP	224	0.4			
Majority	**Con**	**19,649**	**33.1**	**+4.8**	**28.4**	**14,768**

Electorate: 74,459 **Voters:** 59,317 **Turnout:** 79.7 **Swing:** 2.0 to Lab from Con

KETTERING

Roger Freeman: *Conservative. Born: 1942. Educated: Whitgift School; Oxford. Jobs: accountant. First Elected: 1983. Posts: Minister for Public Transport. Status: married, two children.*

CON HOLD		1992 election			1987 election	
		Votes	%	+/-	%	Votes
Roger Freeman*	Con	29,115	52.0	+0.9	51.1	26,532
Philip Hope	Lab	17,961	32.1	+12.4	19.7	10,229
Richard Denton-White	Lib Dem	8,962	16.0	-13.3	29.3	15,205
Majority	**Con**	**11,154**	**19.9**	**-1.9**	**21.8**	**11,327**

Electorate: 67,853 **Voters:** 56,038 **Turnout:** 82.6 **Swing:** 5.7 to Lab from Con

CONSTITUENCIES

KILMARNOCK & LOUDOUN

William McKelvey: Labour. Born: 1934. Educated: Morgan Academy; Dundee College of Technology. Jobs: party agent, shop steward. First Elected: 1979. Union: AEU. Posts: chairman, Scottish Affairs Select Committee. Status: married, two children.

LAB HOLD		1992 election Votes	%	+/-	1987 election %	Votes
William McKelvey*	Lab	22,210	44.8	-3.7	48.5	23,713
Alex Neil	SNP	15,231	30.7	+12.5	18.2	8,881
Richard Wilkinson	Con	9,438	19.0	-0.6	19.6	9,586
Kate Philbrick	Lib Dem	2,722	5.5	-8.2	13.7	6,698
Majority	**Lab**	**6,979**	**14.1**	**-14.8**	**28.9**	**14,127**

Electorate: 62,002 **Voters:** 49,601 **Turnout:** 80.0 **Swing:** 8.1 to SNP from Lab

KINCARDINE & DEESIDE

George Kynoch: Conservative. Born: 1946. Educated: Glenalmond; Bristol University. Jobs: company director. First Elected: 1992. Posts: member, Scottish Affairs Select Committee. Status: married, two children.

CON REGAIN		1992 election Votes	%	+/-	1987 election %	Votes
George Kynoch	Con	22,924	43.7	+3.1	40.6	19,438
Nicol Stephen*	Lib Dem	18,429	35.1	-1.2	36.3	17,375
Allan Macartney	SNP	5,927	11.3	+4.9	6.4	3,082
Malcolm Savidge	Lab	4,795	9.1	-6.8	15.9	7,624
Steve Campbell	Green	381	0.7	+0.1	0.6	299
Majority	**Con**	**4,495**	**8.6**	**+4.3**	**4.3**	**2,063**

Electorate: 66,617 **Voters:** 52,456 **Turnout:** 78.7 **Swing:** 2.1 to Con from LDm

BY-ELECTION November 1991: LIBDEM GAIN. N Stephen (LibDem) 20,779 (49.0%), M. Humphrey (Con) 12,955 (30.6%), A. Macartney (SNP) 4,705 (11.1%), LibDem majority 7,824 (18.5%), SWING 11.4% to LibDem from Con

KINGSTON UPON THAMES

Norman Lamont: Conservative. Born: 1942. Educated: Loretto School; Cambridge. First Elected: 1972. Posts: Chancellor of the Exchequer. Status: married, two children.

CON HOLD		1992 election Votes	%	+/-	1987 election %	Votes
Norman Lamont*	Con	20,675	51.6	-4.6	56.2	24,198
Derek Osbourne	Lib Dem	10,522	26.3	-3.9	30.2	13,012
Robert Markless	Lab	7,748	19.3	+6.2	13.2	5,676
Adrian Amer	Lib	771	1.9			
David Beaupre	Loony	212	0.5			
Graham Woollcoombe	NLP	81	0.2			
Anthony Scholefield	Anti Fed	42	0.1			
Majority	**Con**	**10,153**	**25.4**	**-0.6**	**26.0**	**11,186**

Electorate: 51,077 **Voters:** 40,051 **Turnout:** 78.4 **Swing:** 0.3 to LDm from Con

KINGSWOOD

Roger Berry: Labour. Born: 1948. Educated: Bristol University. Jobs: economics lecturer. Union: MSF. First Elected: 1992.

LAB GAIN		1992 election			1987 election	
		Votes	%	+/-	%	Votes
Roger Berry	Lab	26,774	44.5	+7.1	37.4	21,907
Robert Hayward*	Con	24,404	40.6	-4.3	44.9	26,300
Jeanne Pinkerton	Lib Dem	8,967	14.9	-2.8	17.7	10,382
Majority	**Lab**	**2,370**	**3.9**	**+11.4**	**7.5**	**4,393**

Electorate: 71,727 **Voters:** 60,145 **Turnout:** 83.8 **Swing:** 5.7 to Lab from Con

KIRKCALDY

Lewis Moonie: Labour. Born: 1947. Educated: Nicholson Institute, Stornaway; St Andrew's University. Jobs: doctor. First Elected: 1987. Posts: Labour spokesman on the citizen's charter and women. Status: married, two children.

LAB HOLD		1992 election			1987 election	
		Votes	%	+/-	%	Votes
Lewis Moonie*	Lab	17,887	46.0	-3.5	49.6	20,281
Stewart Hosie	SNP	8,761	22.5	+10.8	11.7	4,794
Stephen Wolsey	Con	8,476	21.8	+0.5	21.3	8,711
Sue Leslie	Lib Dem	3,729	9.6	-7.8	17.4	7,118
Majority	**Lab**	**9,126**	**23.5**	**-4.8**	**28.3**	**11,570**

Electorate: 51,762 **Voters:** 38,853 **Turnout:** 75.1 **Swing:** 7.2 to SNP from Lab

KNOWSLEY NORTH

George Howarth: Labour. Born: 1949. Educated: Huyton Hey Secondary School; Liverpool Polytechnic. Jobs: teacher. First Elected: 1986. Union: AEU. Status: married, three children.

LAB HOLD		1992 election			1987 election	
		Votes	%	+/-	%	Votes
George Howarth*	Lab	27,517	77.5	+7.6	69.9	27,454
Simon Mabey	Con	5,114	14.4	+1.9	12.5	4,922
James Murray	Lib Dem	1,515	4.3	-11.9	16.2	6,356
Kathleen Lappin	Lib	1,180	3.3			
Veeva Ruben	NLP	179	0.5			
Majority	**Lab**	**22,403**	**63.1**	**+9.4**	**53.7**	**21,098**

Electorate: 48,761 **Voters:** 35,505 **Turnout:** 72.8 **Swing:** 2.9 to Lab from Con

KNOWSLEY SOUTH

Eddie O'Hara: Labour. Born: 1937. Educated: Liverpool Collegiate School; Oxford. Jobs: classics teacher. First Elected: 1990. Posts: member, Education Select Committee. Status: married, three children.

LAB HOLD		1992 election			1987 election	
		Votes	%	+/-	%	Votes
Eddie O'Hara*	Lab	31,933	68.6	+4.1	64.5	31,378
Leslie Byrom	Con	9,922	21.3	-0.3	21.6	10,532
Ian Smith	Lib Dem	4,480	9.6	-4.3	13.9	6,760
Michelangelo Raiano	NLP	217	0.5			
Majority	**Lab**	**22,011**	**47.3**	**+4.5**	**42.8**	**20,846**

Electorate: 62,260 **Voters:** 46,552 **Turnout:** 74.8 **Swing:** 2.2 to Lab from Con

BY-ELECTION September 1990: LAB HOLD. E. O'Hara (Lab) 14,581 (68.8%), L. Byrom (Con) 3,214 (15.2%), C. Hancox (LibDem) 1,809 (8.5%), Lab majority 11,367 (53.6%), SWING 5.4% to Lab from Con

LAGAN VALLEY

James Molyneaux: Ulster Unionist Party. Born: 1920. Educated: Aldergrove School; Antrim. First Elected: 1970. Posts: leader, Ulster Unionist Party.

UUP HOLD		1992 election			1987 election	
		Votes	%	+/-	%	Votes
James Molyneaux*	UUP	29,772	60.8	-9.2	70.0	29,101
Seamus Close	All	6,207	12.7	-1.1	13.8	5,728
Hugh Lewsley	SDLP	4,626	9.4	+2.5	6.9	2,888
Timothy Coleridge	Con	4,423	9.0			
Pat Rice	Sinn Fein	3,346	6.8	+0.4	6.4	2,656
Anne-Marie Lowry	WP	582	1.2	-1.7	2.9	1,215
Majority	**UUP**	**23,565**	**48.1**	**-8.1**	**56.2**	**23,373**

Electorate: 72,645 **Voters:** 48,956 **Turnout:** 67.4 **Swing:** 4.0 to All from UUP

LANCASHIRE WEST

Colin Pickthall: Labour. Born: 1944. Educated: Ulverston Grammar School; University of Wales, Lancaster University. Jobs: lecturer. First Elected: 1992. Posts: member, Agriculture Affairs Select Committee. Status: married, two children.

LAB GAIN		1992 election			1987 election	
		Votes	%	+/-	%	Votes
Colin Pickthall	Lab	30,128	47.1	+5.6	41.5	25,147
Kenneth Hind*	Con	28,051	43.9	+0.2	43.7	26,500
Peter Reilly	Lib Dem	4,884	7.6	-7.2	14.8	8,972
Philip Pawley	Green	546	0.9			
Bevin Morris	NLP	336	0.5			
Majority	**Lab**	**2,077**	**3.2**	**+1.0**	**2.2**	**1,353**

Electorate: 77,462 **Voters:** 63,945 **Turnout:** 82.6 **Swing:** 2.7 to Lab from Con

LANCASTER

Dame Elaine Kellett-Bowman: *Conservative. Born: 1924. Educated: Queen Mary's School, Lytham; Oxford. Jobs: barrister, Euro MP. First Elected: 1970. Status: married, four children.*

CON HOLD

		1992 election Votes	%	+/-	1987 election %	Votes
Dame Elaine Kellett-Bowman*	Con	21,084	45.6	-1.1	46.7	21,142
Ruth Henig	Lab	18,131	39.2	+6.8	32.4	14,689
John Humberstone	Lib Dem	6,524	14.1	-5.8	19.9	9,003
Gina Dowding	Green	433	0.9	-0.1	1.0	473
Robert Barcis	NLP	83	0.2			
Majority	**Con**	**2,953**	**6.4**	**-7.9**	**14.2**	**6,453**

Electorate: 58,714 **Voters:** 46,255 **Turnout:** 78.8 **Swing:** 3.9 to Lab from Con

LANGBAURGH

Michael Bates: *Conservative. Born: 1961. Educated: Gateshead College. Jobs: pensions consultant. First Elected: 1992. Status: married, two children.*

CON REGAIN

		1992 election Votes	%	+/-	1987 election %	Votes
Michael Bates	Con	30,018	45.4	+3.7	41.7	26,047
Ashok Kumar*	Lab	28,454	43.1	+4.7	38.4	23,959
Peter Allen	Lib Dem	7,615	11.5	-8.4	19.9	12,405
Majority	**Con**	**1,564**	**2.4**	**-1.0**	**3.3**	**2,088**

Electorate: 79,566 **Voters:** 66,087 **Turnout:** 83.1 **Swing:** 0.5 to Lab from Con

BY-ELECTION November 1991: LAB GAIN. A. Kumar (Lab) 22,442 (42.9%), M. Bates (Con) 20,467 (39.1%), P. Allan (LibDem) 8,421 (16.1%), Lab majority 1,975 (3.8%), swing 3.6% to Lab from Con

LEEDS CENTRAL

Derek Fatchett: *Labour. Born: 1945. Educated: Lincoln School; Birmingham University. Jobs: lecturer. First Elected: 1983. Posts: Labour spokesman on industry and small business. Union: MSF. Status: married, two children.*

LAB HOLD

		1992 election Votes	%	+/-	1987 election %	Votes
Derek Fatchett*	Lab	23,673	62.2	+6.6	55.6	21,270
Tessa Holdroyd	Con	8,653	22.7	-2.8	25.5	9,765
David Pratt	Lib Dem	5,713	15.0	-2.9	17.9	6,853
Majority	**Lab**	**15,020**	**39.5**	**+9.4**	**30.1**	**11,505**

Electorate: 62,058 **Voters:** 38,039 **Turnout:** 61.3 **Swing:** 4.7 to Lab from Con

LEEDS EAST

George Mudie: Labour. Born: 1945. Educated: local state schools. Jobs: trade union official. First Elected: 1992. Union: NUPE. Status: married, two children.

LAB HOLD		1992 election			1987 election	
		Votes	%	+/-	%	Votes
George Mudie	Lab	24,929	57.7	+9.0	48.7	20,932
Neil Carmichael	Con	12,232	28.3	+1.8	26.5	11,406
Peter Wrigley	Lib Dem	6,040	14.0	-10.8	24.7	10,630
Majority	**Lab**	**12,697**	**29.4**	**+7.2**	**22.2**	**9,526**

Electorate: 61,695 **Voters:** 43,201 **Turnout:** 70.0 **Swing:** 3.6 to Lab from Con

LEEDS NORTH EAST

Timothy Kirkhope: Conservative. Born: 1945. Educated: Royal Grammar School; Newcastle. Jobs: solicitor. First Elected: 1987. Posts: Government Whip. Status: married, four children.

CON HOLD		1992 election			1987 election	
		Votes	%	+/-	%	Votes
Timothy Kirkhope*	Con	22,462	45.4	-0.2	45.6	22,196
Fabian Hamilton	Lab	18,218	36.8	+11.6	25.3	12,292
Christopher Walmsley	Lib Dem	8,274	16.7	-11.6	28.3	13,777
John Noble	Green	546	1.1	+0.2	0.9	416
Majority	**Con**	**4,244**	**8.6**	**-8.7**	**17.3**	**8,419**

Electorate: 64,372 **Voters:** 49,500 **Turnout:** 76.9 **Swing:** 5.9 to Lab from Con

LEEDS NORTH WEST

Dr Keith Hampson: Conservative. Born: 1943. Educated: Grammar School; Bishop Auckland; Bristol University. Jobs: political adviser, lecturer. First Elected: 1974. Posts: member, Select Committee on Trade and Industry. Status: married.

CON HOLD		1992 election			1987 election	
		Votes	%	+/-	%	Votes
Keith Hampson*	Con	21,750	43.0	-0.5	43.5	22,480
Barbara Pearce	Lib Dem	14,079	27.8	-5.6	33.5	17,279
Sue Egan	Lab	13,782	27.3	+5.5	21.7	11,210
David Webb	Green	519	1.0	-0.3	1.3	663
Noel Nowosielski	Lib	427	0.8			
Majority	**Con**	**7,671**	**15.2**	**+5.1**	**10.1**	**5,201**

Electorate: 69,406 **Voters:** 50,557 **Turnout:** 72.8 **Swing:** 2.5 to Con from LDm

LEEDS SOUTH & MORLEY

John Gunnell: *Labour. Born: 1933. Educated: King Edward's School, Birmingham; Leeds University. Jobs: teacher. First Elected: 1992. Union: GMB. Status: married, four children.*

LAB HOLD		1992 election			1987 election	
		Votes	%	+/-	%	Votes
John Gunnell	Lab	23,896	52.2	+2.6	49.6	21,551
Richard Booth	Con	16,524	36.1	+1.9	34.1	14,840
Joan Walmsley	Lib Dem	5,062	11.1	-5.3	16.3	7,099
Robert Thurston	NLP	327	0.7			
Majority	**Lab**	**7,372**	**16.1**	**+0.7**	**15.4**	**6,711**

Electorate: 63,107 **Voters:** 45,809 **Turnout:** 72.6 **Swing:** 0.3 to Lab from Con

LEEDS WEST

John Battle: *Labour. Born: 1951. Educated: Leeds University. Jobs: researcher. First Elected: 1987. Posts: Labour spokesman on housing; member, Environment Select Committee. Union: MSF. Status: married, three children.*

LAB HOLD		1992 election			1987 election	
		Votes	%	+/-	%	Votes
John Battle*	Lab	26,310	55.1	+11.9	43.2	21,032
Paul Bartlett	Con	12,482	26.2	+3.0	23.2	11,276
George Howard	Lib Dem	4,252	8.9	-24.7	33.6	16,340
Michael Meadowcroft	Lib	3,980	8.3			
Alison Mander	Green	569	1.2			
Robert Tenny	NF	132	0.3			
Majority	**Lab**	**13,828**	**29.0**	**+19.3**	**9.6**	**4,692**

Electorate: 67,084 **Voters:** 47,725 **Turnout:** 71.1 **Swing:** 4.5 to Lab from Con

LEICESTER EAST

Keith Vaz: *Labour. Born: 1956. Educated: Latymer Upper School; Cambridge. Jobs: solicitor. First Elected: 1987. Posts: Labour spokesman on local government; member, Home Affairs Select Committee. Union: NUPE.*

LAB HOLD		1992 election			1987 election	
		Votes	%	+/-	%	Votes
Keith Vaz*	Lab	28,123	56.5	+10.4	46.2	24,074
Jeffery Stevens	Con	16,807	33.8	-8.7	42.5	22,150
Sheila Mitchell	Lib Dem	4,043	8.1	-3.2	11.4	5,935
Murray Frankland	Green	453	0.9			
Dennis Taylor	Homeland	308	0.6			
Majority	**Lab**	**11,316**	**22.8**	**+19.1**	**3.7**	**1,924**

Electorate: 63,434 **Voters:** 49,734 **Turnout:** 78.4 **Swing:** 9.5 to Lab from Con

LEICESTER SOUTH

James Marshall: Labour. Born: 1941. Educated: Sheffield City Grammar School, Leeds University. Jobs: research scientist. First Elected: 1974. Status: married, two children.

LAB HOLD		1992 election			1987 election	
		Votes	%	+/-	%	Votes
James Marshall*	Lab	27,934	52.3	+8.1	44.2	24,901
Michael Dutt	Con	18,494	34.6	-6.2	40.8	23,024
Anne Crumbie	Lib Dem	6,271	11.7	-2.0	13.8	7,773
McWhirter John	Green	554	1.0	+0.3	0.7	390
Patricia Saunders	NLP	154	0.3			
Majority	**Lab**	**9,440**	**17.7**	**+14.3**	**3.3**	**1,877**

Electorate: 71,120 **Voters:** 53,407 **Turnout:** 75.1 **Swing:** 7.2 to Lab from Con

LEICESTER WEST

Greville Janner: Labour. Born: 1928. Educated: St Paul's School, Cambridge. Jobs: barrister. First Elected: 1970. Posts: member, Employment Select Committee. Status: married, three children.

LAB HOLD		1992 election			1987 election	
		Votes	%	+/-	%	Votes
Greville Janner*	Lab	22,574	46.8	+2.3	44.5	22,156
John Guthrie	Con	18,596	38.5	-3.5	42.1	20,955
Geoffrey Walker	Lib Dem	6,402	13.3	-0.2	13.5	6,708
Claire Wintram	Green	517	1.1			
Jenny Rosta	NLP	171	0.4			
Majority	**Lab**	**3,978**	**8.2**	**+5.8**	**2.4**	**1,201**

Electorate: 65,510 **Voters:** 48,260 **Turnout:** 73.7 **Swing:** 2.9 to Lab from Con

LEICESTERSHIRE NORTH WEST

David Ashby: Conservative. Born: 1940. Educated: Royal Grammar School, High Wycombe, Bristol University. Jobs: barrister, company director. First Elected: 1983. Posts: member, Home Affairs Select Committee. Status: married, one child.

CON HOLD		1992 election			1987 election	
		Votes	%	+/-	%	Votes
David Ashby*	Con	28,379	45.5	-2.1	47.6	27,872
David Taylor	Lab	27,400	43.9	+9.7	34.3	20,044
Jeremy Beckett	Lib Dem	6,353	10.2	-7.0	17.1	10,034
John Fawcett	NLP	229	0.4			
Majority	**Con**	**979**	**1.6**	**-11.8**	**13.4**	**7,828**

Electorate: 72,414 **Voters:** 62,361 **Turnout:** 86.1 **Swing:** 5.9 to Lab from Con

LEIGH

Lawrence Cunliffe: Labour. Born: 1929. Educated: St Edmund's RC School, Worsley. Jobs: mine engineer. First Elected: 1979. Union: NUM. Status: divorced, five children.

LAB HOLD

		1992 election			1987 election	
		Votes	%	+/-	%	Votes
Lawrence Cunliffe*	Lab	32,225	61.3	+2.7	58.6	30,064
Joseph Egerton	Con	13,398	25.5	-0.8	26.3	13,458
Robert Bleakley	Lib Dem	6,621	12.6	-2.5	15.1	7,745
Adrian Tayler	NLP	320	0.6			
Majority	**Lab**	**18,827**	**35.8**	**+3.4**	**32.4**	**16,606**

Electorate: 70,064 **Voters:** 52,564 **Turnout:** 75.0 **Swing:** 1.7 to Lab from Con

LEOMINSTER

Peter Temple-Morris: Conservative. Born: 1938. Educated: Malvern College, Cambridge. Jobs: barrister. First Elected: 1974. Status: married, four children.

CON HOLD

		1992 election			1987 election	
		Votes	%	+/-	%	Votes
Peter Temple-Morris*	Con	32,783	56.6	-1.2	57.9	31,396
David Short	Lib Dem	16,103	27.8	-4.1	31.9	17,321
Chris Chappell	Lab	6,874	11.9	+3.7	8.2	4,444
Felicity Norman	Green	1,503	2.6	+0.6	2.0	1,102
Capt Edmund Carlise	Anti Fed	640	1.1			
Majority	**Con**	**16,680**	**28.8**	**+2.9**	**25.9**	**14,075**

Electorate: 70,873 **Voters:** 57,903 **Turnout:** 81.7 **Swing:** 1.4 to Con from LDm

LEWES

Tim Rathbone: Conservative. Born: 1933. Educated: Eton, Oxford. Jobs: advertising, public relations. First Elected: 1974. Posts: delegate, Council of Europe, Western European Union. Status: married, three children.

CON HOLD

		1992 election			1987 election	
		Votes	%	+/-	%	Votes
Tim Rathbone*	Con	33,042	54.6	-2.2	56.8	32,016
Norman Baker	Lib Dem	20,867	34.5	+1.9	32.6	18,396
Alison Chapman	Lab	5,758	9.5	+0.7	8.8	4,973
Anthony Beaumont	Green	719	1.2	-0.5	1.7	970
Norman Clinch	NLP	87	0.1			
Majority	**Con**	**12,175**	**20.1**	**-4.0**	**24.2**	**13,620**

Electorate: 73,918 **Voters:** 60,473 **Turnout:** 81.8 **Swing:** 2.0 to LDm from Con

LEWISHAM, DEPTFORD

Joan Ruddock: Labour. Born: 1943. Educated: Pontypool Grammar School, London University. Jobs: director, voluntary organisations. First Elected: 1987. Posts: Labour spokeswoman on prisons and criminal justice. Union: TGWU. Status: separated

LAB HOLD		1992 election			1987 election	
		Votes	%	+/-	%	Votes
Joan Ruddock*	Lab	22,574	60.9	+11.3	49.6	18,724
Teresa O'Neill	Con	10,336	27.9	-3.8	31.7	11,953
Johanna Brightwell	Lib Dem	4,181	11.3	-6.0	17.2	6,513
Majority	**Lab**	**12,238**	**33.0**	**+15.1**	**17.9**	**6,771**

Electorate: 57,014 **Voters:** 37,091 **Turnout:** 65.1 **Swing:** 7.5 to Lab from Con

LEWISHAM EAST

Bridget Prentice: Labour. Born: 1952. Educated: Our Lady School, Glasgow, Glasgow University. Jobs: teacher. First Elected: 1992. Status: married.

LAB GAIN		1992 election			1987 election	
		Votes	%	+/-	%	Votes
Bridget Prentice	Lab	19,576	45.4	+11.2	34.2	15,059
Colin Moynihan*	Con	18,481	42.8	-2.3	45.1	19,873
Julian Hawkins	Lib Dem	4,877	11.3	-9.4	20.7	9,118
Gilda Mansour	NLP	196	0.5			
Majority	**Lab**	**1,095**	**2.5**	**-8.4**	**10.9**	**4,814**

Electorate: 57,674 **Voters:** 43,130 **Turnout:** 74.8 **Swing:** 6.7 to Lab from Con

LEWISHAM WEST

Jim Dowd: Labour. Born: 1951. Educated: Sedgehill Comprehensive School, London. Jobs: telecom engineer. First Elected: 1992. Union: MSF.

LAB GAIN		1992 election			1987 election	
		Votes	%	+/-	%	Votes
Jim Dowd	Lab	20,378	47.0	+9.1	37.9	17,223
John Maples*	Con	18,569	42.8	-3.4	46.2	20,995
Eileen Neale	Lib Dem	4,295	9.9	-6.0	15.9	7,247
Paul Coulam	Anti Fed	125	0.3			
Majority	**Lab**	**1,809**	**4.2**	**-4.1**	**8.3**	**3,772**

Electorate: 59,317 **Voters:** 43,367 **Turnout:** 73.1 **Swing:** 6.2 to Lab from Con

LEYTON

Harry Cohen: Labour. Born: 1949. Educated: George Gascoyne Secondary School. First Elected: 1983. Status: married.

LAB HOLD		1992 election			1987 election	
		Votes	%	+/-	%	Votes
Harry Cohen*	Lab	20,334	52.7	+11.5	41.2	16,536
Christine Smith	Con	8,850	22.9	-6.2	29.1	11,692
Jonathan Fryer	Lib Dem	8,180	21.2	-8.5	29.6	11,895
Louis de Pinna	Lib	561	1.5			
Khalid Pervez	Green	412	1.1			
Richard Archer	NLP	256	0.7			
Majority	**Lab**	**11,484**	**29.8**	**+18.2**	**11.6**	**4,641**

Electorate: 57,271 **Voters:** 38,593 **Turnout:** 67.4 **Swing:** 8.8 to Lab from Con

LINCOLN

Kenneth Carlisle: Conservative. Born: 1941. Educated: Harrow, Oxford. Jobs: barrister. First Elected: 1979. Posts: Minister for Roads and Traffic. Status: married.

CON HOLD		1992 election			1987 election	
		Votes	%	+/-	%	Votes
Kenneth Carlisle*	Con	28,792	46.1	-0.4	46.5	27,097
Nick Butler	Lab	26,743	42.8	+9.2	33.7	19,614
David Harding-Price	Lib Dem	6,316	10.1	-9.3	19.4	11,319
Sue Wiggin	Lib	603	1.0			
Majority	**Con**	**2,049**	**3.3**	**-9.6**	**12.8**	**7,483**

Electorate: 78,905 **Voters:** 62,454 **Turnout:** 79.2 **Swing:** 4.8 to Lab from Con

LINDSEY EAST

Sir Peter Tapsell: Conservative. Born: 1930. Educated: Tonbridge School, Oxford. Jobs: political researcher. First Elected: 1959. Status: married.

CON HOLD		1992 election			1987 election	
		Votes	%	+/-	%	Votes
Sir Peter Tapsell*	Con	31,916	51.1	-1.1	52.2	29,048
Jim Dodsworth	Lib Dem	20,070	32.1	-4.6	36.7	20,432
David Shepherd	Lab	9,477	15.2	+4.0	11.1	6,206
Rosemary Robinson	Green	1,018	1.6			
Majority	**Con**	**11,846**	**19.0**	**+3.5**	**15.5**	**8,616**

Electorate: 80,026 **Voters:** 62,481 **Turnout:** 78.1 **Swing:** 1.7 to Con from LDm

LINLITHGOW

Tam Dalyell: Labour. Born: 1932. Educated: Eton, Cambridge. First Elected: 1962. Union: RMT. Status: married, two children.

LAB HOLD		1992 election			1987 election	
		Votes	%	+/-	%	Votes
Tam Dalyell*	Lab	21,603	45.0	-2.4	47.3	21,869
Kenny MacAskill	SNP	14,577	30.3	+5.4	24.9	11,496
Elizabeth Forbes	Con	8,424	17.5	+2.7	14.8	6,828
Mike Falchikov	Lib Dem	3,446	7.2	-5.5	12.6	5,840
Majority	**Lab**	**7,026**	**14.6**	**-7.8**	**22.5**	**10,373**

Electorate: 61,082 **Voters:** 48,050 **Turnout:** 78.7 **Swing:** 3.9 to SNP from Lab

LITTLEBOROUGH & SADDLEWORTH

Geoffrey Dickens: Conservative. Born: 1931. Educated: Byron Court School; Harrow & Acton Technical Colleges. Jobs: company director. First Elected: 1979. Status: married, two children.

CON HOLD		1992 election			1987 election	
		Votes	%	+/-	%	Votes
Geoffrey Dickens*	Con	23,682	44.2	+1.2	43.1	22,027
Chris Davies	Lib Dem	19,188	35.9	+4.9	30.9	15,825
Allen Brett	Lab	10,649	19.9	-6.1	26.0	13,299
Majority	**Con**	**4,494**	**8.4**	**-3.7**	**12.1**	**6,202**

Electorate: 65,576 **Voters:** 53,519 **Turnout:** 81.6 **Swing:** 1.9 to LDm from Con

LIVERPOOL, BROADGREEN

Jane Kennedy: Labour. Born: 1958. Educated: Haughton Comprehensive School, Liverpool University. Jobs: trade union official. First Elected: 1992. Union: NUPE. Status: married, two children.

LAB HOLD		1992 election			1987 election	
		Votes	%	+/-	%	Votes
Jane Kennedy	Lab	18,062	43.2	-5.4	48.6	23,262
Rosemary Cooper	Lib Dem	11,035	26.4	-9.6	35.9	17,215
Terry Fields*	Soc Lab	5,952	14.2			
Helen Roche	Con	5,405	12.9	-2.6	15.5	7,413
Steve Radford	Lib	1,211	2.9			
Ann Brennan	NLP	149	0.4			
Majority	**Lab**	**7,027**	**16.8**	**+4.2**	**12.6**	**6,047**

Electorate: 60,080 **Voters:** 41,814 **Turnout:** 69.6 **Swing:** 2.1 to Lab from LDm

LIVERPOOL, GARSTON

Eddie Loyden: Labour. Born: 1923. Educated: Friary School, Liverpool. First Elected: 1974. Union: TGWU. Status: married, three children.

LAB HOLD		1992 election			1987 election	
		Votes	%	+/-	%	Votes
Eddie Loyden*	Lab	23,212	57.1	+3.6	53.6	24,848
John Backhouse	Con	10,933	26.9	+3.0	23.9	11,071
Bill Roberts	Lib Dem	5,398	13.3	-9.1	22.4	10,370
Tony Conrad	Lib	894	2.2			
Peter Chandler	NLP	187	0.5			
Majority	**Lab**	**12,279**	**30.2**	**+0.5**	**29.7**	**13,777**

Electorate: 57,538 **Voters:** 40,624 **Turnout:** 70.6 **Swing:** 0.3 to Lab from Con

LIVERPOOL, MOSSLEY HILL

David Alton: Liberal Democrat. Born: 1951. Educated: Edmund Campion School, Hornchurch, Christ's College of Education, Liverpool. Jobs: teacher. First Elected: 1979. Status: married, one child.

LIB DEM HOLD		1992 election			1987 election	
		Votes	%	+/-	%	Votes
David Alton*	Lib Dem	19,809	47.9	+4.2	43.7	20,012
Neville Bann	Lab	17,203	41.6	+2.7	38.8	17,786
Stephen Syder	Con	4,269	10.3	-7.2	17.5	8,005
Byron Rigby	NLP	114	0.3			
Majority	**Lib Dem**	**2,606**	**6.3**	**+1.4**	**4.9**	**2,226**

Electorate: 60,409 **Voters:** 41,395 **Turnout:** 68.5 **Swing:** 0.7 to LDm from Lab

LIVERPOOL, RIVERSIDE

Bob Parry: Labour. Born: 1933. Educated: Bishop Goss RC School, Liverpool. Jobs: building worker, trade union official. First Elected: 1970. Posts: delegate, Council of Europe, Western European Union. Union: TGWU. Status: widower.

LAB HOLD		1992 election			1987 election	
		Votes	%	+/-	%	Votes
Bob Parry*	Lab	20,550	75.9	+2.7	73.2	25,505
Andrew Zsigmond	Con	3,113	11.5	-2.3	13.8	4,816
Mohammad Akbar Ali	Lib Dem	2,498	9.2	-2.0	11.2	3,912
Lawrence Brown	Green	738	2.7			
John Collins	NLP	169	0.6			
Majority	**Lab**	**17,437**	**64.4**	**+5.0**	**59.4**	**20,689**

Electorate: 49,595 **Voters:** 27,068 **Turnout:** 54.6 **Swing:** 2.5 to Lab from Con

LIVERPOOL, WALTON

Peter Kilfoyle: Labour. Born: 1946. Educated: St Edward's College, Liverpool, Durham University. Jobs: teacher, party organiser. First Elected: 1991. Union: TGWU, MSF. Status: married, five children.

LAB HOLD		1992 election			1987 election	
		Votes	%	+/-	%	Votes
Peter Kilfoyle*	Lab	34,214	72.4	+8.0	64.4	34,661
Berkeley Greenwood	Con	5,915	12.5	-1.9	14.4	7,738
Joseph Lang	Lib Dem	5,672	12.0	-9.2	21.2	11,408
Tom Newall	Lib	963	2.0			
David Carson	Prot Ref	393	0.8			
Dianne Raiano	NLP	98	0.2			
Majority	**Lab**	**28,299**	**59.9**	**+16.7**	**43.2**	**23,253**

Electorate: 70,102 **Voters:** 47,255 **Turnout:** 67.4 **Swing:** 4.9 to Lab from Con
BY-ELECTION July 1991: LAB HOLD. P. Kilfoyle (Lab) 21,317 (53.1%), P. Clark (LibDem) 14,457 (36.0%), L. Mahood (Real Lab) 2,613 (6.5%), Lab majority 6,860 (17.1%), swing 13.1% to LibDem from Lab

LIVERPOOL, WEST DERBY

Bob Wareing: Labour. Born: 1930. Educated: Alsop High School, Bolton College of Education. Jobs: lecturer. First Elected: 1983. Union: MSF. Posts: member, Foreign Affairs Select Committee. Status: widower

LAB HOLD		1992 election			1987 election	
		Votes	%	+/-	%	Votes
Bob Wareing*	Lab	27,014	68.2	+2.9	65.3	29,021
Stephen Fitzsimmons	Con	6,589	16.6	-2.5	19.2	8,525
Gillian Bundred	Lib Dem	4,838	12.2	-3.3	15.5	6,897
Derek Curtis	Lib	1,021	2.6			
Christopher Higgins	NLP	154	0.4			
Majority	**Lab**	**20,425**	**51.6**	**+5.4**	**46.1**	**20,496**

Electorate: 56,718 **Voters:** 39,616 **Turnout:** 69.8 **Swing:** 2.7 to Lab from Con

LIVINGSTON

Robin Cook: Labour. Born: 1946. Educated: Aberdeen Grammar School, Edinburgh University. Jobs: tutor organiser. First Elected: 1974. Posts: Shadow Trade and Industry Secretary. Union: RMT. Status: married, two children.

LAB HOLD		1992 election			1987 election	
		Votes	%	+/-	%	Votes
Robin Cook*	Lab	20,245	44.4	-1.2	45.6	19,110
Peter Johnston	SNP	12,140	26.6	+10.0	16.6	6,969
Hugh Gordon	Con	8,824	19.4	+0.6	18.7	7,860
Fred Mackintosh	Lib Dem	3,911	8.6	-10.5	19.1	8,005
Alpin Ross-Smith	Green	469	1.0			
Majority	**Lab**	**8,105**	**17.8**	**-8.7**	**26.5**	**11,105**

Electorate: 61,092 **Voters:** 45,589 **Turnout:** 74.6 **Swing:** 5.6 to SNP from Lab

LLANELLI

Denzil Davies: Labour. Born: 1938. Educated: Queen Elizabeth Grammar School, Carmarthen; Oxford. Jobs: barrister. First Elected: 1970. Union: MSF. Posts: member, Public Accounts Committee. Status: married, two children.

LAB HOLD		1992 election			1987 election	
		Votes	%	+/-	%	Votes
Denzil Davies*	Lab	27,802	54.9	-4.2	59.2	29,506
Graham Down	Con	8,532	16.9	-0.3	17.2	8,571
Marc Phillips	Plaid Cymru	7,878	15.6	+5.4	10.2	5,088
Keith Evans	Lib Dem	6,404	12.7	-0.8	13.5	6,714
Majority	**Lab**	**19,270**	**38.1**	**-3.9**	**42.0**	**20,935**

Electorate: 65,058 **Voters:** 50,616 **Turnout:** 77.8 **Swing:** 2.0 to Con from Lab

LONDONDERRY EAST

William Ross: United Ulster Unionist Party. Born: 1936. Educated: Dungiven Primary School. Jobs: farmer. First Elected: 1974. Posts: UUP Whip; member, Statutory Instruments Select Committee. Status: married, four children.

UUP HOLD		1992 election			1987 election	
		Votes	%	+/-	%	Votes
William Ross*	UUP	30,370	57.6	-2.9	60.5	29,532
Archie Doherty	SDLP	11,843	22.5	+3.3	19.2	9,375
Pauline Kennedy	Sinn Fein	5,320	10.1	-1.1	11.2	5,464
Paddy McGowan	All	3,613	6.9	+0.2	6.6	3,237
Alan Elder	Con	1,589	3.0			
Majority	**UUP**	**18,527**	**35.1**	**-6.2**	**41.3**	**20,157**

Electorate: 75,559 **Voters:** 52,735 **Turnout:** 69.8 **Swing:** 3.1 to SDLP from UUP

LOUGHBOROUGH

Stephen Dorrell: Conservative. Born: 1952. Educated: Uppingham School, Oxford. Jobs: company director. First Elected: 1979. Posts: Financial Secretary to the Treasury. Status: married, one child.

CON HOLD		1992 election			1987 election	
		Votes	%	+/-	%	Votes
Stephen Dorrell*	Con	30,064	50.7	-4.0	54.7	31,931
Andrew Reed	Lab	19,181	32.4	+7.9	24.5	14,283
Tony Stott	Lib Dem	8,953	15.1	-4.6	19.7	11,499
Ian Sinclair	Green	817	1.4	+0.3	1.1	656
Peter Reynolds	NLP	233	0.4			
Majority	**Con**	**10,883**	**18.4**	**-11.9**	**30.2**	**17,648**

Electorate: 75,450 **Voters:** 59,248 **Turnout:** 78.5 **Swing:** 5.9 to Lab from Con

LUDLOW

Christopher Gill: Conservative. Born: 1936. Educated: Shrewsbury School. Jobs: farmer, meat processor. First Elected: 1987. Posts: member, Agriculture Select Committee. Status: married, three children.

CON HOLD		1992 election			1987 election	
		Votes	%	+/-	%	Votes
Christopher Gill*	Con	28,719	51.5	-2.4	53.9	27,499
David Phillips	Lib Dem	14,567	26.1	-4.8	31.0	15,800
Beryl Mason	Lab	11,709	21.0	+5.9	15.1	7,724
Nick Appleton-Fox	Green	758	1.4			
Majority	**Con**	**14,152**	**25.4**	**+2.5**	**22.9**	**11,699**

Electorate: 68,935 **Voters:** 55,753 **Turnout:** 80.9 **Swing:** 1.2 to Con from LDm

LUTON NORTH

John Carlisle: Conservative. Born: 1942. Educated: Bedford College, St Lawrence College, Ramsgate. Jobs: commodities dealer. First Elected: 1979. Status: married, two children.

CON HOLD		1992 election			1987 election	
		Votes	%	+/-	%	Votes
John Carlisle*	Con	33,777	53.7	-0.2	53.8	30,997
Tony McWalter	Lab	20,683	32.9	+6.1	26.8	15,424
Jane Jackson	Lib Dem	7,570	12.0	-7.4	19.4	11,166
Roger Jones	Green	633	1.0			
Keith Buscombe	NLP	292	0.5			
Majority	**Con**	**13,094**	**20.8**	**-6.2**	**27.0**	**15,573**

Electorate: 76,857 **Voters:** 62,955 **Turnout:** 81.9 **Swing:** 3.1 to Lab from Con

LUTON SOUTH

Graham Bright: Conservative. Born: 1942. Educated: Hassenbrook Comprehensive School, Thurrock Technical College. Jobs: company director. First Elected: 1979. Posts: PPS to the Prime Minister. Status: married, one child.

CON HOLD		1992 election			1987 election	
		Votes	%	+/-	%	Votes
Graham Bright*	Con	25,900	44.8	-1.4	46.2	24,762
Bill McKenzie	Lab	25,101	43.5	+6.8	36.7	19,647
David Rogers	Lib Dem	6,020	10.4	-6.7	17.1	9,146
Lyn Bliss	Green	550	1.0			
David Cooke	NLP	191	0.3			
Majority	**Con**	**799**	**1.4**	**-8.2**	**9.6**	**5,115**

Electorate: 73,016 **Voters:** 57,762 **Turnout:** 79.1 **Swing:** 4.1 to Lab from Con

MACCLESFIELD

Nicholas Winterton: *Conservative. Born: 1938. Educated: Rugby. Jobs: sales executive. First Elected: 1971. Posts: member, chairmens' panel. Status: married, three children.*

CON HOLD		1992 election Votes	%	+/-	1987 election %	Votes
Nicholas Winterton*	Con	36,447	57.9	+1.5	56.4	33,208
Martina Longworth	Lab	13,680	21.7	+2.1	19.6	11,563
Paul Beatty	Lib Dem	12,600	20.0	-4.0	24.0	14,116
Cheryl Penn	NLP	268	0.4			
Majority	**Con**	**22,767**	**36.1**	**+3.7**	**32.4**	**19,092**

Electorate: 76,548 **Voters:** 62,995 **Turnout:** 82.3 **Swing:** 0.3 to Lab from Con

MAIDSTONE

Ann Widdecombe: *Conservative. Born: 1947. Educated: La Sainte Union Convent, Bath; Birmingham and Oxford Universities. Jobs: university administrator. First Elected: 1987. Posts: Social Security minister. Status: single.*

CON HOLD		1992 election Votes	%	+/-	1987 election %	Votes
Ann Widdecombe*	Con	31,611	54.2	+1.7	52.4	29,100
Paula Yates	Lib Dem	15,325	26.3	-7.5	33.8	18,736
Anne Logan	Lab	10,517	18.0	+5.5	12.5	6,935
Penny Kemp	Green	707	1.2	-0.1	1.3	717
Frederick Ingram	NLP	172	0.3			
Majority	**Con**	**16,286**	**27.9**	**+9.2**	**18.7**	**10,364**

Electorate: 72,834 **Voters:** 58,332 **Turnout:** 80.1 **Swing:** 4.6 to Con from LDm

MAKERFIELD

Ian McCartney: *Labour. Born: 1951. Educated: local state schools. Jobs: party organiser. First Elected: 1987. Posts: Labour spokesman on the NHS. Union: TGWU. Status: married, three children.*

LAB HOLD		1992 election Votes	%	+/-	1987 election %	Votes
Ian McCartney*	Lab	32,832	60.4	+4.1	56.3	30,190
Davina Dickson	Con	14,714	27.1	-0.2	27.3	14,632
Stephen Jeffers	Lib Dem	5,097	9.4	-7.1	16.5	8,838
Stella Cairns	Lib	1,309	2.4			
Christopher Davies	NLP	397	0.7			
Majority	**Lab**	**18,118**	**33.3**	**+4.3**	**29.0**	**15,558**

Electorate: 71,425 **Voters:** 54,349 **Turnout:** 76.1 **Swing:** 2.2 to Lab from Con

MANCHESTER, BLACKLEY

Ken Eastham: Labour. Born: 1927. Educated: Openshaw Technical College. First Elected: 1979. Posts: member, Employment Select Committee. Union: AEU. Status: married, one child.

LAB HOLD		1992 election			1987 election	
		Votes	%	+/-	%	Votes
Ken Eastham*	Lab	23,031	60.2	+7.7	52.4	22,476
William Hobhouse	Con	10,642	27.8	-1.0	28.8	12,354
Simon Wheale	Lib Dem	4,324	11.3	-7.5	18.8	8,041
Michael Kennedy	NLP	288	0.8			
Majority	**Lab**	**12,389**	**32.4**	**+8.7**	**23.6**	**10,122**

Electorate: 55,234 **Voters:** 38,285 **Turnout:** 69.3 **Swing:** 4.4 to Lab from Con

MANCHESTER CENTRAL

Bob Litherland: Labour. Born: 1930. Educated: North Manchester Grammar School. First Elected: 1979. Posts: delegate, Council of Europe, Western European Union. Status: married, two children.

LAB HOLD		1992 election			1987 election	
		Votes	%	+/-	%	Votes
Bob Litherland*	Lab	23,336	72.7	+4.5	68.2	27,428
Peter Davies	Con	5,299	16.5	-2.3	18.8	7,561
Mark Clayton	Lib Dem	3,151	9.8	-3.2	13.0	5,250
Andy Buchanan	CL	167	0.5			
Vivienne Mitchell	NLP	167	0.5			
Majority	**Lab**	**18,037**	**56.2**	**+6.8**	**49.4**	**19,867**

Electorate: 56,446 **Voters:** 32,120 **Turnout:** 56.9 **Swing:** 3.4 to Lab from Con

MANCHESTER, GORTON

Gerald Kaufman: Labour. Born: 1930. Educated: Leeds Grammar School, Oxford. Jobs: journalist. First Elected: 1970. Posts: chairman, National Heritage Select Committee. Union: GMB. Status: single

LAB HOLD		1992 election			1987 election	
		Votes	%	+/-	%	Votes
Gerald Kaufman*	Lab	23,671	62.3	+7.9	54.4	24,615
Jonathan Bullock	Con	7,392	19.5	-3.8	23.3	10,550
Phil Harris	Lib Dem	5,327	14.0	-7.7	21.7	9,830
Terry Henderson	Lib	767	2.0			
Mick Daw	Green	595	1.6			
Pam Lawrence	Rev Comm	108	0.3			
Philip Mitchell	NLP	84	0.2			
Colleen Smith	Int Comm	30	0.1			
Majority	**Lab**	**16,279**	**42.9**	**+11.8**	**31.1**	**14,065**

Electorate: 62,410 **Voters:** 37,974 **Turnout:** 60.8 **Swing:** 5.9 to Lab from Con

MANCHESTER, WITHINGTON

Keith Bradley: Labour. Born: 1950. Educated: Bishop Vesey's Grammar School, Manchester Polytechnic. Jobs: health administrator. First Elected: 1987. Posts: Labour spokesman on social security. Union: MSF. Status: married, two children.

LAB HOLD		1992 election			1987 election	
		Votes	%	+/-	%	Votes
Keith Bradley*	Lab	23,962	52.7	+9.7	42.9	21,650
Eric Farthing	Con	14,227	31.3	-5.0	36.2	18,259
Gordon Hennell	Lib Dem	6,457	14.2	-5.6	19.8	9,978
Brian Candeland	Green	725	1.6	+0.6	1.0	524
Clive Menhinick	NLP	128	0.3			
Majority	**Lab**	**9,735**	**21.4**	**+14.7**	**6.7**	**3,391**

Electorate: 63,838 **Voters:** 45,499 **Turnout:** 71.3 **Swing:** 7.3 to Lab from Con

MANCHESTER, WYTHENSHAWE

Alf Morris: Labour. Born: 1928. Educated: Ruskin and St. Catherine's Colleges, Oxford. Jobs: teacher. First Elected: 1964. Union: GMB. Status: married, four children.

LAB HOLD		1992 election			1987 election	
		Votes	%	+/-	%	Votes
Alf Morris*	Lab	22,591	60.5	+3.7	56.8	23,881
Kevin McKenna	Con	10,595	28.4	-0.2	28.6	12,026
Stephen Fenn	Lib Dem	3,633	9.7	-4.3	14.1	5,921
Guy Otten	Green	362	1.0			
Elspeth Martin	NLP	133	0.4			
Majority	**Lab**	**11,996**	**32.1**	**+4.0**	**28.2**	**11,855**

Electorate: 53,548 **Voters:** 37,314 **Turnout:** 69.7 **Swing:** 2.0 to Lab from Con

MANSFIELD

Alan Meale: Labour. Born: 1949. Educated: Ruskin College, Oxford. Jobs: trade union official, political adviser. First Elected: 1987. Union: MSF. Status: married, two children.

LAB HOLD		1992 election			1987 election	
		Votes	%	+/-	%	Votes
Alan Meale*	Lab	29,932	54.4	+16.9	37.5	19,610
Gary Mond	Con	18,208	33.1	-4.3	37.4	19,554
Stuart Thompstone	Lib Dem	6,925	12.6	-9.6	22.2	11,604
Majority	**Lab**	**11,724**	**21.3**	**+21.2**	**0.1**	**56**

Electorate: 66,964 **Voters:** 55,065 **Turnout:** 82.2 **Swing:** 10.6 to Lab from Con

MEDWAY

Dame Peggy Fenner: *Conservative. Born: 1922. Educated: LCC School, Brockley. First Elected: 1970. Posts: delegate, Council of Europe, Western European Union. Status: married, one child.*

CON HOLD		1992 election Votes	%	+/-	1987 election %	Votes
Dame Peggy Fenner*	Con	25,924	52.3	+1.3	51.0	23,889
Robert Marshall-Andrews	Lab	17,138	34.6	+4.8	29.8	13,960
Cyril Trice	Lib Dem	4,751	9.6	-8.5	18.1	8,450
Mark Austin	Lib	1,480	3.0			
Paul Kember	NLP	234	0.5			
Majority	**Con**	**8,786**	**17.7**	**-3.5**	**21.2**	**9,929**

Electorate: 61,736 **Voters:** 49,527 **Turnout:** 80.2 **Swing:** 1.7 to Lab from Con

MEIRIONNYDD NANT CONWY

Elfyn Llwyd: *Plaid Cymru. Born: 1951. Educated: Llanrwst Grammar School, University College, Aberystwyth. Jobs: solicitor. First Elected: 1992. Posts: member, Welsh Affairs Select Committee. Status: married, two children.*

PLAID CYMRU HOLD		1992 election Votes	%	+/-	1987 election %	Votes
Elfyn Llwyd	Plaid Cymru	11,608	44.0	+3.9	40.0	10,392
Gwyn Lewis	Con	6,995	26.5	-1.9	28.4	7,366
Rhys Williams	Lab	4,978	18.8	+1.9	16.9	4,397
Ruth Parry	Lib Dem	2,358	8.9	-5.8	14.7	3,814
Bill Pritchard	Green	471	1.8			
Majority	**Plaid Cymru**	**4,613**	**17.5**	**+5.8**	**11.7**	**3,026**

Electorate: 32,413 **Voters:** 26,410 **Turnout:** 81.5 **Swing:** 2.9 to PC from Con

MERIDEN

Iain Mills: *Conservative. Born: 1940. Educated: Rhodesia, University of Capetown. Jobs: company director. First Elected: 1979. Posts: member, Employment Select Committee. Status: married.*

CON HOLD		1992 election Votes	%	+/-	1987 election %	Votes
Iain Mills*	Con	33,462	55.1	+0.0	55.1	31,935
Nick Stephens	Lab	18,763	30.9	+4.8	26.1	15,115
Judy Morris	Lib Dem	8,489	14.0	-4.8	18.8	10,896
Majority	**Con**	**14,699**	**24.2**	**-4.8**	**29.0**	**16,820**

Electorate: 76,994 **Voters:** 60,714 **Turnout:** 78.9 **Swing:** 2.4 to Lab from Con

MERTHYR TYDFIL & RHYMNEY

Ted Rowlands: Labour. Born: 1940. Educated: Rhondda Grammar School, London University. Jobs: lecturer. First Elected: 1966. Posts: member, Foreign Affairs Select Committee. Union: MSF. Status: married, three children.

LAB HOLD

		1992 election Votes	%	+/-	1987 election %	Votes
Ted Rowlands*	Lab	31,710	71.6	-3.8	75.4	33,477
Robyn Rowland	Lib Dem	4,997	11.3	+3.2	8.0	3,573
Mark Hughes	Con	4,904	11.1	-0.8	11.9	5,270
Alun Cox	Plaid Cymru	2,704	6.1	+1.4	4.7	2,085
Majority	**Lab**	**26,713**	**60.3**	**-3.2**	**63.5**	**28,207**

Electorate: 58,430 **Voters:** 44,315 **Turnout:** 75.8 **Swing:** 3.5 to LDm from Lab

MIDDLESBROUGH

Stuart Bell: Labour. Born: 1938. Educated: Hookergate Grammar School, Durham. Jobs: colliery clerk, journalist, barrister. First Elected: 1983. Posts: Labour spokesman on trade and industry. Union: GMB. Status: married, three children.

LAB HOLD

		1992 election Votes	%	+/-	1987 election %	Votes
Stuart Bell*	Lab	26,343	64.1	+4.4	59.7	25,747
Paul Rayner	Con	10,559	25.7	+0.7	25.0	10,789
Rosamund Jordan	Lib Dem	4,201	10.2	-5.1	15.3	6,594
Majority	**Lab**	**15,784**	**38.4**	**+3.7**	**34.7**	**14,958**

Electorate: 58,844 **Voters:** 41,103 **Turnout:** 69.9 **Swing:** 1.9 to Lab from Con

MIDLOTHIAN

Eric Clarke: Labour. Born: 1933. Educated: local state schools. Jobs: miner, trade union official. First elected: 1992. Union: NUM. Posts: member, Scottish Affairs Select Committee. Status: married, three children.

LAB HOLD

		1992 election Votes	%	+/-	1987 election %	Votes
Eric Clarke	Lab	20,588	43.9	-4.4	48.3	22,553
Andrew Lumsden	SNP	10,254	21.9	+11.3	10.6	4,947
Jeff Stoddart	Con	9,443	20.1	+1.9	18.2	8,527
Paul Sewell	Lib Dem	6,164	13.1	-8.9	22.0	10,300
Iain Morrice	Green	476	1.0	+0.1	0.9	412
Majority	**Lab**	**10,334**	**22.0**	**-4.2**	**26.2**	**12,253**

Electorate: 60,255 **Voters:** 46,925 **Turnout:** 77.9 **Swing:** 7.8 to SNP from Lab

MILTON KEYNES NORTH EAST

Peter Butler: *Conservative. Born: 1951. Educated: Adams Grammar School, Newport, Shropshire; Oxford. Jobs: teacher, solicitor. First Elected: 1992. Posts: member, Home Affairs Select Committee. Status: married, three children.*

CON GAIN		1992 election Votes	%	+/-	1987 election %	Votes
Peter Butler	Con	26,212	51.6			
Maggie Cosin	Lab	12,036	23.7			
Peter Gaskell	Lib Dem	11,693	23.0			
Alan Francis	Green	529	1.0			
Margaret Kavanagh-Dowsett	Ind C	249	0.5			
Martin Simson	NLP	79	0.2			
Majority	**Con**	**14,176**	**27.9**			

Electorate: 62,748 **Voters:** 50,798 **Turnout:** 81.0

MILTON KEYNES SOUTH WEST

Barry Legg: *Conservative. Born: 1949. Educated: Sir Thomas Rich's Grammar School, Gloucester; Manchester University. Jobs: tax accountant. First Elected: 1992. Posts: member, Treasury Select Committee. Status: married, three children.*

CON GAIN		1992 election Votes	%	+/-	1987 election %	Votes
Barry Legg	Con	23,840	46.6			
Kevin Wilson	Lab	19,153	37.4			
Chris Pym	Lib Dem	7,429	14.5			
Caroline Field	Green	525	1.0			
Hugh Kelly	NLP	202	0.4			
Majority	**Con**	**4,687**	**9.2**			

Electorate: 66,422 **Voters:** 51,149 **Turnout:** 77.0

MITCHAM & MORDEN

Angela Rumbold: *Conservative. Born: 1932. Educated: Notting Hill & Ealing High School; Perse School for Girls, Cambridge; London University. Jobs: company director. First Elected: 1982. Posts: deputy chairman, Conservative Party. Status: married, three children.*

CON HOLD		1992 election Votes	%	+/-	1987 election %	Votes
Angela Rumbold*	Con	23,789	46.5	-1.7	48.2	23,002
Siobhain McDonagh	Lab	22,055	43.1	+7.9	35.2	16,819
John Field	Lib Dem	4,687	9.2	-7.5	16.6	7,930
Tom Walsh	Green	655	1.3			
Majority	**Con**	**1,734**	**3.4**	**-9.6**	**12.9**	**6,183**

Electorate: 63,723 **Voters:** 51,186 **Turnout:** 80.3 **Swing:** 4.8 to Lab from Con

MOLE VALLEY

Kenneth Baker: Conservative. Born: 1934. Educated: St Paul's School; Oxford. First Elected: 1968. Status: married, three children.

CON HOLD		1992 election		+/-	1987 election	
		Votes	%		%	Votes
Kenneth Baker*	Con	32,549	59.3	-1.5	60.8	31,689
Mike Watson	Lib Dem	16,599	30.2	+0.3	29.9	15,613
Tim Walsh	Lab	5,291	9.6	+0.3	9.3	4,846
Judith Thomas	NLP	442	0.8			
Majority	**Con**	**15,950**	**29.1**	**-1.8**	**30.8**	**16,076**

Electorate: 66,949 **Voters:** 54,881 **Turnout:** 82.0 **Swing:** 0.9 to LDm from Con

MONKLANDS EAST

John Smith: Labour. Born: 1938. Educated: Dunoon Grammar School, Glasgow University. Jobs: barrister. First Elected: 1970. Posts: Leader of the Opposition. Union: GMB. Status: married, three children.

LAB HOLD		1992 election		+/-	1987 election	
		Votes	%		%	Votes
John Smith*	Lab	22,266	61.3	+0.3	61.0	22,649
Jim Wright	SNP	6,554	18.0	+5.1	12.9	4,790
Stewart Walters	Con	5,830	16.0	-0.8	16.9	6,260
Philip Ross	Lib Dem	1,679	4.6	-4.6	9.3	3,442
Majority	**Lab**	**15,712**	**43.2**	**-0.9**	**44.1**	**16,389**

Electorate: 48,391 **Voters:** 36,329 **Turnout:** 75.1 **Swing:** 2.4 to SNP from Lab

MONKLANDS WEST

Tom Clarke: Labour. Born: 1941. Educated: Columba High School, Coatbridge. Jobs: administrator. First Elected: 1982. Posts: Shadow Scottish Secretary. Union: GMB.

LAB HOLD		1992 election		+/-	1987 election	
		Votes	%		%	Votes
Tom Clarke*	Lab	23,384	61.3	-1.0	62.3	24,499
Keith Bovey	SNP	6,319	16.6	+5.7	10.8	4,260
Andrew Lownie	Con	6,074	15.9	+0.2	15.7	6,166
Shiona Hamilton	Lib Dem	2,382	6.2	-5.0	11.2	4,408
Majority	**Lab**	**17,065**	**44.7**	**-1.9**	**46.6**	**18,333**

Electorate: 49,269 **Voters:** 38,159 **Turnout:** 77.5 **Swing:** 3.4 to SNP from Lab

MONMOUTH

Roger Evans: *Conservative. Born: 1947. Educated: West Hartlepool Grammar School; City of Norwich School; Bristol Grammar School; Cambridge. Jobs: barrister. First Elected: 1992. Posts: member, Welsh Affairs Select Committee. Status: married, two children.*

CON REGAIN		1992 election			1987 election	
		Votes	%	+/-	%	Votes
Roger Evans	Con	24,059	47.3	-0.3	47.5	22,387
Huw Edwards*	Lab	20,855	41.0	+13.3	27.7	13,037
Frances David	Lib Dem	5,562	10.9	-13.1	24.0	11,313
Mel Witherden	Green/PC	431	0.8	†		
Majority	**Con**	**3,204**	**6.3**	**-13.6**	**19.9**	**9,350**

Electorate: 59,147 **Voters:** 50,907 **Turnout:** 86.1 **Swing:** 6.8 to Lab from Con
† *Plaid Cymru candidate polled 363 (0.8%) in 1987*
BY-ELECTION May 1991: LAB GAIN. H. Edwards (Lab) 17,733 (39.3%), R. Evans (Con) 15,327 (34.0%), F. David (LibDem) 11,164 (24.8%), Lab majority 2,406 (5.3%), swing 12.6% to Lab from Con

MONTGOMERY

Alex Carlile: *Liberal Democrat. Born: 1948. Educated: Epsom College, London University. Jobs: barrister. First Elected: 1983. Posts: member, Welsh Affairs Select Committee; LibDem spokesman on Welsh Affairs. Status: married, three children.*

LIB DEM HOLD		1992 election			1987 election	
		Votes	%	+/-	%	Votes
Alex Carlile*	Lib Dem	16,031	48.5	+1.9	46.6	14,729
Jeannie France-Hayhurst	Con	10,822	32.7	-5.8	38.5	12,171
Steve Wood	Lab	4,115	12.4	+2.0	10.5	3,304
Hugh Parsons	Plaid Cymru	1,581	4.8	+0.3	4.5	1,412
Patrick Adams	Green	508	1.5			
Majority	**Lib Dem**	**5,209**	**15.8**	**+7.7**	**8.1**	**2,558**

Electorate: 41,386 **Voters:** 33,057 **Turnout:** 79.9 **Swing:** 3.8 to LDm from Con

MORAY

Margaret Ewing: *Scottish National Party. Born: 1945. Educated: Biggar High School, Glasgow University. Jobs: teacher. First Elected: 1974. Posts: SNP parliamentary leader; member, Electoral Legislation Select Committee. Status: married.*

SNP HOLD		1992 election			1987 election	
		Votes	%	+/-	%	Votes
Margaret Ewing*	SNP	20,299	44.3	+1.1	43.2	19,510
Roma Hossack	Con	17,455	38.1	+3.1	35.0	15,825
Conal Smith	Lab	5,448	11.9	+0.6	11.3	5,118
Brinsley Sheridan	Lib Dem	2,634	5.7	-4.7	10.5	4,724
Majority	**SNP**	**2,844**	**6.2**	**-2.0**	**8.2**	**3,685**

Electorate: 63,255 **Voters:** 45,836 **Turnout:** 72.5 **Swing:** 1.0 to Con from SNP

MORECAMBE & LUNESDALE

Mark Lennox-Boyd: *Conservative. Born: 1943. Educated: Eton, Oxford. Jobs: barrister. First Elected: 1979. Posts: Foreign Office minister. Status: married, one child.*

CON HOLD		1992 election			1987 election	
		Votes	%	+/-	%	Votes
Mark Lennox-Boyd*	Con	22,507	50.9	-1.7	52.7	22,327
Jean Yates	Lab	10,998	24.9	+2.4	22.5	9,535
Tony Saville	Lib Dem	9,584	21.7	-3.2	24.9	10,542
Mark Turner	MBI	916	2.1			
Richard Marriott	NLP	205	0.5			
Majority	**Con**	**11,509**	**26.0**	**-1.8**	**27.8**	**11,785**

Electorate: 56,426 **Voters:** 44,210 **Turnout:** 78.4 **Swing:** 2.1 to Lab from Con

MOTHERWELL NORTH

Dr John Reid: *Labour. Born: 1947. Educated: Coatbridge, Stirling University. Jobs: political researcher. First Elected: 1987. Union: TGWU. Posts: Labour spokesman on defence and disarmament.. Status: married, two children.*

LAB HOLD		1992 election			1987 election	
		Votes	%	+/-	%	Votes
John Reid*	Lab	27,852	63.4	-3.6	66.9	29,825
David Clark	SNP	8,942	20.3	+6.4	14.0	6,230
Robert Hargrave	Con	5,011	11.4	+0.3	11.1	4,939
Harriet Smith	Lib Dem	2,145	4.9	-3.1	8.0	3,558
Majority	**Lab**	**18,910**	**43.0**	**-9.9**	**53.0**	**23,595**

Electorate: 57,290 **Voters:** 43,950 **Turnout:** 76.7 **Swing:** 5.0 to SNP from Lab

MOTHERWELL SOUTH

Dr Jeremy Bray: *Labour. Born: 1930. Educated: Aberystwyth Grammar School, Cambridge. Jobs: technical officer, personnel director. First Elected: 1962. Posts: member, Science and Technology Select Committee. Union: TGWU. Status: married, four children.*

LAB HOLD		1992 election			1987 election	
		Votes	%	+/-	%	Votes
Jeremy Bray*	Lab	21,771	57.1	-1.2	58.3	22,957
Kay Ullrich	SNP	7,758	20.4	+5.0	15.3	6,027
Gordon McIntosh	Con	6,097	16.0	+1.5	14.5	5,704
Alex Mackie	Lib Dem	2,349	6.2	-5.2	11.3	4,463
David Lettice	YSOR	146	0.4			
Majority	**Lab**	**14,013**	**36.8**	**-6.2**	**43.0**	**16,930**

Electorate: 50,042 **Voters:** 38,121 **Turnout:** 76.2 **Swing:** 3.1 to SNP from Lab

NEATH

Peter Hain: Labour. Born: 1950. Educated: Emanuel School,.Wandsworth; Sussex and London Universities. Jobs: trade union researcher. First Elected: 1991. Union: GMB. Status: married, two children.

LAB HOLD		1992 election			1987 election	
		Votes	%	+/-	%	Votes
Peter Hain*	Lab	30,903	68.0	+4.6	63.4	27,612
David Adams	Con	6,928	15.2	-0.9	16.1	7,034
Dewi Evans	Plaid Cymru	5,145	11.3	+4.9	6.4	2,792
Michael Phillips	Lib Dem	2,467	5.4	-8.6	14.1	6,132
Majority	**Lab**	**23,975**	**52.8**	**+5.5**	**47.2**	**20,578**

Electorate: 56,392 **Voters:** 45,443 **Turnout:** 80.6 **Swing:** 2.8 to Lab from Con

BY-ELECTION April 1991: LAB HOLD. P. Hain (Lab) 17,962 (51.8%), D. Evans (Plaid Cymru) 8,132 (23.4%), R. Evans (Con) 2,995 (8.6%), Lab majority 9,830 (28.4%), SWING 14.3% to Plaid Cymru from Lab

NEWARK

Richard Alexander: Conservative. Born: 1934. Educated: Eastbourne Grammar School, London University. Jobs: solicitor. First Elected: 1979. Posts: member, Agriculture Select Committee. Status: married, two children.

CON HOLD		1992 election			1987 election	
		Votes	%	+/-	%	Votes
Richard Alexander*	Con	28,494	50.4	-3.1	53.5	28,070
Dave Barton	Lab	20,265	35.8	+8.1	27.7	14,527
Peter Harris	Lib Dem	7,342	13.0	-5.8	18.8	9,833
Patricia Wood	Green	435	0.8			
Majority	**Con**	**8,229**	**14.6**	**-11.3**	**25.8**	**13,543**

Electorate: 68,801 **Voters:** 56,536 **Turnout:** 82.2 **Swing:** 5.6 to Lab from Con

NEWBURY

Judith Chaplin: Conservative. Born: 1939. Educated: Wycombe Abbey School, Cambridge. Jobs: farmer, school proprietor, political adviser. First Elected: 1992. Posts: member, Treasury Select Committee. Status: married, four children.

CON HOLD		1992 election			1987 election	
		Votes	%	+/-	%	Votes
Judith Chaplin	Con	37,135	55.9	-4.2	60.1	35,266
David Rendel	Lib Dem	24,778	37.3	+5.6	31.7	18,608
Richard Hall	Lab	3,962	6.0	-2.2	8.1	4,765
Jim Wallis	Green	539	0.8			
Majority	**Con**	**12,357**	**18.6**	**-9.8**	**28.4**	**16,658**

Electorate: 80,252 **Voters:** 66,414 **Turnout:** 82.8 **Swing:** 4.9 to LDm from Con

NEWCASTLE-UNDER-LYME

Llin Golding: *Labour. Born: 1933. Educated: Caerphilly Girls' Grammar School. Jobs: radiographer. First Elected: 1986. Posts: Labour spokeswoman on social security. Union: NUPE. Status: married, three children.*

LAB HOLD		1992 election			1987 election	
		Votes	%	+/-	%	Votes
Llin Golding*	Lab	25,652	47.9	+7.4	40.5	21,618
Andrew Brierley	Con	15,813	29.6	+1.7	27.9	14,863
Alan Thomas	Lib Dem	11,727	21.9	-9.0	30.9	16,486
Richard Lines	NLP	314	0.6			
Majority	**Lab**	**9,839**	**18.4**	**+8.8**	**9.6**	**5,132**

Electorate: 66,595 **Voters:** 53,506 **Turnout:** 80.3 **Swing:** 2.9 to Lab from Con

NEWCASTLE UPON TYNE C

Jim Cousins: *Labour. Born: 1944. Educated: Oxford. Jobs: lecturer. First Elected: 1987. Posts: Labour spokesman on trade and industry; member, Trade and Industry Select Committee. Union: MSF. Status: married, four children.*

LAB HOLD		1992 election			1987 election	
		Votes	%	+/-	%	Votes
Jim Cousins*	Lab	21,123	49.4	+5.2	44.2	20,416
Michael Summersby	Con	15,835	37.0	-1.8	38.8	17,933
Lembit Opik	Lib Dem	5,816	13.6	-2.2	15.8	7,304
Majority	**Lab**	**5,288**	**12.4**	**+7.0**	**5.4**	**2,483**

Electorate: 59,973 **Voters:** 42,774 **Turnout:** 71.3 **Swing:** 3.5 to Lab from Con

NEWCASTLE UPON TYNE E

Nick Brown: *Labour. Born: 1950. Educated: Secondary Modern School, Tunbridge Wells Technical High School, Manchester University. Jobs: industry, trade union official. First Elected: 1983. Posts: Deputy Shadow Leader of the Commons; Shadow Paymaster General. Union: GMB.*

LAB HOLD		1992 election			1987 election	
		Votes	%	+/-	%	Votes
Nick Brown*	Lab	24,342	60.2	+3.8	56.4	23,677
Jeremy Lucas	Con	10,465	25.9	-0.8	26.6	11,177
Alan Thompson	Lib Dem	4,883	12.1	-4.0	16.0	6,728
Gareth Edwards	Green	744	1.8			
Majority	**Lab**	**13,877**	**34.3**	**+4.5**	**29.8**	**12,500**

Electorate: 57,165 **Voters:** 40,434 **Turnout:** 70.7 **Swing:** 2.3 to Lab from Con

NEWCASTLE UPON TYNE NORTH

Douglas Henderson: Labour. Born: 1949. Educated: Waid Academy, Fife; Strathclyde University. Jobs: trade union official. First Elected: 1987. Posts: Labour spokesman on local government. Union: GMB. Status: married, one child.

LAB HOLD		1992 election Votes	%	+/-	1987 election %	Votes
Douglas Henderson*	Lab	25,121	49.4	+6.7	42.7	22,424
Ian Gordon	Con	16,175	31.8	+7.2	24.6	12,915
Peter Maughan	Lib Dem	9,542	18.8	-13.9	32.7	17,181
Majority	**Lab**	**8,946**	**17.6**	**+7.6**	**10.0**	**5,243**

Electorate: 66,187 **Voters:** 50,838 **Turnout:** 76.8 **Swing:** 0.3 to Con from Lab

NEW FOREST

Sir Patrick McNair-Wilson: Conservative. Born: 1929. Educated: Eton. Jobs: army officer. First Elected: 1964. Status: married, five children.

CON HOLD		1992 election Votes	%	+/-	1987 election %	Votes
Sir Patrick McNair-Wilson*	Con	37,986	62.4	-2.3	64.7	37,188
Jean Vernon-Jackson	Lib Dem	17,581	28.9	+2.0	26.9	15,456
Michael Shutler	Lab	4,989	8.2	-0.3	8.4	4,856
Felicity Carter	NLP	350	0.6			
Majority	**Con**	**20,405**	**33.5**	**-4.3**	**37.8**	**21,732**

Electorate: 75,413 **Voters:** 60,906 **Turnout:** 80.8 **Swing:** 2.1 to LDm from Con

NEWHAM NORTH EAST

Ron Leighton: Labour. Born: 1930. Educated: Ruskin College, Oxford. First Elected: 1979. Posts: chairman, Employment Select Committee. Status: married, three children.

LAB HOLD		1992 election Votes	%	+/-	1987 election %	Votes
Ron Leighton*	Lab	20,952	58.3	+6.4	51.9	20,220
Jeremy Galbraith	Con	10,966	30.5	-0.2	30.7	11,984
Jonathan Aves	Lib Dem	4,020	11.2	-6.2	17.4	6,772
Majority	**Lab**	**9,986**	**27.8**	**+6.7**	**21.1**	**8,236**

Electorate: 59,555 **Voters:** 35,938 **Turnout:** 60.3 **Swing:** 3.3 to Lab from Con

NEWHAM NORTH WEST

Tony Banks: Labour. Born: 1943. Educated: local state schools, York University. Jobs: trade union researcher. First Elected: 1983. Posts: Labour spokesman on transport and London affairs; delegate, Council of Europe, Western European Union. Union: TGWU. Status: married.

LAB HOLD

		1992 election Votes	%	+/-	1987 election %	Votes
Tony Banks*	Lab	15,911	61.1	+5.7	55.4	15,677
Mark Prisk	Con	6,740	25.9	+0.5	25.4	7,181
Andrew Sawdon	Lib Dem	2,445	9.4	-8.0	17.4	4,920
Amanda Standford	Green	587	2.3	+0.5	1.8	497
Toby Jug	Loony G	252	1.0			
David O'Sullivan	Int Comm	100	0.4			
Majority	**Lab**	**9,171**	**35.2**	**+5.2**	**30.0**	**8,496**

Electorate: 46,471 **Voters:** 26,035 **Turnout:** 56.0 **Swing:** 2.6 to Lab from Con

NEWHAM SOUTH

Nigel Spearing: Labour. Born: 1930. Educated: Latymer Upper School; Cambridge. Jobs: teacher. First Elected: 1970. Posts: member, Select Committee on European Legislation. Status: married, three children.

LAB HOLD

		1992 election Votes	%	+/-	1987 election %	Votes
Nigel Spearing*	Lab	14,358	46.6	+3.1	43.5	12,935
Jacqueline Foster	Con	11,856	38.5	+4.3	34.2	10,169
Alec Kellaway	Lib Dem	4,572	14.9	-7.4	22.2	6,607
Majority	**Lab**	**2,502**	**8.1**	**-1.2**	**9.3**	**2,766**

Electorate: 51,143 **Voters:** 30,786 **Turnout:** 60.2 **Swing:** 0.6 to Con from Lab

NEWPORT EAST

Roy Hughes: Labour. Born: 1925. Educated: Pontllanfraith Grammar School; Ruskin College Oxford. First Elected: 1966. Union: TGWU. Posts: member, chairmen's panel. Status: married, three children.

LAB HOLD

		1992 election Votes	%	+/-	1987 election %	Votes
Roy Hughes*	Lab	23,050	55.0	+5.9	49.1	20,518
Angela Emmett	Con	13,151	31.4	-0.8	32.2	13,454
William Oliver	Lib Dem	4,991	11.9	-5.7	17.7	7,383
Stephen Ainley	Green/PC	716	1.7	†		
Majority	**Lab**	**9,899**	**23.6**	**+6.7**	**16.9**	**7,064**

Electorate: 51,603 **Voters:** 41,908 **Turnout:** 81.2 **Swing:** 3.4 to Lab from Con

† Plaid Cymru candidate polled 458 (1.1%) in 1987

NEWPORT WEST

Paul Flynn*: Labour. Born: 1935. Educated: University College, Cardiff. Jobs: chemist, broadcaster. First Elected: 1987. Status: married, three children.*

LAB HOLD		1992 election			1987 election	
		Votes	%	+/-	%	Votes
Paul Flynn*	Lab	24,139	53.1	+7.1	46.1	20,887
Andrew Taylor	Con	16,360	36.0	-4.1	40.1	18,179
Andrew Toye	Lib Dem	4,296	9.5	-3.6	13.0	5,903
Peter Keelan	Plaid Cymru	653	1.4	+0.6	0.8	377
Majority	**Lab**	**7,779**	**17.1**	**+11.1**	**6.0**	**2,708**

Electorate: 54,871 **Voters:** 45,448 **Turnout:** 82.8 **Swing:** 5.6 to Lab from Con

NEWRY & ARMAGH

Seamus Mallon*: Social Democratic and Labour Party. Born: 1936. Educated: Abbey Grammar School, Armagh. Jobs: head teacher. First Elected: 1986. Posts: deputy leader SDLP. Status: married, one child.*

SDLP HOLD		1992 election			1987 election	
		Votes	%	+/-	%	Votes
Seamus Mallon*	SDLP	26,073	49.6	+1.5	48.1	25,137
Jim Speers	UUP	18,982	36.1	-1.8	37.9	19,812
Brendan Curran	Sinn Fein	6,547	12.5	+0.6	11.8	6,173
Eileen Bell	All	972	1.8	+0.6	1.3	664
Majority	**SDLP**	**7,091**	**13.5**	**+3.3**	**10.2**	**5,325**

Electorate: 67,508 **Voters:** 52,574 **Turnout:** 77.9 **Swing:** 1.6 to SDLP from UUP

NORFOLK MID

Richard Ryder*: Conservative. Born: 1949. Educated: Radley; Cambridge. Jobs: political adviser. First Elected: 1983. Posts: Government Chief Whip. Status: married, one child.*

CON HOLD		1992 election			1987 election	
		Votes	%	+/-	%	Votes
Richard Ryder*	Con	35,620	54.3	-2.4	56.7	32,758
Michael Castle	Lab	16,672	25.4	+7.6	17.8	10,272
John Gleed	Lib Dem	13,072	19.9	-5.6	25.5	14,750
Corrie Waite	NLP	226	0.3			
Majority	**Con**	**18,948**	**28.9**	**-2.3**	**31.2**	**18,008**

Electorate: 80,336 **Voters:** 65,590 **Turnout:** 81.6 **Swing:** 5.0 to Lab from Con

NORFOLK NORTH

Ralph Howell: Conservative. Born: 1923. Educated: Diss Grammar School. Jobs: farmer. First Elected: 1970. Posts: executive member, 1922 Committee. Status: married, three children.

CON HOLD		1992 election Votes	%	+/-	1987 election %	Votes
Ralph Howell*	Con	28,810	48.3	-5.0	53.3	28,822
Norman Lamb	Lib Dem	16,265	27.3	+2.3	25.0	13,512
Michael Cullingham	Lab	13,850	23.2	+3.3	19.9	10,765
Angie Zelter	Green	559	0.9	-0.8	1.8	960
Susan Jackson	NLP	167	0.3			
Majority	**Con**	**12,545**	**21.0**	**-7.3**	**28.3**	**15,310**

Electorate: 73,780 **Voters:** 59,651 **Turnout:** 80.8 **Swing:** 3.6 to LDm from Con

NORFOLK NORTH WEST

Henry Bellingham: Conservative. Born: 1955. Educated: Eton; Cambridge. Jobs: barrister. First Elected: 1983. Posts: PPS. Status: single.

CON HOLD		1992 election Votes	%	+/-	1987 election %	Votes
Henry Bellingham*	Con	32,554	52.1	+1.6	50.6	29,393
George Turner	Lab	20,990	33.6	+16.1	17.5	10,184
Alan Waterman	Lib Dem	8,599	13.8	-18.2	31.9	18,568
Simon Pink	NLP	330	0.5			
Majority	**Con**	**11,564**	**18.5**	**-0.1**	**18.6**	**10,825**

Electorate: 77,438 **Voters:** 62,473 **Turnout:** 80.7 **Swing:** 7.3 to Lab from Con

NORFOLK SOUTH

John MacGregor: Conservative. Born: 1937. Educated: Merchiston Castle School, Edinburgh; St Andrew's University. Jobs: political adviser. First Elected: 1974. Posts: Transport Secretary. Status: married, three children.

CON HOLD		1992 election Votes	%	+/-	1987 election %	Votes
John MacGregor*	Con	36,081	52.6	-0.8	53.4	33,912
C. Brocklebank Fowler	Lib Dem	18,516	27.0	-6.9	33.9	21,494
Clive Needle	Lab	12,422	18.1	+5.4	12.7	8,047
Stephanie Ross	Green	702	1.0			
Neil Clark	NLP	320	0.5			
Roger Peacock	Ind	304	0.4			
Roger Watkins	Ind C	232	0.3			
Majority	**Con**	**17,565**	**25.6**	**+6.0**	**19.6**	**12,418**

Electorate: 81,647 **Voters:** 68,577 **Turnout:** 84.0 **Swing:** 3.0 to Con from LDm

NORFOLK SOUTH WEST

Gillian Shephard: Conservative. Born: 1940. Educated: North Walsham Girls' High School; Oxford. Jobs: schools inspector. First Elected: 1987. Posts: Employment Secretary. Status: married.

CON HOLD		1992 election			1987 election	
		Votes	%	+/-	%	Votes
Gillian Shephard*	Con	33,637	54.6	-3.0	57.6	32,519
Mary Page	Lab	16,706	27.1	+6.1	21.0	11,844
John Marsh	Lib Dem	11,237	18.2	-3.2	21.4	12,083
Majority	**Con**	**16,931**	**27.5**	**-8.7**	**36.2**	**20,436**

Electorate: 77,652 **Voters:** 61,580 **Turnout:** 79.3 **Swing:** 4.6 to Lab from Con

NORMANTON

William O'Brien: Labour. Born: 1929. Educated: St Joseph's School, Castleford; Leeds University. Jobs: miner. First Elected: 1983. Posts: Labour spokesman on Northern Ireland. Union: NUM. Status: married, three children.

LAB HOLD		1992 election			1987 election	
		Votes	%	+/-	%	Votes
William O'Brien*	Lab	25,936	51.8	+2.3	49.5	23,303
Robert Sturdy	Con	16,986	33.9	-0.1	34.1	16,016
Mitchell Galdas	Lib Dem	7,137	14.3	-2.1	16.4	7,717
Majority	**Lab**	**8,950**	**17.9**	**+2.4**	**15.5**	**7,287**

Electorate: 65,562 **Voters:** 50,059 **Turnout:** 76.4 **Swing:** 1.2 to Lab from Con

NORTHAMPTON NORTH

Tony Marlow: Conservative. Born: 1940. Educated: Wellington College; Sandhurst; Cambridge. Jobs: management consultant. First Elected: 1979. Posts: member, European Legislation Select Committee. Status: married, five children.

CON HOLD		1992 election			1987 election	
		Votes	%	+/-	%	Votes
Tony Marlow*	Con	24,865	45.8	-2.2	48.0	24,816
Janet Thomas	Lab	20,957	38.6	+8.5	30.1	15,560
Richard Church	Lib Dem	8,236	15.2	-5.5	20.7	10,690
Barry Spivack	NLP	232	0.4			
Majority	**Con**	**3,908**	**7.2**	**-10.7**	**17.9**	**9,256**

Electorate: 69,139 **Voters:** 54,290 **Turnout:** 78.5 **Swing:** 5.4 to Lab from Con

NORTHAMPTON SOUTH

Michael Morris: *Conservative. Born: 1936. Educated: Bedford School; Cambridge. Jobs: advertising. First Elected: 1974. Posts: Deputy Speaker. Status: married, three children.*

CON HOLD		1992 election			1987 election	
		Votes	%	+/-	%	Votes
Michael Morris*	Con	36,882	55.3	-0.4	55.7	31,864
John Dickie	Lab	19,909	29.8	+5.3	24.6	14,061
Graham Mabbutt	Lib Dem	9,912	14.9	-3.7	18.6	10,639
Majority	**Con**	**16,973**	**25.4**	**-5.7**	**31.1**	**17,803**

Electorate: 83,477 **Voters:** 66,703 **Turnout:** 79.9 **Swing:** 2.8 to Lab from Con

NORTHAVON

Sir John Cope: *Conservative. Born: 1937. Educated: Oakham School, Rutland. Jobs: political researcher, accountant. First Elected: 1974. Posts: Paymaster-General. Status: married, two children.*

CON HOLD		1992 election			1987 election	
		Votes	%	+/-	%	Votes
Sir John Cope*	Con	35,338	50.3	-4.1	54.4	34,224
Heather Larkins	Lib Dem	23,477	33.4	+1.7	31.7	19,954
June Norris	Lab	10,290	14.6	+0.7	13.9	8,762
Jay Greene	Green	789	1.1			
Paul Marx	Lib	380	0.5			
Majority	**Con**	**11,861**	**16.9**	**-5.8**	**22.7**	**14,270**

Electorate: 83,496 **Voters:** 70,274 **Turnout:** 84.2 **Swing:** 2.9 to LDm from Con

NORWICH NORTH

Patrick Thompson: *Conservative. Born: 1935. Educated: Felsted School, Essex; Cambridge. Jobs: teacher. First Elected: 1983. Posts: member, Statutory Instruments Select Committee. Status: married.*

CON HOLD		1992 election			1987 election	
		Votes	%	+/-	%	Votes
Patrick Thompson*	Con	22,419	43.3	-2.6	45.8	22,772
Ian Gibson	Lab	22,153	42.8	+12.6	30.2	14,996
David Harrison	Lib Dem	6,706	12.9	-11.0	24.0	11,922
Lou Betts	Green	433	0.8			
Robert Arnold	NLP	93	0.2			
Majority	**Con**	**266**	**0.5**	**-15.1**	**15.6**	**7,776**

Electorate: 63,308 **Voters:** 51,804 **Turnout:** 81.8 **Swing:** 7.6 to Lab from Con

CONSTITUENCIES

NORWICH SOUTH

John Garrett: Labour. Born: 1931. Educated: Sir George Monoux School, London; Oxford. Jobs: market researcher. First Elected: 1974. Posts: member, Treasury Select Committee. Union: TGWU. Status: married, two children.

LAB HOLD		1992 election			1987 election	
		Votes	%	+/-	%	Votes
John Garrett*	Lab	24,965	48.7	+10.8	37.9	19,666
David Baxter	Con	18,784	36.6	-0.6	37.3	19,330
Christopher Thomas	Lib Dem	6,609	12.9	-12.0	24.9	12,896
Adrian Holmes	Green	803	1.6			
Bryan Parsons	NLP	104	0.2			
Majority	**Lab**	**6,181**	**12.1**	**+11.4**	**0.6**	**336**

Electorate: 63,603 **Voters:** 51,265 **Turnout:** 80.6 **Swing:** 5.7 to Lab from Con

NORWOOD

John Fraser: Labour. Born: 1934. Educated: Sloane Grammar School, Chelsea. Jobs: solicitor. First Elected: 1966. Posts: Labour spokesman on legal affairs. Union: GMB. Status: married, three children.

LAB HOLD		1992 election			1987 election	
		Votes	%	+/-	%	Votes
John Fraser*	Lab	18,391	53.2	+4.7	48.4	18,359
Julian Samways	Con	11,175	32.3	-3.7	36.0	13,636
Sandra Lawman	Lib Dem	4,087	11.8	-2.9	14.7	5,579
Shane Collins	Green	790	2.3			
Mark Leighton	NLP	138	0.4			
Majority	**Lab**	**7,216**	**20.9**	**+8.4**	**12.5**	**4,723**

Electorate: 52,496 **Voters:** 34,581 **Turnout:** 65.9 **Swing:** 4.2 to Lab from Con

NOTTINGHAM EAST

John Heppell: Labour. Born: 1948. Educated: Rutherford Grammar School; Ashington Technical College. Jobs: full-time councillor. First Elected: 1992. Union: RMT. Status: married, three children.

LAB GAIN		1992 election			1987 election	
		Votes	%	+/-	%	Votes
John Heppell	Lab	25,026	52.6	+10.6	42.0	19,706
Michael Knowles*	Con	17,346	36.4	-6.5	42.9	20,162
Tim Ball	Lib Dem	3,695	7.8	-6.9	14.7	6,883
Andrew Jones	Green	667	1.4			
Charles Roylance	Lib	598	1.3			
John Ashforth	NLP	283	0.6			
Majority	**Lab**	**7,680**	**16.1**	**+17.1**	**1.0**	**456**

Electorate: 67,939 **Voters:** 47,615 **Turnout:** 70.1 **Swing:** 8.6 to Lab from Con

NOTTINGHAM NORTH

Graham Allen: Labour. Born: 1953. Educated: Forest Fields Grammar School; City of London Polytechnic; Leeds University. Jobs: political researcher. First Elected: 1987. Posts: Labour spokesman on home affairs. Union: TGWU.

LAB HOLD		1992 election			1987 election	
		Votes	%	+/-	%	Votes
Graham Allen*	Lab	29,052	55.7	+10.8	44.9	22,713
Ian Bridge	Con	18,309	35.1	-6.5	41.6	21,048
Tony Skelton	Lib Dem	4,477	8.6	-3.1	11.7	5,912
Alwyn Cadman	NLP	274	0.5			
Majority	**Lab**	**10,743**	**20.6**	**+17.3**	**3.3**	**1,665**

Electorate: 69,494 **Voters:** 52,112 **Turnout:** 75.0 **Swing:** 8.7 to Lab from Con

NOTTINGHAM SOUTH

Alan Simpson: Labour. Born: 1948. Educated: Bootle Grammar School; Nottingham Polytechnic. Jobs: researcher. First Elected: 1992. Union: NUPE. Status: married, three children.

LAB GAIN		1992 election			1987 election	
		Votes	%	+/-	%	Votes
Alan Simpson	Lab	25,771	47.7	+7.2	40.5	21,687
Martin Brandon-Bravo*	Con	22,590	41.8	-2.9	44.7	23,921
Gareth David Long	Lib Dem	5,408	10.0	-4.8	14.8	7,917
Julianne Christou	NLP	263	0.5			
Majority	**Lab**	**3,181**	**5.9**	**+10.1**	**4.2**	**2,234**

Electorate: 72,796 **Voters:** 54,032 **Turnout:** 74.2 **Swing:** 5.0 to Lab from Con

NUNEATON

Bill Olner: Labour. Born: 1942. Educated: local state schools. Jobs: engineer. First Elected: 1992. Union: AEU. Status: married.

LAB GAIN		1992 election			1987 election	
		Votes	%	+/-	%	Votes
Bill Olner	Lab	27,157	45.8	+11.2	34.6	18,975
Lewis Stevens*	Con	25,526	43.0	-1.9	44.9	24,630
Ruth Merritt	Lib Dem	6,671	11.2	-8.0	19.2	10,550
Majority	**Lab**	**1,631**	**2.7**	**+13.0**	**10.3**	**5,655**

Electorate: 70,906 **Voters:** 59,354 **Turnout:** 83.7 **Swing:** 6.5 to Lab from Con

OGMORE

Ray Powell: Labour. Born: 1928. Educated: Pentre Grammar School; London School of Economics. Jobs: shop worker, small business. First Elected: 1979. Posts: Labour Whip. Union: USDAW. Status: married, two children.

LAB HOLD		1992 election			1987 election	
		Votes	%	+/-	%	Votes
Ray Powell*	Lab	30,186	71.7	+2.4	69.4	28,462
David Edwards	Con	6,359	15.1	+0.1	15.0	6,170
John Warman	Lib Dem	2,868	6.8	-2.8	9.6	3,954
Laura McAllister	Plaid Cymru	2,667	6.3	+2.0	4.4	1,791
Majority	**Lab**	**23,827**	**56.6**	**+2.3**	**54.3**	**22,292**

Electorate: 52,195 **Voters:** 42,080 **Turnout:** 80.6 **Swing:** 1.1 to Lab from Con

OLD BEXLEY & SIDCUP

Sir Edward Heath: Conservative. Born: 1916. Educated: Chatham House School, Ramsgate; Oxford. First Elected: 1950. Posts: Father of the House. Status: single.

CON HOLD		1992 election			1987 election	
		Votes	%	+/-	%	Votes
Edward Heath*	Con	24,450	60.3	-1.8	62.1	24,350
Donna Brierly	Lab	8,751	21.6	+4.3	17.3	6,762
David Nicolle	Lib Dem	6,438	15.9	-4.7	20.6	8,076
Barry Rose	Alt C	733	1.8			
Robert Stephens	NLP	148	0.4			
Majority	**Con**	**15,699**	**38.7**	**-2.8**	**41.5**	**16,274**

Electorate: 49,449 **Voters:** 40,520 **Turnout:** 81.9 **Swing:** 3.1 to Lab from Con

OLDHAM CENTRAL & ROYTON

Bryan Davies: Labour. Born: 1939. Educated: Redditch County High School; London University. Jobs: party official. First Elected: 1974. Union: TGWU. Posts: member, National Heritage Select Committee. Status: married, three children.

LAB HOLD		1992 election			1987 election	
		Votes	%	+/-	%	Votes
Bryan Davies	Lab	23,246	51.1	+2.9	48.1	21,759
Trish Morris	Con	14,640	32.2	-2.1	34.3	15,480
Ann Dunn	Lib Dem	7,224	15.9	-1.7	17.6	7,956
Ian Dalling	NLP	403	0.9			
Majority	**Lab**	**8,606**	**18.9**	**+5.0**	**13.9**	**6,279**

Electorate: 61,333 **Voters:** 45,513 **Turnout:** 74.2 **Swing:** 2.5 to Lab from Con

OLDHAM WEST

Michael Meacher: *Labour. Born: 1939. Educated: Berkhamsted School; Oxford. Jobs: lecturer. First Elected: 1970. Posts: Shadow minister for development and co-operation. Union: COHSE. Status: married, four children.*

LAB HOLD		1992 election			1987 election	
		Votes	%	+/-	%	Votes
Michael Meacher*	Lab	21,580	52.8	+3.4	49.4	20,291
Jonathan Gillen	Con	13,247	32.4	-2.5	34.9	14,324
John Smith	Lib Dem	5,525	13.5	-2.3	15.8	6,478
Sheila Dalling	NLP	551	1.3			
Majority	**Lab**	**8,333**	**20.4**	**+5.9**	**14.5**	**5,967**

Electorate: 54,063 **Voters:** 40,903 **Turnout:** 75.7 **Swing:** 2.9 to Lab from Con

ORKNEY & SHETLAND

Jim Wallace: *Liberal Democrat. Born: 1954. Educated: Annan Academy; Cambridge and Edinburgh Universities. Jobs: barrister. First Elected: 1983. Posts: LibDem Scottish Spokesman. Status: married, two children.*

LIBDEM HOLD		1992 election			1987 election	
		Votes	%	+/-	%	Votes
Jim Wallace*	Lib Dem	9,575	46.4	+4.8	41.7	8,881
Paul McCormick	Con	4,542	22.0	-1.2	23.3	4,959
John Aberdein	Lab	4,093	19.8	+1.1	18.7	3,995
Frances McKie	SNP	2,301	11.2			
Christian Wharton	NLP	115	0.6			
Majority	**Lib Dem**	**5,033**	**24.4**	**+6.0**	**18.4**	**3,922**

Electorate: 31,472 **Voters:** 20,626 **Turnout:** 65.5 **Swing:** 3.0 to LDm from Con

ORPINGTON

John Horam: *Conservative. Born: 1939. Educated: Silcoates School, Wakefield; Cambridge. Jobs: economic consultant. First Elected: 1970 (as Labour). Posts: member, Public Accounts Committee. Status: married.*

CON HOLD		1992 election			1987 election	
		Votes	%	+/-	%	Votes
John Horam	Con	27,421	57.2	-1.1	58.2	27,261
Chris Maines	Lib Dem	14,486	30.2	-0.8	31.0	14,529
Stephen Cowan	Lab	5,512	11.5	+0.8	10.7	5,020
Robin Almond	Lib	539	1.1			
Majority	**Con**	**12,935**	**27.0**	**-0.2**	**27.2**	**12,732**

Electorate: 57,318 **Voters:** 47,958 **Turnout:** 83.7 **Swing:** 0.1 to LDm from Con

CONSTITUENCIES

OXFORD EAST

Andrew Smith: Labour. Born: 1951. Educated: Reading School; Oxford. First Elected: 1987. Posts: Shadow Economic Secretary to the Treasury. Union: USDAW. Status: married.

LAB HOLD		1992 election Votes	%	+/-	1987 election %	Votes
Andrew Smith*	Lab	23,702	50.4	+7.4	43.0	21,103
Mark Mayall	Con	16,164	34.4	-6.0	40.4	19,815
Martin Horwood	Lib Dem	6,105	13.0	-2.6	15.6	7,648
Caroline Lucas	Green	933	2.0	+1.1	0.9	441
Ann Wilson	NLP	101	0.2			
Keith Thompson	Rev Comm	48	0.1			
Majority	**Lab**	**7,538**	**16.0**	**+13.4**	**2.6**	**1,288**

Electorate: 63,075 **Voters:** 47,053 **Turnout:** 74.6 **Swing:** 6.7 to Lab from Con

OXFORD WEST & ABINGDON

John Patten: Conservative. Born: 1945. Educated: Wimbledon College; Cambridge. Jobs: lecturer. First Elected: 1979. Posts: Education Secretary. Status: married, one child.

CON HOLD		1992 election Votes	%	+/-	1987 election %	Votes
John Patten*	Con	25,163	45.4	-1.0	46.4	25,171
Sir William Goodhart	Lib Dem	21,624	39.0	+1.6	37.4	20,293
Bruce Kent	Lab	7,652	13.8	-1.1	14.9	8,108
Mike Woodin	Green	660	1.2	-0.1	1.3	695
Roger Jenking	Lib	194	0.3			
Susan Nelson	Anti Fed	98	0.2			
Geoffrey Wells	NLP	75	0.1			
Majority	**Con**	**3,539**	**6.4**	**-2.6**	**9.0**	**4,878**

Electorate: 72,328 **Voters:** 55,466 **Turnout:** 76.7 **Swing:** 1.3 to LDm from Con

PAISLEY NORTH

Irene Adams: Labour. Born: 1947. Educated: Stanley Green High School, Paisley. First Elected: 1990. Union: GMB. Status: widow, three children.

LAB HOLD		1992 election Votes	%	+/-	1987 election %	Votes
Irene Adams*	Lab	17,269	50.7	-4.8	55.5	20,193
Roger Mullin	SNP	7,940	23.3	+10.4	12.9	4,696
David Sharpe	Con	5,576	16.4	+0.6	15.8	5,751
Eileen McCartin	Lib Dem	2,779	8.2	-7.6	15.8	5,741
David Mellor	Green	412	1.2			
Nicholas Brennan	NLP	81	0.2			
Majority	**Lab**	**9,329**	**27.4**	**-12.3**	**39.7**	**14,442**

Electorate: 46,403 **Voters:** 34,057 **Turnout:** 73.4 **Swing:** 7.6 to SNP from Lab

BY-ELECTION November 1990: LAB HOLD. I Adams (Lab) 11,353 (44.0%), R. Mullin (SNP) 7,583 (29.4%), E. Marwick (Con) 3,835 (14.8%), Lab majority 3,770 (14.6%), SWING 14.0% to Lab from Con

PAISLEY SOUTH

Gordon McMaster: Labour. Born: 1960. Educated: local state schools. Jobs: horticulture lecturer. First Elected: 1990. Union: TGWU. Status: single.

LAB HOLD

		1992 election Votes	%	+/-	1987 election %	Votes
Gordon McMaster*	Lab	18,202	50.7	-5.5	56.2	21,611
Iain Lawson	SNP	8,653	24.1	+10.1	14.0	5,398
Sheila Laidlaw	Con	5,703	15.9	+1.2	14.7	5,644
Alan Reid	Lib Dem	3,271	9.1	-6.0	15.1	5,826
Stephen Porter	NLP	93	0.3			
Majority	**Lab**	**9,549**	**26.6**	**-14.4**	**41.0**	**15,785**

Electorate: 47,889 **Voters:** 35,922 **Turnout:** 75.0 **Swing:** 7.8 to SNP from Lab

BY-ELECTION November 1990: LAB HOLD. G. McMaster (Lab) 12,485 (46.1%), I. Lawson (SNP) 7,455 (27.5%), J. Workman (Con) 3,627 (13.4%), Lab majority 5,030 (18.6%), SWING 11.8% to SNP from Lab

PECKHAM

Harriet Harman: Labour. Born: 1950. Educated: St Paul's; York University. Jobs: solicitor. First Elected: 1982. Posts: Shadow Chief Secretary to the Treasury. Union: TGWU. Status: married, three children.

LAB HOLD

		1992 election Votes	%	+/-	1987 election %	Votes
Harriet Harman*	Lab	19,391	61.8	+7.2	54.5	17,965
Christopher Frazer	Con	7,386	23.5	-2.2	25.7	8,476
Rose Colley	Lib Dem	4,331	13.8	-4.0	17.8	5,878
Gilbert Dacres	WRP	146	0.5			
Victor Emmanuel	Whiplash	140	0.4			
Majority	**Lab**	**12,005**	**38.2**	**+9.4**	**28.8**	**9,489**

Electorate: 58,269 **Voters:** 31,394 **Turnout:** 53.9 **Swing:** 4.7 to Lab from Con

PEMBROKE

Nick Ainger: Labour. Born: 1949. Educated: local state schools. Jobs: rigger. First Elected: 1992. Union: TGWU. Status: married, one child.

LAB GAIN

		1992 election Votes	%	+/-	1987 election %	Votes
Nick Ainger	Lab	26,253	43.3	+12.3	31.0	17,614
Nicholas Bennett*	Con	25,498	42.0	+1.1	41.0	23,314
Peter Berry	Lib Dem	6,625	10.9	-15.2	26.1	14,832
Conrad Bryant	Plaid Cymru	1,627	2.7	+0.7	2.0	1,119
Roger Coghill	Green	484	0.8			
Michael Stoddart	Anti Fed	158	0.3			
Majority	**Lab**	**755**	**1.2**	**-11.2**	**10.0**	**5,700**

Electorate: 73,187 **Voters:** 60,645 **Turnout:** 82.9 **Swing:** 5.6 to Lab from Con

PENDLE

Gordon Prentice: Labour. Born: 1951. Educated: Glasgow University. Jobs: party official. First Elected: 1992. Union: TGWU. Status: married.

LAB GAIN		1992 election			1987 election	
		Votes	%	+/-	%	Votes
Gordon Prentice	Lab	23,497	44.2	+8.9	35.3	18,370
John Lee*	Con	21,384	40.3	-0.1	40.4	21,009
Alan Davies	Lib Dem	7,976	15.0	-9.3	24.3	12,662
Val Thome	Anti Fed	263	0.5			
Majority	**Lab**	**2,113**	**4.0**	**+9.0**	**5.1**	**2,639**

Electorate: 64,063 **Voters:** 53,120 **Turnout:** 82.9 **Swing:** 4.5 to Lab from Con

PENRITH & THE BORDER

David Maclean: Conservative. Born: 1953. Educated: Fortrose Academy; Aberdeen University. First Elected: 1983. Posts: Minister for the Environment and the Countryside. Status: married.

CON HOLD		1992 election			1987 election	
		Votes	%	+/-	%	Votes
David Maclean*	Con	33,808	57.5	-2.7	60.3	33,148
Geyve Walker	Lib Dem	15,359	26.1	-2.6	28.7	15,782
John Metcalfe	Lab	8,871	15.1	+4.0	11.0	6,075
Robert Gibson	Green	610	1.0			
Ian Docker	NLP	129	0.2			
Majority	**Con**	**18,449**	**31.4**	**-0.2**	**31.6**	**17,366**

Electorate: 73,769 **Voters:** 58,777 **Turnout:** 79.7 **Swing:** No Swing

PERTH & KINROSS

Sir Nicholas Fairbairn: Conservative. Born: 1933. Educated: Loretto School; Edinburgh University. Jobs: barrister. First Elected: 1974. Posts: member, Scottish Affairs Select Committee, Defence Select Committee. Status: married, three children.

CON HOLD		1992 election			1987 election	
		Votes	%	+/-	%	Votes
Sir Nicholas Fairbairn*	Con	20,195	40.2	+0.5	39.6	18,716
Roseanna Cunningham	SNP	18,101	36.0	+8.4	27.6	13,040
Merv Rolfe	Lab	6,267	12.5	-3.4	15.9	7,490
Malcolm Black	Lib Dem	5,714	11.4	-5.5	16.9	7,969
Majority	**Con**	**2,094**	**4.2**	**-7.9**	**12.0**	**5,676**

Electorate: 65,410 **Voters:** 50,277 **Turnout:** 76.9 **Swing:** 3.9 to SNP from Con

PETERBOROUGH

Dr Brian Mawhinney: *Conservative. Born: 1940. Educated: Royal Belfast Academical Institution, Queen's University. Jobs: lecturer. First Elected: 1979. Posts: Minister of State for Health.*

CON HOLD

		1992 election Votes	%	+/-	1987 election %	Votes
Brian Mawhinney*	Con	31,827	48.3	-1.1	49.4	30,624
Julie Owens	Lab	26,451	40.2	+6.5	33.6	20,840
Amanda Taylor	Lib Dem	5,208	7.9	-8.2	16.1	9,984
Erbie Murat	Lib	1,557	2.4			
Richard Heaton	BNP	311	0.5			
Pam Beasley	PP	271	0.4			
Charles Brettell	NLP	215	0.3			
Majority	**Con**	**5,376**	**8.2**	**-7.6**	**15.8**	**9,784**

Electorate: 87,638 **Voters:** 65,840 **Turnout:** 75.1 **Swing:** 3.8 to Lab from Con

PLYMOUTH, DEVONPORT

David Jamieson: *Labour. Born: 1947. Educated: Tudor Grange Grammar School, Solihull; Open University. Jobs: teacher. First Elected: 1992. Posts: member, Education Select Committee. Status: married, three children.*

LAB GAIN

		1992 election Votes	%	+/-	1987 election %	Votes
David Jamieson	Lab	24,953	48.7	+20.3	28.5	14,166
Keith Simpson	Con	17,541	34.2	+5.0	29.3	14,569
Murdoch Mactaggart	Lib Dem	6,315	12.3	-29.9	42.3	21,039
Harold Luscombe	Soc Dem	2,152	4.2			
Francis Lyons	NLP	255	0.5			
Majority	**Lab**	**7,412**	**14.5**	**+27.5**	**13.0**	**6,470**

Electorate: 65,799 **Voters:** 51,216 **Turnout:** 77.8

PLYMOUTH, DRAKE

Dame Janet Fookes: *Conservative. Born: 1936. Educated: Hastings & St Leonard's Ladies' College; London University. Jobs: teacher. First Elected: 1970. Posts: Deputy Speaker.*

CON HOLD

		1992 election Votes	%	+/-	1987 election %	Votes
Dame Janet Fookes*	Con	17,075	43.7	+2.4	41.3	16,195
Peter Telford	Lab	15,062	38.6	+14.5	24.1	9,451
Valerie Cox	Lib Dem	5,893	15.1	-18.2	33.3	13,070
David Stanbury	Soc Dem	476	1.2			
Anne Harrison	Green	441	1.1	-0.1	1.3	493
Tom Pringle	NLP	95	0.2			
Majority	**Con**	**2,013**	**5.2**	**-2.8**	**8.0**	**3,125**

Electorate: 51,667 **Voters:** 39,042 **Turnout:** 75.6 **Swing:** 6.0 to Lab from Con

PLYMOUTH, SUTTON

Gary Streeter: Conservative. Born: 1955. Educated: Tiverton Grammar School; London University. Jobs: solicitor. First Elected: 1992. Posts: member, Environment Select Committee. Status: married, two children.

CON HOLD		1992 election Votes	%	+/-	1987 election %	Votes
Gary Streeter	Con	27,070	49.5	+3.7	45.8	23,187
Andrew Pawley	Lab	15,120	27.6	+11.2	16.4	8,310
Julian Brett-Freeman	Lib Dem	12,291	22.5	-15.4	37.8	19,174
Jeremy Bowler	NLP	256	0.5			
Majority	**Con**	**11,950**	**21.8**	**+13.9**	**7.9**	**4,013**

Electorate: 67,430 **Voters:** 54,737 **Turnout:** 81.2 **Swing:** 3.8 to Lab from Con

PONTEFRACT & CASTLEFORD

Geoffrey Lofthouse: Labour. Born: 1925. Educated: Featherstone Secondary School; Leeds University. Jobs: personnel manager. First Elected: 1978. Posts: Deputy Speaker. Union: NUM. Status: widower, one child.

LAB HOLD		1992 election Votes	%	+/-	1987 election %	Votes
Geoffrey Lofthouse*	Lab	33,546	69.9	+3.0	66.9	31,656
Anthony Rockall	Con	10,051	20.9	-0.3	21.2	10,030
David Ryan	Lib Dem	4,410	9.2	-2.1	11.3	5,334
Majority	**Lab**	**23,495**	**48.9**	**+3.2**	**45.7**	**21,626**

Electorate: 64,648 **Voters:** 48,007 **Turnout:** 74.3 **Swing:** 1.6 to Lab from Con

PONTYPRIDD

Dr Kim Howells: Labour. Born: 1946. Educated: Mountain Ash Grammar School; Hornsey College of Art; Cambridge College of Advanced Technology; Warwick University. Jobs: trade union researcher, broadcaster. First Elected: 1989. Union: NUM. Posts: member, Public Accounts Committee. Status: married, three children.

LAB HOLD		1992 election Votes	%	+/-	1987 election %	Votes
Kim Howells*	Lab	29,722	60.8	+4.5	56.3	26,422
Peter Donnelly	Con	9,925	20.3	+0.8	19.5	9,135
Delme Bowen	Plaid Cymru	4,448	9.1	+3.8	5.3	2,498
Steve Belzak	Lib Dem	4,180	8.5	-10.3	18.9	8,865
Emma Jackson	Green	615	1.3			
Majority	**Lab**	**19,797**	**40.5**	**+3.6**	**36.8**	**17,287**

Electorate: 61,685 **Voters:** 48,890 **Turnout:** 79.3 **Swing:** 1.8 to Lab from Con
BY-ELECTION February 1989: LAB HOLD. K. Howells (Lab) 20,549 (53.4%), S. Morgan (Plaid Cymru) 9,755 (25.3%), N. Evans (Con) 5,212 (13.5%), Lab majority 10,794 (28%), SWING 11.5% to Plaid Cymru from Lab

POOLE

John Ward: *Conservative. Born: 1925. Educated: Romford Technical College; St Andrew's University. Jobs: engineer. First Elected: 1979. Posts: delegate, Council of Europe, Western European Union. Status: married, two children.*

CON HOLD

		1992 election Votes	%	+/-	1987 election %	Votes
John Ward*	Con	33,445	53.2	-4.3	57.5	34,159
Brian Clements	Lib Dem	20,614	32.8	+0.2	32.6	19,351
Haydn White	Lab	6,912	11.0	+1.1	9.9	5,901
Michael Steen	Ind C	1,620	2.6			
Alistair Bailey	NLP	303	0.5			
Majority	**Con**	**12,831**	**20.4**	**-4.5**	**24.9**	**14,808**

Electorate: 79,221 **Voters:** 62,894 **Turnout:** 79.4 **Swing:** 2.3 to LDm from Con

PORTSMOUTH NORTH

Peter Griffiths: *Conservative. Born: 1928. Educated: West Bromwich Grammar School; London University. Jobs: teacher, lecturer. First Elected: 1964. Status: married, two children.*

CON HOLD

		1992 election Votes	%	+/-	1987 election %	Votes
Peter Griffiths*	Con	32,240	52.6	-2.7	55.3	33,297
Alan Burnett	Lab	18,359	29.9	+10.0	20.0	12,016
Alex Bentley	Lib Dem	10,101	16.5	-8.3	24.7	14,896
Helen Palmer	Green	628	1.0			
Majority	**Con**	**13,881**	**22.6**	**-7.9**	**30.6**	**18,401**

Electorate: 79,592 **Voters:** 61,328 **Turnout:** 77.1 **Swing:** 6.4 to Lab from Con

PORTSMOUTH SOUTH

David Martin: *Conservative. Born: 1945. Educated: Norwood School, Exeter; Cambridge. Jobs: barrister. First Elected: 1987. Posts: PPS. Status: married, four children.*

CON HOLD

		1992 election Votes	%	+/-	1987 election %	Votes
David Martin*	Con	22,798	42.5	-0.8	43.3	23,534
Mike Hancock	Lib Dem	22,556	42.0	-0.9	42.9	23,329
Sydney Rapson	Lab	7,857	14.6	+1.7	13.0	7,047
Aleksander Zivkovic	Green	349	0.7			
William Trend	NLP	91	0.2			
Majority	**Con**	**242**	**0.5**	**+0.1**	**0.4**	**205**

Electorate: 77,645 **Voters:** 53,651 **Turnout:** 69.1 **Swing:** No Swing

PRESTON

Audrey Wise: Labour. Born: 1935. Educated: Rutherford High School. First Elected: 1974. Posts: president of USDAW; member, Health Select Committee. Status: married, two children.

LAB HOLD		1992 election Votes	%	+/-	1987 election %	Votes
Audrey Wise*	Lab	24,983	54.3	+1.8	52.5	23,341
Simon O'Toole	Con	12,808	27.8	-0.7	28.5	12,696
Bill Chadwick	Lib Dem	7,897	17.2	-1.8	19.0	8,452
Janet Ayliffe	NLP	341	0.7			
Majority	**Lab**	**12,175**	**26.5**	**+2.5**	**23.9**	**10,645**

Electorate: 64,158 **Voters:** 46,029 **Turnout:** 71.7 **Swing:** 1.3 to Lab from Con

PUDSEY

Sir Giles Shaw: Conservative. Born: 1931. Educated: Sedbergh School; Cambridge. Jobs: marketing director. First Elected: 1974. Posts: treasurer, 1922 Committee; chairman, Science and Technology Select Committee. Status: married, three children.

CON HOLD		1992 election Votes	%	+/-	1987 election %	Votes
Sir Giles Shaw*	Con	25,067	44.1	-1.4	45.5	25,457
Arthur Giles	Lab	16,095	28.3	+7.9	20.5	11,461
David Shutt	Lib Dem	15,153	26.7	-7.3	34.0	19,021
Jean Wynne	Green	466	0.8			
Majority	**Con**	**8,972**	**15.8**	**+4.3**	**11.5**	**6,436**

Electorate: 70,847 **Voters:** 56,781 **Turnout:** 80.1 **Swing:** 4.6 to Lab from Con

PUTNEY

David Mellor: Conservative. Born: 1949. Educated: Swanage Grammar School; Cambridge. Jobs: barrister. First Elected: 1979. Posts: National Heritage Secretary. Status: married, two children.

CON HOLD		1992 election Votes	%	+/-	1987 election %	Votes
David Mellor*	Con	25,188	52.2	+1.7	50.5	24,197
Judith Chegwidden	Lab	17,662	36.6	+0.5	36.1	17,290
John Martyn	Lib Dem	4,636	9.6	-2.8	12.4	5,934
Keith Hagenbach	Green	618	1.3	+0.2	1.1	508
Paul Levy	NLP	139	0.3			
Majority	**Con**	**7,526**	**15.6**	**+1.2**	**14.4**	**6,907**

Electorate: 61,914 **Voters:** 48,243 **Turnout:** 77.9 **Swing:** 0.6 to Con from Lab

RAVENSBOURNE

Sir John Hunt: *Conservative. Born: 1929. Educated: Dulwich College. Jobs: stockbroker. First Elected: 1964. Status: single.*

CON HOLD		1992 election			1987 election	
		Votes	%	+/-	%	Votes
Sir John Hunt*	Con	29,506	63.4	+0.5	63.0	28,295
Paul Booth	Lib Dem	9,792	21.0	-4.3	25.3	11,376
Erny Dyer	Lab	6,182	13.3	+2.0	11.3	5,087
Ian Mouland	Green	617	1.3			
Peter White	Lib	318	0.7			
John Shepheard	NLP	105	0.2			
Majority	**Con**	**19,714**	**42.4**	**+4.7**	**37.6**	**16,919**

Electorate: 57,259 **Voters:** 46,520 **Turnout:** 81.2 **Swing:** 2.4 to Con from LDm

READING EAST

Sir Gerry Vaughan: *Conservative. Born: 1923. Educated: London University. Jobs: doctor. First Elected: 1970. Posts: member, Science and Technology Select Committee. Status: married, two children.*

CON HOLD		1992 election			1987 election	
		Votes	%	+/-	%	Votes
Sir Gerry Vaughan*	Con	29,148	53.8	+0.0	53.8	28,515
Gill Parker	Lab	14,593	27.0	+5.5	21.5	11,371
Denis Thair	Lib Dem	9,528	17.6	-5.6	23.2	12,298
Anne McCubbin	Green	861	1.6	+0.3	1.3	667
Majority	**Con**	**14,555**	**26.9**	**-3.7**	**30.6**	**16,217**

Electorate: 72,151 **Voters:** 54,130 **Turnout:** 75.0 **Swing:** 2.7 to Lab from Con

READING WEST

Sir Tony Durant: *Conservative. Born: 1928. Educated: Bryanston School. Jobs: company director, banker. First Elected: 1974. Posts: executive member, 1922 Committee. Status: married, two children.*

CON HOLD		1992 election			1987 election	
		Votes	%	+/-	%	Votes
Sir Tony Durant*	Con	28,048	52.9	-2.4	55.3	28,122
Peter Ruhemann	Lab	14,750	27.8	+6.6	21.3	10,819
Keith Lock	Lib Dem	9,572	18.1	-4.3	22.4	11,369
Phil Unsworth	Green	613	1.2	+0.1	1.1	542
Majority	**Con**	**13,298**	**25.1**	**-7.8**	**32.9**	**16,753**

Electorate: 67,937 **Voters:** 52,983 **Turnout:** 78.0 **Swing:** 4.5 to Lab from Con

REDCAR

Dr Marjorie Mowlam: Labour. Born: 1949. Educated: Coundon Court Comprehensive, Coventry; Durham University. Jobs: administrator, lecturer. First Elected: 1987. Posts: Shadow minister for the Citizen's Charter and women. Union: COHSE. Status: single.

LAB HOLD		1992 election			1987 election	
		Votes	%	+/-	%	Votes
Marjorie Mowlam*	Lab	27,184	56.0	+8.6	47.3	22,824
Robert Goodwill	Con	15,607	32.1	+0.8	31.3	15,089
Chris Abbott	Lib Dem	5,789	11.9	-9.4	21.4	10,298
Majority	**Lab**	**11,577**	**23.8**	**+7.8**	**16.0**	**7,735**

Electorate: 62,494 **Voters:** 48,580 **Turnout:** 77.7 **Swing:** 3.9 to Lab from Con

REIGATE

Sir George Gardiner: Conservative. Born: 1935. Educated: Harvey Grammar School, Folkestone; Oxford. Jobs: journalist, company director. First Elected: 1974. Posts: executive member, 1922 Committee. Status: married, three children.

CON HOLD		1992 election			1987 election	
		Votes	%	+/-	%	Votes
Sir George Gardiner*	Con	32,220	57.1	-2.2	59.3	30,925
Barry Newsome	Lib Dem	14,556	25.8	+1.3	24.4	12,752
Helen Young	Lab	9,150	16.2	+1.9	14.3	7,460
Mark Dilcliff	Soc Dem	513	0.9			
Majority	**Con**	**17,664**	**31.3**	**-3.5**	**34.8**	**18,173**

Electorate: 71,853 **Voters:** 56,439 **Turnout:** 78.5 **Swing:** 1.8 to LDm from Con

RENFREW WEST & INVERCLYDE

Tommy Graham: Labour. Born: 1943. Educated: Crookston Castle Secondary School. Jobs: engineer, manager. First Elected: 1987. Union: USDAW. Status: married, two children.

LAB HOLD		1992 election			1987 election	
		Votes	%	+/-	%	Votes
Tommy Graham*	Lab	17,085	36.6	-2.1	38.7	17,525
Annabel Goldie	Con	15,341	32.9	+3.1	29.8	13,462
Colin Campbell	SNP	9,444	20.2	+10.1	10.1	4,578
Sandy Nimmo	Lib Dem	4,668	10.0	-11.4	21.4	9,669
Duncan Maltman	NLP	149	0.3			
Majority	**Lab**	**1,744**	**3.7**	**-5.2**	**9.0**	**4,063**

Electorate: 58,122 **Voters:** 46,687 **Turnout:** 80.3 **Swing:** 2.6 to Con from Lab

RHONDDA

Allan Rogers: Labour. Born: 1932. Educated: Bargoed Secondary School; University College, Swansea. Jobs: tutor, geologist, Euro MP. First Elected: 1983. Posts: Labour spokesman on foreign and commonwealth affairs. Union: COHSE. Status: married, four children.

LAB HOLD		1992 election			1987 election	
		Votes	%	+/-	%	Votes
Allan Rogers*	Lab	34,243	74.5	+1.2	73.3	34,857
Geraint Davies	Plaid Cymru	5,427	11.8	+2.9	9.0	4,261
John Richards	Con	3,588	7.8	+0.2	7.6	3,612
Paul Nicholls-Jones	Lib Dem	2,431	5.3	-3.0	8.3	3,935
Mark Fisher	Comm GB	245	0.5			
Majority	**Lab**	**28,816**	**62.7**	**-1.6**	**64.4**	**30,596**

Electorate: 59,955 **Voters:** 45,934 **Turnout:** 76.6 **Swing:** 0.8 to Plaid Cymru from Lab

RIBBLE VALLEY

Nigel Evans: Conservative. Born: 1957. Educated: Dynevor School, Swansea; University College, Swansea. Jobs: retailer. First Elected: 1992. Status: single.

CON REGAIN		1992 election			1987 election	
		Votes	%	+/-	%	Votes
Nigel Evans	Con	29,178	52.4	-8.5	60.9	30,136
Michael Carr*	Lib Dem	22,636	40.6	+19.2	21.4	10,608
Ronald Pickup	Lab	3,649	6.5	-11.2	17.7	8,781
David Beesley	Loony G	152	0.3			
Nicky Holmes	NLP	112	0.2			
Majority	**Con**	**6,542**	**11.7**	**-27.7**	**39.4**	**19,528**

Electorate: 64,996 **Voters:** 55,727 **Turnout:** 85.7 **Swing:** 13.8 to LDm from Con

BY-ELECTION March 1991: LIBDEM GAIN. M. Carr (LibDem) 22,377 (48.5%), N. Evans (Con) 17,776 (38.5%), J. Farringdon (Lab) 4,356 (9.4%), LibDem majority 4,601 (10.0%), SWING 24.8% to LibDem from Con

RICHMOND & BARNES

Jeremy Hanley: Conservative. Born: 1945. Educated: Rugby. Jobs: accountant. First Elected: 1983. Posts: Northern Ireland minister. Status: married, three children.

CON HOLD		1992 election			1987 election	
		Votes	%	+/-	%	Votes
Jeremy Hanley*	Con	22,894	50.7	+3.0	47.7	21,729
Jenny Tonge	Lib Dem	19,025	42.2	-1.7	43.8	19,963
Donald Touhig	Lab	2,632	5.8	-1.3	7.1	3,227
Judy Maciejowska	Green	376	0.8	-0.5	1.3	610
Charles Cunningham	NLP	89	0.2			
Richard Meacock	QFL	62	0.1			
Angela Ellis-Jones	Anti Fed	47	0.1			
Majority	**Con**	**3,869**	**8.6**	**+4.7**	**3.9**	**1,766**

Electorate: 53,081 **Voters:** 45,125 **Turnout:** 85.0 **Swing:** 2.3 to Con from LDm

RICHMOND, YORKS

William Hague: Conservative. Born: 1961. Educated: Wath-upon-Dearne Comprehensive; Oxford. Jobs: political adviser, business consultant. First Elected: 1989. Posts: PPS. Status: single.

CON HOLD		1992 election Votes	%	+/-	1987 election %	Votes
William Hague*	Con	40,202	61.9	+0.6	61.2	34,995
George Irwin	Lib Dem	16,698	25.7	-1.3	27.0	15,419
Ross Cranston	Lab	7,523	11.6	-0.2	11.8	6,737
Michael Barr	Ind	570	0.9			
Majority	**Con**	**23,504**	**36.2**	**+1.9**	**34.3**	**19,576**

Electorate: 82,879 **Voters:** 64,993 **Turnout:** 78.4 **Swing:** 1.0 to Con from LDm

BY-ELECTION February 1989: W. Hague (Con) 19,543 (37.2%), M. Potter (SDP) 16,909 (32.2%), B. Pearce (Lib Dem) 11,589 (22.1%), Con majority 2,634 (5.0%)

ROCHDALE

Liz Lynne: Liberal Democrat. Born: 1948. Educated: Dorking Grammar School. Jobs: speech consultant, actress. First Elected: 1992.. Posts: LibDem spokeswoman on health and community care. Status: single.

LIBDEM HOLD		1992 election Votes	%	+/-	1987 election %	Votes
Liz Lynne	Lib Dem	22,776	42.8	-0.6	43.4	22,245
David Williams	Lab	20,937	39.4	+1.4	38.0	19,466
Duncan Goldie-Scott	Con	8,626	16.2	-2.4	18.6	9,561
Kenneth Henderson	BNP	620	1.2			
Vincent Lucker	NLP	211	0.4			
Majority	**Lib Dem**	**1,839**	**3.5**	**-2.0**	**5.4**	**2,779**

Electorate: 69,522 **Voters:** 53,170 **Turnout:** 76.5 **Swing:** 1.0 to Lab from LDm

ROCHFORD

Dr Michael Clark: Conservative. Born: 1935. Educated: King Edward VI School, East Retford; London University. Jobs: management consultant, industrial chemist. First Elected: 1983. Posts: member, Trade and Industry Select Committee. Status: married, two children.

CON HOLD		1992 election Votes	%	+/-	1987 election %	Votes
Michael Clark*	Con	38,967	61.1	+0.6	60.4	35,872
Nicholas Harris	Lib Dem	12,931	20.3	-7.0	27.3	16,178
Donald Quinn	Lab	10,537	16.5	+4.2	12.3	7,308
Linda Farmer	Lib	1,362	2.1			
Majority	**Con**	**26,036**	**40.8**	**+7.6**	**33.2**	**19,694**

Electorate: 76,869 **Voters:** 63,797 **Turnout:** 83.0 **Swing:** 3.8 to Con from LDm

ROMFORD

Sir Michael Neubert: Conservative. Born: 1933. Educated: Bromley Grammar School; Royal College of Music; Cambridge. Jobs: tour operator, musician. First Elected: 1974. Status: married, one child.

CON HOLD		1992 election			1987 election	
		Votes	%	+/-	%	Votes
Sir Michael Neubert*	Con	23,834	56.6	+0.6	56.0	22,745
Eileen Gordon	Lab	12,414	29.5	+6.6	22.8	9,274
Pat Atherton	Lib Dem	5,329	12.7	-7.5	20.2	8,195
Fred Gibson	Green	546	1.3	+0.3	0.9	385
Majority	**Con**	**11,420**	**27.1**	**-6.1**	**33.2**	**13,471**

Electorate: 54,001 **Voters:** 42,123 **Turnout:** 78.0 **Swing:** 3.0 to Lab from Con

ROMSEY & WATERSIDE

Michael Colvin: Conservative. Born: 1932. Educated: Eton; Sandhurst; Royal Agricultural College. Jobs: army officer, advertising, farmer. First Elected: 1979. Posts: member, Defence Select Committee. Status: married, three children.

CON HOLD		1992 election			1987 election	
		Votes	%	+/-	%	Votes
Michael Colvin*	Con	37,375	54.4	-2.0	56.4	35,303
George Dawson	Lib Dem	22,071	32.1	+0.1	32.0	20,031
Angela Mawle	Lab	8,688	12.6	+1.1	11.5	7,213
John Spottiswood	Green	577	0.8			
Majority	**Con**	**15,304**	**22.3**	**-2.1**	**24.4**	**15,272**

Electorate: 82,628 **Voters:** 68,711 **Turnout:** 83.2 **Swing:** 1.1 to LDm from Con

ROSS, CROMARTY & SKYE

Charles Kennedy: Liberal Democrat. Born: 1959. Educated: Lochaber High School; Glasgow University. Jobs: teacher. First Elected: 1983. Posts: President of LibDems, European spokesman. Status: single.

LIBDEM HOLD		1992 election			1987 election	
		Votes	%	+/-	%	Votes
Charles Kennedy*	Lib Dem	17,066	41.6	-7.8	49.4	18,809
James Gray	Con	9,436	23.0	+3.3	19.7	7,490
Rob Gibson	SNP	7,618	18.6	+6.8	11.8	4,492
James MacDonald	Lab	6,275	15.3	-3.8	19.1	7,287
David Jardine	Green	642	1.6			
Majority	**Lib Dem**	**7,630**	**18.6**	**-11.1**	**29.7**	**11,319**

Electorate: 55,524 **Voters:** 41,037 **Turnout:** 73.9 **Swing:** 5.6 to Con from LDm

ROSSENDALE & DARWEN

Janet Anderson: Labour. Born: 1949. Educated: Kingsfield Comprehensive; Polytechnic of Central London. Jobs: political researcher, secretary. First Elected: 1992. Union: TGWU. Status: married, three children.

LAB GAIN		1992 election			1987 election	
		Votes	%	+/-	%	Votes
Janet Anderson	Lab	28,028	43.9	+5.6	38.3	23,074
David Trippier*	Con	27,908	43.7	-2.9	46.6	28,056
Kevin Connor	Lib Dem	7,226	11.3	-3.8	15.1	9,097
Jim Gaffney	Green	596	0.9			
Peter Gorrod	NLP	125	0.2			
Majority	**Lab**	**120**	**0.2**	**+8.5**	**8.3**	**4,982**

Electorate: 76,909 **Voters:** 63,883 **Turnout:** 83.1 **Swing:** 4.2 to Lab from Con

ROTHER VALLEY

Kevin Barron: Labour. Born: 1946. Educated: Maltby Hall Secondary School; Ruskin College, Oxford. Jobs: colliery electrician. First Elected: 1983. Union: NUM. Status: married, three children.

LAB HOLD		1992 election			1987 election	
		Votes	%	+/-	%	Votes
Kevin Barron*	Lab	30,977	60.5	+4.1	56.4	28,292
Toby Horton	Con	13,755	26.9	+1.9	24.9	12,502
Kevin Smith	Lib Dem	6,483	12.7	-5.8	18.4	9,240
Majority	**Lab**	**17,222**	**33.6**	**+2.2**	**31.5**	**15,790**

Electorate: 68,303 **Voters:** 51,215 **Turnout:** 75.0 **Swing:** 1.1 to Lab from Con

ROTHERHAM

Jimmy Boyce: Labour. Born: 1947. Educated: St Mirrens Academy; Sheffield University. Jobs: foundry worker, tiler. First Elected: 1992. Union: AEU. Status: separated.

LAB HOLD		1992 election			1987 election	
		Votes	%	+/-	%	Votes
Jimmy Boyce	Lab	27,933	63.9	+4.3	59.7	25,422
Stephen Yorke	Con	10,372	23.7	+1.7	22.1	9,410
David Wildgoose	Lib Dem	5,375	12.3	-5.9	18.2	7,766
Majority	**Lab**	**17,561**	**40.2**	**+2.6**	**37.6**	**16,012**

Electorate: 60,937 **Voters:** 43,680 **Turnout:** 71.7 **Swing:** 1.3 to Lab from Con

ROXBURGH & BERWICKSHIRE

Archy Kirkwood: *Liberal Democrat. Born: 1946. Educated: Cranhill School; Heriot Watt University. Jobs: solicitor. First Elected: 1983. Posts: LibDem Chief Whip and spokesman on social security. Status: married, two children.*

LIBDEM HOLD		1992 election Votes	%	+/-	1987 election %	Votes
Archy Kirkwood*	Lib Dem	15,852	46.9	-2.3	49.2	16,388
Shirley Finlay-Maxwell	Con	11,595	34.3	-2.9	37.2	12,380
Marshall Douglas	SNP	3,437	10.2	+5.4	4.8	1,586
Stephen Lambert	Lab	2,909	8.6	-0.2	8.8	2,944
Majority	**Lib Dem**	**4,257**	**12.6**	**+0.6**	**12.0**	**4,008**

Electorate: 43,485 **Voters:** 33,793 **Turnout:** 77.7 **Swing:** 0.3 to LDm from Con

RUGBY & KENILWORTH

James Pawsey: *Conservative. Born: 1933. Educated: Coventry Technical College. Jobs: company director. First Elected: 1979. Posts: executive member, 1922 Committee. Status: married, six children.*

CON HOLD		1992 election Votes	%	+/-	1987 election %	Votes
James Pawsey*	Con	34,110	52.4	+0.8	51.6	31,485
John Airey	Lab	20,863	32.0	+7.1	24.9	15,221
Jeremy Roodhouse	Lib Dem	9,934	15.3	-8.2	23.5	14,343
Stuart Withers	NLP	202	0.3			
Majority	**Con**	**13,247**	**20.3**	**-6.3**	**26.6**	**16,264**

Electorate: 77,766 **Voters:** 65,109 **Turnout:** 83.7 **Swing:** 3.1 to Lab from Con

RUISLIP & NORTHWOOD

John Wilkinson: *Conservative. Born: 1940. Educated: Eton; Cambridge. Jobs: political researcher, aeronautics industry. First Elected: 1970. Status: married, one child.*

CON HOLD		1992 election Votes	%	+/-	1987 election %	Votes
John Wilkinson*	Con	28,097	63.3	+0.7	62.6	27,418
Rachel Brooks	Lab	8,306	18.7	+5.2	13.5	5,913
Harry Davies	Lib Dem	7,739	17.4	-6.4	23.9	10,447
Michael Sheehan	NLP	214	0.5			
Majority	**Con**	**19,791**	**44.6**	**+5.9**	**38.8**	**16,971**

Electorate: 54,151 **Voters:** 44,356 **Turnout:** 81.9 **Swing:** 2.3 to Lab from Con

RUSHCLIFFE

Kenneth Clarke: Conservative. Born: 1940. Educated: Nottingham High School; Cambridge. Jobs: barrister. First Elected: 1970. Posts: Home Secretary. Status: married, two children.

CON HOLD		1992 election			1987 election	
		Votes	%	+/-	%	Votes
Kenneth Clarke*	Con	34,448	54.4	-4.4	58.8	34,214
Alan Chewings	Lab	14,682	23.2	+6.6	16.5	9,631
Andrew Wood	Lib Dem	12,660	20.0	-3.0	23.0	13,375
Simon Anthony	Green	775	1.2	-0.5	1.7	991
Morgan Maelor-Jones	Ind C	611	1.0			
David Richards	NLP	150	0.2			
Majority	**Con**	**19,766**	**31.2**	**-4.6**	**35.8**	**20,839**

Electorate: 76,253 **Voters:** 63,326 **Turnout:** 83.0 **Swing:** 5.5 to Lab from Con

RUTLAND & MELTON

Alan Duncan: Conservative. Born: 1957. Educated: Merchant Taylors; Oxford. Jobs: crude oil trader. First Elected: 1992. Status: single.

CON HOLD		1992 election			1987 election	
		Votes	%	+/-	%	Votes
Alan Duncan	Con	38,603	59.0	-3.0	62.0	37,073
Joan Taylor	Lab	13,068	20.0	+5.5	14.5	8,680
Richard Lustig	Lib Dem	12,682	19.4	-4.1	23.5	14,051
Jim Berreen	Green	861	1.3			
Robert Grey	NLP	237	0.4			
Majority	**Con**	**25,535**	**39.0**	**+0.5**	**38.5**	**23,022**

Electorate: 80,976 **Voters:** 65,451 **Turnout:** 80.8 **Swing:** 4.2 to Lab from Con

RYEDALE

John Greenway: Conservative. Born: 1946. Educated: Sir John Deane's School, Northwich. Jobs: policeman, insurance broker. First Elected: 1987. Posts: member, Home Affairs Select Committee. Status: married, three children.

CON HOLD		1992 election			1987 election	
		Votes	%	+/-	%	Votes
John Greenway*	Con	39,888	56.1	+2.7	53.3	35,149
Elizabeth Shields	Lib Dem	21,449	30.1	-8.4	38.6	25,409
John Healey	Lab	9,812	13.8	+5.7	8.1	5,340
Majority	**Con**	**18,439**	**25.9**	**+11.1**	**14.8**	**9,740**

Electorate: 87,048 **Voters:** 71,149 **Turnout:** 81.7 **Swing:** 5.6 to Con from LDm

SAFFRON WALDEN

Alan Haselhurst: *Conservative. Born: 1937. Educated: King Edward VI School, Birmingham; Oxford. Jobs: director of voluntary organisations. First Elected: 1970. Posts: member, Transport Select Committee, European Legislation Select Committee. Status: married, three children.*

CON HOLD		1992 election Votes	%	+/-	1987 election %	Votes
Alan Haselhurst*	Con	35,272	56.6	-1.1	57.7	33,354
Mark Hayes	Lib Dem	17,848	28.6	-0.3	29.0	16,752
John Kotz	Lab	8,933	14.3	+2.8	11.5	6,674
Michael Miller	NLP	260	0.4			
Majority	**Con**	**17,424**	**28.0**	**-0.8**	**28.7**	**16,602**

Electorate: 74,878 **Voters:** 62,313 **Turnout:** 83.2 **Swing:** 0.4 to LDm from Con

ST ALBANS

Peter Lilley: *Conservative. Born: 1943. Educated: Dulwich College; Cambridge. Jobs: oil analyst, economic consultant. First Elected: 1983. Posts: Social Security Secretary. Status: married.*

CON HOLD		1992 election Votes	%	+/-	1987 election %	Votes
Peter Lilley*	Con	32,709	52.8	+0.3	52.5	31,726
Monica Howes	Lib Dem	16,305	26.3	-8.2	34.5	20,845
Kerry Pollard	Lab	12,016	19.4	+7.9	11.5	6,922
Craig Simmons	Green	734	1.2	-0.1	1.3	788
David Lucas	NLP	161	0.3			
Majority	**Con**	**16,404**	**26.5**	**+8.5**	**18.0**	**10,881**

Electorate: 74,188 **Voters:** 61,925 **Turnout:** 83.5 **Swing:** 4.2 to Con from LDm

ST HELENS NORTH

John Evans: *Labour. Born: 1930. Educated: Jarrow Central School. Jobs: shipyard worker. First Elected: 1974. Posts: member, Labour National Executive. Union: AEU. Status: married, three children.*

LAB HOLD		1992 election Votes	%	+/-	1987 election %	Votes
John Evans*	Lab	31,930	57.9	+4.3	53.7	28,989
Brendan Anderson	Con	15,686	28.5	+1.2	27.3	14,729
John Beirne	Lib Dem	7,224	13.1	-6.0	19.1	10,300
Anne Lynch	NLP	287	0.5			
Majority	**Lab**	**16,244**	**29.5**	**+3.1**	**26.4**	**14,260**

Electorate: 71,261 **Voters:** 55,127 **Turnout:** 77.4 **Swing:** 1.5 to Lab from Con

ST HELENS SOUTH

Gerald Bermingham: Labour. Born: 1940. Educated: Wellingborough Grammar School; Sheffield University. Jobs: teacher, solicitor, barrister. First Elected: 1983. Posts: member, Home Affairs Select Committee. Union: GMB. Status: married, two children.

LAB HOLD		1992 election			1987 election	
		Votes	%	+/-	%	Votes
Gerald Bermingham*	Lab	30,391	61.0	+6.4	54.6	27,027
Patricia Buzzard	Con	12,182	24.5	-2.3	26.7	13,226
Brian Spencer	Lib Dem	6,933	13.9	-4.8	18.7	9,252
Harriet Jump	NLP	295	0.6			
Majority	**Lab**	**18,209**	**36.6**	**+8.7**	**27.9**	**13,801**

Electorate: 67,507 **Voters:** 49,801 **Turnout:** 73.8 **Swing:** 4.3 to Lab from Con

ST IVES

David Harris: Conservative. Born: 1937. Educated: Mount Radford School, Exeter. Jobs: journalist. First Elected: 1983. Posts: member, Foreign Affairs Select Committee, Social Security Select Committee. Status: married, two children.

CON HOLD		1992 election			1987 election	
		Votes	%	+/-	%	Votes
David Harris*	Con	24,528	42.9	-5.4	48.3	25,174
Andrew George	Lib Dem	22,883	40.1	+6.2	33.8	17,619
Stephen Warran	Lab	9,144	16.0	-1.8	17.8	9,275
Graham Stephens	Lib	577	1.0			
Majority	**Con**	**1,645**	**2.9**	**-11.6**	**14.5**	**7,555**

Electorate: 71,152 **Voters:** 57,132 **Turnout:** 80.3 **Swing:** 5.8 to LDm from Con

SALFORD EAST

Stanley Orme: Labour. Born: 1923. Educated: elementary and technical schools. Jobs: engineer. First Elected: 1964. Union: AEU. Posts: member, Trade and Industry Select Committee. Status: married.

LAB HOLD		1992 election			1987 election	
		Votes	%	+/-	%	Votes
Stanley Orme*	Lab	20,327	60.0	+1.2	58.8	22,555
David Berens	Con	9,092	26.8	-0.5	27.4	10,499
Norman Owen	Lib Dem	3,836	11.3	-2.0	13.3	5,105
Mark Stanley	Green	463	1.4			
Christopher Craig	NLP	150	0.4			
Majority	**Lab**	**11,235**	**33.2**	**+1.7**	**31.4**	**12,056**

Electorate: 52,616 **Voters:** 33,868 **Turnout:** 64.4 **Swing:** 0.9 to Lab from Con

SALISBURY

Robert Key: *Conservative. Born: 1945. Educated: Sherborne; Cambridge. Jobs: teacher. First Elected: 1983. Posts: National Heritage minister. Status: married, three children.*

CON HOLD		1992 election			1987 election	
		Votes	%	+/-	%	Votes
Robert Key*	Con	31,546	52.0	-2.9	54.9	31,612
Paul Sample	Lib Dem	22,573	37.2	+2.2	35.0	20,169
Steve Fear	Lab	5,483	9.0	-0.4	9.5	5,455
Sherwood Elcock	Green	609	1.0			
Stephen Fletcher	Ind	233	0.4	-0.3	0.6	372
Tim Abbott	Wessex	117	0.2			
Annie Martell	NLP	93	0.2			
Majority	**Con**	**8,973**	**14.8**	**-5.1**	**19.9**	**11,443**

Electorate: 75,916 **Voters:** 60,654 **Turnout:** 79.9 **Swing:** 2.5 to LDm from Con

SCARBOROUGH

John Sykes: *Conservative. Born: 1956. Educated: Giggleswick School. Jobs: company director. First Elected: 1992. Status: married, three children.*

CON HOLD		1992 election			1987 election	
		Votes	%	+/-	%	Votes
John Sykes	Con	29,334	49.8	-0.9	50.7	27,672
David Billing	Lab	17,600	29.9	+6.2	23.6	12,913
Bromley Davenport	Lib Dem	11,133	18.9	-6.8	25.7	14,046
Dick Richardson	Green	876	1.5			
Majority	**Con**	**11,734**	**19.9**	**-5.0**	**24.9**	**13,626**

Electorate: 76,364 **Voters:** 58,943 **Turnout:** 77.2 **Swing:** 3.6 to Lab from Con

SEDGEFIELD

Tony Blair: *Labour. Born: 1953. Educated: Fettes College; Oxford. Jobs: barrister. First Elected: 1983. Posts: Shadow Home Secretary. Union: TGWU. Status: married, three children.*

LAB HOLD		1992 election			1987 election	
		Votes	%	+/-	%	Votes
Tony Blair*	Lab	28,453	60.5	+4.5	56.0	25,965
Nicholas Jopling	Con	13,594	28.9	+1.1	27.8	12,907
Garry Huntington	Lib Dem	4,982	10.6	-5.5	16.1	7,477
Majority	**Lab**	**14,859**	**31.6**	**+3.4**	**28.2**	**13,058**

Electorate: 61,024 **Voters:** 47,029 **Turnout:** 77.1 **Swing:** 1.7 to Lab from Con

SELBY

Michael Alison: *Conservative. Born: 1926. Educated: Eton; Oxford. Jobs: merchant banker. First Elected: 1964. Posts: Second Church Estates Commissioner. Status: married, three children.*

CON HOLD		1992 election			1987 election	
		Votes	%	+/-	%	Votes
Michael Alison*	Con	31,067	50.2	-1.4	51.6	28,611
John Grogan	Lab	21,559	34.8	+8.1	26.7	14,832
Ted Batty	Lib Dem	9,244	14.9	-6.7	21.7	12,010
Majority	**Con**	**9,508**	**15.4**	**-9.5**	**24.8**	**13,779**

Electorate: 77,178 **Voters:** 61,870 **Turnout:** 80.2 **Swing:** 4.7 to Lab from Con

SEVENOAKS

Mark Wolfson: *Conservative. Born: 1934. Educated: Eton; Cambridge. Jobs: merchant banker, personnel director. First Elected: 1979. Posts: PPS. Status: married, two children.*

CON HOLD		1992 election			1987 election	
		Votes	%	+/-	%	Votes
Mark Wolfson*	Con	33,245	57.5	-1.4	58.9	32,945
Roger Walshe	Lib Dem	14,091	24.4	-3.5	27.9	15,600
Jeannie Evans	Lab	9,470	16.4	+3.2	13.2	7,379
Margot Lawrence	Green	786	1.4			
Peter Wakeling	NLP	210	0.4			
Majority	**Con**	**19,154**	**33.1**	**+2.1**	**31.0**	**17,345**

Electorate: 71,050 **Voters:** 57,802 **Turnout:** 81.4 **Swing:** 1.1 to Con from LDm

SHEFFIELD, ATTERCLIFFE

Clive Betts: *Labour. Born: 1950. Educated: King Edward VII School, Sheffield; Cambridge. Jobs: local government officer. First Elected: 1992. Union: TGWU. Status: single.*

LAB HOLD		1992 election			1987 election	
		Votes	%	+/-	%	Votes
Clive Betts	Lab	28,563	57.5	-0.3	57.8	28,266
Gordon Millward	Con	13,083	26.3	+3.7	22.7	11,075
Helen Woolley	Lib Dem	7,283	14.7	-4.9	19.5	9,549
Gordon Ferguson	Green	751	1.5			
Majority	**Lab**	**15,480**	**31.2**	**-4.0**	**35.2**	**17,191**

Electorate: 69,177 **Voters:** 49,680 **Turnout:** 71.8 **Swing:** 2.0 to Con from Lab

SHEFFIELD, BRIGHTSIDE

David Blunkett: Labour. Born: 1947. Educated: Sheffield School for the Blind; Sheffield University. Jobs: office worker, tutor. First Elected: 1987. Posts: Shadow Health Secretary. Union: NUPE. Status: divorced, three children.

LAB HOLD		1992 election			1987 election	
		Votes	%	+/-	%	Votes
David Blunkett*	Lab	29,771	70.4	+0.5	69.9	31,208
Timothy Loughton	Con	7,090	16.8	+1.1	15.7	7,017
Richard Franklin	Lib Dem	5,273	12.5	-1.9	14.4	6,434
David Hyland	Int Comm	150	0.4			
Majority	**Lab**	**22,681**	**53.6**	**-0.5**	**54.2**	**24,191**

Electorate: 63,810 **Voters:** 42,284 **Turnout:** 66.3 **Swing:** 0.3 to Con from Lab

SHEFFIELD CENTRAL

Richard Caborn: Labour. Born: 1943. Educated: Hurfield Comprehensive; Sheffield Polytechnic. Jobs: engineer, Euro MP. First Elected: 1983. Posts: member, Trade and Industry Select Committee. Union: AEU. Status: married, two children.

LAB HOLD		1992 election			1987 election	
		Votes	%	+/-	%	Votes
Richard Caborn*	Lab	22,764	68.7	+0.9	67.7	25,872
Vernon Davies	Con	5,470	16.5	-0.6	17.1	6,530
Andrew Sangar	Lib Dem	3,856	11.6	-2.3	13.9	5,314
Graham Wroe	Green	750	2.3			
Martin Clarke	EUVJJ	212	0.6			
Josephine O'Brien	CL	92	0.3			
Majority	**Lab**	**17,294**	**52.2**	**+1.5**	**50.6**	**19,342**

Electorate: 59,059 **Voters:** 33,144 **Turnout:** 56.1 **Swing:** 0.8 to Lab from Con

SHEFFIELD, HALLAM

Irvine Patnick: Conservative. Born: 1929. Educated: Central Technical School; Sheffield Polytechnic. Jobs: property developer, company director. First Elected: 1987. Posts: Government Whip. Status: married, two children.

CON HOLD		1992 election			1987 election	
		Votes	%	+/-	%	Votes
Irvine Patnick*	Con	24,693	45.5	-0.8	46.3	25,649
Peter Gold	Lib Dem	17,952	33.1	+0.6	32.5	18,012
Veronica Hardstaff	Lab	10,930	20.1	-0.2	20.4	11,290
Michael Baker	Green	473	0.9	+0.0	0.8	459
Richard Hurford	NLP	101	0.2			
Theresa Clifford	Rev Comm	99	0.2			
Majority	**Con**	**6,741**	**12.4**	**-1.4**	**13.8**	**7,637**

Electorate: 76,584 **Voters:** 54,248 **Turnout:** 70.8 **Swing:** 0.7 to LDm from Con

SHEFFIELD, HEELEY

Bill Michie: Labour. Born: 1935. Educated: Abbeydale Secondary School; Sheffield. Jobs: electrician. First Elected: 1983. Union: AEU. Status: married, two children.

LAB HOLD		1992 election			1987 election	
		Votes	%	+/-	%	Votes
Bill Michie*	Lab	28,005	55.7	+2.3	53.4	28,425
David Beck	Con	13,051	25.9	-0.3	26.3	13,985
Peter Moore	Lib Dem	9,247	18.4	-1.9	20.3	10,811
Majority	**Lab**	**14,954**	**29.7**	**+2.6**	**27.1**	**14,440**

Electorate: 70,953 **Voters:** 50,303 **Turnout:** 70.9 **Swing:** 1.3 to Lab from Con

SHEFFIELD, HILLSBOROUGH

Helen Jackson: Labour. Born: 1939. Educated: Berkhamsted School; Oxford. Jobs: tutor. First Elected: 1992. Posts: member, Environment Select Committee. Union: TGWU. Status: married, three children.

LAB HOLD		1992 election			1987 election	
		Votes	%	+/-	%	Votes
Helen Jackson	Lab	27,568	46.2	+2.1	44.0	26,208
David Chadwick	Lib Dem	20,500	34.3	-4.2	38.5	22,922
Sidney Cordle	Con	11,640	19.5	+2.0	17.5	10,396
Majority	**Lab**	**7,068**	**11.8**	**+6.3**	**5.5**	**3,286**

Electorate: 77,343 **Voters:** 59,708 **Turnout:** 77.2 **Swing:** 3.2 to Lab from LDm

SHERWOOD

Paddy Tipping: Labour. Born: 1949. Educated: Hipperholme Grammar School; Nottingham University. Jobs: social worker, full-time councillor. First Elected: 1992. Union: NUPE. Status: married, two children.

LAB GAIN		1992 election			1987 election	
		Votes	%	+/-	%	Votes
Paddy Tipping	Lab	29,788	47.5	+9.3	38.2	22,321
Andrew Stewart*	Con	26,878	42.9	-3.0	45.9	26,816
John Howard	Lib Dem	6,039	9.6	-6.3	16.0	9,343
Majority	**Lab**	**2,910**	**4.6**	**+12.3**	**7.7**	**4,495**

Electorate: 73,354 **Voters:** 62,705 **Turnout:** 85.5 **Swing:** 6.2 to Lab from Con

SHIPLEY

Sir Marcus Fox: Conservative. Born: 1927. Educated: Wheelwright Grammar School, Dewsbury. Jobs: bank clerk, company director. First Elected: 1970. Posts: vice-chairman, 1922 Committee; chairman, Selection Committee. Status: married, two children.

CON HOLD

		1992 election			1987 election	
		Votes	%	+/-	%	Votes
Sir Marcus Fox*	Con	28,463	50.4	+0.9	49.5	26,941
Annie Lockwood	Lab	16,081	28.5	+5.2	23.3	12,669
John Cole	Lib Dem	11,288	20.0	-6.3	26.3	14,311
Colin Harris	Green	680	1.2	+0.3	0.9	507
Majority	**Con**	**12,382**	**21.9**	**-1.3**	**23.2**	**12,630**

Electorate: 68,816 **Voters:** 56,512 **Turnout:** 82.1 **Swing:** 2.2 to Lab from Con

SHOREHAM

Michael Stephen: Conservative. Born: 1942. Educated: King Henry VIII School, Coventry; Stanford and Harvard Universities. Jobs: barrister, army officer. First Elected: 1992. Status: married.

CON HOLD

		1992 election			1987 election	
		Votes	%	+/-	%	Votes
Michael Stephen	Con	32,670	56.5	-4.4	60.9	33,660
Martin King	Lib Dem	18,384	31.8	+1.8	30.0	16,590
Paul Godwin	Lab	6,123	10.6	+1.4	9.1	5,053
Bill Weights	Lib	459	0.8			
Jeffrey Dreben	NLP	200	0.3			
Majority	**Con**	**14,286**	**24.7**	**-6.2**	**30.9**	**17,070**

Electorate: 71,252 **Voters:** 57,836 **Turnout:** 81.2 **Swing:** 3.1 to LDm from Con

SHREWSBURY & ATCHAM

Derek Conway: Conservative. Born: 1953. Educated: Beacon Hill School; Gateshead Technical College, Newcastle Polytechnic. Jobs: grocer, advertising. First Elected: 1983. Status: married, three children.

CON HOLD

		1992 election			1987 election	
		Votes	%	+/-	%	Votes
Derek Conway*	Con	26,681	45.8	-2.0	47.8	26,027
Kenneth Hemsley	Lib Dem	15,716	27.0	-4.2	31.2	16,963
Liz Owen	Lab	15,157	26.0	+6.2	19.8	10,797
Geoff Hardy	Green	677	1.2	+0.0	1.2	660
Majority	**Con**	**10,965**	**18.8**	**+2.2**	**16.6**	**9,064**

Electorate: 70,620 **Voters:** 58,231 **Turnout:** 82.5 **Swing:** 1.1 to Con from LDm

SHROPSHIRE NORTH

John Biffen: *Conservative. Born: 1930. Educated: Dr Morgan's Grammar School, Bridgwater; Cambridge. Jobs: economist, company director. First Elected: 1961. Status: married.*

CON HOLD		1992 election			1987 election	
		Votes	%	+/-	%	Votes
John Biffen*	Con	32,443	50.5	-1.7	52.2	30,385
John Stevens	Lib Dem	16,232	25.3	-2.2	27.4	15,970
Robert Hawkins	Lab	15,550	24.2	+3.8	20.4	11,866
Majority	**Con**	**16,211**	**25.2**	**+0.5**	**24.8**	**14,415**

Electorate: 82,675 **Voters:** 64,225 **Turnout:** 77.7 **Swing:** 0.2 to Con from LDm

SKIPTON & RIPON

David Curry: *Conservative. Born: 1944. Educated: Ripon Grammar School; Oxford. Jobs: journalist, Euro MP. First Elected: 1987. Posts: Minister of State for Agriculture. Status: married, three children.*

CON HOLD		1992 election			1987 election	
		Votes	%	+/-	%	Votes
David Curry*	Con	35,937	58.4	-0.6	59.0	33,128
Richard Hall	Lib Dem	16,607	27.0	-1.4	28.4	15,954
Katharine Allott	Lab	8,978	14.6	+3.4	11.2	6,264
Majority	**Con**	**19,330**	**31.4**	**+0.8**	**30.6**	**17,174**

Electorate: 75,628 **Voters:** 61,522 **Turnout:** 81.3 **Swing:** 0.4 to Con from LDm

SLOUGH

John Watts: *Conservative. Born: 1947. Educated: Bishopshalt School, Hillingdon; Cambridge. Jobs: accountant. First Elected: 1983. Posts: chairman, Treasury Select Committee. Status: married, four children.*

CON HOLD		1992 election			1987 election	
		Votes	%	+/-	%	Votes
John Watts*	Con	25,793	44.6	-2.3	46.9	26,166
Eddie Lopez	Lab	25,279	43.7	+4.1	39.6	22,076
Peter Mapp	Lib Dem	4,041	7.0	-6.4	13.4	7,490
John Clark	Lib	1,426	2.5			
Declan Alford	Ind Lab	699	1.2			
Andy Carmichael	NF	290	0.5			
Martin Creese	NLP	153	0.3			
Elizabeth Smith	ERIP	134	0.2			
Majority	**Con**	**514**	**0.9**	**-6.4**	**7.3**	**4,090**

Electorate: 73,889 **Voters:** 57,815 **Turnout:** 78.2 **Swing:** 3.2 to Lab from Con

SOLIHULL

John Taylor: *Conservative. Born: 1941. Educated: Bromsgrove School. Jobs: solicitor, company director. First Elected: 1983. Posts: minister in Lord Chancellor's department. Status: married.*

CON HOLD

		1992 election Votes	%	+/-	1987 election %	Votes
John Taylor*	Con	38,385	60.8	-0.2	61.1	35,844
Michael Southcombe	Lib Dem	13,239	21.0	-3.0	24.0	14,058
Nicola Kutapan	Lab	10,544	16.7	+1.7	15.0	8,791
Clifford Hards	Green	925	1.5			
Majority	**Con**	**25,146**	**39.9**	**+2.7**	**37.1**	**21,786**

Electorate: 77,303 **Voters:** 63,093 **Turnout:** 81.6 **Swing:** 1.4 to Con from LDm

SOMERTON & FROME

Mark Robinson: *Conservative. Born: 1946. Educated: Harrow; Oxford. Jobs: barrister, banker. First Elected: 1983. Posts: member, Welsh Affairs Select Committee. Status: married.*

CON HOLD

		1992 election Votes	%	+/-	1987 election %	Votes
Mark Robinson	Con	28,052	47.5	-6.2	53.7	29,351
David Heath	Lib Dem	23,711	40.2	+3.9	36.3	19,813
Bob Ashford	Lab	6,154	10.4	+0.4	10.0	5,461
Leona Graham	Green	742	1.3			
Jean Pollock	Lib	388	0.7			
Majority	**Con**	**4,341**	**7.4**	**-10.1**	**17.5**	**9,538**

Electorate: 71,354 **Voters:** 59,047 **Turnout:** 82.8 **Swing:** 5.1 to LDm from Con

SOUTHAMPTON, ITCHEN

John Denham: *Labour. Born: 1953. Educated: Woodroffe Comprehensive, Lyme Regis; Southampton University. Jobs: consultant to voluntary organisations. First Elected: 1992. Union: MSF. Status: married, two children.*

LAB GAIN

		1992 election Votes	%	+/-	1987 election %	Votes
John Denham	Lab	24,402	44.0	+11.9	32.1	17,703
Christopher Chope*	Con	23,851	43.0	-1.3	44.3	24,419
James Hodgson	Lib Dem	7,221	13.0	-10.6	23.6	13,006
Majority	**Lab**	**551**	**1.0**	**+13.2**	**12.2**	**6,716**

Electorate: 72,104 **Voters:** 55,474 **Turnout:** 76.9 **Swing:** 6.6 to Lab from Con

SOUTHAMPTON, TEST

James Hill: Conservative. Born: 1926. Educated: Regent's Park Secondary School; Southampton University. Jobs: pilot, company director. First Elected: 1970. Posts: member, chairmen's panel. Status: married, five children.

CON HOLD		1992 election			1987 election	
		Votes	%	+/-	%	Votes
James Hill*	Con	24,504	43.4	-2.2	45.6	25,722
Alan Whitehead	Lab	23,919	42.4	+9.1	33.3	18,768
Diana Maddock	Lib Dem	7,391	13.1	-8.1	21.2	11,950
Jonathan Michaelis	Green	535	0.9			
David Plummer	NLP	101	0.2			
Majority	**Con**	**585**	**1.0**	**-11.3**	**12.3**	**6,954**

Electorate: 72,932 **Voters:** 56,450 **Turnout:** 77.4 **Swing:** 5.6 to Lab from Con

SOUTHEND EAST

Sir Teddy Taylor: Conservative. Born: 1937. Educated: Glasgow High School; Glasgow University. Jobs: industrial relations officer. First Elected: 1964. Status: married, three children.

CON HOLD		1992 election			1987 election	
		Votes	%	+/-	%	Votes
Sir Teddy Taylor*	Con	24,591	58.8	+0.8	58.0	23,753
Graham Bramley	Lab	11,480	27.4	+9.6	17.8	7,296
Jackie Horne	Lib Dem	5,107	12.2	-12.0	24.2	9,906
Brian Lynch	Lib	673	1.6			
Majority	**Con**	**13,111**	**31.3**	**-2.5**	**33.8**	**13,847**

Electorate: 56,708 **Voters:** 41,851 **Turnout:** 73.8 **Swing:** 4.4 to Lab from Con

SOUTHEND WEST

Paul Channon: Conservative. Born: 1935. Educated: Eton; Oxford. Jobs: company director. First Elected: 1959. Posts: member, National Heritage Select Committee. Status: married, two children.

CON HOLD		1992 election			1987 election	
		Votes	%	+/-	%	Votes
Paul Channon*	Con	27,319	54.7	+0.3	54.4	28,003
Nina Stimson	Lib Dem	15,417	30.9	-7.2	38.1	19,603
Geoffrey Viney	Lab	6,139	12.3	+4.7	7.6	3,899
Alan Farmer	Lib	495	1.0			
Chris Keene	Green	451	0.9			
Peter Warburton	NLP	127	0.3			
Majority	**Con**	**11,902**	**23.8**	**+7.5**	**16.3**	**8,400**

Electorate: 64,198 **Voters:** 49,948 **Turnout:** 77.8 **Swing:** 3.8 to Con from LDm

SOUTH HAMS

Anthony Steen: Conservative. Born: 1939. Educated: Westminster; London University. Jobs: lecturer, barrister, charity director. First Elected: 1974. Status: married, two children.

CON HOLD		1992 election Votes	%	+/-	1987 election %	Votes
Anthony Steen*	Con	35,951	53.4	-2.0	55.4	34,218
Vaughan Evans	Lib Dem	22,240	33.0	-1.1	34.1	21,072
Eleanor Cohen	Lab	8,091	12.0	+3.8	8.2	5,060
Christopher Titmuss	Green	846	1.3	-0.6	1.9	1,178
Linda Summerville	NLP	227	0.3			
Majority	**Con**	**13,711**	**20.4**	**-0.9**	**21.3**	**13,146**

Electorate: 83,061 **Voters:** 67,355 **Turnout:** 81.1 **Swing:** 0.5 to LDm from Con

SOUTHPORT

Matthew Banks: Conservative. Born: 1961. Educated: Calday Grange Grammar School; Sheffield Polytechnic; Sandhurst. Jobs: army officer, public relations, political adviser. Posts: member, Transport Select Committee. First Elected: 1992. Status: single.

CON GAIN		1992 election Votes	%	+/-	1987 election %	Votes
Matthew Banks	Con	26,081	47.0	+2.5	44.5	24,261
Ronnie Fearn*	Lib Dem	23,018	41.5	-6.4	47.9	26,110
James King	Lab	5,637	10.2	+3.8	6.4	3,483
Justin Walker	Green	545	1.0	-0.2	1.2	653
Geoffrey Clements	NLP	159	0.3			
Majority	**Con**	**3,063**	**5.5**	**+8.9**	**3.4**	**1,849**

Electorate: 71,443 **Voters:** 55,440 **Turnout:** 77.6 **Swing:** 4.5 to Con from LDm

SOUTH RIBBLE

Robert Atkins: Conservative. Born: 1946. Educated: Highgate School. Jobs: insurance broker, sales executive. First Elected: 1979. Posts: Minister of State for Northern Ireland. Status: married, two children.

CON HOLD		1992 election Votes	%	+/-	1987 election %	Votes
Robert Atkins*	Con	30,828	47.5	+0.3	47.2	28,133
Geoffrey Smith	Lab	24,855	38.3	+5.2	33.1	19,703
Simon Jones	Lib Dem	8,928	13.8	-6.0	19.7	11,746
Ronald Decter	NLP	269	0.4			
Majority	**Con**	**5,973**	**9.2**	**-4.9**	**14.1**	**8,430**

Electorate: 78,173 **Voters:** 64,880 **Turnout:** 83.0 **Swing:** 2.5 to Lab from Con

CONSTITUENCIES

SOUTH SHIELDS

Dr David Clark: Labour. Born: 1939. Educated: Windermere Grammar School; Manchester University. Jobs: forester, lecturer. First Elected: 1970. Posts: Shadow Defence Secretary. Union: NUPE. Status: married, one child.

LAB HOLD		1992 election			1987 election	
		Votes	%	+/-	%	Votes
David Clark*	Lab	24,876	59.8	+1.9	57.9	24,882
Jonathan Howard	Con	11,399	27.4	+1.7	25.7	11,031
Arthur Preece	Lib Dem	5,344	12.8	-2.6	15.5	6,654
Majority	**Lab**	**13,477**	**32.4**	**+0.2**	**32.2**	**13,851**

Electorate: 59,392 **Voters:** 41,619 **Turnout:** 70.1 **Swing:** No Swing

SOUTHWARK & BERMONDSEY

Simon Hughes: Liberal Democrat. Born: 1951. Educated: Christ College, Brecon; Cambridge. Jobs: barrister. First Elected: 1983. Posts: LibDem spokesman on environment and energy. Status: single.

LIBDEM HOLD		1992 election			1987 election	
		Votes	%	+/-	%	Votes
Simon Hughes*	Lib Dem	21,459	56.9	+9.4	47.4	17,072
Richard Balfe	Lab	11,614	30.8	-8.9	39.7	14,293
Andrew Raca	Con	3,794	10.1	-2.5	12.6	4,522
Stephen Tyler	BNP	530	1.4			
Terry Blackham	NF	168	0.4			
Graham Barnett	NLP	113	0.3			
John Grogan	CL	56	0.1			
Majority	**Lib Dem**	**9,845**	**26.1**	**+18.4**	**7.7**	**2,779**

Electorate: 60,251 **Voters:** 37,734 **Turnout:** 62.6 **Swing:** 9.2 to LDm from Lab

SPELTHORNE

David Wilshire: Conservative. Born: 1943. Educated: Kingswood School, Bath; Cambridge. Jobs: political adviser. First Elected: 1987. Status: married, one child.

CON HOLD		1992 election			1987 election	
		Votes	%	+/-	%	Votes
David Wilshire*	Con	32,627	58.5	-1.5	60.0	32,440
Ann Leedham	Lab	12,784	22.9	+5.9	17.1	9,227
Roger Roberts	Lib Dem	9,202	16.5	-6.4	22.9	12,390
Julia Wassell	Green	580	1.0			
Dave Rea	Loony	338	0.6			
David Ellis	NLP	195	0.3			
Majority	**Con**	**19,843**	**35.6**	**-1.5**	**37.1**	**20,050**

Electorate: 69,343 **Voters:** 55,726 **Turnout:** 80.4 **Swing:** 3.7 to Lab from Con

STAFFORD

Bill Cash: *Conservative. Born: 1940. Educated: Stonyhurst College; Oxford. Jobs: solicitor. First Elected: 1984. Posts: member, European Legislation Select Committee. Status: married, three children.*

CON HOLD		1992 election			1987 election	
		Votes	%	+/-	%	Votes
Bill Cash*	Con	30,876	49.9	-1.5	51.3	29,541
David Kidney	Lab	19,976	32.3	+11.1	21.2	12,177
Jamie Calder	Lib Dem	10,702	17.3	-10.2	27.5	15,834
Christopher Peat	Hardcore	178	0.3			
Philip Lines	NLP	176	0.3			
Majority	**Con**	**10,900**	**17.6**	**-6.2**	**23.8**	**13,707**

Electorate: 74,663 **Voters:** 61,908 **Turnout:** 82.9 **Swing:** 6.3 to Lab from Con

STAFFORDSHIRE MID

Michael Fabricant: *Conservative. Born: 1950. Educated: Brighton, Hove and Sussex Grammar School; Loughborough, Sussex and London Universities. Jobs: broadcaster, company director. First Elected: 1992. Status: single.*

CON REGAIN		1992 election			1987 election	
		Votes	%	+/-	%	Votes
Michael Fabricant	Con	31,227	49.7	-1.0	50.6	28,644
Sylvia Heal*	Lab	24,991	39.7	+15.0	24.7	13,990
Barry Stamp	Lib Dem	6,432	10.2	-12.9	23.2	13,114
Dinah Grice	NLP	239	0.4			
Majority	**Con**	**6,236**	**9.9**	**-16.0**	**25.9**	**14,654**

Electorate: 73,414 **Voters:** 62,889 **Turnout:** 85.7 **Swing:** 8.0 to Lab from Con

BY-ELECTION March 1990: LAB GAIN. S. Heal (Lab) 27,649 (49.1%), C. Prior (Con) 18,200 (32.3%), T. Jones (Lib Dem) 6,315 (11.2%), Lab majority 9,499 (16.8%), SWING 21.4% to Lab from Con

STAFFORDSHIRE MOORLANDS

David Knox: *Conservative. Born: 1933. Educated: Lockerbie Academy; London University. Jobs: economic adviser, management consultant. First Elected: 1970. Posts: member, European Legislation Select Committee. Status: married.*

CON HOLD		1992 election			1987 election	
		Votes	%	+/-	%	Votes
David Knox*	Con	29,240	46.6	-6.3	52.9	31,613
James Siddelley	Lab	21,830	34.8	+6.0	28.8	17,186
Christina Jebb	Lib Dem	9,326	14.9	-3.5	18.3	10,950
Michael Howson	Anti Fed	2,121	3.4			
Paul Davies	NLP	261	0.4			
Majority	**Con**	**7,410**	**11.8**	**-12.3**	**24.1**	**14,427**

Electorate: 75,036 **Voters:** 62,778 **Turnout:** 83.7 **Swing:** 6.2 to Lab from Con

STAFFORDSHIRE SOUTH

Patrick Cormack: *Conservative. Born: 1939. Educated: Havelock School; Grimsby; Hull University. Jobs: teacher. First Elected: 1970. Posts: member, National Heritage Select Committee, chairmen's panel. editor, House Magazine. Status: married, two children.*

CON HOLD		1992 election			1987 election	
		Votes	%	+/-	%	Votes
Patrick Cormack*	Con	40,266	59.7	-1.2	60.9	37,708
Bruce Wylie	Lab	17,633	26.1	+7.1	19.1	11,805
Ian Sadler	Lib Dem	9,584	14.2	-5.9	20.1	12,440
Majority	**Con**	**22,633**	**33.5**	**-7.2**	**40.8**	**25,268**

Electorate: 82,758 **Voters:** 67,483 **Turnout:** 81.5 **Swing:** 4.1 to Lab from Con

STAFFORDSHIRE SOUTH EAST

David Lightbown: *Conservative. Born: 1932. Educated: Derby School of Art; Derby Technical College. Jobs: engineering company director. First Elected: 1983. Posts: Government Whip. Status: married.*

CON HOLD		1992 election			1987 election	
		Votes	%	+/-	%	Votes
David Lightbown*	Con	29,180	50.7	+3.5	47.2	25,115
Brian Jenkins	Lab	21,988	38.2	+12.1	26.1	13,874
Gilbert Penlington	Lib Dem	5,540	9.6	-17.1	26.7	14,230
Jill Taylor	Soc Dem	895	1.6			
Majority	**Con**	**7,192**	**12.5**	**-8.0**	**20.5**	**10,885**

Electorate: 70,199 **Voters:** 57,603 **Turnout:** 82.1 **Swing:** 4.3 to Lab from Con

STALYBRIDGE & HYDE

Tom Pendry: *Labour. Born: 1934. Educated: St Augustine's School, Ramsgate; Oxford. Jobs: electrical engineer, trade union official. First Elected: 1970. Posts: Labour spokesman on sport; member, Environment Select Committee. Union: NUPE. Status: married, two children.*

LAB HOLD		1992 election			1987 election	
		Votes	%	+/-	%	Votes
Tom Pendry*	Lab	26,207	52.3	+3.9	48.4	24,401
Simon Mort	Con	17,376	34.7	-2.5	37.1	18,738
Ian Kirk	Lib Dem	4,740	9.5	-5.0	14.5	7,311
Robert Powell	Lib	1,199	2.4			
Darren Poyzer	Loony	337	0.7			
Edward Blomfield	NLP	238	0.5			
Majority	**Lab**	**8,831**	**17.6**	**+6.4**	**11.2**	**5,663**

Electorate: 68,189 **Voters:** 50,097 **Turnout:** 73.5 **Swing:** 3.2 to Lab from Con

STAMFORD & SPALDING

Quentin Davies: *Conservative. Born: 1944. Educated: Leighton Park; Cambridge. Jobs: diplomat, merchant banker. First Elected: 1987. Posts: member, Treasury Select Committee. Status: married, two children.*

CON HOLD		1992 election			1987 election	
		Votes	%	+/-	%	Votes
Quentin Davies*	Con	35,965	59.0	+2.5	56.5	31,016
Chris Burke	Lab	13,096	21.5	+8.9	12.5	6,882
Bryan Lee	Lib Dem	11,939	19.6	-11.4	31.0	17,009
Majority	**Con**	**22,869**	**37.5**	**+12.0**	**25.5**	**14,007**

Electorate: 75,153 **Voters:** 61,000 **Turnout:** 81.2 **Swing:** 3.2 to Lab from Con

STEVENAGE

Timothy Wood: *Conservative. Born: 1940. Educated: King James's Grammar School, Knaresborough; Manchester University. Jobs: computer industry manager. First Elected: 1983. Posts: Government Whip. Status: married, two children.*

CON HOLD		1992 election			1987 election	
		Votes	%	+/-	%	Votes
Timothy Wood*	Con	26,652	45.7	+3.6	42.1	23,541
Judith Church	Lab	21,764	37.3	+11.9	25.4	14,229
Andrew Reilly	Lib Dem	9,668	16.6	-15.9	32.5	18,201
Andrew Calcraft	NLP	233	0.4			
Majority	**Con**	**4,888**	**8.4**	**-1.2**	**9.5**	**5,340**

Electorate: 70,233 **Voters:** 58,317 **Turnout:** 83.0 **Swing:** 4.1 to Lab from Con

STIRLING

Michael Forsyth: *Conservative. Born: 1954. Educated: Arbroath High School; St Andrew's University. Jobs: company director. First Elected: 1983. Posts: Minister of State for Employment. Status: married, two children.*

CON HOLD		1992 election			1987 election	
		Votes	%	+/-	%	Votes
Michael Forsyth*	Con	19,174	40.0	+2.2	37.8	17,191
Kate Phillips	Lab	18,471	38.5	+2.0	36.5	16,643
Gerry Fisher	SNP	6,558	13.7	+2.9	10.8	4,897
Willie Robertson	Lib Dem	3,337	7.0	-8.0	14.9	6,804
Bill Thomson	Green	342	0.7			
Russ Sharp	Loony	68	0.1			
Majority	**Con**	**703**	**1.5**	**+0.3**	**1.2**	**548**

Electorate: 58,266 **Voters:** 47,950 **Turnout:** 82.3 **Swing:** 0.1 to Con from Lab

STOCKPORT

Ann Coffey: Labour. Born: 1946. Educated: South Bank Polytechnic, London; Manchester University. Jobs: social worker, local government officer. First Elected: 1992. Status: divorced, one child.

LAB GAIN		1992 election			1987 election	
		Votes	%	+/-	%	Votes
Ann Coffey	Lab	21,096	44.1	+8.8	35.3	16,557
Tony Favell*	Con	19,674	41.2	-0.2	41.4	19,410
Anne Corris	Lib Dem	6,539	13.7	-8.4	22.1	10,365
Judith Filmore	Green	436	0.9	-0.3	1.2	573
David Saunders	NLP	50	0.1			
Majority	**Lab**	**1,422**	**3.0**	**+9.0**	**6.1**	**2,853**

Electorate: 58,095 **Voters:** 47,795 **Turnout:** 82.3 **Swing:** 4.5 to Lab from Con

STOCKTON NORTH

Frank Cook: Labour. Born: 1935. Educated: Corby School, Sunderland; De La Salle College, Manchester. Jobs: gravedigger, engineer, teacher. First Elected: 1983. Posts: member, Defence Select Committee. Union: MSF. Status: married, four children.

LAB HOLD		1992 election			1987 election	
		Votes	%	+/-	%	Votes
Frank Cook*	Lab	27,918	52.3	+3.2	49.1	26,043
Simon Fowler	Con	17,444	32.7	+0.2	32.5	17,242
Suzanne Fletcher	Lib Dem	7,454	14.0	-4.4	18.3	9,712
Ken McGarvey	Ind Lab	550	1.0			
Majority	**Lab**	**10,474**	**19.6**	**+3.0**	**16.6**	**8,801**

Electorate: 69,451 **Voters:** 53,366 **Turnout:** 76.8 **Swing:** 1.5 to Lab from Con

STOCKTON SOUTH

Tim Devlin: Conservative. Born: 1959. Educated: Dulwich College; London School of Economics. Jobs: accountant, barrister. Posts: PPS. First Elected: 1987. Status: married.

CON HOLD		1992 election			1987 election	
		Votes	%	+/-	%	Votes
Tim Devlin*	Con	28,418	45.2	+10.2	35.0	20,833
John Scott	Lab	25,049	39.8	+8.6	31.3	18,600
Kay Kirkham	Lib Dem	9,410	15.0	-18.8	33.7	20,059
Majority	**Con**	**3,369**	**5.4**	**+4.1**	**1.3**	**774**

Electorate: 75,959 **Voters:** 62,877 **Turnout:** 82.8 **Swing:** 0.8 to Con from Lab

STOKE-ON-TRENT CENTRAL

Mark Fisher: Labour. Born: 1944. Educated: Eton; Cambridge. Jobs: scriptwriter, administrator. First Elected: 1983. Union: MSF. Status: married, four children.

LAB HOLD		1992 election			1987 election	
		Votes	%	+/-	%	Votes
Mark Fisher*	Lab	25,897	58.0	+5.5	52.5	23,842
Nicolas Gibb	Con	12,477	27.9	-3.1	31.0	14,072
Martin Dent	Lib Dem	6,073	13.6	-2.8	16.4	7,462
Nicholas Pullen	NLP	196	0.4			
Majority	**Lab**	**13,420**	**30.1**	**+8.5**	**21.5**	**9,770**

Electorate: 65,527 **Voters:** 44,643 **Turnout:** 68.1 **Swing:** 4.3 to Lab from Con

STOKE-ON-TRENT NORTH

Joan Walley: Labour. Born: 1949. Educated: Biddulph Grammar School; Hull University. Jobs: researcher. First Elected: 1987. Posts: Labour spokeswoman on maritime and road transport. Union: COHSE. Status: married, two children.

LAB HOLD		1992 election			1987 election	
		Votes	%	+/-	%	Votes
Joan Walley*	Lab	30,464	56.7	+9.6	47.1	25,459
Laurence Harris	Con	15,687	29.2	-2.1	31.3	16,946
John Redfern	Lib Dem	7,167	13.3	-8.2	21.6	11,665
Alan Morrison	NLP	387	0.7			
Majority	**Lab**	**14,777**	**27.5**	**+11.8**	**15.7**	**8,513**

Electorate: 73,141 **Voters:** 53,705 **Turnout:** 73.4 **Swing:** 5.9 to Lab from Con

STOKE-ON-TRENT SOUTH

George Stevenson: Labour. Born: 1938. Educated: Queensberry Road Secondary Modern, Stoke. Jobs: miner, bus driver, Euro MP. First Elected: 1992. Posts: member, Agriculture Select Committee. Union: TGWU. Status: married, three children.

LAB HOLD		1992 election			1987 election	
		Votes	%	+/-	%	Votes
George Stevenson	Lab	26,380	49.8	+2.3	47.5	24,794
Roger Ibbs	Con	19,471	36.7	-1.1	37.8	19,741
Fred Jones	Lib Dem	6,870	13.0	-1.7	14.7	7,669
Elizabeth Lines	NLP	291	0.5			
Majority	**Lab**	**6,909**	**13.0**	**+3.4**	**9.7**	**5,053**

Electorate: 71,316 **Voters:** 53,012 **Turnout:** 74.3 **Swing:** 1.7 to Lab from Con

STRANGFORD

John Taylor: Ulster Unionist Party. Born: 1937. Educated: Royal School, Armagh; Queen's University, Belfast. Jobs: civil engineer, company director, Euro MP. First Elected: 1983. Status: married, six children.

UUP HOLD		1992 election			1987 election	
		Votes	%	+/-	%	Votes
John Taylor*	UUP	19,517	43.6	-32.4	75.9	28,199
Sammy Wilson	DUP	10,606	23.7			
Keiran McCarthy	All	7,585	16.9	-3.4	20.3	7,553
Stephen Eyre	Con	6,782	15.1			
David Shaw	NLP	295	0.7			
Majority	**UUP**	**8,911**	**19.9**	**-35.7**	**55.6**	**20,646**

Electorate: 68,870 **Voters:** 44,785 **Turnout:** 65.0

STRATFORD-ON-AVON

Alan Howarth: Conservative. Born: 1944. Educated: Rugby; Cambridge. Jobs: teacher. First Elected: 1983. Posts: member, National Heritage Select Committee. Status: married, four children.

CON HOLD		1992 election			1987 election	
		Votes	%	+/-	%	Votes
Alan Howarth*	Con	40,251	59.2	-2.7	61.9	38,483
Nicholas Fogg	Lib Dem	17,359	25.5	-2.3	27.9	17,318
Sheila Brookes	Lab	8,932	13.1	+2.9	10.2	6,335
Richard Roughan	Green	729	1.1			
Andrew Saunders	Ind C	573	0.8			
Michael Twite	NLP	130	0.2			
Majority	**Con**	**22,892**	**33.7**	**-0.4**	**34.1**	**21,165**

Electorate: 82,824 **Voters:** 67,974 **Turnout:** 82.1 **Swing:** 0.2 to LDm from Con

STRATHKELVIN & BEARSDEN

Sam Galbraith: Labour. Born: 1945. Educated: Greenock High School; Glasgow University. Jobs: neuro-surgeon. First Elected: 1987. Posts: Labour spokesman on employment. Union: MSF. Status: married.

LAB HOLD		1992 election			1987 election	
		Votes	%	+/-	%	Votes
Sam Galbraith*	Lab	21,267	42.3	+4.1	38.1	19,639
Michael Hirst	Con	18,105	36.0	+2.6	33.4	17,187
Tom Chalmers	SNP	6,275	12.5	+5.4	7.1	3,654
Barbara Waterfield	Lib Dem	4,585	9.1	-12.3	21.4	11,034
David Whitley	NLP	90	0.2			
Majority	**Lab**	**3,162**	**6.3**	**+1.5**	**4.8**	**2,452**

Electorate: 61,116 **Voters:** 50,322 **Turnout:** 82.3 **Swing:** 0.8 to Lab from Con

STREATHAM

Keith Hill: Labour. Born: 1943. Educated: City of Leicester Grammar School; Oxford. Jobs: lecturer, political researcher, trade union official. First Elected: 1992. Posts: member, Transport Select Committee. Union: RMT. Status: married.

LAB GAIN		1992 election			1987 election	
		Votes	%	+/-	%	Votes
Keith Hill	Lab	18,925	47.0	+7.8	39.2	16,509
Sir William Shelton*	Con	16,608	41.3	-3.6	44.9	18,916
John Pindar	Lib Dem	3,858	9.6	-6.2	15.8	6,663
Roger Baker	Green	443	1.1			
Abdesalam Hankin	Islamic	154	0.4			
Cynthia Payne	ADS	145	0.4			
John Parsons	NLP	97	0.2			
Majority	**Lab**	**2,317**	**5.7**	**+11.4**	**5.7**	**2,407**

Electorate: 56,825 **Voters:** 40,230 **Turnout:** 70.8 **Swing:** 5.7 to Lab from Con

STRETFORD

Tony Lloyd: Labour. Born: 1950. Educated: Stretford Grammar School; Nottingham University. Jobs: lecturer. First Elected: 1983. Posts: Labour spokesman on training and education. Union: Graphic Print Media Union. Status: married, three children.

LAB HOLD		1992 election			1987 election	
		Votes	%	+/-	%	Votes
Tony Lloyd*	Lab	22,300	59.5	+4.4	55.2	22,831
Charles Rae	Con	11,163	29.8	-2.6	32.4	13,429
Francis Beswick	Lib Dem	3,722	9.9	-2.4	12.4	5,125
Andrew Boyton	NLP	268	0.7			
Majority	**Lab**	**11,137**	**29.7**	**+7.0**	**22.7**	**9,402**

Electorate: 54,467 **Voters:** 37,453 **Turnout:** 68.8 **Swing:** 3.5 to Lab from Con

STROUD

Roger Knapman: Conservative. Born: 1944. Educated: Allhallows School, Lyme Regis; Royal Agricultural College. Jobs: surveyor, farmer. First Elected: 1987. Posts: PPS. Status: married, two children.

CON HOLD		1992 election			1987 election	
		Votes	%	+/-	%	Votes
Roger Knapman*	Con	32,201	46.2	-4.0	50.2	32,883
David Drew	Lab	18,796	26.9	+8.4	18.5	12,145
Myles Robinson	Lib Dem	16,751	24.0	-7.3	31.3	20,508
Sue Atkinson	Green	2,005	2.9			
Majority	**Con**	**13,405**	**19.2**	**+0.3**	**18.9**	**12,375**

Electorate: 82,553 **Voters:** 69,753 **Turnout:** 84.5 **Swing:** 6.2 to Lab from Con

SUFFOLK CENTRAL

Michael Lord: Conservative. Born: 1938. Educated: William Hulme's Grammar School, Manchester; Cambridge. Jobs: farmer, arboriculturist. First Elected: 1983. Status: married, two children.

CON HOLD		1992 election Votes	%	+/-	1987 election %	Votes
Michael Lord*	Con	32,917	49.6	-4.1	53.7	32,422
Lesley Henniker-Major	Lib Dem	16,886	25.4	-1.3	26.7	16,132
John Harris	Lab	15,615	23.5	+3.9	19.6	11,817
John Matthiessen	Green	800	1.2			
Julia Wilmot	NLP	190	0.3			
Majority	**Con**	**16,031**	**24.1**	**-2.8**	**27.0**	**16,290**

Electorate: 82,735 **Voters:** 66,408 **Turnout:** 80.3 **Swing:** 1.4 to LDm from Con

SUFFOLK COASTAL

John Gummer: Conservative. Born: 1939. Educated: King's School, Rochester; Cambridge. Jobs: company director. First Elected: 1970. Posts: Minister of Agriculture, Fisheries and Food. Status: married, four children.

CON HOLD		1992 election Votes	%	+/-	1987 election %	Votes
John Gummer*	Con	34,680	53.6	-2.1	55.7	32,834
Peter Monk	Lib Dem	15,395	23.8	-6.0	29.8	17,554
Terry Hodgson	Lab	13,508	20.9	+8.1	12.8	7,534
Tony Slade	Green	943	1.5	-0.3	1.8	1,049
Felicity Kaplan	NLP	232	0.4			
Majority	**Con**	**19,285**	**29.8**	**+3.9**	**25.9**	**15,280**

Electorate: 79,333 **Voters:** 64,758 **Turnout:** 81.6 **Swing:** 1.9 to Con from LDm

SUFFOLK SOUTH

Tim Yeo: Conservative. Born: 1945. Educated: Charterhouse; Cambridge. Jobs: company director, charity director. First Elected: 1983. Posts: Health minister. Status: married, two children.

CON HOLD		1992 election Votes	%	+/-	1987 election %	Votes
Tim Yeo*	Con	34,793	50.2	-3.3	53.4	33,972
Kathy Pollard	Lib Dem	17,504	25.2	-2.6	27.9	17,729
Stephen Hesford	Lab	16,623	24.0	+5.3	18.7	11,876
Tom Aisbitt	NLP	420	0.6			
Majority	**Con**	**17,289**	**24.9**	**-0.6**	**25.5**	**16,243**

Electorate: 84,833 **Voters:** 69,340 **Turnout:** 81.7 **Swing:** 0.3 to LDm from Con

SUNDERLAND NORTH

William Etherington: Labour. Born: 1941. Educated: Monkwearmouth Grammar School. Jobs: fitter. First Elected: 1992. Union: NUM. Status: married, three children.

LAB HOLD

		1992 election			1987 election	
		Votes	%	+/-	%	Votes
William Etherington	Lab	30,481	60.7	+5.0	55.8	29,767
Judith Barnes	Con	13,477	26.9	-1.4	28.3	15,095
Vic Halom	Lib Dem	5,389	10.7	-5.2	16.0	8,518
Win Lundgren	Lib	841	1.7			
Majority	**Lab**	**17,004**	**33.9**	**+6.4**	**27.5**	**14,672**

Electorate: 72,874 **Voters:** 50,188 **Turnout:** 68.9 **Swing:** 3.2 to Lab from Con

SUNDERLAND SOUTH

Chris Mullin: Labour. Born: 1947. Educated: Hull University. Jobs: journalist. First Elected: 1987. Posts: member, Home Affairs Select Committee. Union: MSF. Status: married.

LAB HOLD

		1992 election			1987 election	
		Votes	%	+/-	%	Votes
Chris Mullin*	Lab	29,399	57.9	+3.9	54.1	28,823
George Howe	Con	14,898	29.4	-1.0	30.4	16,210
John Lennox	Lib Dem	5,844	11.5	-3.1	14.6	7,768
Terry Scouler	Green	596	1.2	+0.2	1.0	516
Majority	**Lab**	**14,501**	**28.6**	**+4.9**	**23.7**	**12,613**

Electorate: 72,607 **Voters:** 50,737 **Turnout:** 69.9 **Swing:** 2.5 to Lab from Con

SURBITON

Richard Tracey: Conservative. Born: 1943. Educated: King Edward VI School, Stratford; Birmingham University. Jobs: broadcaster. First Elected: 1983. Status: married, four children.

CON HOLD

		1992 election			1987 election	
		Votes	%	+/-	%	Votes
Richard Tracey*	Con	19,033	54.4	-1.4	55.9	19,861
Barbara Janke	Lib Dem	9,394	26.9	-1.6	28.5	10,120
Robin Hutchinson	Lab	6,384	18.3	+3.9	14.4	5,111
William Parker	NLP	161	0.5			
Majority	**Con**	**9,639**	**27.6**	**+0.2**	**27.4**	**9,741**

Electorate: 42,421 **Voters:** 34,972 **Turnout:** 82.4 **Swing:** No Swing

SURREY EAST

Peter Ainsworth: Conservative. Born: 1956. Educated: Bradfield College; Oxford. Jobs: political adviser. First Elected: 1992. Status: married, three children.

CON HOLD		1992 election			1987 election	
		Votes	%	+/-	%	Votes
Peter Ainsworth	Con	29,767	62.3	-1.1	63.4	29,126
Bob Tomlin	Lib Dem	12,111	25.4	+1.4	23.9	11,000
Gill Roles	Lab	5,075	10.6	+0.2	10.4	4,779
Ian Kilpatrick	Green	819	1.7	-0.6	2.3	1,044
Majority	**Con**	**17,656**	**37.0**	**-2.5**	**39.4**	**18,126**

Electorate: 57,878 **Voters:** 47,772 **Turnout:** 82.5 **Swing:** 1.2 to LDm from Con

SURREY NORTH WEST

Sir Michael Grylls: Conservative. Born: 1934. Educated: Royal Naval College; Paris University. Jobs: company director. First Elected: 1970. Status: married, two children.

CON HOLD		1992 election			1987 election	
		Votes	%	+/-	%	Votes
Sir Michael Grylls*	Con	41,772	63.8	-0.2	64.0	38,535
Chris Clark	Lib Dem	13,378	20.4	-4.4	24.8	14,960
Mark Hayhurst	Lab	8,886	13.6	+2.4	11.2	6,751
Yvonne Hockey	Green	1,441	2.2			
Majority	**Con**	**28,394**	**43.4**	**+4.2**	**39.1**	**23,575**

Electorate: 83,648 **Voters:** 65,477 **Turnout:** 78.3 **Swing:** 2.1 to Con from LDm

SURREY SOUTH WEST

Virginia Bottomley: Conservative. Born: 1948. Educated: Putney High School; Essex University. Jobs: researcher, social worker. First Elected: 1984. Posts: Health Secretary. Status: married, three children.

CON HOLD		1992 election			1987 election	
		Votes	%	+/-	%	Votes
Virginia Bottomley*	Con	35,008	58.5	-0.9	59.5	34,024
Neil Sherlock	Lib Dem	20,033	33.5	-0.9	34.4	19,681
Phil Kelly	Lab	3,840	6.4	+0.8	5.6	3,224
Nigel Bedrock	Green	710	1.2			
Keith Campbell	NLP	147	0.2			
Donald Newman	Anglo Sax	98	0.2			
Majority	**Con**	**14,975**	**25.0**	**-0.0**	**25.1**	**14,343**

Electorate: 72,288 **Voters:** 59,836 **Turnout:** 82.8 **Swing:** No Swing

SUSSEX MID

Timothy Renton: *Conservative. Born: 1932. Educated: Eton; Oxford. Jobs: company director. First Elected: 1974. Status: married, five children.*

CON HOLD

		1992 election			1987 election	
		Votes	%	+/-	%	Votes
Timothy Renton*	Con	39,524	59.0	-2.1	61.1	37,781
Margaret Collins	Lib Dem	18,996	28.4	-3.1	31.5	19,489
Linda Gregory	Lab	6,951	10.4	+3.0	7.4	4,573
Hugh Stevens	Green	772	1.2			
Peter Berry	Loony	392	0.6			
Peter Hodkin	PR	246	0.4			
Alexander Hankey	NLP	89	0.1			
Majority	**Con**	**20,528**	**30.7**	**+1.1**	**29.6**	**18,292**

Electorate: 80,827 **Voters:** 66,970 **Turnout:** 82.9 **Swing:** 0.5 to Con from LDm

SUTTON & CHEAM

Lady Olga Maitland: *Conservative. Born: 1944. Educated: School of St Mary & St Anne, Abbots Bromley; Lycée Français. Jobs: journalist. First Elected: 1992. Posts: member, Education Select Committee. Status: married, three children.*

CON HOLD

		1992 election			1987 election	
		Votes	%	+/-	%	Votes
Lady Olga Maitland	Con	27,710	55.2	-5.6	60.8	29,710
Paul Burstow	Lib Dem	16,954	33.8	+5.1	28.6	13,992
Geoff Martin	Lab	4,980	9.9	-0.7	10.6	5,202
Jim Duffy	Green	444	0.9			
Angela Hatchard	NLP	133	0.3			
Majority	**Con**	**10,756**	**21.4**	**-10.7**	**32.1**	**15,718**

Electorate: 60,949 **Voters:** 50,221 **Turnout:** 82.4 **Swing:** 5.4 to LDm from Con

SUTTON COLDFIELD

Sir Norman Fowler: *Conservative. Born: 1938. Educated: King Edward VI School, Chelmsford; Cambridge. Jobs: journalist. First Elected: 1970. Posts: chairman, Conservative Party. Status: married, two children.*

CON HOLD

		1992 election			1987 election	
		Votes	%	+/-	%	Votes
Sir Norman Fowler*	Con	37,001	65.2	+1.2	64.0	34,475
James Whorwood	Lib Dem	10,965	19.3	-5.4	24.7	13,292
Jan Bott-Obi	Lab	8,490	15.0	+3.6	11.3	6,104
Huw Meads	NLP	324	0.6			
Majority	**Con**	**26,036**	**45.9**	**+6.5**	**39.3**	**21,183**

Electorate: 71,410 **Voters:** 56,780 **Turnout:** 79.5 **Swing:** 3.3 to Con from LDm

SWANSEA EAST

Donald Anderson: Labour. Born: 1939. Educated: Swansea Grammar School; University College, Swansea. Jobs: diplomat, barrister. First Elected: 1966. Union: RMT. Status: married, three children.

LAB HOLD		**1992 election**			**1987 election**	
		Votes	%	+/-	%	Votes
Donald Anderson*	Lab	31,179	69.7	+6.0	63.7	27,478
Henri Davies	Con	7,697	17.2	-1.7	18.9	8,140
Bob Barton	Lib Dem	4,248	9.5	-5.3	14.8	6,380
Eleanor Bonner-Evans	Plaid Cymru	1,607	3.6	+0.9	2.7	1,145
Majority	**Lab**	**23,482**	**52.5**	**+7.7**	**44.8**	**19,338**

Electorate: 59,196 **Voters:** 44,731 **Turnout:** 75.6 **Swing:** 3.8 to Lab from Con

SWANSEA WEST

Alan Williams: Labour. Born: 1930. Educated: Cardiff High School; Cardiff College of Technology; Oxford. Jobs: lecturer. First Elected: 1964. Posts: member, Public Accounts Committee. Union: TSSA. Status: married, three children.

LAB HOLD		**1992 election**			**1987 election**	
		Votes	%	+/-	%	Votes
Alan Williams*	Lab	23,238	53.0	+4.5	48.5	22,089
Roy Perry	Con	13,760	31.4	-1.6	33.0	15,027
Martyn Shrewsbury	Lib Dem	4,620	10.5	-4.9	15.4	7,019
David Lloyd	Plaid Cymru	1,668	3.8	+1.8	2.0	902
Brig Oubridge	Green	564	1.3	+0.3	1.0	469
Majority	**Lab**	**9,478**	**21.6**	**+6.1**	**15.5**	**7,062**

Electorate: 59,785 **Voters:** 43,850 **Turnout:** 73.3 **Swing:** 3.0 to Lab from Con

SWINDON

Simon Coombs: Conservative. Born: 1947. Educated: Wycliffe College, Stroud; Reading University. Jobs: marketing manager. First Elected: 1983. Posts: PPS. Status: married.

CON HOLD		**1992 election**			**1987 election**	
		Votes	%	+/-	%	Votes
Simon Coombs*	Con	31,749	43.3	-0.6	43.8	29,385
Jim D'Avila	Lab	28,923	39.4	+2.8	36.6	24,528
Simon Cordon	Lib Dem	11,737	16.0	-3.6	19.6	13,114
Bill Hughes	Green	647	0.9			
Roly Gillard	Loony G	236	0.3			
Vince Farrar	Ind	78	0.1			
Majority	**Con**	**2,826**	**3.9**	**-3.4**	**7.2**	**4,857**

Electorate: 90,067 **Voters:** 73,370 **Turnout:** 81.5 **Swing:** 1.7 to Lab from Con

TATTON

Neil Hamilton: Conservative. Born: 1949. Educated: Amman Valley Grammar School; University College, Aberystwyth; Cambridge University. Jobs: barrister, economist. First Elected: 1983. Posts: Corporate Affairs minister. Status: married.

CON HOLD		1992 election			1987 election	
		Votes	%	+/-	%	Votes
Neil Hamilton*	Con	31,658	55.1	+0.5	54.6	30,128
Jonathan Kelly	Lab	15,798	27.5	+6.2	21.3	11,760
Cathy Hancox	Lib Dem	9,597	16.7	-6.9	23.6	13,034
Michael Gibson	FP	410	0.7	+0.2	0.5	263
Majority	**Con**	**15,860**	**27.6**	**-3.4**	**31.0**	**17,094**

Electorate: 71,085 **Voters:** 57,463 **Turnout:** 80.8 **Swing:** 2.8 to Lab from Con

TAUNTON

David Nicholson: Conservative. Born: 1944. Educated: Queen Elizabeth Grammar School, Blackburn; Oxford. Jobs: political researcher. First Elected: 1987. Posts: member, Public Accounts Committee. Status: married, three children.

CON HOLD		1992 election			1987 election	
		Votes	%	+/-	%	Votes
David Nicholson*	Con	29,576	46.0	-5.3	51.4	30,248
Jackie Ballard	Lib Dem	26,240	40.8	+7.1	33.7	19,868
Jean Hole	Lab	8,151	12.7	-2.2	14.9	8,754
Philip Leavey	NLP	279	0.4			
Majority	**Con**	**3,336**	**5.2**	**-12.4**	**17.6**	**10,380**

Electorate: 78,036 **Voters:** 64,246 **Turnout:** 82.3 **Swing:** 6.2 to LDm from Con

TAYSIDE NORTH

Bill Walker: Conservative. Born: 1929. Educated: Trades College, Dundee; College of Art, Dundee. Jobs: pilot, company director. First Elected: 1979. Posts: vice-chairman, Scottish Conservative Party. Status: married, three children.

CON HOLD		1992 election			1987 election	
		Votes	%	+/-	%	Votes
Bill Walker*	Con	20,283	46.7	+1.3	45.4	18,307
John Swinney	SNP	16,288	37.5	+4.5	32.9	13,291
Simon Horner	Lib Dem	3,791	8.7	-4.2	12.9	5,201
Stuart Maclennan	Lab	3,094	7.1	-1.7	8.8	3,550
Majority	**Con**	**3,995**	**9.2**	**-3.2**	**12.4**	**5,016**

Electorate: 55,969 **Voters:** 43,456 **Turnout:** 77.6 **Swing:** 1.6 to SNP from Con

TEIGNBRIDGE

Patrick Nicholls: Conservative. Born: 1948. Educated: Redrice College, Andover. Jobs: solicitor. First Elected: 1983. Posts: member, Social Security Select Committee. Status: married, three children.

CON HOLD		1992 election			1987 election	
		Votes	%	+/-	%	Votes
Patrick Nicholls*	Con	31,272	50.0	-3.2	53.2	30,693
Richard Younger-Ross	Lib Dem	22,416	35.9	+0.7	35.1	20,268
Robert Kennedy	Lab	8,128	13.0	+1.9	11.1	6,413
Alan Hope	Loony	437	0.7	+0.2	0.5	312
Nicholas Hayes	NLP	234	0.4			
Majority	**Con**	**8,856**	**14.2**	**-3.9**	**18.1**	**10,425**

Electorate: 74,892 **Voters:** 62,487 **Turnout:** 83.4 **Swing:** 1.9 to LDm from Con

THANET NORTH

Roger Gale: Conservative. Born: 1943. Educated: Hardye's School, Dorchester; Guildhall School of Music and Drama. Jobs: broadcaster. First Elected: 1983. Status: married, three children.

CON HOLD		1992 election			1987 election	
		Votes	%	+/-	%	Votes
Roger Gale*	Con	30,867	57.2	-0.8	58.0	29,225
Alan Bretman	Lab	12,657	23.5	+6.8	16.7	8,395
Joanna Phillips	Lib Dem	9,563	17.7	-5.6	23.3	11,745
Hazel Dawe	Green	873	1.6	-0.4	2.0	996
Majority	**Con**	**18,210**	**33.7**	**-1.0**	**34.7**	**17,480**

Electorate: 70,978 **Voters:** 53,960 **Turnout:** 76.0 **Swing:** 3.8 to Lab from Con

THANET SOUTH

Jonathan Aitken: Conservative. Born: 1942. Educated: Eton; Oxford. Jobs: journalist, company director. First Elected: 1974. Posts: Minister for Defence Procurement. Status: married, three children.

CON HOLD		1992 election			1987 election	
		Votes	%	+/-	%	Votes
Jonathan Aitken*	Con	25,253	51.7	-2.6	54.3	25,135
Mark James	Lab	13,740	28.1	+7.2	20.9	9,673
Bill Pitt	Lib Dem	8,948	18.3	-6.4	24.8	11,452
Sue Peckham	Green	871	1.8			
Majority	**Con**	**11,513**	**23.6**	**-6.0**	**29.6**	**13,683**

Electorate: 62,441 **Voters:** 48,812 **Turnout:** 78.2 **Swing:** 4.9 to Lab from Con

THURROCK

Andrew MacKinlay: Labour. Born: 1949. Educated: Salesian College, Chertsey. Jobs: local government officer, trade union official. First Elected: 1992. Posts: member, Transport Select Committee. Union: TGWU. Status: married, three children.

LAB GAIN		1992 election			1987 election	
		Votes	%	+/-	%	Votes
Andrew MacKinlay	Lab	24,791	45.9	+4.8	41.0	19,837
Tim Janman*	Con	23,619	43.7	+1.2	42.5	20,527
Alan Banton	Lib Dem	5,145	9.5	-7.0	16.5	7,970
Charles Rogers	Pensioners	391	0.7			
Peter Compobassi	Anti Fed	117	0.2			
Majority	**Lab**	**1,172**	**2.2**	**+3.6**	**1.4**	**690**

Electorate: 69,171 **Voters:** 54,063 **Turnout:** 78.2 **Swing:** 1.8 to Lab from Con

TIVERTON

Angela Browning: Conservative. Born: 1946. Educated: Westwood Grammar School; Reading College of Technology. Jobs: nurse, sales manager. First Elected: 1992. Posts: member, Agriculture Select Committee. Status: married, two children.

CON HOLD		1992 election			1987 election	
		Votes	%	+/-	%	Votes
Angela Browning	Con	30,376	51.5	-3.4	54.9	29,875
David Cox	Lib Dem	19,287	32.7	-5.3	38.0	20,663
Susan Gibb	Lab	5,950	10.1	+3.8	6.3	3,400
David Morrish	Lib	2,225	3.8			
Phil Foggitt	Green	1,007	1.7			
Brendan Rhodes	NLP	96	0.2			
Majority	**Con**	**11,089**	**18.8**	**+1.9**	**16.9**	**9,212**

Electorate: 71,024 **Voters:** 58,941 **Turnout:** 83.0 **Swing:** 0.9 to Con from LDm

TONBRIDGE & MALLING

Sir John Stanley: Conservative. Born: 1942. Educated: Repton, Oxford. Jobs: researcher, company director. First Elected: 1974. Posts: member, Foreign Affairs Select Committee. Status: married, three children.

CON HOLD		1992 election			1987 election	
		Votes	%	+/-	%	Votes
Sir John Stanley*	Con	36,542	57.2	+0.3	56.9	33,990
Paul Roberts	Lib Dem	14,984	23.5	-6.0	29.4	17,561
Margaret O'Neill	Lab	11,533	18.1	+5.0	13.1	7,803
Jim Tidy	Green	612	1.0			
Janet Hovarth	NLP	221	0.3			
Majority	**Con**	**21,558**	**33.7**	**+6.2**	**27.5**	**16,429**

Electorate: 77,292 **Voters:** 63,892 **Turnout:** 82.7 **Swing:** 3.1 to Con from LDm

CONSTITUENCIES

TOOTING

Tom Cox: Labour. Born: 1930. Educated: London School of Economics. Jobs: miner, electrician. First Elected: 1970. Posts: delegate, Council of Europe, Western European Union. Union: EEPTU. Status: single.

LAB HOLD		1992 election			1987 election	
		Votes	%	+/-	%	Votes
Tom Cox*	Lab	24,601	48.2	+3.9	44.2	21,457
Martin Winters	Con	20,494	40.1	-1.1	41.3	20,016
Bob Bunce	Lib Dem	3,776	7.4	-5.8	13.2	6,423
Carmel Martin	Lib	1,340	2.6			
Paul Owens	Green	694	1.4	+0.1	1.3	621
Farrakh Anklesalria	NLP	119	0.2			
Michael Whitelaw	CD	64	0.1			
Majority	**Lab**	**4,107**	**8.0**	**+5.1**	**3.0**	**1,441**

Electorate: 68,306 **Voters:** 51,088 **Turnout:** 74.8 **Swing:** 2.5 to Lab from Con

TORBAY

Rupert Allason: Conservative. Born: 1951. Educated: Downside School; Grenoble University. Jobs: journalist, author. First Elected: 1987. Status: married, two children.

CON HOLD		1992 election			1987 election	
		Votes	%	+/-	%	Votes
Rupert Allason*	Con	28,624	49.9	-4.1	54.0	29,029
Adrian Sanders	Lib Dem	22,837	39.8	+2.2	37.6	20,209
Peter Truscott	Lab	5,503	9.6	+1.2	8.4	4,538
Bob Jones	NF	268	0.5			
Alison Thomas	NLP	157	0.3			
Majority	**Con**	**5,787**	**10.1**	**-6.3**	**16.4**	**8,820**

Electorate: 71,171 **Voters:** 57,389 **Turnout:** 80.6 **Swing:** 3.2 to LDm from Con

TORFAEN

Paul Murphy: Labour. Born: 1948. Educated: West Monmouth School, Pontypool; Oxford. Jobs: lecturer. First Elected: 1987. Posts: Labour spokesman on Welsh affairs. Union: TGWU. Status: single.

LAB HOLD		1992 election			1987 election	
		Votes	%	+/-	%	Votes
Paul Murphy*	Lab	30,352	64.1	+5.4	58.7	26,577
Mark Watkins	Con	9,598	20.3	+1.2	19.1	8,632
Malcolm Hewson	Lib Dem	6,178	13.1	-6.9	19.9	9,027
John Cox	Green/PC	1,210	2.6		†	
Majority	**Lab**	**20,754**	**43.8**	**+5.1**	**38.8**	**17,550**

Electorate: 61,104 **Voters:** 47,338 **Turnout:** 77.5 **Swing:** 2.1 to Lab from Con

† Plaid Cymru candidate polled 577 (1.3%) in 1987

TOTTENHAM

Bernie Grant: Labour. Born: 1944. Educated: Tottenham Technical College; Heriot Watt University. Jobs: clerk, telephonist, housing officer. First Elected: 1987. Union: NUPE. Status: divorced, three children.

LAB HOLD		1992 election			1987 election	
		Votes	%	+/-	%	Votes
Bernie Grant*	Lab	25,309	56.5	+12.9	43.6	21,921
Andrew Charalambous	Con	13,341	29.8	-5.6	35.4	17,780
Alex L'Estrange	Lib Dem	5,120	11.4	-6.4	17.9	8,983
Peter Budge	Green	903	2.0	+0.5	1.5	744
Margaret Obomanu	NLP	150	0.3			
Majority	**Lab**	**11,968**	**26.7**	**+18.5**	**8.2**	**4,141**

Electorate: 68,319 **Voters:** 44,823 **Turnout:** 65.6 **Swing:** 9.2 to Lab from Con

TRURO

Matthew Taylor: Liberal Democrat. Born: 1963. Educated: University College School, London; Oxford. Jobs: political adviser. First Elected: 1987. Posts: LibDem spokesman on Citizen's Charter. Status: single.

LIBDEM HOLD		1992 election			1987 election	
		Votes	%	+/-	%	Votes
Matthew Taylor*	Lib Dem	31,230	50.5	+1.5	49.0	28,368
Nicholas St Aubyn	Con	23,660	38.3	-2.6	40.8	23,615
James Geach	Lab	6,078	9.8	-0.3	10.2	5,882
Liam Keating	Green	569	0.9			
Chris Tankard	Lib	208	0.3			
Margot Hartley	NLP	108	0.2			
Majority	**Lib Dem**	**7,570**	**12.2**	**+4.0**	**8.2**	**4,753**

Electorate: 75,101 **Voters:** 61,853 **Turnout:** 82.4 **Swing:** 2.0 to LDm from Con

TUNBRIDGE WELLS

Sir Patrick Mayhew: Conservative. Born: 1929. Educated: Tonbridge School; Oxford. Jobs: barrister. First Elected: 1974. Posts: Northern Ireland Secretary. Status: married, four children.

CON HOLD		1992 election			1987 election	
		Votes	%	+/-	%	Votes
Sir Patrick Mayhew*	Con	34,162	56.9	-1.5	58.4	33,111
Tony Clayton	Lib Dem	17,030	28.4	-1.6	30.0	16,989
Ted Goodman	Lab	8,300	13.8	+2.3	11.6	6,555
Ted Fenna	NLP	267	0.4			
Roy Edey	ISS	236	0.4			
Majority	**Con**	**17,132**	**28.6**	**+0.1**	**28.5**	**16,122**

Electorate: 76,808 **Voters:** 59,995 **Turnout:** 78.1 **Swing:** No Swing

TWEEDDALE ETTRICK & LAUDERDALE

Sir David Steel: Liberal Democrat. Born: 1938. Educated: George Watson's College; Edinburgh University. Jobs: broadcaster. First Elected: 1965. Posts: LibDem spokesman on foreign affairs. Status: married, four children.

LIBDEM HOLD

		1992 election Votes	%	+/-	1987 election %	Votes
Sir David Steel*	Lib Dem	12,296	39.9	-10.0	49.9	14,599
Lloyd Beat	Con	9,776	31.7	+2.1	29.6	8,657
Christine Creech	SNP	5,244	17.0	+7.9	9.1	2,660
Alan Dunton	Lab	3,328	10.8	-0.6	11.4	3,320
John Hein	Lib	177	0.6			
Majority	**Lib Dem**	**2,520**	**8.2**	**-12.1**	**20.3**	**5,942**

Electorate: 39,493 **Voters:** 30,821 **Turnout:** 78.0 **Swing:** 6.1 to Con from LDm

TWICKENHAM

Toby Jessel: Conservative. Born: 1934. Educated: Royal Naval College, Dartmouth; Oxford. First Elected: 1970. Posts: delegate, Council of Europe. Status: married.

CON HOLD

		1992 election Votes	%	+/-	1987 election %	Votes
Toby Jessel*	Con	26,804	50.4	-1.4	51.9	27,331
Vincent Cable	Lib Dem	21,093	39.7	+1.3	38.3	20,204
Michael Gold	Lab	4,919	9.3	+0.9	8.4	4,415
Gary Gill	NLP	152	0.3			
David Griffith	DLC	103	0.2			
Adrian Miners	Lib	85	0.2			
Majority	**Con**	**5,711**	**10.7**	**-2.8**	**13.5**	**7,127**

Electorate: 63,072 **Voters:** 53,156 **Turnout:** 84.3 **Swing:** 1.4 to LDm from Con

TYNE BRIDGE

David Clelland: Labour. Born: 1943. Educated: Gateshead and Hebburn Technical Colleges. Jobs: electrical tester. First Elected: 1985. Union: AEU. Status: married, two children.

LAB HOLD

		1992 election Votes	%	+/-	1987 election %	Votes
David Clelland*	Lab	22,328	67.2	+4.1	63.0	23,131
C. Liddell-Grainger	Con	7,118	21.4	+0.8	20.6	7,558
John Burt	Lib Dem	3,804	11.4	-4.9	16.4	6,005
Majority	**Lab**	**15,210**	**45.7**	**+3.3**	**42.4**	**15,573**

Electorate: 53,079 **Voters:** 33,250 **Turnout:** 62.6 **Swing:** 1.7 to Lab from Con

TYNEMOUTH

Neville Trotter: Conservative. Born: 1932. Educated: Shrewsbury School; Durham University. Jobs: company director, accountant. First Elected: 1974. Posts: member, Defence Select Committee. Status: married, one child.

CON HOLD		1992 election			1987 election	
		Votes	%	+/-	%	Votes
Neville Trotter*	Con	27,731	46.0	+2.8	43.2	25,113
Patrick Cosgrove	Lab	27,134	45.0	+6.2	38.8	22,530
Philip Selby	Lib Dem	4,855	8.1	-9.9	18.0	10,446
A. Buchanan-Smith	Green	543	0.9			
Majority	**Con**	**597**	**1.0**	**-3.5**	**4.4**	**2,583**

Electorate: 74,955 **Voters:** 60,263 **Turnout:** 80.4 **Swing:** 1.7 to Lab from Con

ULSTER MID

Rev William McCrea: Democratic Unionist Party. Born: 1948. Educated: Cookstown Grammar School. Jobs: civil servant, church minister, gospel singer. First Elected: 1983. Status: married, five children.

DUP HOLD		1992 election			1987 election	
		Votes	%	+/-	%	Votes
Rev William McCrea*	DUP	23,181	42.3	-1.8	44.2	23,004
Denis Haughey	SDLP	16,994	31.0	+4.8	26.2	13,644
Barry McElduff	Sinn Fein	10,248	18.7	-5.2	23.9	12,449
Johnny McLoughlin	Ind	1,996	3.6			
Ann Gormley	All	1,506	2.8	-0.8	3.5	1,846
Harry Hutchinson	LTU	389	0.7			
Tommy Owens	WP	285	0.5	-1.7	2.2	1,133
Jim Anderson	NLP	164	0.3			
Majority	**DUP**	**6,187**	**11.3**	**-6.7**	**18.0**	**9,360**

Electorate: 69,071 **Voters:** 54,763 **Turnout:** 79.3 **Swing:** 3.3 to SDLP from DUP

UPMINSTER

Sir Nicholas Bonsor: Conservative. Born: 1942. Educated: Eton; Oxford. Jobs: barrister. First Elected: 1979. Posts: chairman, British Field Sports Society; member, Defence Select Committee. Status: married, five children.

CON HOLD		1992 election			1987 election	
		Votes	%	+/-	%	Votes
Sir Nicholas Bonsor*	Con	28,791	55.8	+0.0	55.8	27,946
Terry Ward	Lab	14,970	29.0	+6.9	22.1	11,069
Terry Hurlstone	Lib Dem	7,848	15.2	-6.9	22.1	11,089
Majority	**Con**	**13,821**	**26.8**	**-6.9**	**33.6**	**16,857**

Electorate: 64,138 **Voters:** 51,609 **Turnout:** 80.5 **Swing:** 3.5 to Lab from Con

CONSTITUENCIES

UPPER BANN

David Trimble: *Ulster Unionist Party. Born: 1944. Educated: Bangor Grammar School; Queen's University, Belfast. Jobs: lecturer. First Elected: 1990. Status: married, three children.*

UUP HOLD		1992 election			1987 election	
		Votes	%	+/-	%	Votes
David Trimble*	UUP	26,824	59.0	-2.5	61.5	26,037
Brid Rodgers	SDLP	10,661	23.4	+2.9	20.5	8,676
Brendan Curran	Sinn Fein	2,777	6.1	-1.3	7.4	3,126
William Ramsey	All	2,541	5.6	-0.3	5.9	2,487
Colette Jones	Con	1,556	3.4			
Tom French	WP	1,120	2.5	-2.3	4.7	2,004
Majority	**UUP**	**16,163**	**35.5**	**-5.5**	**41.0**	**17,361**

Electorate: 67,446 **Voters:** 45,479 **Turnout:** 67.4 **Swing:** 2.7 to SDLP from UUP

BY-ELECTION May 1990: UUP HOLD. D Trimble (UUP) 20,547 (58%), B. Rodgers (SDLP) 6,698 (18.9%), S. Campbell (Sinn Fein) 2,033 (5.7%), UUP majority 13, 949 (39.1%), SWING 1.0% to SDLP from UUP

UXBRIDGE

Michael Shersby: *Conservative. Born: 1933. Educated: John Lyon School. Jobs: industry. First Elected: 1972. Posts: member, Public Accounts Committee. Status: married, two children.*

CON HOLD		1992 election			1987 election	
		Votes	%	+/-	%	Votes
Michael Shersby*	Con	27,487	56.4	+0.0	56.5	27,292
Robert Evans	Lab	14,308	29.4	+6.0	23.4	11,323
Steve Carey	Lib Dem	5,900	12.1	-6.8	19.0	9,164
Ian Flindall	Green	538	1.1	+0.0	1.1	549
Michael O'Rourke	BNP	350	0.7			
Ashley Deans	NLP	120	0.2			
Majority	**Con**	**13,179**	**27.1**	**-6.0**	**33.0**	**15,969**

Electorate: 61,744 **Voters:** 48,703 **Turnout:** 78.9 **Swing:** 3.0 to Lab from Con

VALE OF GLAMORGAN

Walter Sweeney: *Conservative. Born: 1949. Educated: Lawrence Sheriff School, Rugby; Cambridge. Jobs: solicitor. First Elected: 1992. Posts: member, Welsh Affairs Select Committee. Status: single.*

CON REGAIN		1992 election			1987 election	
		Votes	%	+/-	%	Votes
Walter Sweeney	Con	24,220	44.3	-2.4	46.8	24,229
John Smith*	Lab	24,201	44.3	+9.6	34.7	17,978
Keith Davies	Lib Dem	5,045	9.2	-7.4	16.7	8,633
David Haswell	Plaid Cymru	1,160	2.1	+0.3	1.8	946
Majority	**Con**	**19**	**0.0**	**-12.0**	**12.1**	**6,251**

Electorate: 66,672 **Voters:** 54,626 **Turnout:** 81.9 **Swing:** 6.0 to Lab from Con

BY-ELECTION May 1989: LAB GAIN. J. Smith (Lab) 23,342 (48.9%), R. Richards (Con) 17,314 (36.3%), F. Leavers (Lib Dem) 2,017 (4.2%), Lab majority 6,028 (12.6%), SWING 12.4% to Lab from Con

VAUXHALL

Kate Hoey: Labour. Born: 1946. Educated: Belfast Royal Academy; Ulster College of Physical Education. Jobs: lecturer. First Elected: 1989. Posts: Labour spokeswoman on Citizen's charter and women. Union: TGWU. Status: single.

LAB HOLD		1992 election			1987 election	
		Votes	%	+/-	%	Votes
Kate Hoey*	Lab	21,328	54.7	+4.6	50.2	21,364
Bernard Gentry	Con	10,840	27.8	-1.2	29.0	12,345
Michael Tuffrey	Lib Dem	5,678	14.6	-3.7	18.2	7,764
Penny Shepherd	Green	803	2.1	+0.3	1.8	770
Abdul Khan	DOS	156	0.4			
Susannah Hill	Rev Comm	152	0.4			
Majority	**Lab**	**10,488**	**26.9**	**+5.7**	**21.2**	**9,019**

Electorate: 62,473 **Voters:** 38,957 **Turnout:** 62.4 **Swing:** 2.9 to Lab from Con
BY-ELECTION June 1989: LAB HOLD. K. Hoey (Lab) 15,191 (52.8%), M. Keegan (Con) 5,425 (18.8%), M. Tuffrey (Lib Dem) 5,043 (17.5%), Lab majority 9,766 (34%), SWING 6.4% to Lab from Con

WAKEFIELD

David Hinchliffe: Labour. Born: 1948. Educated: Wakefield Technical College; Leeds Polytechnic; Bradford University. Jobs: social work tutor. First Elected: 1987. Posts: Labour spokesman on community care; member, Health Select Committee. Union: NUPE. Status: married, two children.

LAB HOLD		1992 election			1987 election	
		Votes	%	+/-	%	Votes
David Hinchliffe*	Lab	26,964	50.6	+4.0	46.6	24,509
David Fanthorpe	Con	20,374	38.3	-3.0	41.3	21,720
Tim Wright	Lib Dem	5,900	11.1	-1.0	12.1	6,350
Majority	**Lab**	**6,590**	**12.4**	**+7.1**	**5.3**	**2,789**

Electorate: 69,794 **Voters:** 53,238 **Turnout:** 76.3 **Swing:** 3.5 to Lab from Con

WALLASEY

Angela Eagle: Labour. Born: 1961. Educated: Formby High School; Oxford. Jobs: trade union official. First Elected: 1992. Union: COHSE. Status: single.

LAB GAIN		1992 election			1987 election	
		Votes	%	+/-	%	Votes
Angela Eagle	Lab	26,531	49.0	+7.0	41.9	22,512
Lynda Chalker*	Con	22,722	41.9	-0.5	42.5	22,791
Neil Thomas	Lib Dem	4,177	7.7	-7.9	15.6	8,363
Sally Davis	Green	650	1.2			
Geoffrey Gay	NLP	105	0.2			
Majority	**Lab**	**3,809**	**7.0**	**+7.5**	**0.5**	**279**

Electorate: 65,676 **Voters:** 54,185 **Turnout:** 82.5 **Swing:** 3.8 to Lab from Con

WALLSEND

Stephen Byers: Labour. Born: 1953. Educated: Chester City Grammar School; Liverpool Polytechnic. Jobs: lecturer. First Elected: 1992. Posts: chairman, Council of Local Education Authorities. Status: single.

LAB HOLD		1992 election			1987 election	
		Votes	%	+/-	%	Votes
Stephen Byers	Lab	33,439	57.9	+1.0	56.8	32,709
Mary Gibbon	Con	13,969	24.2	+1.0	23.2	13,325
Michael Huscroft	Lib Dem	10,369	17.9	-2.1	20.0	11,508
Majority	**Lab**	**19,470**	**33.7**	**+0.0**	**33.7**	**19,384**

Electorate: 77,941 **Voters:** 57,777 **Turnout:** 74.1 **Swing:** No Swing

WALSALL NORTH

David Winnick: Labour. Born: 1933. Educated: London School of Economics. Jobs: clerk, advertising, administrator. First Elected: 1966. Union: GMB-APEX Status: divorced.

LAB HOLD		1992 election			1987 election	
		Votes	%	+/-	%	Votes
David Winnick*	Lab	24,387	46.7	+4.2	42.6	21,458
Robert Syms	Con	20,563	39.4	+0.4	39.0	19,668
Alan Powis	Lib Dem	6,629	12.7	-5.7	18.4	9,285
Ken Reynolds	NF	614	1.2			
Majority	**Lab**	**3,824**	**7.3**	**+3.8**	**3.6**	**1,790**

Electorate: 69,604 **Voters:** 52,193 **Turnout:** 75.0 **Swing:** 1.9 to Lab from Con

WALSALL SOUTH

Bruce George: Labour. Born: 1942. Educated: Mountain Ash Grammar School; Swansea and Warwick Universities. Jobs: lecturer. First Elected: 1974. Posts: member, Defence Select Committee. Status: single.

LAB HOLD		1992 election			1987 election	
		Votes	%	+/-	%	Votes
Bruce George*	Lab	24,133	48.2	+3.3	44.9	22,629
Laurence Jones	Con	20,955	41.9	-0.8	42.7	21,513
Grant Williams	Lib Dem	4,132	8.3	-4.1	12.4	6,241
Richard Clarke	Green	673	1.3			
John Oldbury	NLP	167	0.3			
Majority	**Lab**	**3,178**	**6.3**	**+4.1**	**2.2**	**1,116**

Electorate: 65,642 **Voters:** 50,060 **Turnout:** 76.3 **Swing:** 2.1 to Lab from Con

WALTHAMSTOW

Neil Gerrard: Labour. Born: 1942. Educated: Manchester Grammar School; Oxford. Jobs: teacher, lecturer. First Elected: 1992. Status: divorced, two children.

LAB GAIN

		1992 election Votes	%	+/-	1987 election %	Votes
Neil Gerrard	Lab	16,251	45.7	+11.0	34.7	12,236
Hugo Summerson*	Con	13,229	37.2	-1.8	39.0	13,748
Peter Leighton	Lib Dem	5,142	14.5	-10.7	25.1	8,852
Jean Lambert	Green	594	1.7			
Vernon Wilkinson	Lib	241	0.7			
Andrew Planton	NLP	94	0.3			
Majority	**Lab**	**3,022**	**8.5**	**+12.8**	**4.3**	**1,512**

Electorate: 49,140 **Voters:** 35,551 **Turnout:** 72.3 **Swing:** 6.4 to Lab from Con

WANSBECK

John Thompson: Labour. Born: 1928. Educated: Bothal Secondary Modern School; Ashington Mining College. Jobs: electrical engineer. First Elected: 1983. Posts: Labour whip; delegate, Council of Europe, Western European Union. Union: NUM. Status: married, two children.

LAB HOLD

		1992 election Votes	%	+/-	1987 election %	Votes
John Thompson*	Lab	30,046	59.7	+2.2	57.5	28,080
Glen Sanderson	Con	11,872	23.6	+4.2	19.4	9,490
Brian Priestley	Lib Dem	7,691	15.3	-7.8	23.1	11,291
Nicholas Best	Green	710	1.4			
Majority	**Lab**	**18,174**	**36.1**	**+1.8**	**34.4**	**16,789**

Electorate: 63,457 **Voters:** 50,319 **Turnout:** 79.3 **Swing:** 1.0 to Con from Lab

WANSDYKE

Jack Aspinwall: Conservative. Born: 1933. Educated: Prescot Grammar School; Bootle; Marconi College, Chelmsford. Jobs: publican, company director. First Elected: 1979. Posts: member, Transport Select Committee. Status: married.

CON HOLD

		1992 election Votes	%	+/-	1987 election %	Votes
Jack Aspinwall*	Con	31,389	48.2	-3.3	51.6	31,537
Dan Norris	Lab	18,048	27.7	+4.5	23.3	14,231
Doreen Darby	Lib Dem	14,834	22.8	-2.4	25.2	15,393
Francis Hayden	Green	800	1.2			
Majority	**Con**	**13,341**	**20.5**	**-5.9**	**26.4**	**16,144**

Electorate: 77,156 **Voters:** 65,071 **Turnout:** 84.3 **Swing:** 3.9 to Lab from Con

WANSTEAD & WOODFORD

James Arbuthnot: Conservative. Born: 1952. Educated: Eton; Cambridge. Jobs: barrister. First Elected: 1987. Posts: Government Whip. Status: married, two children.

CON HOLD		1992 election			1987 election	
		Votes	%	+/-	%	Votes
James Arbuthnot*	Con	26,204	60.0	-1.3	61.3	25,701
Lyn Brown	Lab	9,319	21.3	+4.7	16.6	6,958
Gary Staight	Lib Dem	7,362	16.8	-5.3	22.1	9,289
Francis Roads	Green	637	1.5			
Anthony Brickell	NLP	178	0.4			
Majority	**Con**	**16,885**	**38.6**	**-0.5**	**39.1**	**16,412**

Electorate: 55,821 **Voters:** 43,700 **Turnout:** 78.3 **Swing:** 3.0 to Lab from Con

WANTAGE

Robert Jackson: Conservative. Born: 1946. Educated: Rhodesia; Oxford. Jobs: political adviser, Euro MP. First Elected: 1983. Posts: Civil Service minister. Status: married.

CON HOLD		1992 election			1987 election	
		Votes	%	+/-	%	Votes
Robert Jackson*	Con	30,575	54.1	+0.2	54.0	27,951
Bob Morgan	Lib Dem	14,102	25.0	-5.5	30.5	15,795
Vivian Woodell	Lab	10,955	19.4	+3.8	15.5	8,055
Robert Ely	Green	867	1.5			
Majority	**Con**	**16,473**	**29.2**	**+5.7**	**23.5**	**12,156**

Electorate: 68,328 **Voters:** 56,499 **Turnout:** 82.7 **Swing:** 2.8 to Con from LDm

WARLEY EAST

Andrew Faulds: Labour. Born: 1923. Educated: King Edward VI School, Louth; Glasgow University. Jobs: actor. First Elected: 1966. Union: Equity. Status: married, one child.

LAB HOLD		1992 election			1987 election	
		Votes	%	+/-	%	Votes
Andrew Faulds*	Lab	19,891	53.6	+3.4	50.2	19,428
Giles Marshall	Con	12,097	32.6	-3.2	35.8	13,843
Alan Harrod	Lib Dem	4,547	12.3	-1.7	14.0	5,396
Alan Groucott	NLP	561	1.5			
Majority	**Lab**	**7,794**	**21.0**	**+6.6**	**14.4**	**5,585**

Electorate: 51,717 **Voters:** 37,096 **Turnout:** 71.7 **Swing:** 3.3 to Lab from Con

WARLEY WEST

John Spellar: Labour. Born: 1947. Educated: local state schools; Oxford. Jobs: trade union official. First Elected: 1982. Union: EEPTU. Status: married, one child.

LAB HOLD		1992 election			1987 election	
		Votes	%	+/-	%	Votes
John Spellar	Lab	21,386	50.6	+1.4	49.2	19,825
Sarah Whitehouse	Con	15,914	37.7	+1.8	35.8	14,432
Elaine Todd	Lib Dem	4,945	11.7	-3.3	15.0	6,027
Majority	**Lab**	**5,472**	**13.0**	**-0.4**	**13.4**	**5,393**

Electorate: 57,164 **Voters:** 42,245 **Turnout:** 73.9 **Swing:** 0.2 to Con from Lab

WARRINGTON NORTH

Doug Hoyle: Labour. Born: 1930. Educated: Adlington School; Horwich Technical College. Jobs: sales engineer. First Elected: 1974. Posts: chairman Parliamentary Labour Party; member, Trade and Industry Select Committee. Union: MSF. Status: widower, one child.

LAB HOLD		1992 election			1987 election	
		Votes	%	+/-	%	Votes
Doug Hoyle*	Lab	33,019	54.3	+6.1	48.2	27,422
Colin Daniels	Con	20,397	33.6	-0.6	34.1	19,409
Ian Greenhalgh	Lib Dem	6,965	11.5	-6.2	17.7	10,046
Brian Davies	NLP	400	0.7			
Majority	**Lab**	**12,622**	**20.8**	**+6.7**	**14.1**	**8,013**

Electorate: 78,548 **Voters:** 60,781 **Turnout:** 77.4 **Swing:** 3.3 to Lab from Con

WARRINGTON SOUTH

Mike Hall: Labour. Born: 1952. Educated: St Damian's Secondary Modern School; Stretford Technical College; Victoria University, Manchester; University of Wales, Bangor. Jobs: scientific assistant, teacher. First Elected: 1992. Posts: member, Public Accounts Committee. Status: married, one child.

LAB GAIN		1992 election			1987 election	
		Votes	%	+/-	%	Votes
Mike Hall	Lab	27,819	43.6	+7.8	35.9	21,200
Chris Butler*	Con	27,628	43.3	+1.4	42.0	24,809
Peter Walker	Lib Dem	7,978	12.5	-9.7	22.2	13,112
Stephen Benson	NLP	321	0.5			
Majority	**Lab**	**191**	**0.3**	**+6.4**	**6.1**	**3,609**

Electorate: 77,694 **Voters:** 63,746 **Turnout:** 82.0 **Swing:** 3.2 to Lab from Con

WARWICK & LEAMINGTON

Sir Dudley Smith: *Conservative. Born: 1926. Educated: Chichester High School. Jobs: journalist, company executive. First Elected: 1959. Posts: delegate, Council of Europe, Western European Union. Status: married, three children.*

CON HOLD		1992 election			1987 election	
		Votes	%	+/-	%	Votes
Sir Dudley Smith*	Con	28,093	48.3	-1.4	49.8	27,530
Matthew Taylor	Lab	19,158	33.0	+9.4	23.5	13,019
Sarah Boad	Lib Dem	9,645	16.6	-7.9	24.5	13,548
Janet Alty	Green	803	1.4	-0.8	2.2	1,214
Ronald Newby	Ind	251	0.4			
James Brewster	NLP	156	0.3			
Majority	**Con**	**8,935**	**15.4**	**-9.9**	**25.3**	**13,982**

Electorate: 71,259 **Voters:** 58,106 **Turnout:** 81.5 **Swing:** 5.4 to Lab from Con

WARWICKSHIRE NORTH

Mike O'Brien: *Labour. Born: 1954. Educated: Blessed Edward Oldcorne RC School; Worcester Technical College; North Staffs. Polytechnic. Jobs: lecturer, solicitor. First Elected: 1992. Posts: member, Home Affairs Select Committee. Union: GMB. Status: married, one child.*

LAB GAIN		1992 election			1987 election	
		Votes	%	+/-	%	Votes
Mike O'Brien	Lab	27,599	46.1	+6.0	40.1	22,624
Francis Maude*	Con	26,145	43.6	-1.4	45.1	25,453
Noel Mitchell	Lib Dem	6,167	10.3	-4.6	14.8	8,382
Majority	**Lab**	**1,454**	**2.4**	**+7.4**	**5.0**	**2,829**

Electorate: 71,473 **Voters:** 59,911 **Turnout:** 83.8 **Swing:** 3.7 to Lab from Con

WATFORD

Tristan Garel-Jones: *Conservative. Born: 1941. Educated: King's School, Canterbury; Madrid University. Jobs: merchant banker, language school principal. First Elected: 1979. Posts: Minister of State at the Foreign Office. Status: married, five children.*

CON HOLD		1992 election			1987 election	
		Votes	%	+/-	%	Votes
Tristan Garel-Jones*	Con	29,072	48.8	+0.1	48.7	27,912
Michael Jackson	Lab	19,482	32.7	+4.5	28.2	16,176
Mark Oaten	Lib Dem	10,231	17.2	-5.9	23.0	13,202
Jeremy Hywel-Davies	Green	566	1.0			
Leslie Davis	NLP	176	0.3			
Majority	**Con**	**9,590**	**16.1**	**-4.4**	**20.5**	**11,736**

Electorate: 72,291 **Voters:** 59,527 **Turnout:** 82.3 **Swing:** 2.2 to Lab from Con

WAVENEY

David Porter: *Conservative. Born: 1948. Educated: Lowestoft Grammar School. Jobs: teacher, party agent. First Elected: 1987. Posts: member, Education Select Committee. Status: married, four children.*

CON HOLD		1992 election		+/-	1987 election	
		Votes	%		%	Votes
David Porter*	Con	33,174	48.2	-0.2	48.4	31,067
Ezra Leverett	Lab	26,472	38.4	+8.4	30.0	19,284
Adrian Rogers	Lib Dem	8,925	13.0	-8.6	21.6	13,845
David Hook	NLP	302	0.4			
Majority	**Con**	**6,702**	**9.7**	**-8.6**	**18.4**	**11,783**

Electorate: 84,181 **Voters:** 68,873 **Turnout:** 81.8 **Swing:** 4.3 to Lab from Con

WEALDEN

Sir Geoffrey Johnson Smith: *Conservative. Born: 1924. Educated: Charterhouse; Oxford. Jobs: broadcaster, company director. First Elected: 1959. Posts: vice-chairman, 1922 Committee, leader UK delegation to NATO Assembly. Status: married, three children.*

CON HOLD		1992 election		+/-	1987 election	
		Votes	%		%	Votes
Sir Geoffrey Johnson Smith*	Con	37,263	61.7	-2.5	64.2	35,154
Michael Skinner	Lib Dem	16,332	27.1	-0.4	27.5	15,044
Steve Billcliffe	Lab	5,579	9.2	+0.9	8.3	4,563
Ian Guy-Moore	Green	1,002	1.7			
Roger Graham	NLP	182	0.3			
Majority	**Con**	**20,931**	**34.7**	**-2.0**	**36.7**	**20,110**

Electorate: 74,665 **Voters:** 60,358 **Turnout:** 80.8 **Swing:** 1.0 to LDm from Con

WELLINGBOROUGH

Peter Fry: *Conservative. Born: 1931. Educated: Royal Grammar School, High Wycombe; Oxford. Jobs: insurance broker, political adviser, company director. First Elected: 1969. Status: married, two children.*

CON HOLD		1992 election		+/-	1987 election	
		Votes	%		%	Votes
Peter Fry*	Con	32,302	53.4	+0.6	52.7	29,038
Philip Sawford	Lab	20,486	33.9	+6.7	27.2	14,968
Julie Trevor	Lib Dem	7,714	12.7	-7.3	20.1	11,047
Majority	**Con**	**11,816**	**19.5**	**-6.0**	**25.6**	**14,070**

Electorate: 73,875 **Voters:** 60,502 **Turnout:** 81.9 **Swing:** 3.0 to Lab from Con

WELLS

David Heathcoat-Amory: *Conservative. Born: 1949. Educated: Eton; Oxford. Jobs: accountant, farmer, finance director. First Elected: 1983. Status: married, three children.*

CON HOLD

		1992 election Votes	%	+/-	1987 election %	Votes
David Heathcoat-Amory*	Con	28,620	49.6	-4.0	53.5	28,624
Humphrey Temperley	Lib Dem	21,971	38.0	+0.5	37.6	20,083
John Pilgrim	Lab	6,126	10.6	+1.9	8.7	4,637
Mike Fenner	Green	1,042	1.8			
Majority	**Con**	**6,649**	**11.5**	**-4.5**	**16.0**	**8,541**

Electorate: 69,833 **Voters:** 57,759 **Turnout:** 82.7 **Swing:** 2.2 to LDm from Con

WELWYN HATFIELD

David Evans: *Conservative. Born: 1935. Educated: Tottenham Technical College. Jobs: footballer, cricketer, company director. First Elected: 1987. Posts: PPS. Status: married, three children.*

CON HOLD

		1992 election Votes	%	+/-	1987 election %	Votes
David Evans*	Con	29,447	48.4	+2.7	45.6	27,164
Ray Little	Lab	20,982	34.5	+8.1	26.4	15,699
Robin Parker	Lib Dem	10,196	16.7	-10.6	27.3	16,261
Eva Lucas	NLP	264	0.4			
Majority	**Con**	**8,465**	**13.9**	**-4.4**	**18.3**	**10,903**

Electorate: 72,146 **Voters:** 60,889 **Turnout:** 84.4 **Swing:** 2.7 to Lab from Con

WENTWORTH

Peter Hardy: *Labour. Born: 1931. Educated: Wath-upon-Dearne Grammar School; Sheffield University. Jobs: teacher. First Elected: 1970. Posts: delegate, Council of Europe. Union: NACODS. Status: married, two children.*

LAB HOLD

		1992 election Votes	%	+/-	1987 election %	Votes
Peter Hardy*	Lab	32,939	68.5	+3.4	65.2	30,205
Michael Brennan	Con	10,490	21.8	+0.0	21.8	10,113
Christine Roderick	Lib Dem	4,629	9.6	-3.4	13.0	6,031
Majority	**Lab**	**22,449**	**46.7**	**+3.4**	**43.3**	**20,092**

Electorate: 64,914 **Voters:** 48,058 **Turnout:** 74.0 **Swing:** 1.7 to Lab from Con

WEST BROMWICH EAST

Peter Snape: Labour. Born: 1942. Educated: St. Joseph's and St. Winifred's Schools, Stockport; St. Bede's College, Manchester; Dial Stone Secondary Modern. Jobs: signalman, soldier. First Elected: 1974. Posts: Labour spokesman on railways. Union: RMT. Status: divorced, two children.

LAB HOLD

		1992 election Votes	%	+/-	1987 election %	Votes
Peter Snape*	Lab	19,913	46.5	+3.8	42.6	18,162
Crispin Blunt	Con	17,100	39.9	-0.4	40.3	17,179
Martyn Smith	Lib Dem	5,360	12.5	-4.5	17.1	7,268
John Lord	NF	477	1.1			
Majority	**Lab**	**2,813**	**6.6**	**+4.3**	**2.3**	**983**

Electorate: 56,940 **Voters:** 42,850 **Turnout:** 75.3 **Swing:** 2.1 to Lab from Con

WEST BROMWICH WEST

Betty Boothroyd: Labour. Born: 1929. Educated: Dewsbury Technical College. Jobs: political assistant. First Elected: 1973. Posts: Speaker. Union: GMB. Status: single.

LAB HOLD

		1992 election Votes	%	+/-	1987 election %	Votes
Betty Boothroyd*	Lab	22,251	54.8	+4.3	50.5	19,925
Desmond Swayne	Con	14,421	35.5	-1.6	37.2	14,672
Sarah Broadbent	Lib Dem	3,925	9.7	-2.7	12.4	4,877
Majority	**Lab**	**7,830**	**19.3**	**+6.0**	**13.3**	**5,253**

Electorate: 57,655 **Voters:** 40,597 **Turnout:** 70.4 **Swing:** 3.0 to Lab from Con

WESTBURY

David Faber: Conservative. Born: 1961. Educated: Eton; Oxford. Jobs: political adviser, marketing consultant. First Elected: 1992. Posts: member, Social Security Select Committee. Status: married.

CON HOLD

		1992 election Votes	%	+/-	1987 election %	Votes
David Faber	Con	36,568	50.4	-1.2	51.6	34,256
Vivienne Rayner	Lib Dem	23,962	33.1	-3.3	36.4	24,159
William Stallard	Lab	9,642	13.3	+1.3	12.0	7,982
Paul Macdonald	Lib	1,440	2.0			
Patrick French	Green	888	1.2			
Majority	**Con**	**12,606**	**17.4**	**+2.2**	**15.2**	**10,097**

Electorate: 87,356 **Voters:** 72,500 **Turnout:** 83.0 **Swing:** 1.1 to Con from LDm

WESTERN ISLES

Calum MacDonald: Labour. Born: 1956. Educated: Nicolson Institute; Edinburgh University. Jobs: lecturer. First Elected: 1987. Union: TGWU. Status: single.

LAB HOLD		1992 election Votes	%	+/-	1987 election %	Votes
Calum MacDonald*	Lab	7,664	47.8	+5.1	42.7	7,041
Frances MacFarlane	SNP	5,961	37.2	+8.7	28.5	4,701
Bob Heany	Con	1,362	8.5	+0.4	8.1	1,336
Neil Mitchison	Lib Dem	552	3.4	-17.3	20.7	3,419
Andrew Price	Ind	491	3.1			
Majority	**Lab**	**1,703**	**10.6**	**-3.6**	**14.2**	**2,340**

Electorate: 22,784 **Voters:** 16,030 **Turnout:** 70.4 **Swing:** 1.8 to SNP from Lab

WESTMINSTER NORTH

Sir John Wheeler: Conservative. Born: 1940. Educated: County School, Suffolk. Jobs: assistant prison governor. First Elected: 1979. Status: married, two children.

CON HOLD		1992 election Votes	%	+/-	1987 election %	Votes
Sir John Wheeler*	Con	21,828	49.0	+1.6	47.3	19,941
Jennifer Edwards	Lab	18,095	40.6	+1.1	39.5	16,631
Justin Wigoder	Lib Dem	3,341	7.5	-4.6	12.1	5,116
Amelia Burke	Green	1,017	2.3	+1.2	1.1	450
Jonathan Hinde	NLP	159	0.4			
Michael Kelly	Anti Fed	137	0.3			
Majority	**Con**	**3,733**	**8.4**	**+0.5**	**7.9**	**3,310**

Electorate: 58,847 **Voters:** 44,577 **Turnout:** 75.8 **Swing:** 0.3 to Con from Lab

WESTMORLAND & LONSDALE

Michael Jopling: Conservative. Born: 1930. Educated: Cheltenham School; Newcastle University. Jobs: farmer, company director. First Elected: 1964. Posts: member, Foreign Affairs Select Committee. Status: married, three children.

CON HOLD		1992 election Votes	%	+/-	1987 election %	Votes
Michael Jopling*	Con	31,798	56.9	-0.7	57.6	30,259
Stan Collins	Lib Dem	15,362	27.5	-1.7	29.2	15,339
Dickon Abbott	Lab	8,436	15.1	+1.8	13.3	6,968
Robert Johnstone	NLP	287	0.5			
Majority	**Con**	**16,436**	**29.4**	**+1.0**	**28.4**	**14,920**

Electorate: 71,865 **Voters:** 55,883 **Turnout:** 77.8 **Swing:** 0.5 to Con from LDm

WESTON-SUPER-MARE

Jerry Wiggin: *Conservative. Born: 1937. Educated: Eton; Cambridge. Jobs: farmer, company director. First Elected: 1969. Posts: chairman, Agriculture Select Committee. Status: married, two children.*

CON HOLD

		1992 election Votes	%	+/-	1987 election %	Votes
Jerry Wiggin*	Con	30,022	47.7	-1.7	49.4	28,547
Brian Cotter	Lib Dem	24,680	39.3	+3.7	35.6	20,549
David Murray	Lab	6,913	11.0	-0.4	11.4	6,584
Richard Lawson	Green	1,262	2.0	-1.6	3.6	2,067
Majority	**Con**	**5,342**	**8.5**	**-5.4**	**13.9**	**7,998**

Electorate: 78,839 **Voters:** 62,877 **Turnout:** 79.8 **Swing:** 2.7 to LDm from Con

WIGAN

Roger Stott: *Labour. Born: 1943. Educated: Greenbank Secondary Modern School; Rochdale Technical College, Ruskin College, Oxford. Jobs: seaman, telephone engineer. First Elected: 1973. Posts: Labour spokesman on Northern Ireland. Union: NCU. Status: married, three children.*

LAB HOLD

		1992 election Votes	%	+/-	1987 election %	Votes
Roger Stott*	Lab	34,910	63.0	+1.5	61.5	33,955
Edward Hess	Con	13,068	23.6	-0.9	24.5	13,493
George Davies	Lib Dem	6,111	11.0	-3.0	14.0	7,732
Kevin White	Lib	1,116	2.0			
Annie Taylor	NLP	197	0.4			
Majority	**Lab**	**21,842**	**39.4**	**+2.3**	**37.1**	**20,462**

Electorate: 72,739 **Voters:** 55,402 **Turnout:** 76.2 **Swing:** 1.2 to Lab from Con

WILTSHIRE NORTH

Richard Needham: *Conservative. Born: 1942. Educated: Eton. Jobs: company director. First Elected: 1979. Posts: Minister for Trade. Status: married, three children.*

CON HOLD

		1992 election Votes	%	+/-	1987 election %	Votes
Richard Needham*	Con	39,028	55.6	+0.5	55.2	35,309
Christine Napier	Lib Dem	22,640	32.3	-5.8	38.1	24,370
Christine Reid	Lab	6,945	9.9	+3.1	6.8	4,343
Lydia Howitt	Green	850	1.2			
George Hawkins	Lib	622	0.9			
Sebastion Martienssen	Bastion	66	0.1			
Majority	**Con**	**16,388**	**23.4**	**+6.3**	**17.1**	**10,939**

Electorate: 85,851 **Voters:** 70,151 **Turnout:** 81.7 **Swing:** 3.1 to Con from LDm

WIMBLEDON

Dr Charles Goodson-Wickes: Conservative. Born: 1945. Educated: Charterhouse. Jobs: doctor, barrister. First Elected: 1987. Posts: PPS. Posts: deputy chairman, Conservative Party. Status: married, two children.

CON HOLD		1992 election Votes	%	+/-	1987 election %	Votes
Charles Goodson-Wickes*	Con	26,331	53.0	+2.1	50.9	24,538
Kingsley Abrams	Lab	11,570	23.3	+1.7	21.6	10,428
Alison Willott	Lib Dem	10,569	21.3	-6.2	27.5	13,237
Vaughan Flood	Green	860	1.7			
Hugh Godfrey	NLP	181	0.4			
Graham Hadley	Ind	170	0.3			
Majority	**Con**	**14,761**	**29.7**	**+6.3**	**23.4**	**11,301**

Electorate: 61,917 **Voters:** 49,681 **Turnout:** 80.2 **Swing:** 0.2 to Con from Lab

WINCHESTER

Gerald Malone: Conservative. Born: 1950. Educated: St Aloysius College, Glasgow; Glasgow University. Jobs: solicitor, broadcaster, company director. First Elected: 1983. Status: married, two children.

CON HOLD		1992 election Votes	%	+/-	1987 election %	Votes
Gerald Malone	Con	33,113	50.1	-2.3	52.3	32,195
Tony Barron	Lib Dem	24,992	37.8	-2.4	40.2	24,716
Peter Jenks	Lab	4,917	7.4	+0.9	6.5	4,028
John Browne*	Ind C	3,095	4.7			
Majority	**Con**	**8,121**	**12.3**	**+0.1**	**12.2**	**7,479**

Electorate: 79,218 **Voters:** 66,117 **Turnout:** 83.5 **Swing:** No Swing

WINDSOR & MAIDENHEAD

Michael Trend: Conservative. Born: 1952. Educated: Westminster; Oxford. Jobs: journalist. First Elected: 1992. Posts: member, Health Select Committee. Status: married, two children.

CON HOLD		1992 election Votes	%	+/-	1987 election %	Votes
Michael Trend	Con	35,075	55.5	-1.3	56.8	33,980
Jeremy Hyde	Lib Dem	22,147	35.1	+8.1	27.0	16,144
Catherine Attlee	Lab	4,975	7.9	-3.3	11.2	6,678
Robert Williams	Green	510	0.8	-0.4	1.2	711
David Askwith	Loony	236	0.4			
Edith Bigg	Ind	110	0.2			
Mike Grenville	NLP	108	0.2			
Majority	**Con**	**12,928**	**20.5**	**-9.4**	**29.8**	**17,836**

Electorate: 77,327 **Voters:** 63,161 **Turnout:** 81.7 **Swing:** 4.7 to LDm from Con

WIRRAL SOUTH

Barry Porter: *Conservative. Born: 1939. Educated: Birkenhead School; Oxford. Jobs: solicitor, company director. First Elected: 1979. Posts: member, Trade and Industry Select Committee. Status: married, five children.*

CON HOLD

		1992 election			1987 election	
		Votes	%	+/-	%	Votes
Barry Porter*	Con	25,590	50.8	+0.6	50.2	24,821
Helen Southworth	Lab	17,407	34.6	+6.6	28.0	13,858
Ed Cunniffe	Lib Dem	6,581	13.1	-8.7	21.8	10,779
Nigel Birchenough	Green	584	1.2			
George Griffiths	NLP	182	0.4			
Majority	**Con**	**8,183**	**16.3**	**-5.9**	**22.2**	**10,963**

Electorate: 61,116 **Voters:** 50,344 **Turnout:** 82.4 **Swing:** 3.0 to Lab from Con

WIRRAL WEST

David Hunt: *Conservative. Born: 1942. Educated: Liverpool College; Bristol University. Jobs: solicitor. First Elected: 1976. Posts: Secretary of State for Wales. Status: married, four children.*

CON HOLD

		1992 election			1987 election	
		Votes	%	+/-	%	Votes
David Hunt*	Con	26,852	52.7	+0.8	51.9	25,736
Helen Stephenson	Lab	15,788	31.0	+4.7	26.3	13,013
John Thornton	Lib Dem	7,420	14.6	-5.6	20.2	10,015
Garnette Bowler	Green	700	1.4	-0.3	1.6	806
Nigel Broome	NLP	188	0.4			
Majority	**Con**	**11,064**	**21.7**	**-4.0**	**25.7**	**12,723**

Electorate: 62,453 **Voters:** 50,948 **Turnout:** 81.6 **Swing:** 2.0 to Lab from Con

WITNEY

Douglas Hurd: *Conservative. Born: 1930. Educated: Eton; Cambridge. Jobs: diplomat, author. First Elected: 1974. Posts: Foreign Secretary. Status: married, five children.*

CON HOLD

		1992 election			1987 election	
		Votes	%	+/-	%	Votes
Douglas Hurd*	Con	36,256	56.4	-1.1	57.5	33,458
James Plaskitt	Lab	13,688	21.3	+4.6	16.7	9,733
Ian Blair	Lib Dem	13,393	20.8	-4.9	25.8	14,994
Charlotte Beckford	Green	716	1.1			
Sally Catling	NLP	134	0.2			
Marilyn Brown	FTA	119	0.2			
Majority	**Con**	**22,568**	**35.1**	**+3.4**	**31.7**	**18,464**

Electorate: 78,521 **Voters:** 64,306 **Turnout:** 81.9 **Swing:** 2.8 to Lab from Con

WOKING

Cranley Onslow: Conservative. Born: 1926. Educated: Harrow; Oxford. Jobs: diplomat. First Elected: 1964. Posts: member, Trade and Industry Select Committee. Status: married, four children.

CON HOLD		1992 election			1987 election	
		Votes	%	+/-	%	Votes
Cranley Onslow*	Con	37,744	58.9	+0.9	58.1	35,990
Dorothy Buckrell	Lib Dem	17,902	28.0	-3.4	31.4	19,446
James Dalgleish	Lab	8,080	12.6	+2.1	10.5	6,537
Teresa Macintyre	NLP	302	0.5			
Majority	**Con**	**19,842**	**31.0**	**+4.3**	**26.7**	**16,544**

Electorate: 80,842 **Voters:** 64,028 **Turnout:** 79.2 **Swing:** 2.1 to Con from LDm

WOKINGHAM

John Redwood: Conservative. Born: 1951. Educated: Kent College, Canterbury; Oxford. Jobs: investment analyst, political adviser. First Elected: 1987. Posts: Minister for Local Government and Inner Cities. Status: married, two children.

CON HOLD		1992 election			1987 election	
		Votes	%	+/-	%	Votes
John Redwood*	Con	43,497	61.4	+0.0	61.4	39,808
Paul Simon	Lib Dem	17,788	25.1	-4.8	29.9	19,421
Nelson Bland	Lab	8,846	12.5	+3.8	8.7	5,622
Peter Owen	Loony	531	0.7			
Philip Harriss	WUWC	148	0.2			
Majority	**Con**	**25,709**	**36.3**	**+4.9**	**31.4**	**20,387**

Electorate: 85,914 **Voters:** 70,810 **Turnout:** 82.4 **Swing:** 2.4 to Con from LDm

WOLVERHAMPTON NE

Ken Purchase: Labour. Born: 1939. Educated: local state schools. Jobs: local government officer, engineering. First Elected: 1992. Union: TGWU. Status: married, two children.

LAB GAIN		1992 election			1987 election	
		Votes	%	+/-	%	Votes
Ken Purchase	Lab	24,106	49.3	+7.6	41.7	19,653
Maureen Hicks*	Con	20,167	41.2	-0.9	42.1	19,857
Malcolm Gwinnett	Lib Dem	3,546	7.3	-8.9	16.2	7,623
Kenneth Bullman	Lib	1,087	2.2			
Majority	**Lab**	**3,939**	**8.1**	**+8.5**	**0.4**	**204**

Electorate: 62,695 **Voters:** 48,906 **Turnout:** 78.0 **Swing:** 4.2 to Lab from Con

WOLVERHAMPTON SE

Dennis Turner: *Labour. Born: 1942. Educated: Stonefield Secondary School. Jobs: co-operative director. First Elected: 1987. Posts: member, Education Select Committee. Union: ISC. Status: married, two children.*

LAB HOLD		1992 election			1987 election	
		Votes	%	+/-	%	Votes
Dennis Turner*	Lab	23,215	56.7	+7.8	48.9	19,760
Philip Bradbourn	Con	12,975	31.7	-1.4	33.1	13,362
Richard Whitehouse	Lib Dem	3,881	9.5	-8.5	18.0	7,258
Catherine Twelvetrees	Lib	850	2.1			
Majority	**Lab**	**10,240**	**25.0**	**+9.2**	**15.8**	**6,398**

Electorate: 56,158 **Voters:** 40,921 **Turnout:** 72.9 **Swing:** 4.6 to Lab from Con

WOLVERHAMPTON SW

Nick Budgen: *Conservative. Born: 1937. Educated: St Edward School; Oxford, Cambridge University. Jobs: barrister, farmer. First Elected: 1974. Posts: member, Treasury Select Committee. Status: married, two children.*

CON HOLD		1992 election			1987 election	
		Votes	%	+/-	%	Votes
Nick Budgen*	Con	25,969	49.3	-1.4	50.7	26,235
Simon Murphy	Lab	21,003	39.9	+9.1	30.7	15,917
Mark Wiggin	Lib Dem	4,470	8.5	-10.1	18.6	9,616
Colin Hallmark	Lib	1,237	2.3			
Majority	**Con**	**4,966**	**9.4**	**-10.5**	**19.9**	**10,318**

Electorate: 67,288 **Voters:** 52,679 **Turnout:** 78.3 **Swing:** 5.3 to Lab from Con

WOODSPRING

Dr Liam Fox: *Conservative. Born: 1961. Educated: St Bride's High School, East Kilbride; Glasgow University. Jobs: doctor. First Elected: 1992. Posts: member, Scottish Affairs Select Committee. Status: single.*

CON HOLD		1992 election			1987 election	
		Votes	%	+/-	%	Votes
Liam Fox	Con	35,175	54.5	-2.1	56.6	34,134
Nan Kirsen	Lib Dem	17,666	27.4	+0.4	27.0	16,282
Ronald Stone	Lab	9,942	15.4	+1.0	14.4	8,717
Nicholas Brown	Lib	836	1.3			
Rosey Knifton	Green	801	1.2	-0.8	2.0	1,208
Bryan Lee	NLP	100	0.2			
Majority	**Con**	**17,509**	**27.1**	**-2.4**	**29.6**	**17,852**

Electorate: 77,534 **Voters:** 64,520 **Turnout:** 83.2 **Swing:** 1.2 to LDm from Con

WOOLWICH

John Austin-Walker: *Labour. Born: 1944. Educated: Glyn County Grammar School, Epsom; London University. Jobs: lab technician, party agent, social worker. First Elected: 1992. Union: MSF. Status: married, three children.*

LAB GAIN		1992 election			1987 election	
		Votes	%	+/-	%	Votes
John Austin-Walker	Lab	17,551	44.2	+7.2	37.0	15,200
John Cartwright*	Soc Dem	15,326	38.6	-3.1	41.7	17,137
Kevin Walmsley	Con	6,598	16.6	-4.6	21.2	8,723
Sarah Hayward	NLP	220	0.6			
Majority	**Lab**	**2,225**	**5.6**	**+10.9**	**4.7**	**1,937**

Electorate: 55,977 **Voters:** 39,695 **Turnout:** 70.9 **Swing:** 5.1 to Lab from SDP

WORCESTER

Peter Luff: *Conservative. Born: 1955. Educated: Windsor Grammar School; Cambridge. Jobs: political adviser, public relations. First Elected: 1992. Posts: member, Welsh Affairs Select Committee. Status: married, two children.*

CON HOLD		1992 election			1987 election	
		Votes	%	+/-	%	Votes
Peter Luff	Con	27,883	46.4	-1.8	48.2	25,504
Roger Berry	Lab	21,731	36.2	+7.7	28.4	15,051
John Caiger	Lib Dem	9,561	15.9	-7.5	23.4	12,386
Mike Foster	Green	592	1.0			
Martin Soden	Brewer	343	0.6			
Majority	**Con**	**6,152**	**10.2**	**-9.5**	**19.7**	**10,453**

Electorate: 74,211 **Voters:** 60,110 **Turnout:** 81.0 **Swing:** 4.8 to Lab from Con

WORCESTERSHIRE MID

Eric Forth: *Conservative. Born: 1944. Educated: Jordanhill College School; Glasgow University. Jobs: management consultant, computer industry, Euro MP. First Elected: 1983. Posts: Education minister. Status: married, two children.*

CON HOLD		1992 election			1987 election	
		Votes	%	+/-	%	Votes
Eric Forth*	Con	33,964	49.7	-1.9	51.6	31,854
Jacqui Smith	Lab	24,094	35.3	+7.8	27.4	16,943
David Barwick	Lib Dem	9,745	14.3	-6.7	21.0	12,954
Paul Davis	NLP	520	0.8			
Majority	**Con**	**9,870**	**14.4**	**-9.7**	**24.1**	**14,911**

Electorate: 84,269 **Voters:** 68,323 **Turnout:** 81.1 **Swing:** 4.9 to Lab from Con

WORCESTERSHIRE SOUTH

Michael Spicer: Conservative. Born: 1943. Educated: Wellington College; Cambridge. Jobs: economist, company director. First Elected: 1974. Status: married, three children.

CON HOLD		1992 election			1987 election	
		Votes	%	+/-	%	Votes
Michael Spicer*	Con	34,792	54.1	-1.2	55.3	32,277
Paul Chandler	Lib Dem	18,641	29.0	-2.9	31.9	18,632
Nigel Knowles	Lab	9,727	15.1	+4.2	10.9	6,374
Guy Woodford	Green	1,178	1.8	+0.0	1.9	1,089
Majority	**Con**	**16,151**	**25.1**	**+1.7**	**23.4**	**13,645**

Electorate: 80,423 **Voters:** 64,338 **Turnout:** 80.0 **Swing:** 0.9 to Con from LDm

WORKINGTON

Dale Campbell-Savours: Labour. Born: 1943. Educated: Keswick School; Sorbonne. Jobs: export agent, company director. First Elected: 1979. Posts: Labour spokesman on agriculture and food. Union: COHSE. Status: married, three children.

LAB HOLD		1992 election			1987 election	
		Votes	%	+/-	%	Votes
Dale Campbell-Savours*	Lab	26,719	56.9	+4.5	52.4	24,019
Stuart Sexton	Con	16,270	34.7	-2.4	37.1	17,000
Christine Neale	Lib Dem	3,028	6.4	-4.1	10.6	4,853
David Langstaff	Loony	755	1.6			
Nicola Escott	NLP	183	0.4			
Majority	**Lab**	**10,449**	**22.3**	**+7.0**	**15.3**	**7,019**

Electorate: 57,597 **Voters:** 46,955 **Turnout:** 81.5 **Swing:** 3.5 to Lab from Con

WORSLEY

Terry Lewis: Labour. Born: 1935. Educated: Mount Carmel School, Salford. Jobs: personnel officer. First Elected: 1983. Posts: member, chairmen's panel. Union: TGWU. Status: married, one child.

LAB HOLD		1992 election			1987 election	
		Votes	%	+/-	%	Votes
Terry Lewis*	Lab	29,418	52.4	+4.3	48.1	27,157
Neil Cameron	Con	19,406	34.6	-0.5	35.1	19,820
Bob Boyd	Lib Dem	6,490	11.6	-5.3	16.8	9,507
Philip Connolly	Green	677	1.2			
Gregg Phillips	NLP	176	0.3			
Majority	**Lab**	**10,012**	**17.8**	**+4.8**	**13.0**	**7,337**

Electorate: 72,244 **Voters:** 56,167 **Turnout:** 77.7 **Swing:** 2.4 to Lab from Con

WORTHING

Terence Higgins: *Conservative. Born: 1928. Educated: Alleyn's School, Dulwich; Cambridge. Jobs: economist, company director. First Elected: 1964. Posts: executive member, 1922 Committee. Status: married, two children.*

CON HOLD		1992 election			1987 election	
		Votes	%	+/-	%	Votes
Terence Higgins*	Con	34,198	57.0	-4.7	61.7	34,573
Sue Bucknall	Lib Dem	17,665	29.4	+0.7	28.7	16,072
Jim Deen	Lab	6,679	11.1	+1.5	9.6	5,387
Pauline Beever	Green	806	1.3			
Nicholas Goble	Lib	679	1.1			
Majority	**Con**	**16,533**	**27.5**	**-5.5**	**33.0**	**18,501**

Electorate: 77,540 **Voters:** 60,027 **Turnout:** 77.4 **Swing:** 2.7 to LDm from Con

WREKIN, THE

Bruce Grocott: *Labour. Born: 1940. Educated: Hemel Hempstead Grammar School; Leicester and Manchester Universities. Jobs: lecturer, broadcaster. First Elected: 1974. Posts: Labour spokesman on foreign and Commonwealth affairs. Union: COHSE. Status: married, two children.*

LAB HOLD		1992 election			1987 election	
		Votes	%	+/-	%	Votes
Bruce Grocott*	Lab	33,865	48.3	+5.5	42.8	27,681
Elizabeth Holt	Con	27,217	38.8	-1.8	40.6	26,225
Anthony West	Lib Dem	8,032	11.5	-5.2	16.6	10,737
Robert Saunders	Green	1,008	1.4			
Majority	**Lab**	**6,648**	**9.5**	**+7.2**	**2.3**	**1,456**

Electorate: 90,892 **Voters:** 70,122 **Turnout:** 77.1 **Swing:** 3.6 to Lab from Con

WREXHAM

Dr John Marek: *Labour. Born: 1940. Educated: Chatham House Grammar School; London University. Jobs: lecturer. First Elected: 1983. Union: RMT. Status: married.*

LAB HOLD		1992 election			1987 election	
		Votes	%	+/-	%	Votes
John Marek*	Lab	24,830	48.3	+4.4	43.9	22,144
Owen Paterson	Con	18,114	35.2	-0.4	35.6	17,992
Andrew Thomas	Lib Dem	7,074	13.8	-5.7	19.4	9,808
Gareth Wheatley	Plaid Cymru	1,415	2.8	+1.7	1.1	539
Majority	**Lab**	**6,716**	**13.1**	**+4.8**	**8.2**	**4,152**

Electorate: 63,720 **Voters:** 51,433 **Turnout:** 80.7 **Swing:** 2.4 to Lab from Con

WYCOMBE

Ray Whitney: *Conservative. Born: 1930. Educated: Wellingborough School; Sandhurst; London University. Jobs: army officer, diplomat. First Elected: 1978. Status: married, two children.*

CON HOLD		1992 election			1987 election	
		Votes	%	+/-	%	Votes
Ray Whitney*	Con	30,081	53.1	-0.7	53.9	28,209
Tim Andrews	Lib Dem	13,005	23.0	-4.5	27.5	14,390
John Huddart	Lab	12,222	21.6	+2.9	18.7	9,773
John Laker	Green	686	1.2			
Alan Page	Soc Dem	449	0.8			
Trevor Anton	NLP	168	0.3			
Majority	**Con**	**17,076**	**30.2**	**+3.8**	**26.4**	**13,819**

Electorate: 72,564 **Voters:** 56,611 **Turnout:** 78.0 **Swing:** 1.9 to Con from LDm

WYRE

Keith Mans: *Conservative. Born: 1946. Educated: Berkhamsted School; Open University. Jobs: retailer, RAF pilot. First Elected: 1987. Posts: PPS. Status: married, three children.*

CON HOLD		1992 election			1987 election	
		Votes	%	+/-	%	Votes
Keith Mans*	Con	29,449	54.6	+1.6	53.0	26,800
David Borrow	Lab	17,785	33.0	+11.8	21.2	10,725
John Ault	Lib Dem	6,420	11.9	-12.1	24.0	12,139
Roger Perry	NLP	260	0.5			
Majority	**Con**	**11,664**	**21.6**	**-7.4**	**29.0**	**14,661**

Electorate: 67,778 **Voters:** 53,914 **Turnout:** 79.5 **Swing:** 5.1 to Lab from Con

WYRE FOREST

Anthony Coombs: *Conservative. Born: 1952. Educated: Charterhouse; Oxford. Jobs: company director. First Elected: 1987. Posts: PPS. Status: married, one child.*

CON HOLD		1992 election			1987 election	
		Votes	%	+/-	%	Votes
Anthony Coombs*	Con	28,983	47.8	+0.7	47.1	25,877
Ross Maden	Lab	18,642	30.8	+11.9	18.9	10,365
Mark Jones	Lib Dem	12,958	21.4	-12.6	34.0	18,653
Majority	**Con**	**10,341**	**17.1**	**+3.9**	**13.2**	**7,224**

Electorate: 73,550 **Voters:** 60,583 **Turnout:** 82.4 **Swing:** 5.6 to Lab from Con

YEOVIL

Paddy Ashdown: Liberal Democrat. Born: 1941. Educated: Bedford School. Jobs: armed forces, diplomat, company manager. First Elected: 1983. Posts: leader of the LibDems. Status: married, two children.

LIBDEM HOLD		1992 election			1987 election	
		Votes	%	+/-	%	Votes
Paddy Ashdown*	Lib Dem	30,958	51.7	+0.3	51.4	28,841
Julian Davidson	Con	22,125	36.9	-4.3	41.3	23,141
Vivien Nelson	Lab	5,765	9.6	+2.3	7.3	4,099
Jay Risbridger	Green	639	1.1			
David Sutch	Loony	338	0.6			
Reginald Simmerson	APAKBI	70	0.1			
Majority	**Lib Dem**	**8,833**	**14.7**	**+4.6**	**10.2**	**5,700**

Electorate: 73,057 **Voters:** 59,895 **Turnout:** 82.0 **Swing:** 2.3 to LDm from Con

YNYS MON

Ieuan Wyn Jones: Plaid Cymru. Born: 1949. Educated: Ysgol y Berwyn, Bala; Liverpool Polytechnic. Jobs: solicitor. First Elected: 1987. Posts: member, Agriculture Select Committee. Status: married, three children.

PLAID CYMRU HOLD		1992 election			1987 election	
		Votes	%	+/-	%	Votes
Ieuan Wyn Jones*	Plaid Cymru	15,984	37.1	-6.1	43.2	18,580
Gwynn Price Rowlands	Con	14,878	34.6	+1.3	33.2	14,282
Robin Jones	Lab	10,126	23.5	+6.6	16.9	7,255
Pauline Badger	Lib Dem	1,891	4.4	-2.3	6.7	2,863
Susan Parry	NLP	182	0.4			
Majority	**Plaid Cymru**	**1,106**	**2.6**	**-7.4**	**10.0**	**4,298**

Electorate: 53,412 **Voters:** 43,061 **Turnout:** 80.6 **Swing:** 3.7 to Con from PC

YORK

Hugh Bayley: Labour. Born: 1952. Educated: Haileybury School; Bristol and York Universities. Jobs: trade union official, lecturer. First Elected: 1992. Union: BECTU. Status: married, two children.

LAB GAIN		1992 election			1987 election	
		Votes	%	+/-	%	Votes
Hugh Bayley	Lab	31,525	49.1	+7.7	41.4	25,733
Conal Gregory*	Con	25,183	39.2	-2.4	41.6	25,880
Karen Anderson	Lib Dem	6,811	10.6	-5.3	15.9	9,898
Stephen Kenwright	Green	594	0.9	-0.1	1.0	637
Pamela Orr	NLP	54	0.1			
Majority	**Lab**	**6,342**	**9.9**	**+10.1**	**0.2**	**147**

Electorate: 79,242 **Voters:** 64,167 **Turnout:** 81.0 **Swing:** 5.1 to Lab from Con

ANALYSIS

THE CABINET
AS AT MAY 1992

		Age	Salary (£)
Prime Minister	John Major	49	76,234
Lord Chancellor	Lord Mackay of Clashfern	64	106,750
Foreign Secretary	Douglas Hurd	62	63,047
Chancellor	Norman Lamont	49	63,047
Home Secretary	Kenneth Clarke	51	63,047
Board of Trade	Michael Heseltine	59	63,047
Transport Secretary	John MacGregor	55	63,047
Defence Secretary	Malcolm Rifkind	45	63,047
Lord Privy Seal	John Wakeham	59	50,558
Lord President	Antony Newton	54	63,047
Minister of Agriculture	John Gummer	52	63,047
Environment Secretary	Michael Howard	50	63,047
Welsh Secretary	David Hunt	49	63,047
Social Security	Peter Lilley	48	63,047
Chancellor of Duchy of Lancaster	William Waldegrave	45	63,047
Scottish Secretary	Ian Lang	51	63,047
National Heritage Secretary	David Mellor	43	63,047
Northern Ireland Secretary	Sir Patrick Mayhew	62	63,047
Education Secretary	John Patten	46	63,047
Health Secretary	Virginia Bottomley	44	63,047
Employment Secretary	Gillian Shephard	52	63,047
Chief Secretary	Michael Portillo	38	63,047

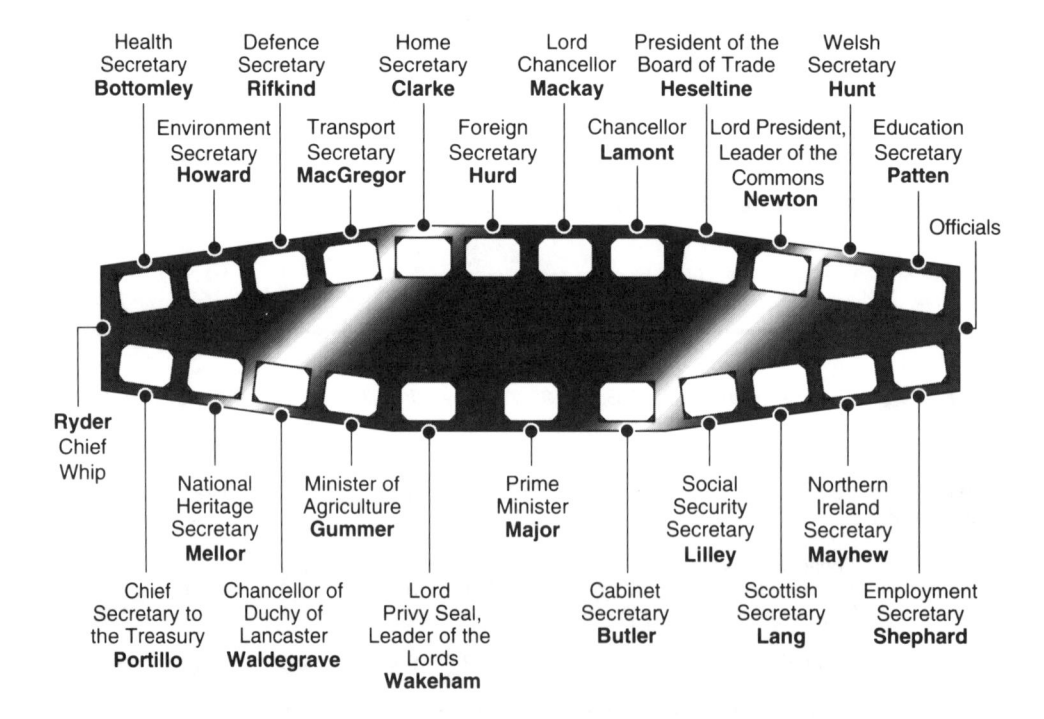

Health Secretary **Bottomley**
Defence Secretary **Rifkind**
Home Secretary **Clarke**
Lord Chancellor **Mackay**
President of the Board of Trade **Heseltine**
Welsh Secretary **Hunt**
Environment Secretary **Howard**
Transport Secretary **MacGregor**
Foreign Secretary **Hurd**
Chancellor **Lamont**
Lord President, Leader of the Commons **Newton**
Education Secretary **Patten**
Officials

Ryder Chief Whip
National Heritage Secretary **Mellor**
Minister of Agriculture **Gummer**
Prime Minister **Major**
Social Security Secretary **Lilley**
Northern Ireland Secretary **Mayhew**
Chief Secretary to the Treasury **Portillo**
Chancellor of Duchy of Lancaster **Waldegrave**
Lord Privy Seal, Leader of the Lords **Wakeham**
Cabinet Secretary **Butler**
Scottish Secretary **Lang**
Employment Secretary **Shephard**

THE GOVERNMENT
AS AT MAY 1992

		Age	Salary (£)
AGRICULTURE			
Minister of Agriculture	**John Gummer**	**52**	**63,047**
Minister of State	David Curry	47	51,402
Parliamentary Secretary	Nicholas Soames	44	44,611
Parliamentary Secretary	Earl Howe	41	37,689
DEFENCE			
Secretary of State	**Malcolm Rifkind**	**45**	**63,047**
Armed Forces Minister	Archie Hamilton	50	51,402
Procurement Minister	Jonathan Aitken	49	51,402
Under Secretary	Lord Cranbourne	46	37,689
EDUCATION			
Secretary of State	**John Patten**	**46**	**63,047**
Minister of State	Baroness Blatch	54	44,945
Under Secretary	Nigel Forman	49	44,611
Under Secretary	Eric Forth	47	44,611
EMPLOYMENT			
Secretary of State	**Gillian Shephard**	**52**	**63,047**
Minister of State	Michael Forsyth	37	51,402
Under Secretary	Patrick McLoughlin	44	44,611
Under Secretary	Viscount Ullswater	50	37,689
ENVIRONMENT			
Secretary of State	**Michael Howard**	**50**	**63,047**
Minister for Housing	Sir George Young	50	51,402
Minister for Local Govt & Inner Cities	John Redwood	40	51,402
Minister for Environment & Countryside	David Maclean	38	51,402
Under Secretary	Tony Baldry	41	44,611
Under Secretary	Robin Squire	47	44,611
Under Secretary	Lord Strathclyde	32	37,689
FOREIGN & COMMONWEALTH			
Foreign Secretary	**Douglas Hurd**	**62**	**63,047**
Overseas Development	Baroness Chalker	49	44,945
Minister of State	Douglas Hogg	47	51,402
Minister of State	Tristan Garel-Jones	51	51,402
Minister of State	Alastair Goodlad	48	51,402
Under Secretary	Mark Lennox-Boyd	38	44,611
HEALTH			
Secretary of State	**Virginia Bottomley**	**44**	**63,047**
Minister of State	Dr Brian Mawhinney	51	51,402
Under Secretary	Baroness Cumberlege	49	37,689
Under Secretary	Tim Yeo	47	44,611
Under Secretary	Thomas Sackville	41	44,611
HOME OFFICE			
Home Secretary	**Kenneth Clarke**	**51**	**63,047**
Minister of State	Peter Lloyd	54	51,402
Minister of State	Michael Jack	45	51,402
Minister of State	Earl Ferrers	62	44,945
Under Secretary	Charles Wardle	52	44,611
HERITAGE			
Secretary of State	**David Mellor**	**43**	**63,047**
Minister of State	Robert Key	46	51,402

THE GOVERNMENT
AS AT MAY 1992

		Age	Salary (£)
NORTHERN IRELAND			
Secretary of State	**Sir Patrick Mayhew**	62	63,047
Minister of State	Robert Atkins	46	51,402
Minister of State	Michael Mates	57	51,402
Under Secretary	Jeremy Hanley	47	44,611
Under Secretary	Earl of Arran	53	37,689
PUBLIC SERVICE & SCIENCE			
Chancellor of the Duchy of Lancaster	**William Waldegrave**	45	63,047
Under Secretary	Robert Jackson	45	44,611
SCOTTISH OFFICE			
Secretary of State	**Ian Lang**	51	63,047
Minister of State	Lord Fraser	46	44,945
Under Secretary	Sir Hector Monro	69	44,611
Under Secretary	Lord James Douglas Hamilton	49	44,611
Under Secretary	Allan Stewart	49	44,611
SOCIAL SECURITY			
Secretary of State	**Peter Lilley**	48	63,047
Minister of State	Nicholas Scott	59	51,402
Under Secretary	Alistair Burt	36	44,611
Under Secretary	Lord Henley	38	37,689
Under Secretary	Ann Widdecombe	44	44,611
DEPARTMENT OF TRADE & INDUSTRY			
President of the Board of Trade	**Michael Heseltine**	59	63,047
Minister for Industry	Tim Sainsbury	59	51,402
Minister for Energy	Tim Eggar	40	51,402
Minister for Trade	Richard Needham	50	51,402
Technology minister	Edward Leigh	41	44,611
Corporate affairs minister	Neil Hamilton	43	44,611
Consumer affairs and small firms minister	Baroness Denton	56	37,689
TRANSPORT			
Transport Secretary	**John MacGregor**	55	63,047
Minister for Public Transport	Roger Freeman	49	51,402
Minister for Aviation & Shipping	Earl of Caithness	43	51,402
Minister for Roads & Traffic	Kenneth Carlisle	51	44,611
Minister for Transport in London	Steve Norris	46	44,611
TREASURY			
Chancellor	**Norman Lamont**	49	63,047
Chief Secretary	Michael Portillo	38	63,047
Financial Secretary	Stephen Dorrell	40	51,402
Paymaster-General	Sir John Cope	54	51,402
Economic Secretary	Tony Nelson	43	51,402
WELSH OFFICE			
Secretary	**David Hunt**	49	63,047
Minister of State	Sir Wyn Roberts	61	51,402
Under Secretary	Gwilym Jones	45	44,611

THE GOVERNMENT
AS AT MAY 1992

LAW OFFICERS

		Age	Salary (£)
Lord Chancellor	**Lord Mackay**	**64**	**106,750**
Parliamentary Secretary	John Taylor	50	44,611
Attorney-General	Sir Nicholas Lyell	53	65,541
Solicitor-General	Sir Derek Spencer	56	57,922
Lord Advocate	Lord Rodger	47	50,638
Solicitor General for Scotland	Thomas Dawson	43	44,342

LEADER OF THE COMMONS

Lord President	**Antony Newton**	**54**	**63,047**

LEADER OF THE LORDS

Lord Privy Seal	**Lord Wakeham**	**59**	**50,558**
Chief Whip	**Richard Ryder**	**43**	**56,369**
Whips	Greg Knight, Irvine Patnick, Nicholas Baker		
	Tim Wood, Tim Boswell, Timothy Kirkhope		
	David Davis, Andrew Mackay, Robert G Hughes		
	James Arbuthnot		

CABINET COMMITTEES

Economic and Domestic Policy (EDP)
"To consider strategic issues relating to the Government's economic and domestic policies."
Prime Minister (John Major) (chairman), Chancellor (Norman Lamont), Home Secretary (Kenneth Clarke), President of the Board of Trade (Michael Heseltine), Lord Privy Seal (John Wakeham), Lord President of the Council (Antony Newton), Environment Secretary (Michael Howard), Welsh Secretary (David Hunt), Chancellor of the Duchy of Lancaster (William Waldegrave), Scottish Secretary (Ian Lang), Northern Ireland Secretary (Sir Patrick Mayhew), Employment Secretary (Gillian Shephard), Chief Secretary to Treasury (Michael Portillo). Other ministers will be invited to attend for items in which they have a departmental interest.

Overseas and Defence Policy (OPD)
"To keep under review the Government's defence and overseas policy."
Prime Minister (chairman), Foreign Secretary (Douglas Hurd), Chancellor, President of the Board of Trade, Defence Secretary (Malcolm Rifkind), Attorney-General (Sir Nicholas Lyell). The Chief of Defence Staff will attend as required, as will the chiefs of staff when necessary.

Ministerial Committee on the Gulf (OPDG)
"To keep under review arrangements for defence and security in the Gulf region and co-ordinate any necessary action."
Prime Minister (chairman), Foreign Secretary, Chancellor, Defence Secretary.

Ministerial Committee on Nuclear Defence Policy (OPDN)
"To keep under review the Government's policy on nuclear defence."
Prime Minister (chairman), Foreign Secretary, Chancellor, Defence Secretary.

Ministerial Committee on European Security (OPDSE)
"To keep under review arrangements for defence and security in Europe."
Prime Minister (chairman), Foreign Secretary, Chancellor, Defence Secretary.

CABINET COMMITTEES

Ministerial Committee on Hong Kong and other Dependent Territories (OPDK)
"To keep under review the implementation of the agreement with the Chinese on the future of Hong Kong and the implications of that agreement for the future Government of Hong Kong and the well-being of its people; to keep under review as necessary the Government's policy towards other Dependent Territories."
Prime Minister (chairman), Foreign Secretary, Chancellor, Home Secretary, President of the Board of Trade, Defence Secretary, Lord President of the Council, Foreign Office Minister (Alastair Goodlad). Others including the Attorney-General, the Governor of Hong Kong, the British Ambassador in Peking and the Minister for Overseas Development are invited to attend as appropriate.

Ministerial Committee on Northern Ireland (NI)
"To oversee the Government's policy on Northern Ireland issues and relations with the Republic of Ireland on these matters."
Prime Minister (chairman), Foreign Secretary, Home Secretary, Defence Secretary, Northern Ireland Secretary, Chief Secretary to Treasury, Attorney-General. Other ministers are invited to attend as the nature of the business requires.

Ministerial Committee on Science and Technology (EDS)
"To review science and technology policy"
Prime Minister (chairman), Foreign Secretary, President of the Board of Trade, Transport Secretary (John MacGregor), Defence Secretary, Minister of Agriculture, Fisheries and Food (John Gummer), Environment Secretary, Chancellor of the Duchy of Lancaster, Scottish Secretary, Education Secretary (John Patten), Health Secretary (Virginia Bottomley), Chief Secretary to Treasury. The chief scientific adviser attends.

Ministerial Committee on the Intelligence Services (IS)
"To keep under review policy on the security and intelligence services."
Prime Minister (chairman), Foreign Secretary, Home Secretary, Defence Secretary, Chancellor of the Duchy of Lancaster. The Chancellor of the Exchequer and the Attorney-General attend as appropriate

Ministerial Committee on Industrial, Commercial and Consumer Affairs (EDI)
"To consider industrial, commercial and consumer issues including questions of competition and deregulation."
Lord Privy Seal (chairman), Chancellor, President of the Board of Trade, Transport Secretary, Lord President of the Council, Agriculture Minister, Environment Secretary, Welsh Secretary, Chancellor of the Duchy of Lancaster, Scottish Secretary, Northern Ireland Secretary, Employment Secretary, Chief Secretary to Treasury.

Ministerial Committee on the Environment (EDE)
"To consider questions of environmental policy."
Lord Privy Seal (chairman), Foreign Secretary, Chancellor, President of the Board of Trade, Transport Secretary, Agriculture Minister, Environment Secretary, Welsh Secretary, Chancellor of the Duchy of Lancaster, Scottish Secretary, National Heritage Secretary (David Mellor), Northern Ireland Secretary, Chief Secretary to Treasury.

Ministerial Committee on Home and Social Affairs (EDH)
"To consider home and social policy issues."
Lord Privy Seal (chairman), Lord Chancellor (Lord Mackay of Clashfern), Home Secretary, President of the Board of Trade, Transport Secretary, Lord President of the Council, Chancellor of the Duchy of Lancaster, Scottish Secretary, National Heritage Secretary, Northern Ireland Secretary, Education Secretary, Health Secretary, Employment Secretary, Chief Secretary to Treasury, Chief Whip (Richard Ryder). Agriculture Minister, the Attorney-General and the Lord Advocate (Lord Rodger) also receive papers and attend as necessary.

CABINET COMMITTEES

Ministerial Committee on Local Government (EDL)
"To consider issues affecting local government, including the annual allocation of resources."
Lord Privy Seal (chairman), Chancellor, Home Secretary, Transport Secretary, Lord President of the Council, Environment Secretary, Welsh Secretary, Social Security Secretary (Peter Lilley), Chancellor of the Duchy of Lancaster, Scottish Secretary, National Heritage Secretary, Education Secretary, Health Secretary, Chief Secretary to Treasury, Local Government Minister (John Redwood).

Ministerial Committee on the Queen's Speeches and Future Legislation (FLG)
"To prepare and submit to the Cabinet drafts of the Queen's Speeches to Parliament and proposals for the Government's legislative programme for each session of Parliament."
Lord President of the Council (chairman), Lord Chancellor, Lord Privy Seal, Chancellor of the Duchy of Lancaster, Attorney-General, Lord Advocate, Chief Whip, Financial Secretary to Treasury (Stephen Dorrell), Captain of the Gentlemen-at-Arms (Lord Hesketh). Foreign Secretary or his representative is invited to attend discussion of the Queen's Speeches.

Ministerial Committee on Legislation(LG)
"To examine all draft Bills; to consider the parliamentary handling of government bills, European Community documents and private members' business and such other related matters as may be necessary; and to keep under review the Government's policy in relation to issues of Parliamentary procedures."
Lord President of the Council (chairman), Lord Chancellor, Lord Privy Seal, Welsh Secretary, Scottish Secretary, Attorney-General, Lord Advocate, Chief Whip, Foreign Office Minister, Home Office Minister, Financial Secretary to Treasury, Captain of the Gentlemen-at-Arms.

Ministerial Committee on Civil Service Pay (EDC)
"To determine the basis of the annual negotiations and consider other matters concerning civil service pay."
Lord President of the Council (chairman), Foreign Secretary, Chancellor, Home Secretary, Defence Secretary, Environment Secretary, Social Security Secretary, Chancellor of the Duchy of Lancaster, Scottish Secretary, Northern Ireland Secretary, Employment Secretary, Financial Secretary to Treasury.

Ministerial Sub-committee on Health Strategy (EDH(H))
"To oversee the development, implementation and monitoring of the Government's health strategy, to co-ordinate the Government's policies on UK-wide issues affecting health and report as necessary to the Ministerial Committee on Home and Social Affairs."
Lord President of the Council (chairman), Agriculture Minister, Environment Secretary, Welsh Secretary, Social Security Secretary, Chancellor of Duchy of Lancaster, Scottish Secretary, Northern Ireland Secretary, Health Secretary, Paymaster-General (Sir John Cope), Minister for Health (Dr Brian Mawhinney), Employment Minister (Michael Forsyth), Junior National Heritage Minister (Robert Key). Home Secretary, Transport Secretary, Education Secretary and President of the Board of Trade receive papers and are invited as appropriate.

Ministerial Sub-committee on Public Sector Pay (EDI(P))
"To co-ordinate the handling of pay issues in the public sector and report as necessary to the Ministerial Committee on Industrial, Commercial and Consumer Affairs."
Lord Privy Seal (chairman), Chancellor, Home Secretary, President of the Board of Trade, Transport Secretary, Environment Secretary, Chancellor of the Duchy of Lancaster, Scottish Secretary, Education Secretary, Health Secretary, Employment Secretary, Chief Secretary to Treasury.

Ministerial Sub-committee on European Questions (OPD(E))
"To consider questions relating to the UK's membership of the EC and to report as necessary to the ministerial committee on defence and overseas policy."
Foreign Secretary (chairman), Chancellor, Home Secretary, President of the Board of Trade, Transport Secretary, Lord President of the Council, Agriculture Minister, Environment Secretary, Welsh Secretary, Scottish Secretary, Northern Ireland Secretary, Employment Secretary, Attorney-General, Chief Whip, Foreign Office Minister (Tristan Garel-Jones). UK's representative to the EC is also in attendance.

CABINET COMMITTEES

Ministerial Sub-committee on Eastern Europe (OPD(AE))
"To consider questions relating to Britain's policy of assisting change in the former Soviet republics and other former Communist countries in Europe and report as necessary to the ministerial committee on defence and overseas policy."
Foreign Secretary (chairman), Chancellor, President of the Board of Trade, Defence Secretary, Agriculture Minister, Environment Secretary, Employment Secretary, Minister for Overseas Development (Baroness Chalker).

Ministerial Sub-committee on Terrorism (OPD(T))
"To keep under review the arrangements for countering terrorism and for dealing with terrorist incidents and their consequences and to report as necessary to the ministerial committee on defence and overseas policy."
Home Secretary (chairman), Foreign Secretary, Defence Secretary, President of the Board of Trade, Transport Secretary, Scottish Secretary, Northern Ireland Secretary, Attorney-General.

Ministerial Sub-committee on London (EDL(L))
"To co-ordinate the Government's policies on London."
Environment Secretary (chairman), Home Office Minister (Michael Jack), Industry Minister (Tim Sainsbury), Minister for Housing and Planning (Sir George Young), Minister for Social Security and Disabled People (Nicholas Scott), Education Minister (Baroness Blatch), Health Minister, Employment Minister, Economic Secretary to Treasury (Tony Nelson), Minister for Transport in London (Steve Norris), National Heritage minister.

Ministerial Sub-committee on Drug Misuse (EDH(D))
"To co-ordinate the Government's national and international policies for tackling drugs misuse and report as necessary to the ministerial committee on home and social affairs."
Lord President of the Council (chairman), Solicitor-General (Sir Derek Spencer), Home Office Minister, Armed Forces Minister (Archie Hamilton), Scottish Office Minister (Lord Fraser), Health Minister, Foreign Office minister (Mark Lennox-Boyd), Welsh Office minister (Gwilym Jones), Schools minister (Eric Forth). Ministers from Employment, Environment and Overseas Development should receive papers and may be invited to attend.

Ministerial Sub-committee on co-ordination of Urban Policy (EDH(U))
"To monitor and co-ordinate Government action on inner cities and report as necessary to the ministerial committee on home and social affairs."
Environment Secretary (chairman), Home Office Minister, Local Government Minister, Economic Secretary to Treasury, Junior Minister of Technology (Edward Leigh), Transport minister (Kenneth Carlisle), Environment minister (Robin Squire), Welsh Office minister, Social Security minister (Alistair Burt), Scottish Office minister (Allan Stewart), National Heritage minister, Northern Ireland minister (Jeremy Hanley), Schools minister, Health minister (Tim Yeo), Employment minister (Patrick McLoughlin). City Action Team ministers are invited for items in which they have an interest.

Ministerial Sub-committee on Alcohol Misuse (EDH(A))
"To review and develop the Government's strategy for combating the misuse of alcohol and to oversee its continuing implementation, and report as necessary to the ministerial committee on home and social affairs." Chancellor of the Duchy of Lancaster (chairman), Paymaster-General, Scottish Office Minister, Minister for Health, Home Office minister, minister for Consumer Affairs and Small Firms (Baroness Denton), Transport minister, Agriculture minister (Nicholas Soames), Welsh Office minister, Northern Ireland minister, Schools minister and Employment minister.

Ministerial Sub-committee on Women's Issues (EDH(W))
"To review and develop the Government's policy and strategy on issues of special concern to women; to oversee their implementation; and to report as necessary to the ministerial committee on home and social affairs."
Employment Secretary (chairman), Paymaster-General, Welsh Minister (Sir Wyn Roberts), Education Minister, minister for Consumer Affairs, Social Security minister, Civil Service minister (Robert Jackson), Scottish Office minister, Northern Ireland minister, Health minister and Employment minister. Ministers representing Lord Chancellor's Department, Home Office, and Environment also receive papers and are invited to attend when appropriate.

THE OPPOSITION
AS AT JULY 1992

Leader of the Opposition	John Smith	Age 54
Shadow leader of the House and Campaigns Co-ordinator	Margaret Beckett	49

CITIZEN'S CHARTER AND WOMEN
Labour spokeswoman	Marjorie Mowlam	43
Labour spokesman	Brian Wilson	44
Labour spokesman	Lewis Moonie	45
Labour spokeswoman	Kate Hoey	46

DEFENCE, DISARMAMENT AND ARMS CONTROL
Shadow Defence Secretary	David Clark	53
Labour spokesman	George Foulkes	50
Labour spokesman	John Reid	45
Labour spokesman	Eric Martlew	43

DEVELOPMENT AND CO-OPERATION
Shadow Overseas Development minister	Michael Meacher	53
Labour spokesman	Tony Worthington	51

DISABLED PEOPLE'S RIGHTS
Labour spokesman	Barry Sheerman	52

EDUCATION
Shadow Education Secretary	Ann Taylor	45
Labour spokesman	Jeff Rooker	51
Labour spokesman	Win Griffiths	49
Labour spokesman on training and education	Tony Lloyd	42

EMPLOYMENT
Shadow employment secretary	Frank Dobson	52
Labour spokesman on training and education	Tony Lloyd	42
Labour spokeswoman	Joyce Quin	48
Labour spokesman	Sam Galbraith	47

ENVIRONMENTAL PROTECTION
Labour spokesman	Chris Smith	41
Labour spokeswoman	Clare Short	46

FOOD, AGRICULTURE AND RURAL AFFAIRS
Shadow Minister of Agriculture	Ron Davies	46
Labour spokesman	Elliot Morley	40
Labour spokesman	Dale Campbell-Savours	49

FOREIGN AND COMMONWEALTH
Shadow Foreign Secretary	Jack Cunningham	53
Labour spokesman on European affairs	George Robertson	46
Labour spokesman	Allan Rogers	60
Labour spokesman	Bruce Grocott	52

HEALTH
Shadow Health Secretary	David Blunkett	45
Shadow health minister	Dawn Primarolo	38
Labour spokesman on community care	David Hinchliffe	44
Labour spokesman on the NHS	Ian McCartney	41

THE OPPOSITION
AS AT JULY 1992

		Age
HOME AFFAIRS		
Shadow Home Secretary	**Tony Blair**	**39**
Labour spokeswoman	Joan Ruddock	49
Labour spokesman	Alun Michael	49
Labour spokesman	Graham Allen	39
LAW OFFICERS		
Shadow Attorney-General	**John Morris**	**61**
Labour spokesman on legal affairs	John Fraser	58
LOCAL GOVERNMENT		
Shadow Environment Secretary (Loc Govt)	**Jack Straw**	**46**
Shadow housing minister	John Battle	41
Shadow local government minister	Doug Henderson	43
Labour spokesman on local government	Keith Vaz	36
Labour spokesman on housing	Peter Pike	55
Labour spokesman on London affairs	Tony Banks	49
LORD CHANCELLOR'S DEPARTMENT		
Labour spokesman	**Paul Boateng**	**41**
NATIONAL HERITAGE		
Shadow National Heritage Secretary	**Bryan Gould**	**53**
Labour spokesman on press and broadcasting	Robin Corbett	59
Labour spokesman on sport	Tom Pendry	58
NORTHERN IRELAND		
Shadow Northern Ireland Secretary	**Kevin McNamara**	**58**
Labour spokesman	Roger Stott	49
Labour spokesman	Bill O'Brien	63
SOCIAL SECURITY		
Shadow Social Security Secretary	**Donald Dewar**	**55**
Labour spokesman	Keith Bradley	42
Labour spokeswoman	Llin Golding	59
SCOTLAND		
Shadow Scottish Secretary	**Tom Clarke**	**51**
Labour spokesman	Henry McLeish	44
Labour spokesman	John McFall	48
Labour spokeswoman	Maria Fyfe	54
TRADE AND INDUSTRY		
Shadow Trade and Industry Secretary	**Robin Cook**	**46**
Shadow minister for energy	Martin O'Neill	47
Labour spokesman on industry and small business	Derek Fatchett	47
Labour spokesman on consumer affairs	Nigel Griffiths	37
Labour spokesman	Stuart Bell	54
Labour spokesman	Jim Cousins	48
TRANSPORT		
Shadow Transport Secretary	**John Prescott**	**54**
Labour spokesman on railways	Peter Snape	50
Labour spokeswoman on maritime & road transport	Joan Walley	43
Labour spokesman on transport in London	Tony Banks	49

THE OPPOSITION
AS AT JULY 1992

TREASURY AND ECONOMIC AFFAIRS

		Age
Shadow Chancellor	**Gordon Brown**	**41**
Shadow Chief Secretary	Harriet Harman	42
Shadow Financial Secretary	Alistair Darling	39
Shadow Economic Secretary	Andrew Smith	41
Shadow Paymaster General	Nick Brown	42

WALES

Shadow Welsh Secretary	**Ann Clwyd**	**55**
Labour spokesman	Paul Murphy	44
Labour spokesman	Rhodri Morgan	53

VOTES CAST

	Con	Lab	LibDem	Nat	Others	TOTAL
East Anglia	635,774	348,353	242,886	–	18,297	1,245,310
East Midlands	1,149,504	992,392	376,603	–	17,851	2,466,350
Greater London	1,630,546	1,332,821	542,733		89,497	3,595,597
North West	1,395,718	1,660,051	582,177	–	56,319	3,694,265
Northern	603,893	914,712	218,236	–	8,704	1,808,545
South East	3,519,048	1,338,297	1,507,299	–	88,144	6,452,788
South West	1,388,921	561,847	916,905	–	52,191	2,919,864
West Midlands	1,390,246	1,203,352	466,048	–	45,124	3,104,770
Yorks & Humberside	1,084,227	1,266,810	481,246	–	25,225	2,857,508
Scotland	751,954	1,142,866	383,856	629,552	23,327	2,931,555
Wales	499,677	865,633	217,457	154,439	11,590	1,748,796
Britain	14,049,282	11,559,734	5,998,378	783,991	453,566	32,827,612
Northern Ireland	44,608	–	–	–	740,485	785,093
United Kingdom	14,093,890	11,559,734	5,998,378	738,991	1,194,091	33,612,705

UNITED KINGDOM
ELECTORS 43,238,929; VOTERS 33,612,705; TURNOUT 77.7%

	SEATS	2nd	3rd	4th	Lost Deposits	Minority* Mandates	Votes Per Seat	VOTES
Con	336	248	50	6	4	125	41,946	41.9
Lab	271	192	161	10	1	103	42,655	34.4
LibDem	20	154	389	68	11	17	299,918	17.8
SNP	3	36	27	6	0	3	209,850	1.9
Plaid Cymru	4	2	5	24	20	3	38,609	0.5
Green	0	0	0	200	253	0	–	0.5
NLP	0	0	0	98	309	0	–	0.2

GREAT BRITAIN
ELECTORS 42,113,786; VOTERS 32,827,612; TURNOUT 77.9%

	SEATS	2nd	3rd	4th	Lost Deposits	Minority* Mandates	Votes Per Seat	VOTES
Con	336	247	49	2	0	125	41,813	42.8
Lab	271	192	161	10	1	103	42,655	35.2
LibDem	20	154	389	68	11	17	299,918	18.3
SNP	3	36	27	6	0	3	209,850	1.9
Plaid Cymru	4	2	5	24	20	3	38,609	0.5
Green	0	0	0	200	253	0	–	0.5
NLP	0	0	0	98	300	0	–	0.2

* Where the winning candidate has less than 50 percent of the vote

ANALYSIS

EAST ANGLIA
ELECTORS 1,556,863; VOTERS 1,245,401; TURNOUT 80.0%

	SEATS	2nd	Position 3rd	4th	Lost Deposits	Minority* Mandates	Votes Per Seat	VOTES
Con	17	3	0	0	0	6	37,398	51.0
Lab	3	9	8	0	0	3	116,117	28.0
LibDem	0	8	12	0	0	0	-	19.5
Green	0	0	0	10	11	0	-	0.6
NLP	0	0	0	6	19	0	-	0.4

EAST MIDLANDS
ELECTORS 3,049,568; VOTERS 2,466,350; TURNOUT 80.9%

	SEATS	2nd	Position 3rd	4th	Lost Deposits	Minority* Mandates	Votes Per Seat	VOTES
Con	28	13	1	0	0	9	41,053	46.6
Lab	14	24	4	0	0	5	65,885	37.4
LibDem	0	5	37	0	0	0	-	15.3
Green	0	0	0	12	12	0	-	0.3
NLP	0	0	0	9	17	0	-	0.2

GREATER LONDON
ELECTORS 4,876,604; VOTERS 3,594,838; TURNOUT 73.7%

	SEATS	2nd	Position 3rd	4th	Lost Deposits	Minority* Mandates	Votes Per Seat	VOTES
Con	48	31	5	0	0	9	33,965	45.4
Lab	35	40	9	0	0	16	38,069	37.1
LibDem	1	11	69	1	0	0	542,733	15.1
Green	0	0	0	38	44	0	-	0.8
NLP	0	0	0	10	47	0	-	0.2

NORTH WEST
ELECTORS 4,780,134; VOTERS 3,694,265; TURNOUT 77.3%

	SEATS	2nd	Position 3rd	4th	Lost Deposits	Minority* Mandates	Votes Per Seat	VOTES
Con	27	43	2	1	0	16	51,693	37.8
Lab	44	22	7	0	0	11	37,728	44.9
LibDem	2	8	63	0	1	2	291,088	15.8
Green	0	0	0	20	22	0	-	0.4
NLP	0	0	0	28	68	0	-	0.4

NORTHERN
ELECTORS 2,366,686; VOTERS 1,808,545; TURNOUT 76.4%

	SEATS	2nd	Position 3rd	4th	Lost Deposits	Minority* Mandates	Votes Per Seat	VOTES
Con	6	29	1	0	0	3	100,648	33.4
Lab	29	4	3	0	0	8	31,541	50.6
LibDem	1	3	32	0	0	1	281,236	15.6
Green	0	0	0	8	8	0	-	0.3
NLP	0	0	0	3	5	0	-	0.1

* Where the winning candidate has less than 50 percent of the vote

SOUTH EAST
ELECTORS 8,041,908; VOTERS 6,455,788; TURNOUT 80.3%

	SEATS	2nd	Position 3rd	4th	Lost Deposits	Minority* Mandates	Votes Per Seat	VOTES
Con	106	3	0	0	0	20	33,198	54.5
Lab	3	41	65	0	1	2	447,099	20.8
LibDem	0	65	44	0	0	0	-	23.3
Green	0	0	0	58	62	0	-	0.7
NLP	0	0	0	22	63	0	-	0.2

SOUTH WEST
ELECTORS 3,600,654; VOTERS 2,919,796; TURNOUT 81.1%

	SEATS	2nd	Position 3rd	4th	Lost Deposits	Minority* Mandates	Votes Per Seat	VOTES
Con	38	10	0	0	0	19	36,550	47.6
Lab	4	9	35	0	0	3	140,461	19.2
LibDem	6	29	13	0	0	4	152,806	31.4
Green	0	0	0	18	26	0	-	0.7
NLP	0	0	0	6	27	0	-	0.2

WEST MIDLANDS
ELECTORS 3,969,970; VOTERS 3,104,770; TURNOUT 78.2%

	SEATS	2nd	Position 3rd	4th	Lost Deposits	Minority* Mandates	Votes Per Seat	VOTES
Con	29	29	0	0	0	15	47,939	44.8
Lab	29	20	9	0	0	14	41,494	38.8
LibDem	0	9	48	1	0	0	-	15.0
Green	0	0	0	17	17	0	-	0.5
NLP	0	0	0	9	16	0	-	0.1

YORKSHIRE AND HUMBERSIDE
ELECTORS 3,788,337; VOTERS 2,857,508; TURNOUT 75.4%

	SEATS	2nd	Position 3rd	4th	Lost Deposits	Minority* Mandates	Votes Per Seat	VOTES
Con	20	33	1	0	0	11	54,211	37.9
Lab	34	12	8	0	0	7	37,259	44.3
LibDem	0	9	45	0	0	0	-	16.8
Green	0	0	0	19	21	0	-	0.5
NLP	0	0	0	5	10	0	-	0.1

SCOTLAND
ELECTORS 3,888,033; VOTERS 2,931,555; TURNOUT 75.4%

	SEATS	2nd	Position 3rd	4th	Lost Deposits	Minority* Mandates	Votes Per Seat	VOTES
Con	11	25	35	1	0	11	68,359	25.7
Lab	49	7	7	9	0	28	23,323	39.0
LibDem	9	3	3	56	9	9	42,650	13.1
SNP	3	36	27	6	0	3	209,850	21.5
Green	0	0	0	0	19	0	-	0.3
NLP	0	0	0	0	19	0	-	0.1

* Where the winning candidate has less than 50 percent of the vote

ANALYSIS

WALES
ELECTORS 2,195,029; VOTERS 1,748,796; TURNOUT 79.7%

	SEATS	Position 2nd	3rd	4th	Lost Deposits	Minority* Mandates	Votes Per Seat	VOTES
Con	6	28	4	0	0	6	83,279	28.6
Lab	27	4	6	1	0	6	32,060	49.5
LibDem	1	4	23	10	1	1	217,457	12.4
Plaid Cymru	4	2	5	24	20	3	38,609	8.8
Green	0	0	0	0	11	0	-	0.3
NLP	0	0	0	0	9	0	-	0.1

NORTHERN IRELAND
ELECTORS 1,125,143; VOTERS 785,093; TURNOUT 69.8%

	SEATS	Position 2nd	3rd	4th	Lost Deposits	Minority* Mandates	Votes Per Seat	VOTES
Ulster Unionist	9	3	1	0	0	5	30,117	34.5
Dem. Unionist	3	3	0	1	0	1	34,346	13.1
Pop. Unionist	1	0	0	0	0	1	19,305	2.5
Con	0	1	1	5	4	0	-	5.7
Alliance	0	2	5	7	5	0	-	8.7
SDLP	4	7	2	1	0	2	46,111	23.5
Sinn Fein	0	1	8	0	5	0	-	10.0
Workers Party	0	0	0	1	8	0	-	0.6
NLP	0	0	0	0	9	0	-	0.3
Other	0	0	0	0	7	0	-	1.2

* Where the winning candidate has less than 50 percent of the vote

ELECTIONS SINCE 1945
UNITED KINGDOM

	VOTES %					SEATS			
	Con	Lab	LDm*	Nat		Con	Lab	LDm*	Nat	TOTAL
1992	41.9	34.4	17.8	2.3		336	271	20	7	651

	Con	Lab	All*	Nat		Con	Lab	All*	Nat	TOTAL
1987	42.3	30.8	22.5	2.0		376	229	22	6	650
1983	42.4	27.6	25.4	1.7		397	209	23	4	650

	Con	Lab	Lib*	Nat		Con	Lab	Lib*	Nat	TOTAL
1979	43.9	36.9	13.8	2.2		339	269	11	4	635
1974 October	35.8	39.2	18.3	3.5		277	319	13	14	635
1974 February	37.9	37.2	19.3	2.6		297	301	14	9	635
1970	46.4	43.1	7.5	2.4		330	288	6	5	630
1966	41.9	48.0	8.6	1.1		253	364	12	1	630
1964	43.4	44.1	11.2	0.9		304	317	9	0	630
1959	49.4	43.8	5.9	0.6		365	258	6	0	630
1955	49.7	46.4	2.7	0.9		345	277	6	2	630
1951	48.0	48.8	2.6	0.4		321	295	6	3	625
1950	43.4	46.1	9.1	0.6		298	315	9	2	625
1945	39.6	48.0	9.0	1.4		210	393	12	6	640

* Liberal Democrat 1992, Alliance 1983 & 1987, Liberal 1945 – 1979

WASTED VOTES

This table shows how many votes fail to count towards the result of the election under the first-past-the-post system. In the first column are the wasted votes cast for candidates who come third or lower and therefore do not even enter into contention for a seat. In the second column are the superfluous votes which just build up the majority of winning candidates above the number of votes they need to win. The third column shows the percentage of a party's votes which are wasted or superfluous.

UNITED KINGDOM

	Wasted votes	Superfluous votes	%
Con	369,735	3,938,198	30.6
Lab	1,417,813	2,811,067	36.6
LibDem	2,910,169	80,543	49.9

EAST ANGLIA

	Wasted votes	Superfluous votes	%
Con	0	261,351	41.1
Lab	102,830	7,023	31.5
LibDem	106,977	0	44.0

EAST MIDLANDS

	Wasted votes	Superfluous votes	%
Con	9,473	333,885	29.9
Lab	42,107	124,222	18.0
LibDem	286,440	0	76.1

GREATER LONDON

	Wasted votes	Superfluous votes	%
Con	30,735	481,052	31.4
Lab	54,134	230,435	21.4
LibDem	373,937	9,844	70.7

NORTH WEST

	Wasted votes	Superfluous votes	%
Con	18,300	218,453	17.0
Lab	54,076	530,627	35.2
LibDem	395,748	4,443	68.7

NORTHERN

	Wasted votes	Superfluous votes	%
Con	7,691	53,847	10.2
Lab	27,240	373,557	43.8
LibDem	214,734	5,042	78.1

ANALYSIS

SOUTH-EAST

	Wasted votes	Superfluous votes	%
Con	0	1,628,472	46.3
Lab	553,223	9,258	41.9
LibDem	395,642	0	26.2

SOUTH-WEST

	Wasted votes	Superfluous votes	%
Con	0	364,319	26.2
Lab	270,696	21,389	52.0
LibDem	137,477	24,548	17.7

WEST MIDLANDS

	Wasted votes	Superfluous votes	%
Con	0	329,699	23.7
Lab	92,988	195,953	24.0
LibDem	319,912	0	68.6

YORKS & HUMBER

	Wasted votes	Superfluous votes	%
Con	11,640	215,141	20.9
Lab	85,544	444,757	41.9
LibDem	319,295	0	66.3

SCOTLAND

	Wasted votes	Superfluous votes	%
Con	227,667	38,618	35.4
Lab	77,961	477,143	48.6
LibDem	205,507	31,458	61.7
SNP	217,330	7,903	35.8

WALES

	Wasted votes	Superfluous votes	%
Con	33,992	13,361	9.5
Lab	57.014	396,653	52.4
LibDem	154,500	5,208	73.4
PC	66,004	23,384	57.0

NORTHERN IRELAND

	Wasted votes	Superfluous votes	%
Con	30,237	0	67.8
UUP	4,766	132,946	50.8
SDLP	11,138	27,023	20.7
DUP	4,414	28,907	32.2
Sinn Fein	61,465	-	78.5
Alliance	51,808	-	75.5

HIGHEST SWINGS 1987-1992 WHERE SEATS HAVE CHANGED PARTIES

Swing	From	to	MP	Constituency
21.3	Lab	SNP	Ian Davidson (Lab)	Glasgow, Govan
13.8	Con	LibDem	Nigel Evans (Con)	Ribble Valley
13.3	LibDem	Plaid Cymru	Cynog Dafis (Plaid Cymru)	Ceredigion & Pembroke North
10.7	Con	LibDem	Nigel Waterson (Con)	Eastbourne
8.6	Con	Lab	John Heppell (Lab)	Nottingham East
8.0	Con	Lab	Michael Fabricant (Con)	Staffordshire Mid
6.9	Con	Lab	Malcolm Wicks (Lab)	Croydon North West
6.8	Con	Lab	John Hutton (Lab)	Barrow & Furness
6.8	Con	Lab	Ms Jean Corston (Lab)	Bristol East
6.8	Con	Lab	Roger Evans (Con)	Monmouth
6.7	Con	Lab	Ms Bridget Prentice (Lab)	Lewisham East
6.6	Con	Lab	John Denham (Lab)	Southampton, Itchen
6.5	Con	Lab	Bill Olner (Lab)	Nuneaton
6.5	Con	Lab	Jon Owen Jones (Lab)	Cardiff Central
6.5	Con	LibDem	Paul Tyler (LibDem)	Cornwall North
6.4	Con	Lab	Ms Anne Campbell (Lab)	Cambridge
6.4	Con	Lab	Neil Gerrard (Lab)	Walthamstow
6.2	Con	Lab	Jim Dowd (Lab)	Lewisham West
6.2	Con	Lab	Alan Keen (Lab)	Feltham & Heston
6.2	Con	Lab	Paddy Tipping (Lab)	Sherwood
6.1	Con	Lab	Ms Barbara Roche (Lab)	Hornsey & Wood Green
6.0	Con	Lab	Walter Sweeney (Con)	Vale of Glamorgan
5.9	Con	Lab	Mike Gapes (Lab)	Ilford South
5.8	Con	Lab	Keith Hill (Lab)	Streatham
5.7	Con	Lab	Roger Berry (Lab)	Kingswood
5.6	Con	Lab	Nick Ainger (Lab)	Pembroke
5.2	Con	LibDem	Nigel Jones (LibDem)	Cheltenham
5.1	Con	Lab	Hugh Bayley (Lab)	York
5.0	Con	Lab	Alan Simpson (Lab)	Nottingham South

HIGHEST SWINGS SINCE 1983 WHICH RESULTED IN A CHANGE OF SITTING PARTY

Swing	From	To	MP	Constituency
25.3	LibDem	Lab	John Battle (Lab)	Leeds West
18.6	Lab	SNP	Ian Davidson (Lab)	Glasgow, Govan
17.6	LibDem	Plaid Cymru	Cynog Dafis (Plaid Cymru)	Ceredigion & Pembroke North
17.5	SNP	Lab	Calum MacDonald (Lab)	Western Isles
16.8	LibDem	Con	Malcolm Moss (Con)	Cambridgeshire North East
14.3	Con	LibDem	Nigel Evans (Con)	Ribble Valley
13.2	Con	Lab	Keith Bradley (Lab)	Manchester, Withington
12.7	Con	Lab	Jon Owen Jones (Lab)	Cardiff Central
12.3	Con	Lab	Rhodri Morgan (Lab)	Cardiff West
12.3	Con	Lab	Keith Vaz (Lab)	Leicester East

1992 WINNERS FROM 3RD OR LOWER POSITION

Constituency	MP	Party	Start position
Cambridge	Ms Anne Campbell	Lab	3rd
Ceredigion & Pembroke North	Cynog Dafis	Plaid Cymru	4th
Plymouth, Devonport	David Jamieson	Lab	3rd

LARGEST ELECTORATES
ENGLAND

Constituency	Electorate	Constituency	Electorate
Isle of Wight	99,838	Stratford-on-Avon	82,824
Huntingdon	92,913	Staffordshire South	82,758
Hampshire East	92,139	Suffolk Central	82,735
Eastleigh	91,736	Shropshire North	82,675
Wrekin, The	90,892	Romsey & Waterside	82,628
Berkshire East	90,365	Stroud	82,553
Swindon	90,067	Crosby	82,537
Devizes	89,745	Brigg & Cleethorpes	82,377
Cirencester & Tewkesbury	88,299	Derbyshire South	82,342
Peterborough	87,638	Chichester	82,124
Westbury	87,356	Faversham	81,977
Ryedale	87,048	Bedfordshire Mid	81,864
Dudley West	86,632	Blaby	81,790
Colchester North	86,479	Aldershot	81,754
Colchester South & Maldon	86,410	Norfolk South	81,647
Wokingham	85,914	Feltham & Heston	81,221
Wiltshire North	85,851	Beverley	81,198
Suffolk South	84,833	Fareham	81,124
Bridlington	84,829	Rutland & Melton	80,976
Cambridgeshire South West	84,418	Woking	80,842
Worcestershire Mid	84,269	Sussex Mid	80,827
Waveney	84,181	Boothferry	80,747
Horsham	84,158	Gloucester	80,578
Surrey North West	83,648	Worcestershire South	80,423
Northavon	83,496	Billericay	80,388
Northampton South	83,477	Norfolk Mid	80,336
Grantham	83,463	Harwich	80,260
Chelmsford	83,441	Newbury	80,252
South Hams	83,061	Bosworth	80,234
Basingstoke	82,952	Hertfordshire North	80,066
Richmond, Yorks	82,879	Lindsey East	80,026

SCOTLAND & WALES

Gordon	80,103	East Lothian	66,699
Pembroke	73,187	Vale of Glamorgan	66,672
Inverness, Nairn & Lochaber	69,468	Kincardine & Deeside	66,617
Carmarthen	68,887	Delyn	66,591
Clwyd North West	67,351	Ceredigion & Pembroke North	66,180

NORTHERN IRELAND

Down South	76,093	Lagan Valley	72,645
Londonderry East	75,559	Fermanagh & South Tyrone	70,192
Foyle	74,585	Antrim North	69,124

SMALLEST ELECTORATES
ENGLAND

Constituency	Electorate	Constituency	Electorate
Kensington	42,129	Chislehurst	53,782
Chelsea	42,371	Romford	54,001
Surbiton	42,421	Barnsley East	54,051
Newham North West	46,471	Oldham West	54,063
Hammersmith	47,229	Ruislip & Northwood	54,151
Greenwich	47,789	Hayes & Harlington	54,449
Hendon South	48,401	Stretford	54,467
Knowsley North	48,761	Hackney North & Stoke Newington	54,655
Coventry South East	48,796	Birmingham, Yardley	54,749
Walthamstow	49,140	Copeland	54,911
Old Bexley & Sidcup	49,449	Berwick-upon-Tweed	54,919
Liverpool, Riverside	49,595	City of London & Westminster South	55,021
Barking	50,454	Carlisle	55,140
Coventry North West	50,670	Dulwich	55,141
Kingston Upon Thames	51,077	Birmingham, Small Heath	55,213
Newham South	51,143	Manchester, Blackley	55,234
Hendon North	51,513	Barnsley Central	55,373
Plymouth, Drake	51,667	Chingford	55,401
Birmingham, Sparkbrook	51,677	Islington South & Finsbury	55,541
Warley East	51,717	Bethnal Green & Stepney	55,675
Eltham	51,989	Hemsworth	55,679
Birmingham, Erdington	52,398	Ilford South	55,741
Norwood	52,496	Croydon Central	55,798
Salford East	52,616	Wanstead & Woodford	55,821
Fulham	52,740	Woolwich	55,977
Finchley	52,907	Brent South	56,034
Birmingham, Edgbaston	53,041	Buckingham	56,063
Tyne Bridge	53,079	Hull West	56,111
Richmond & Barnes	53,081	Wolverhampton South East	56,158
Brent East	53,319	Islington North	56,270
Manchester, Wythenshawe	53,548	Morecambe & Lunesdale	56,426

SCOTLAND & WALES

Constituency	Electorate	Constituency	Electorate
Western Isles	22,784	Tweeddale, Ettrick & Lauderdale	39,493
Caithness & Sutherland	30,905	Glasgow, Garscadden	41,289
Orkney & Shetland	31,472	Montgomery	41,386
Meirionnydd Nant Conwy	32,413	Roxburgh & Berwickshire	43,485
Glasgow, Provan	36,560	Glasgow, Cathcart	44,689

NORTHERN IRELAND

Constituency	Electorate	Constituency	Electorate
Belfast South	52,032	Belfast North	55,062
Belfast East	52,833	Antrim East	62,839
Belfast West	54,609	Upper Bann	67,446

ANALYSIS

HIGHEST TURNOUTS

North-west Leicestershire	86.1
Monmouth	86.1
Brecon & Radnor	85.9
Ribble Valley	85.7
Mid-Staffordshire	85.7
South Derbyshire	85.5
Sherwood	85.5
Richmond & Barnes	85.0
West Derbyshire	85.0
Hazel Grove	84.9

SCOTLAND

Ayr	83.1
Edinburgh West	82.7

NORTHERN IRELAND

South Down	80.8
Mid-Ulster	79.2

LOWEST TURNOUTS

Peckham	53.9
Liverpool Riverside	54.6
Newham North-west	56.0
Sheffield Central	56.1
Manchester Central	56.9
Newham South	60.2
Newham North-east	60.3
Manchester Gorton	60.8
Leeds Central	61.3
East Antrim	62.4

SCOTLAND

Glasgow Central	63.1
Glasgow Maryhill	65.2

WALES

Swansea West	73.3
Cardiff Central	74.4

LARGEST MAJORITIES

Constituency	MP	Party	Majority	%
Huntingdon	John Major	Con	36,230	49.3
Blaenau Gwent	Llewellyn Smith	Lab	30,067	69.2
Bootle	Joe Benton	Lab	29,442	58.6
Hampshire East	Michael Mates	Con	29,165	39.4
Rhondda	Allan Rogers	Lab	28,816	62.7
Berkshire East	Andrew Mackay	Con	28,680	39.0
Surrey North West	Sir Michael Grylls	Con	28,394	43.4
Liverpool, Walton	Peter Kilfoyle	Lab	28,299	59.9
Merthyr Tydfil & Rhymney	Ted Rowlands	Lab	26,713	60.3
Easington	John Cummings	Lab	26,390	56.0
Rochford	Dr Michael Clark	Con	26,036	40.8
Sutton Coldfield	Sir Norman Fowler	Con	26,036	45.9
Wokingham	John Redwood	Con	25,709	36.3
Rutland & Melton	Alan Duncan	Con	25,535	39.0
Blaby	Andrew Robathan	Con	25,347	37.2
Solihull	John Taylor	Con	25,146	39.9
Bedfordshire Mid	Sir Nicholas Lyell	Con	25,138	36.4
Horsham	Sir Peter Hordern	Con	25,072	36.7
Barnsley East	Terry Patchett	Lab	24,777	63.0
Islwyn	Neil Kinnock	Lab	24,728	59.4
Antrim South	Clifford Forsythe	UUP	24,559	58.1
Fareham	Peter Lloyd	Con	24,141	36.4
Neath	Peter Hain	Lab	23,975	52.8
Broxbourne	Marion Roe	Con	23,970	41.6
Ogmore	Ray Powell	Lab	23,827	56.6
Cambridgeshire South East	Jim Paice	Con	23,810	37.6
Beaconsfield	Timothy Smith	Con	23,597	44.6
Lagan Valley	James Molyneaux	UUP	23,565	48.1
Richmond, Yorks	William Hague	Con	23,504	36.2
Pontefract & Castleford	Geoffrey Lofthouse	Lab	23,495	48.9
Swansea East	Donald Anderson	Lab	23,482	52.5
Christchurch	Robert Adley	Con	23,015	39.9
Stratford-on-Avon	Alan Howarth	Con	22,892	33.7
Stamford & Spalding	Quentin Davies	Con	22,869	37.5
Chertsey & Walton	Sir Geoffrey Pattie	Con	22,819	40.2
Macclesfield	Nicholas Winterton	Con	22,767	36.1
Sheffield, Brightside	David Blunkett	Lab	22,681	53.6
Caerphilly	Ron Davies	Lab	22,672	45.5
Staffordshire South	Patrick Cormack	Con	22,633	33.5
Witney	Douglas Hurd	Con	22,568	35.1
Billericay	Teresa Gorman	Con	22,494	34.0
Wentworth	Peter Hardy	Lab	22,449	46.7
Knowsley North	George Howarth	Lab	22,403	63.1
Chesham & Amersham	Ms Cheryl Gillan	Con	22,220	38.8
Hemsworth	Derek Enright	Lab	22,075	52.2
Knowsley South	Eddie O'Hara	Lab	22,011	47.3
Wigan	Roger Stott	Lab	21,842	39.4
Colchester South & Maldon	John Whittingdale	Con	21,821	31.9
Tonbridge & Malling	Sir John Stanley	Con	21,558	33.7
Cynon Valley	Ms Ann Clwyd	Lab	21,364	56.2
Aberavon	John Morris	Lab	21,310	53.2
Bedfordshire South West	David Madel	Con	21,273	32.4
Basingstoke	Andrew Hunter	Con	21,198	30.9
Fylde	Michael Jack	Con	20,991	42.1
Wealden	Sir Geoffrey Johnson Smith	Con	20,931	34.7
Chichester	Anthony Nelson	Con	20,887	32.7
Houghton & Washington	Roland Boyes	Lab	20,808	37.2

ANALYSIS

CONSERVATIVE/LABOUR MARGINALS

Constituency	MP	Majority	%
Vale of Glamorgan	Walter Sweeney	19	0.03
Bristol North West	Michael Stern	45	0.08
Hayes & Harlington	Terry Dicks	53	0.12
Ayr	Phil Gallie	85	0.16
Bolton North East	Peter Thurnham	185	0.38
Norwich North	Patrick Thompson	266	0.51
Corby	William Powell	342	0.60
Slough	John Watts	514	0.89
Tynemouth	Neville Trotter	597	0.99
Southampton, Test	James Hill	585	1.04
Amber Valley	Phillip Oppenheim	712	1.20
Edmonton	Dr Ian Twinn	593	1.24
Luton South	Graham Bright	799	1.38
Dover	David Shaw	833	1.45
Bury South	David Sumberg	788	1.46
Stirling	Michael Forsyth	703	1.47
Leicestershire North West	David Ashby	979	1.57
Bolton West	Tom Sackville	1079	1.81
Chester, City Of	Gyles Brandreth	1101	2.07
Batley & Spen	Elizabeth Peacock	1408	2.31
Langbaurgh	Michael Bates	1564	2.37
Basildon	David Amess	1480	2.75
Coventry South West	John Butcher	1436	2.82
Lincoln	Kenneth Carlisle	2049	3.28
Mitcham & Morden	Angela Rumbold	1734	3.39
Aberdeen South	Raymond Robertson	1517	3.69
Blackpool South	Nicholas Hawkins	1667	3.79
Swindon	Simon Coombs	2826	3.85
Brentford & Isleworth	Niranjan Deva	2086	3.86
Eltham	Peter Bottomley	1666	4.07
Erith & Crayford	David Evennett	2339	4.96
Plymouth, Drake	Dame Janet Fookes	2013	5.16
Harlow	Jerry Hayes	2940	5.19
Stockton South	Tim Devlin	3369	5.36
Elmet	Spencer Batiste	3261	5.60
Cardiff North	Gwilym Jones	2969	6.22
Monmouth	Roger Evans	3204	6.29
Lancaster	Dame Elaine Kellett-Bowman	2953	6.38
Exeter	Sir John Hannam	4045	6.41
Chorley	Den Dover	4246	6.53
Keighley	Gary Waller	3596	6.56
Derbyshire South	Edwina Currie	4658	6.62
Blackpool North	Harold Elletson	3040	6.75
Brighton, Kemptown	Andrew Bowden	3056	6.96
Northampton North	Tony Marlow	3908	7.20
Gloucestershire West	Paul Marland	4958	7.39
Derby North	Greg Knight	4453	7.55
Birmingham, Hall Green	Andrew Hargreaves	3665	7.80
Calder Valley	Sir Donald Thompson	4878	7.98
High Peak	Charles Hendry	4819	8.04
Bury North	Alistair Burt	4764	8.08
Dudley West	Dr John Blackburn	5789	8.14
Peterborough	Dr Brian Mawhinney	5376	8.17
Brighton, Pavilion	Derek Spencer	3675	8.30
Westminster North	Sir John Wheeler	3733	8.37
Stevenage	Timothy Wood	4888	8.38
Leeds North East	Timothy Kirkhope	4244	8.57

CONSERVATIVE/LABOUR MARGINALS

Constituency	MP	Majority	%
Davyhulme	Winston Churchill	4426	8.77
Erewash	Angela Knight	5703	9.00
Milton Keynes South West	Barry Legg	4687	9.16
South Ribble	Robert Atkins	5973	9.21
Battersea	John Bowis	4840	9.26
Gravesham	Jacques Arnold	5493	9.30
Gloucester	Douglas French	6058	9.37
Wolverhampton South West	Nick Budgen	4966	9.43
Edinburgh, Pentlands	Malcolm Rifkind	4290	9.63
Burton	Ivan Lawrence	5996	9.66
Waveney	David Porter	6702	9.73
Staffordshire Mid	Michael Fabricant	6236	9.92
Great Yarmouth	Michael Carttiss	5309	9.98

CONSERVATIVE/LIBDEM MARGINALS

Constituency	MP	Majority	%
Brecon & Radnor	Jonathan Evans	130	0.29
Portsmouth South	David Martin	242	0.45
Hazel Grove	Sir Tom Arnold	929	1.70
Edinburgh West	Lord James Douglas-Hamilton	879	1.80
Isle of Wight	Barry Field	1827	2.29
Conwy	Sir Wyn Roberts	995	2.36
St Ives	David Harris	1645	2.88
Taunton	David Nicholson	3336	5.19
Southport	Matthew Banks	3063	5.52
Falmouth & Camborne	Sebastian Coe	3267	5.70
Devon West & Torridge	Emma Nicholson	3614	5.77
Hereford	Colin Shepherd	3413	6.03
Oxford West & Abingdon	John Patten	3539	6.38
Somerton & Frome	Mark Robinson	4341	7.35
Littleborough & Saddleworth	Geoffrey Dickens	4494	8.40
Weston-super-Mare	Jerry Wiggin	5342	8.50
Kincardine & Deeside	George Kynoch	4495	8.57
Richmond & Barnes	Jeremy Hanley	3869	8.57
Eastbourne	Nigel Waterson	5481	8.89
Torbay	Rupert Allason	5787	10.08
Twickenham	Toby Jessel	5711	10.74
Wells	David Heathcoat-Amory	6649	11.51
Bristol West	William Waldegrave	6071	11.57
Ribble Valley	Nigel Evans	6542	11.74
Winchester	Peter Malone	8121	12.28
Hastings & Rye	Jacqui Lait	6634	12.34
Sheffield, Hallam	Irvine Patnick	6741	12.43
Cornwall South East	Robert Hicks	7704	12.84
Teignbridge	Patrick Nicholls	8856	14.17

CONSERVATIVE/SNP MARGINALS

Constituency	MP	Majority	%
Perth & Kinross	Sir Nicholas Fairbairn	2094	4.16
Galloway & Upper Nithsdale	Ian Lang	2468	5.55
Tayside North	Bill Walker	3995	9.19

ANALYSIS

LABOUR/CONSERVATIVE MARGINALS

Constituency	MP	Majority	%
Rossendale & Darwen	Janet Anderson	120	0.19
Warrington South	Mike Hall	191	0.30
Birmingham, Yardley	Estelle Morris	162	0.38
Ipswich	Jamie Cann	265	0.49
Halifax	Alice Mahon	478	0.83
Ilford South	Mike Gapes	402	0.94
Southampton, Itchen	John Denham	551	0.99
Dewsbury	Ann Taylor	634	1.09
Cambridge	Anne Campbell	580	1.15
Birmingham, Northfield	Richard Burden	630	1.17
Pembroke	Nick Ainger	755	1.24
Thurrock	Andrew MacKinlay	1172	2.17
Warwickshire North	Mike O'Brien	1454	2.43
Cannock & Burntwood	Tony Wright	1506	2.46
Lewisham East	Bridget Prentice	1095	2.54
Nuneaton	Bill Olner	1631	2.75
Stockport	Ann Coffey	1422	2.98
Lancashire West	Colin Pickthall	2077	3.25
Ellesmere Port & Neston	Andrew Miller	1989	3.30
Feltham & Heston	Alan Keen	1995	3.32
Hampstead & Highgate	Glenda Jackson	1440	3.39
Coventry South East	Jim Cunningham	1311	3.59
Delyn	David Hanson	2039	3.67
Birmingham, Selly Oak	Lynne Jones	2060	3.73
Renfrew West & Inverclyde	Tommy Graham	1744	3.74
Croydon North West	Malcolm Wicks	1526	3.77
Kingswood	Roger Berry	2370	3.94
Pendle	Gordon Prentice	2113	3.98
Hyndburn	Greg Pope	1960	3.99
Lewisham West	Jim Dowd	1809	4.17
Crewe & Nantwich	Gwyneth Dunwoody	2695	4.39
Sherwood	Paddy Tipping	2910	4.64

LIBDEM/CONSERVATIVE MARGINALS

Constituency	MP	Majority	%
Gordon	Malcolm Bruce	274	0.46
Devon North	Nick Harvey	794	1.36
Cheltenham	Nigel Jones	1668	2.60
Cornwall North	Paul Tyler	1921	3.07
Bath	Don Foster	3768	7.17
Argyll & Bute	Mrs Ray Michie	2622	7.19
Fife North East	Menzies Campbell	3308	7.91
Tweeddale, Ettrick & Lauderdale	Sir David Steel	2520	8.18

OTHER PARTY/CONSERVATIVE MARGINALS

Constituency	MP	Majority	%
Angus East	Andrew Welsh (SNP)	954	2.01
Ynys Mon	Ieuan Wyn Jones (PC)	1106	2.57
Moray	Margaret Ewing (SNP)	2844	6.20
Banff & Buchan	Alex Salmond (SNP)	4108	8.89

LOWEST WINNING SHARE OF THE VOTE

Winning Share	Party	Over	MP	Constituency
26.0	LibDem	Lab	Sir Russell Johnston	Inverness, Nairn & Lochaber
31.3	Plaid Cymru	LibDem	Cynog Dafis	Ceredigion & Pembroke North
32.6	Lab	Con	Jim Cunningham	Coventry South East
33.7	Con	LibDem	Sir Wyn Roberts	Conwy
34.2	Lab	SNP	Malcolm Chisholm	Edinburgh, Leith
34.9	Lab	Con	Estelle Morris	Birmingham, Yardley
34.9	LibDem	Con	Mrs Ray Michie	Argyll & Bute
36.1	Con	LibDem	Jonathan Evans	Brecon & Radnor
36.6	Lab	Con	Tommy Graham	Renfrew West & Inverclyde
36.6	Lab	Plaid Cymru	Dr Alan Wynne Williams	Carmarthen
36.9	Con	LibDem	Sebastian Coe	Falmouth & Camborne
37.0	Con	LibDem	Lord James Douglas Hamilton	Edinburgh West
37.1	Plaid Cymru	Con	Ieuan Wyn Jones	Ynys Mon
37.4	LibDem	Con	Malcolm Bruce	Gordon
38.5	Con	Lab	Raymond Robertson	Aberdeen South
38.5	Lab	LibDem	George Galloway	Glasgow, Hillhead
38.8	Lab	Con	Alistair Darling	Edinburgh Central
39.7	Lab	Con	Anne Campbell	Cambridge
39.9	LibDem	Con	Sir David Steel	Tweeddale, Ettrick & Lauderdale
40.0	Con	Lab	Michael Forsyth	Stirling
40.1	SNP	Con	Andrew Welsh	Angus East
40.2	Con	SNP	Sir Nicholas Fairbairn	Perth & Kinross
40.7	Con	Lab	Malcolm Rifkind	Edinburgh, Pentlands
40.8	Con	Lab	Phil Gallie	Ayr
41.0	Lab	Con	Brian Wilson	Cunninghame North
41.0	Lab	Soc Dem	Nick Raynsford	Greenwich
41.5	Lab	Con	Nigel Griffiths	Edinburgh South
41.6	LibDem	Con	Charles Kennedy	Ross, Cromarty & Skye
42.0	Lab	Con	Jon Owen Jones	Cardiff Central
42.0	Con	SNP	Ian Lang	Galloway & Upper Nithsdale
42.0	Con	Lab	Graham Riddick	Colne Valley
42.0	Lab	Con	Rachel Squire	Dunfermline West
42.1	Con	Lab	Sir John Hannam	Exeter
42.2	Con	LibDem	William Waldegrave	Bristol West
42.3	Lab	Con	Sam Galbraith	Strathkelvin & Bearsden
42.3	DUP	SDLP	Rev William McCrea	Ulster Mid
42.3	Con	Lab	Michael Stern	Bristol North West
42.5	Con	LibDem	David Martin	Portsmouth South
42.8	LibDem	Lab	Liz Lynne	Rochdale
42.9	Con	LibDem	David Harris	St Ives
42.9	Pop U	Con	James Kilfedder	Down North
43.0	Con	LibDem	Dr Keith Hampson	Leeds North West
43.1	Con	Lab	Sir Hector Monro	Dumfries
43.2	Lab	LibDem	Jane Kennedy	Liverpool, Broadgreen
43.2	UUP	DUP	Roy Beggs	Antrim East
43.3	Con	Lab	Simon Coombs	Swindon
43.3	Con	Lab	Patrick Thompson	Norwich North
43.3	Lab	Con	Nick Ainger	Pembroke
43.4	Con	Lab	James Hill	Southampton, Test
43.4	Lab	SML	James Dunnachie	Glasgow, Pollok
43.5	Lab	Con	Alice Mahon	Halifax
43.5	Lab	Con	Martyn Jones	Clwyd South West
43.6	Con	Lab	Paul Marland	Gloucestershire West
43.6	SDLP	SF	Dr Joe Hendron	Belfast West
43.6	UUP	DUP	John Taylor	Strangford
43.6	Lab	Con	John McFall	Dumbarton

20 BEST SNP VOTES

%	Constituency	%	Constituency
47.5	Banff & Buchan	30.3	Linlithgow
44.3	Moray	28.9	Cumbernauld & Kilsyth
40.1	Angus East	26.9	Clackmannan
37.5	Tayside North	26.6	Livingston
37.2	Western Isles	26.2	Falkirk East
37.1	Glasgow, Govan	25.1	Fife Central
36.4	Galloway & Upper Nithsdale	24.7	Inverness, Nairn & Lochaber
36.0	Perth & Kinross	24.3	Falkirk West
33.4	Dundee East	24.2	Cunninghame South
30.7	Kilmarnock & Loudoun	24.1	Paisley South

10 BEST PLAID CYMRU VOTES

%	Constituency	%	Constituency
59.0	Caernarfon	15.6	Llanelli
44.0	Meirionnydd Nant Conwy	11.8	Rhondda
37.1	Ynys Mon	11.3	Neath
31.5	Carmarthen	11.0	Cynon Valley
31.3	Ceredigion & Pembroke North	9.8	Clwyd South West

10 BEST GREEN VOTES

%	Constituency	%	Constituency
3.8	Islington North	2.4	Birmingham, Sparkbrook
3.2	Hackney North & Stoke Newington	2.4	Birmingham, Smallheath
2.9	Stroud	2.4	Holborn & St Pancras
2.7	Liverpool, Riverside	2.3	Norwood
2.6	Leominster	2.3	Westminster North

10 BEST LIBERAL VOTES

%	Constituency	%	Constituency
8.3	Leeds West	2.6	Tooting
3.8	Tiverton	2.6	Liverpool, West Derby
3.3	Knowsley North	2.5	Slough
3.0	Medway	2.5	Denton & Reddish
2.9	Liverpool, Broadgreen	2.4	Makerfield

10 BEST LOONY VOTES

%	Constituency	%	Constituency
2.25	Honiton	0.97	Newham North West
1.61	Workington	0.77	Cannock & Burntwood
1.31	Islwyn	0.75	Wokingham
1.05	Antrim South	0.71	Bradford North
0.99	Huntingdon	0.70	Teignbridge

SCHOOLS

Eton	36
Rugby	8
Harrow	7
Latymer Upper	5
Bradfield College	4
George Watson's, Edinburgh	4
King Edward's, Birmingham	4
Merchant Taylors	4
Shrewsbury	4
Wellington	4
Westminster	4
Winchester	4

UNIVERSITIES

Oxford	104
Cambridge	78
London	36
Wales	18
Glasgow	13
Edinburgh	12
Hull	11
St Andrew's	9
Durham	8
Leeds	8
Manchester	8
Heriot Watt	7

TRADE UNIONS

TGWU	45
MSF	28
GMB	24
NUM	13
NUPE	11
AEU	11
EETPU	10
COHSE	7
RMT	7

JOBS

Company director	60
Teacher	56
Barrister	53
Lecturer	46
Political adviser/researcher	43
Manual worker	40
Journalist	29
Solicitor	28
Company executive/manager	26
Trade union official	24
Engineering worker	19
Broadcaster	18
Party official/agent	16
Farmer	16
Accountant	15
Voluntary sector worker	14
Banker	14
Management consultant	13
Armed services	12
Stockbroker, financier	10
Miner	10
Economist, statistician	10

UNUSUAL JOBS

Tram conductor	David Marshall, Lab
Crematorium director	Barry Field, Con
Gravedigger	Frank Cook, Lab
Theatre producer	Sir Tom Arnold, Con
Merchant navy steward	John Prescott, Lab
Footballer	David Evans, Con
Neurosurgeon	Sam Galbraith, Lab
River pilot	Malcolm Thornton, Con
Gospel singer	William McCrea, DUP
Telephonist	Bernie Grant, Lab

WOMEN MPS IN THE UK (NUMBER) IN EVERY ELECTION SINCE 1918

1918	1	1959	25
1922	2	1964	29
1923	8	1966	26
1924	4	1970	26
1929	14	1974 Feb	23
1931	15	1974 Oct	27
1935	9	1979	19
1945	24	1983	23
1950	21	1987	41
1951	7	1992	58
1955	24		

NEW WOMEN MPS ELECTED

Anderson, Janet	Lab	Rossendale
Browning, Angela	Con	Tiverton
Campbell, Anne	Lab	Cambridge
Chaplin, Judith	Con	Newbury
Coffey, Ann	Lab	Stockport
Corston, Jean	Lab	Bristol E
Eagle, Angela	Lab	Wallasey
Gillan, Cheryl	Con	Chesham & Amersham
Jackson, Glenda	Lab	Hampstead
Jones, Lynne	Lab	B'ham Selly Oak
Kennedy, Jane	Lab	L'pool Broadgreen
Knight, Angela	Con	Erewash
Lait, Jacqui	Con	Hastings and Rye
Lynne, Elizabeth	LibDem	Rochdale
Maitland, Olga	Con	Sutton and Cheam
Morris, Estelle	Lab	B'ham Yardley
Prentice, Bridget	Lab	Lewisham E
Roche, Barbara	Lab	Hornsey & Wood Green
Squire, Rachel	Lab	Dunfermline W

WOMEN MPS DEFEATED

Chalker, Lynda	Con	Wallasey
Hicks, Maureen	Con	Wolverhampton NE

WOMEN MPS RETIRED

Thatcher, Margaret	Con	Finchley

WOMEN MPS

	1992	1987
Con	20	17
Lab	35	21
LibDem	2	1
SNP	1	1

WOMEN CANDIDATES

Con	62	46
Lab	134	92
LibDem	139	105

MPS FROM ETHNIC MINORITIES

Con	1	0
Lab	5	4
LibDem	0	0

CANDIDATES FROM ETHNIC MINORITIES

Con	7	0
Lab	9	14
LibDem	6	0

NEW MPS FROM ETHNIC MINORITIES

Deva, Nir	Con	Brentford
Khabra, Piara	Lab	Ealing Southall

ETHNIC MINORITY MPS DEFEATED

Kumar, Ashok	Lab	Langbaurgh

YOUNGEST MPS

Age	MP	Party	Constituency
29	Matthew Taylor	LibDem	Truro
30	David Faber	Con	Westbury
30	Nick Harvey	LibDem	Devon North
30	Michael Bates	Con	Langbaurgh
30	Dr Liam Fox	Con	Woodspring
30	Matthew Banks	Con	Southport
31	Harold Elletson	Con	Blackpool North
31	William Hague	Con	Richmond, Yorks
31	Greg Pope	Lab	Hyndburn
31	Angela Eagle	Lab	Wallasey
32	Charles Kennedy	LibDem	Ross, Cromarty & Skye
32	Gordon McMaster	Lab	Paisley South
32	Tim Devlin	Con	Stockton South
32	John Whittingdale	Con	Colchester South & Maldon
32	Raymond Robertson	Con	Aberdeen South
32	Charles Hendry	Con	High Peak
33	Bernard Jenkin	Con	Colchester North
33	Jane Kennedy	Lab	Liverpool, Broadgreen

OLDEST MPS

Age	MP	Party	Constituency
75	Edward Heath	Con	Old Bexley & Sidcup
73	Sir Trevor Skeet	Con	Bedfordshire North
69	Dame Peggy Fenner	Con	Medway
69	Stanley Orme	Lab	Salford East
69	Andrew Faulds	Lab	Warley East
69	Sir Hector Monro	Con	Dumfries
68	Mildred Gordon	Lab	Bow & Poplar
68	Sir Gerry Vaughan	Con	Reading East
68	Robert Sheldon	Lab	Ashton-under-Lyne
68	Ralph Howell	Con	Norfolk North
68	Eddie Loyden	Lab	Liverpool, Garston
68	Jo Richardson	Lab	Barking
67	Tony Benn	Lab	Chesterfield
67	Piara Khabra	Lab	Ealing, Southall
67	Sir Geoffrey Johnson Smith	Con	Wealden
67	Cecil Walker	UUP	Belfast North
67	Dame Elaine Kellett-Bowman	Con	Lancaster
67	Peter Shore	Lab	Bethnal Green & Stepney

LONGEST CONTINUOUS SERVING MPS

First elected	MP	Constituency
1950	Edward Heath	Old Bexley & Sidcup
1959	John Morris	Aberavon
	Paul Channon	Southend West (by election)
1961 (by election)	John Biffen	Shropshire North
1962 (by election)	Tam Dalyell	Linlithgow
1964	Robert Sheldon	Ashton-under-Lyne
	Peter Shore	Bethnal Green and Stepney
	Roy Hattersley	Birmingham Sparkbrook
	Sir Anthony Grant	Cambridgeshire South West
	Harold Walker	Doncaster Central
	Sir Hector Monro	Dumfries
	Sir David Mitchell	Hampshire North West
	Sir Peter Hordern	Horsham
	Sir Russell Johnston	Inverness, Nairn and Lochaber
	Alfred Morris	Manchester Wynthenshawe
	Sir Patrick McNair-Wilson	New Forest
	Sir John Hunt	Ravensbourne
	Stanley Orme	Salford East
	Michael Alison	Selby
	Alan Williams	Swansea West
	Cranley Onslow	Woking
	Terence Higgins	Worthing
1965 (by election)	Sir David Steel	Tweedale, Ettrick and Lauderdale
1966	Dame Jill Knight	Birmingham, Edgbaston
	Joan Lestor	Eccles
	David Howell	Guildford
	Michael Heseltine	Henley
	Kevin McNamara	Hull North
	Edward Rowlands	Methyr Tydfil and Rhymney
	Roy Hughes	Newport East
	John Fraser	Norwood
	Andrew Faulds	Warley East
	Michael Jopling	Westmorland & Lonsdale

The House of Commons

A
ABBOTT, Diane (Lab)	Hackney N
ADAMS, Irene (Lab)	Paisley N
ADLEY, Robert (Con)	Christchurch
AINGER, Nick (Lab)	Pembroke
AINSWORTH, Peter (Con)	Surrey E
AINSWORTH, Robert (Lab)	Coventry NE
AITKEN, Jonathan (Con)	Thanet S
ALEXANDER, Richard (Con)	Newark
ALISON, Michael (Con)	Selby
ALLASON, Rupert (Con)	Torbay
ALLEN, Graham (Lab)	Nottingham N
ALTON, David (LibDem)	Liverpool Mossley
AMESS, David (Con)	Basildon
ANCRAM, Michael (Con)	Devizes
ANDERSON, Donald (Lab)	Swansea E
ANDERSON, Janet (Lab)	Rossendale
ARBUTHNOT, James (Con)	Wanstead and Woodford
ARMSTRONG, Hilary (Lab)	Durham NW
ARNOLD, Jacques (Con)	Gravesham
ARNOLD, Tom (Con)	Hazel Grove
ASHBY, David (Con)	Leicestershire NW
ASHDOWN, Paddy (LibDem)	Yeovil
ASHTON, Joe (Lab)	Bassetlaw
ASPINWALL, Jack (Con)	Wansdyke
ATKINS, Robert (Con)	S Ribble
ATKINSON, David (Con)	Bournemouth E
ATKINSON, Peter (Con)	Hexham
AUSTIN-WALKER, John (Lab)	Woolwich

B
BAKER, Kenneth (Con)	Mole Valley
BAKER, Nicholas (Con)	Dorset N
BALDRY, Tony (Con)	Banbury
BANKS, Matthew (Con)	Southport
BANKS, Robert (Con)	Harrogate
BANKS, Tony (Lab)	Newham NW
BARNES, Harry (Lab)	Derbyshire NE
BARRON, Kevin (Lab)	Rother Valley
BATES, Michael (Con)	Langbaurgh
BATISTE, Spencer (Con)	Elmet
BATTLE, John (Lab)	Leeds W
BAYLEY, Hugh (Lab)	York
BECKETT, Margaret (Lab)	Derby S
BEGGS, Roy (UUP)	E Antrim
BEITH, Alan (LibDem)	Berwick
BELL, Stuart (Lab)	Middlesbrough
BELLINGHAM, Henry (Con)	Norfolk NW
BENDALL, Vivian (Con)	Ilford N
BENN, Tony (Lab)	Chesterfield
BENNETT, Andrew (Lab)	Denton and Reddish
BENTON, Joe (Lab)	Bootle
BERESFORD, Paul (Con)	Croydon Central
BERMINGHAM, Gerald (Lab)	St Helens S
BERRY, Roger (Lab)	Kingswood
BETTS, Clive (Lab)	Sheffield Attercliffe
BIFFEN, John (Con)	Shropshire N
BLACKBURN, John (Con)	Dudley W
BLAIR, Tony (Lab)	Sedgefield
BLUNKETT, David (Lab)	Sheffield Brightside
BOATENG, Paul (Lab)	Brent S
BODY, Richard (Con)	Holland with Boston
BONSOR, Nicholas (Con)	Upminster
BOOTH, Hartley (Con)	Finchley
BOOTHROYD, Betty (Lab)	W Brom W
BOSWELL, Timothy (Con)	Daventry
BOTTOMLEY, Peter (Con)	Eltham
BOTTOMLEY, Virginia (Con)	Surrey SW
BOWDEN, Andrew (Con)	Brighton Kemptown
BOWIS, John (Con)	Battersea
BOYCE, James (Lab)	Rotherham
BOYES, Roland (Lab)	Houghton & Washington
BOYSON, Rhodes (Con)	Brent N
BRADLEY, Keith (Lab)	Manchester Withington
BRANDRETH, Gyles (Con)	Chester
BRAY, Jeremy (Lab)	Motherwell S
BRAZIER, Julian (Con)	Canterbury
BRIGHT, Graham (Con)	Luton S
BROOKE, Peter (Con)	Westminster S
BROWN, Gordon (Lab)	Dunfermline E
BROWN, Michael (Con)	Brigg and Cleethorpes
BROWN, Nick (Lab)	Newcastle E
BROWNING, Angela (Con)	Tiverton
BRUCE, Ian (Con)	Dorset S
BRUCE, Malcolm (LibDem)	Gordon
BUDGEN, Nicholas (Con)	Wolverhampton SW
BURDEN, Richard (Lab)	Birmingham Northfield
BURNS, Simon (Con)	Chelmsford
BURT, Alistair (Con)	Bury N
BUTCHER, John (Con)	Coventry SW
BUTLER, Peter (Con)	Milton Keynes NE
BUTTERFILL, John (Con)	Bournemouth W
BYERS, Stephen (Lab)	Wallsend

C
CABORN, Richard (Lab)	Sheffield Central
CALLAGHAN, Jim (Lab)	Heywood and Middleton
CAMPBELL, Anne (Lab)	Cambridge
CAMPBELL, Menzies (LibDem)	Fife NE
CAMPBELL, Ronnie (Lab)	Blyth Valley
CAMPBELL-SAVOURS, Dale (Lab)	Workington
CANAVAN, Dennis (Lab)	Falkirk W
CANN, James (Lab)	Ipswich
CARLILE, Alex (LibDem)	Montgomery
CARLISLE, John (Con)	Luton N
CARLISLE, Kenneth (Con)	Lincoln
CARRINGTON, Matthew (Con)	Fulham.
CARTTISS, Michael (Con)	Great Yarmouth
CASH, William (Con)	Stafford
CHANNON, Paul (Con)	Southend W
CHAPLIN, Judith (Con)	Newbury
CHAPMAN, Sydney (Con)	Chipping Barnet
CHISHOLM, Malcolm (Lab)	Edinburgh Leith
CHURCHILL, Winston (Con)	Davyhulme
CLAPHAM, Michael (Lab)	Barnsley W
CLAPPISON, James (Con)	Hertsmere
CLARK, David (Lab)	S Shields
CLARK, Michael (Con)	Rochford
CLARKE, Eric (Lab)	Midlothian
CLARKE, Kenneth (Con)	Rushcliffe
CLARKE, Tom (Lab)	Monklands W
CLELLAND, David (Lab)	Tyne Bridge
CLIFTON-BROWN, Geoffrey (Con)	Cirencester
CLWYD, Ann (Lab)	Cynon Valley
COE, Sebastian (Con)	Falmouth
COFFEY, Ann (Lab)	Stockport
COHEN, Harry (Lab)	Leyton
COLVIN, Michael (Con)	Romsey and Waterside
CONGDON, David (Con)	Croydon NE
CONNARTY, Michael (Lab)	Falkirk E
CONWAY, Derek (Con)	Shrewsbury and Atcham
COOK, Frank (Lab)	Stockton N
COOK, Robin (Lab)	Livingston
COOMBS, Anthony (Con)	Wyre Forest
COOMBS, Simon (Con)	Swindon
COPE, John (Con)	Northavon
CORBETT, Robin (Lab)	Birmingham Erdington
CORBYN, Jeremy (Lab)	Islington N
CORMACK, Patrick (Con)	Staffordshire S
CORSTON, Jean (Lab)	Bristol E
COUCHMAN, James (Con)	Gillingham

INDEX OF MPs

COUSINS, Jim (Lab)	Newcastle Central	FLYNN, Paul (Lab)	Newport W
COX, Tom (Lab)	Tooting	FOOKES, Janet (Con)	Plymouth Drake
CRAN, Jim (Con)	Beverley	FORMAN, Nigel (Con)	Carshalton
CRITCHLEY, Julian (Con)	Aldershot	FORSYTH, Michael (Con)	Stirling
CRYER, Bob (Lab)	Bradford S	FORSYTHE, Clifford (UUP)	S Antrim
CUMMINGS, John (Lab)	Easington	FORTH, Eric (Con)	Mid Worcestershire
CUNLIFFE, Lawrence (Lab)	Leigh	FOSTER, Derek (Lab)	Bishop Auckland
CUNNINGHAM, Jim (Lab)	Coventry SE	FOSTER, Don (LibDem)	Bath
CUNNINGHAM, John (Lab)	Copeland	FOULKES, George (Lab)	Carrick
CURRIE, Edwina (Con)	Derbyshire S	FOWLER, Norman (Con)	Sutton Coldfield
CURRY, David (Con)	Skipton and Ripon	FOX, Liam (Con)	Woodspring
		FOX, Marcus (Con)	Shipley
D DAFIS, Cynog (Plaid Cymru)	Ceredigion	FRASER, John (Lab)	Norwood
DALYELL, Tam (Lab)	Linlithgow	FREEMAN, Roger (Con)	Kettering
DARLING, Alistair (Lab)	Edinburgh Central	FRENCH, Douglas (Con)	Gloucester
DAVIDSON, Ian (Lab)	Glasgow Govan	FRY, Peter (Con)	Wellingborough
DAVIES, Bryan (Lab)	Oldham Central	FYFE, Maria (Lab)	Glasgow Maryhill
DAVIES, Denzil (Lab)	Llanelli		
DAVIES, Quentin (Con)	Stamford and Spalding	**G** GALBRAITH, Sam (Lab)	Strathkelvin
DAVIES, Ron (Lab)	Caerphilly	GALE, Roger (Con)	Thanet N
DAVIS, David (Con)	Boothferry	GALLIE, Phil (Con)	Ayr
DAVIS, Terry (Lab)	Birmingham Hodge Hill	GALLOWAY, George (Lab)	Glasgow Hillhead
DAY, Stephen (Con)	Cheadle	GAPES, Mike (Lab)	Ilford
DENHAM, John (Lab)	Southampton Itchen	GARDINER, George (Con)	Reigate
DEVA, Nirj (Con)	Brentford	GAREL-JONES, Tristan (Con)	Watford
DEVLIN, Tim (Con)	Stockton S	GARNIER, Edward (Con)	Harborough
DEWAR, Donald (Lab)	Glasgow Garscadden	GARRETT, John (Lab)	Norwich S
DICKENS, Geoffrey (Con)	Littleborough & Saddleworth	GEORGE, Bruce (Lab)	Walsall S
DICKS, Terry (Con)	Hayes and Harlington	GERRARD, Neil (Lab)	Walthamstow
DIXON, Don (Lab)	Jarrow	GILBERT, John (Lab)	Dudley E
DOBSON, Frank (Lab)	Holborn	GILL, Christopher (Con)	Ludlow
DONOHOE, Brian (Lab)	Cunninghame S	GILLAN, Cheryl (Con)	Chesham & Amersham
DORRELL, Stephen (Con)	Loughborough	GODMAN, Norman (Lab)	Greenock
DOUGLAS-HAMILTON, James (Con)	Edinburgh W	GODSIFF, Roger (Lab)	Birmingham Small Heath
DOVER, Den (Con)	Chorley	GOLDING, Llinos (Lab)	Newcastle-under-Lyme
DOWD, Jim (Lab)	Lewisham W	GOODLAD, Alastair (Con)	Eddisbury
DUNCAN, Alan (Con)	Rutland and Melton	GOODSON-WICKES, Charles (Con)	Wimbledon
DUNCAN-SMITH, Iain (Con)	Chingford	GORDON, Mildred (Lab)	Bow and Poplar
DUNN, Robert (Con)	Dartford	GORMAN, Teresa (Con)	Billericay
DUNNACHIE, James (Lab)	Glasgow Pollok	GORST, John (Con)	Hendon N
DUNWOODY, Gwyneth (Lab)	Crewe and Nantwich	GOULD, Bryan (Lab)	Dagenham
DURANT, Tony (Con)	Reading W	GRAHAM, Tommy (Lab)	Renfrew W
DYKES, Hugh (Con)	Harrow E	GRANT, Anthony (Con)	Cambridgeshire SW
		GRANT, Bernie (Lab)	Tottenham
E EAGLE, Angela (Lab)	Wallasey	GREENWAY, Harry (Con)	Ealing N
EASTHAM, Kenneth (Lab)	Manchester Blackley	GREENWAY, John (Con)	Ryedale
EGGAR, Tim (Con)	Enfield N	GRIFFITHS, Nigel (Lab)	Edinburgh S
ELLETSON, Harold (Con)	Blackpool	GRIFFITHS, Peter (Con)	Portsmouth N
EMERY, Peter (Con)	Honiton	GRIFFITHS, Win (Lab)	Bridgend
ENRIGHT, Derek (Lab)	Hemsworth	GROCOTT, Bruce (Lab)	The Wrekin
ETHERINGTON, William (Lab)	Sunderland N	GRYLLS, Michael (Con)	Surrey NW
EVANS, David (Con)	Welwyn Hatfield	GUMMER, John (Con)	Suffolk Coastal
EVANS, John (Lab)	St Helens N	GUNNELL, John (Lab)	Leeds S and Morley
EVANS, Jonathan (Con)	Brecon and Radnor		
EVANS, Nigel (Con)	Ribble Valley	**H** HAGUE, William (Con)	Richmond
EVANS, Roger (Con)	Monmouth	HAIN, Peter (Lab)	Neath
EVENNETT, David (Con)	Erith and Crayford	HALL, Mike (Lab)	Warrington S
EWING, Margaret (SNP)	Moray	HAMILTON, Archie (Con)	Epsom and Ewell
		HAMILTON, Neil (Con)	Tatton
F FABER, David (Con)	Westbury	HAMPSON, Keith (Con)	Leeds NW
FABRICANT, Michael (Con)	Mid Staffordshire	HANLEY, Jeremy (Con)	Richmond and Barnes
FAIRBAIRN, Nicholas (Con)	Perth	HANNAM, John (Con)	Exeter
FATCHETT, Derek (Lab)	Leeds Central	HANSON, David (Lab)	Delyn
FAULDS, Andrew (Lab)	Warley E	HARDY, Peter (Lab)	Wentworth
FENNER, Peggy (Con)	Medway	HARGREAVES, Andrew (Con)	Birmingham Hall Green
FIELD, Barry (Con)	Isle of Wight	HARMAN, Harriet (Lab)	Peckham
FIELD, Frank (Lab)	Birkenhead	HARRIS, David (Con)	St Ives
FISHBURN, Dudley (Con)	Kensington	HARVEY, Nicholas (LibDem)	Devon N
FISHER, Mark (Lab)	Stoke-on-Trent Central	HASELHURST, Alan (Con)	Saffron Walden

HATTERSLEY, Roy (Lab)	Birmingham Sparkbrook
HAWKINS, Nick (Con)	Blackpool S
HAWKSLEY, Warren (Con)	Halesowen
HAYES, Jerry (Con)	Harlow
HEALD, Oliver (Con)	Hertfordshire N
HEATH, Edward (Con)	Old Bexley
HEATHCOAT-AMORY, David (Con)	Wells
HENDERSON, Douglas (Lab)	Newcastle N
HENDRON, Joe (SDLP)	W Belfast
HENDRY, Charles (Con)	High Peak
HEPPELL, John (Lab)	Nottingham E
HESELTINE, Michael (Con)	Henley
HICKS, Robert (Con)	Cornwall S E
HIGGINS, Terence (Con)	Worthing
HILL, James (Con)	Southampton Test
HILL, Keith (Lab)	Streatham
HINCHLIFFE, David (Lab)	Wakefield
HOEY, Kate (Lab)	Vauxhall
HOGG, Douglas (Con)	Grantham
HOGG, Norman (Lab)	Cumbernauld & Kilsyth
HOME ROBERTSON, John (Lab)	E Lothian
HOOD, Jimmy (Lab)	Clydesdale
HOON, Geoffrey (Lab)	Ashfield
HORAM, John (Con)	Orpington
HORDERN, Peter (Con)	Horsham
HOWARD, Michael (Con)	Folkestone
HOWARTH, Alan (Con)	Stratford-on-Avon
HOWARTH, George (Lab)	Knowsley N
HOWELL, David (Con)	Guildford
HOWELL, Ralph (Con)	Norfolk N
HOWELLS, Kim (Lab)	Pontypridd
HOYLE, Doug (Lab)	Warrington N
HUGHES, Kevin (Lab)	Doncaster N
HUGHES, Robert (Lab)	Aberdeen N
HUGHES, Robert (Con)	Harrow W
HUGHES, Roy (Lab)	Newport E
HUGHES, Simon (LibDem)	Bermondsey
HUME, John (SDLP)	Foyle
HUNT, David (Con)	Wirral W
HUNT, John (Con)	Ravensbourne
HUNTER, Andrew (Con)	Basingstoke
HURD, Douglas (Con)	Witney
HUTTON, John (Lab)	Barrow and Furness
ILLSLEY, Eric (Lab)	Barnsley Central
INGRAM, Adam (Lab)	E Kilbride
JACK, Michael (Con)	Fylde
JACKSON, Glenda (Lab)	Hampstead
JACKSON, Helen (Lab)	Sheffield Hillsborough
JACKSON, Robert (Con)	Wantage
JAMIESON, David (Lab)	Plymouth Devonport
JANNER, Greville (Lab)	Leicester W
JENKIN, Bernard (Con)	Colchester N
JESSEL, Toby (Con)	Twickenham
JOHNSON-SMITH, Geoffrey (Con)	Wealden
JOHNSTON, Russell (LibDem)	Inverness
JONES, Barry (Lab)	Alyn and Deeside
JONES, Gwilym (Con)	Cardiff N
JONES, Ieuan Wyn (Plaid Cymru)	Ynys Mon
JONES, Jon Owen (Lab)	Cardiff Central
JONES, Lynne (Lab)	Birmingham Selly Oak
JONES, Martyn (Lab)	Clwyd SW
JONES, Nigel (LibDem)	Cheltenham
JONES, Robert (Con)	Hertfordshire W
JOPLING, Michael (Con)	Westmorland and Lonsdale
JOWELL, Tessa (Lab)	Dulwich
KAUFMAN, Gerald (Lab)	Manchester Gorton
KEEN, Alan (Lab)	Feltham and Heston
KELLETT-BOWMAN, Elaine (Con)	Lancaster
KENNEDY, Charles (LibDem)	Ross, Cromarty and Skye
KENNEDY, Jane (Lab)	Liverpool Broadgreen
KEY, Robert (Con)	Salisbury
KHABRA, Piara (Lab)	Ealing Southall
KILFEDDER, James (UPUP)	N Down
KILFOYLE, Peter (Lab)	Liverpool Walton
KING, Tom (Con)	Bridgwater
KINNOCK, Neil (Lab)	Islwyn
KIRKHOPE, Timothy (Con)	Leeds NE
KIRKWOOD, Archy (LibDem)	Roxburgh
KNAPMAN, Roger (Con)	Stroud
KNIGHT, Angela (Con)	Erewash
KNIGHT, Greg (Con)	Derby N
KNIGHT, Jill (Con)	Birmingham Edgbaston
KNOX, David (Con)	Staffs Moorlands
KYNOCK, George (Con)	Kincardine and Deeside
LAIT, Jacqui (Con)	Hastings and Rye
LAMONT, Norman (Con)	Kingston
LANG, Ian (Con)	Galloway
LAWRENCE, Ivan (Con)	Burton
LEGG, Barry (Con)	Milton Keynes SW
LEIGH, Edward (Con)	Gainsborough
LEIGHTON, Ron (Lab)	Newham NE
LENNOX-BOYD, Mark (Con)	Morecambe
LESTER, Jim (Con)	Broxtowe
LESTOR, Joan (Lab)	Eccles
LEWIS, Terry (Lab)	Worsley
LIDINGTON, David (Con)	Aylesbury
LIGHTBOWN, David (Con)	Staffs SE
LILLEY, Peter (Con)	St Albans
LITHERLAND, Robert (Lab)	Manchester Central
LIVINGSTONE, Ken (Lab)	Brent E
LLOYD, Peter (Con)	Fareham
LLOYD, Tony (Lab)	Stretford
LLWYD, Elfyn (Plaid Cymru)	Meirionnydd
LOFTHOUSE, Geoffrey (Lab)	Pontefract
LORD, Michael (Con)	Suffolk Central
LOYDEN, Eddie (Lab)	Liverpool Garston
LUFF, Peter (Con)	Worcester
LYELL, Nicholas (Con)	Mid Bedfordshire
LYNNE, Elizabeth (LibDem)	Rochdale
MACDONALD, Calum (Lab)	Western Isles
MACGREGOR, John (Con)	Norfolk S
MACKAY, Andrew (Con)	Berkshire E
MACKINLAY, Andrew (Lab)	Thurrock
MACLEAN, David (Con)	Penrith and the Border
MACLENNAN, Robert (LibDem)	Caithness
MADDEN, Max (Lab)	Bradford W
MADEL, David (Con)	Beds SW
MAGINNIS, Ken (UUP)	Fermanagh
MAHON, Alice (Lab)	Halifax
MAITLAND, Olga (Con)	Sutton and Cheam
MAJOR, John (Con)	Huntingdon
MALLON, Seamus (SDLP)	Newry and Armagh
MALONE, Gerry (Con)	Winchester
MANDELSON, Peter (Lab)	Hartlepool
MANS, Keith (Con)	Wyre
MAREK, John (Lab)	Wrexham
MARLAND, Paul (Con)	Gloucestershire W
MARLOW, Tony (Con)	Northampton N
MARSHALL, David (Lab)	Glasgow Shettleston
MARSHALL, Jim (Lab)	Leicester S
MARSHALL, John (Con)	Hendon S
MARSHALL, Michael (Con)	Arundel

INDEX OF MPs

MARTIN, David (Con)	Portsmouth S
MARTIN, Michael (Lab)	Glasgow Springburn
MARTLEW, Eric (Lab)	Carlisle
MATES, Michael (Con)	Hampshire E
MAWHINNEY, Brian (Con)	Peterborough
MAXTON, John (Lab)	Glasgow Cathcart
MAYHEW, Patrick (Con)	Tunbridge Wells
MCALLION, John (Lab)	Dundee E
MCAVOY, Tommy (Lab)	Glasgow Rutherglen
MCCARTNEY, Ian (Lab)	Makerfield
MCCREA, William (DUP)	Mid Ulster
MCFALL, John (Lab)	Dumbarton
MCGRADY, Eddie (SDLP)	S Down
MCKELVEY, William (Lab)	Kilmarnock & Loudoun
MCLEISH, Henry (Lab)	Fife Central
MCLAUGHLIN, Patrick (Con)	Derbyshire W
MCMASTER, Gordon (Lab)	Paisley S
MCNAIR-WILSON, Patrick (Con)	New Forest
MCNAMARA, Kevin (Lab)	Hull N
MCWILLIAM, John (Lab)	Blaydon
MEACHER, Michael (Lab)	Oldham W
MEALE, Alan (Lab)	Mansfield
MELLOR, David (Con)	Putney
MERCHANT, Piers (Con)	Beckenham
MICHAEL, Alun (Lab)	Cardiff S
MICHIE, Bill (Lab)	Sheffield Heeley
MICHIE, Ray (LibDem)	Argyll and Bute
MILBURN, Alan (Lab)	Darlington
MILLER, Andrew (Lab)	Ellesmere Port
MILLIGAN, Stephen (Con)	Eastleigh
MILLS, Iain (Con)	Meriden
MITCHELL, Andrew (Con)	Gedling
MITCHELL, Austin (Lab)	Great Grimsby
MITCHELL, David (Con)	Hampshire NW
MOATE, Roger (Con)	Faversham
MOLYNEAUX, James (UUP)	Lagan Valley
MONRO, Hector (Con)	Dumfries
MONTGOMERY, Fergus (Con)	Altrincham and Sale
MOONIE, Lewis (Lab)	Kirkcaldy
MORGAN, Rhodri (Lab)	Cardiff W
MORLEY, Elliot (Lab)	Glanford & Scunthorpe
MORRIS, Alf (Lab)	Manchester Wythenshawe
MORRIS, Estelle (Lab)	Birmingham Yardley
MORRIS, John (Lab)	Aberavon
MORRIS, Michael (Con)	Northampton S
MOSS, Malcolm (Con)	Cambridgeshire NE
MOWLAM, Marjorie (Lab)	Redcar
MUDIE, George (Lab)	Leeds E
MULLIN, Chris (Lab)	Sunderland S
MURPHY, Paul (Lab)	Torfaen
N NEEDHAM, Richard (Con)	Wiltshire N
NELSON, Anthony (Con)	Chichester
NEUBERT, Michael (Con)	Romford
NEWTON, Tony (Con)	Braintree
NICHOLLS, Patrick (Con)	Teignbridge
NICHOLSON, David (Con)	Taunton
NICHOLSON, Emma (Con)	Devon W
NORRIS, Steven (Con)	Epping Forest
O O'BRIEN, Mike (Lab)	Warwickshire N
O'BRIEN, William (Lab)	Normanton
O'HARA, Eddie (Lab)	Knowsley S
O'NEILL, Martin (Lab)	Clackmannan
OAKES, Gordon (Lab)	Halton
OLNER, Bill (Lab)	Nuneaton
ONSLOW, Cranley (Con)	Woking
OPPENHEIM, Phillip (Con)	Amber Valley
ORME, Stanley (Lab)	Salford E
OTTAWAY, Richard (Con)	Croydon S
P PAGE, Richard (Con)	Herts SW
PAICE, James (Con)	Cambridgeshire SE
PAISLEY, Ian (DUP)	N Antrim
PARRY, Robert (Lab)	Liverpool Riverside
PATCHETT, Terry (Lab)	Barnsley E
PATNICK, Irvine (Con)	Sheffield Hallam
PATTEN, John (Con)	Oxford W
PATTIE, Geoffrey (Con)	Chertsey and Walton
PAWSEY, James (Con)	Rugby and Kenilworth
PEACOCK, Elizabeth (Con)	Batley and Spen
PENDRY, Tom (Lab)	Stalybridge and Hyde
PICKLES, Eric (Con)	Brentwood
PICKTHALL, Colin (Lab)	Lancashire W
PIKE, Peter (Lab)	Burnley
POPE, Gregory (Lab)	Hyndburn
PORTER, Barry (Con)	Wirral S
PORTER, David (Con)	Waveney
PORTILLO, Michael (Con)	Enfield Southgate
POWELL, Ray (Lab)	Ogmore
POWELL, William (Con)	Corby
PRENTICE, Bridget (Lab)	Lewisham E
PRENTICE, Gordon (Lab)	Pendle
PRESCOTT, John (Lab)	Hull E
PRIMAROLO, Dawn (Lab)	Bristol S
PURCHASE, Kenneth (Lab)	Wolverhampton NE
QUIN, Joyce (Lab)	Gateshead E
R RADICE, Giles (Lab)	Durham N
RANDALL, Stuart (Lab)	Hull W
RATHBONE, Tim (Con)	Lewes
RAYNSFORD, Nick (Lab)	Greenwich
REDMOND, Martin (Lab)	Don Valley
REDWOOD, John (Con)	Wokingham
REID, John (Lab)	Motherwell N
RENTON, Tim (Con)	Mid Sussex
RICHARDS, Rod (Con)	Clwyd NW
RICHARDSON, Jo (Lab)	Barking
RIDDICK, Graham (Con)	Colne Valley
RIFKIND, Malcolm (Con)	Edinburgh Pentlands
ROBATHAN, Andrew (Con)	Blaby
ROBERTS, Wyn (Con)	Conwy
ROBERTSON, George (Lab)	Hamilton
ROBERTSON, Raymond (Con)	Aberdeen S
ROBINSON, Geoffrey (Lab)	Coventry NW
ROBINSON, Mark (Con)	Somerton and Frome
ROBINSON, Peter (DUP)	E Belfast
ROCHE, Barbara (Lab)	Hornsey & Wood Green
ROE, Marion (Con)	Broxbourne
ROGERS, Allan (Lab)	Rhondda
ROOKER, Jeff (Lab)	Birmingham Perry Barr
ROONEY, Terry (Lab)	Bradford N
ROSS, Ernie (Lab)	Dundee W
ROSS, William (UUP)	E Londonderry
ROWE, Andrew (Con)	Mid Kent
ROWLANDS, Ted (Lab)	Merthyr Tydfil
RUDDOCK, Joan (Lab)	Lewisham, Deptford
RUMBOLD, Angela (Con)	Mitcham
RYDER, Richard (Con)	Mid Norfolk
S SACKVILLE, Thomas (Con)	Bolton W
SAINSBURY, Timothy (Con)	Hove
SALMOND, Alex (SNP)	Banff and Buchan

Member	Constituency
SCOTT, Nicholas (Con)	Chelsea
SEDGEMORE, Brian (Lab)	Hackney S
SHAW, David (Con)	Dover
SHAW, Giles (Con)	Pudsey
SHEERMAN, Barry (Lab)	Huddersfield
SHELDON, Robert (Lab)	Ashton-under-Lyne
SHEPHARD, Gillian (Con)	Norfolk SW
SHEPHERD, Colin (Con)	Hereford
SHEPHERD, Richard (Con)	Aldridge-Brownhills
SHERSBY, Michael (Con)	Uxbridge
SHORE, Peter (Lab)	Bethnal Green
SHORT, Clare (Lab)	Birmingham Ladywood
SIMPSON, Alan (Lab)	Nottingham S
SIMS, Roger (Con)	Chislehurst
SKEET, Trevor (Con)	Bedfordshire N
SKINNER, Dennis (Lab)	Bolsover
SMITH, Andrew (Lab)	Oxford E
SMITH, Chris (Lab)	Islington S
SMITH, Dudley (Con)	Warwick & Leamington
SMITH, John (Lab)	Monklands E
SMITH, Llewellyn (Lab)	Blaenau Gwent
SMITH, Tim (Con)	Beaconsfield
SMYTH, Martin (UUP)	S Belfast
SNAPE, Peter (Lab)	W Bromwich E
SOAMES, Nicholas (Con)	Crawley
SOLEY, Clive (Lab)	Hammersmith
SPEARING, Nigel (Lab)	Newham S
SPEED, Keith (Con)	Ashford
SPELLAR, John (Lab)	Warley W
SPENCER, Derek (Con)	Brighton Pavilion
SPICER, James (Con)	Dorset W
SPICER, Michael (Con)	Worcestershire S
SPINK, Robert (Con)	Castle Point
SPRING, Richard (Con)	Bury St Edmunds
SPROAT, Iain (Con)	Harwich
SQUIRE, Rachel (Lab)	Dunfermline W
SQUIRE, Robin (Con)	Hornchurch
STANLEY, John (Con)	Tonbridge and Malling
STEEL, David (LibDem)	Tweeddale
STEEN, Anthony (Con)	S Hams
STEINBERG, Gerry (Lab)	City of Durham
STEPHEN, Michael (Con)	Shoreham
STERN, Michael (Con)	Bristol NW
STEVENSON, George (Lab)	Stoke-on-Trent S
STEWART, Allan (Con)	Eastwood
STOTT, Roger (Lab)	Wigan
STRANG, Gavin (Lab)	Edinburgh E
STRAW, Jack (Lab)	Blackburn
STREETER, Gary (Con)	Plymouth Sutton
SUMBERG, David (Con)	Bury S
SWEENEY, Walter (Con)	Vale of Glamorgan
SYKES, John (Con)	Scarborough

T
Member	Constituency
TAPSELL, Peter (Con)	Lindsey E
TAYLOR, Ann (Lab)	Dewsbury
TAYLOR, Ian (Con)	Esher
TAYLOR, John (Con)	Solihull
TAYLOR, John (UUP)	Strangford
TAYLOR, Matthew (LibDem)	Truro
TAYLOR, Teddy (Con)	Southend E
TEMPLE-MORRIS, Peter (Con)	Leominster
THOMASON, Roy (Con)	Bromsgrove
THOMPSON, Donald (Con)	Calder Valley
THOMPSON, Jack (Lab)	Wansbeck
THOMPSON, Patrick (Con)	Norwich N
THORNTON, Malcolm (Con)	Crosby
THURNHAM, Peter (Con)	Bolton NE
TIPPING, Paddy (Lab)	Sherwood
TOWNEND, John (Con)	Bridlington
TOWNSEND, Cyril (Con)	Bexleyheath
TRACEY, Richard (Con)	Surbiton
TREDINNICK, David (Con)	Bosworth
TREND, Michael (Con)	Windsor and Maidenhead
TRIMBLE, David (UUP)	Upper Bann
TROTTER, Neville (Con)	Tynemouth
TURNER, Dennis (Lab)	Wolverhampton SE
TWINN, Ian (Con)	Edmonton
TYLER, Paul (LibDem)	Cornwall N
VAUGHAN, Gerard (Con)	Reading E
VAZ, Keith (Lab)	Leicester E
VIGGERS, Peter (Con)	Gosport

W
Member	Constituency
WALDEGRAVE, William (Con)	Bristol W
WALDEN, George (Con)	Buckingham
WALKER, Bill (Con)	Tayside N
WALKER, Cecil (UUP)	N Belfast
WALKER, Harold (Lab)	Doncaster Central
WALLACE, Jim (LibDem)	Orkney
WALLER, Gary (Con)	Keighley
WALLEY, Joan (Lab)	Stoke-on-Trent N
WARD, John (Con)	Poole
WARDELL, Gareth (Lab)	Gower
WARDLE, Charles (Con)	Bexhill and Battle
WAREING, Robert (Lab)	Liverpool W Derby
WATERSON, Nigel (Con)	Eastbourne
WATSON, Mike (Lab)	Glasgow Central
WATTS, John (Con)	Slough
WELLS, Bowen (Con)	Hertford and Stortford
WELSH, Andrew (SNP)	Angus E
WHEELER, John (Con)	Westminster N
WHITNEY, Ray (Con)	Wycombe
WHITTINGDALE, John (Con)	Colchester S and Maldon
WICKS, Malcolm (Lab)	Croydon NW
WIDDECOMBE, Ann (Con)	Maidstone
WIGGIN, Jerry (Con)	Weston-super-Mare
WIGLEY, Dafydd (Plaid Cymru)	Caernarfon
WILKINSON, John (Con)	Ruislip Northwood
WILLETTS, David (Con)	Havant
WILLIAMS, Alan (Lab)	Swansea W
WILLIAMS, Alan Wynne (Lab)	Carmarthen
WILSHIRE, David (Con)	Spelthorne
WILSON, Brian (Lab)	Cunninghame N
WINNICK, David (Lab)	Walsall N
WINTERTON, Ann (Con)	Congleton
WINTERTON, Nicholas (Con)	Macclesfield
WISE, Audrey (Lab)	Preston
WOLFSON, Mark (Con)	Sevenoaks
WOOD, Tim (Con)	Stevenage
WORTHINGTON, Tony (Lab)	Clydebank & Milngavie
WRAY, Jimmy (Lab)	Glasgow Provan
WRIGHT, Tony (Lab)	Cannock and Burntwood
YEO, Tim (Con)	Suffolk S
YOUNG, David (Lab)	Bolton SE
YOUNG, George (Con)	Ealing Acton